Windows into the Soul

Windows into the Soul

Surveillance and Society in an Age of High Technology

GARY T. MARX

The University of Chicago Press
Chicago and London

Gary T. Marx is professor emeritus at the Massachusetts Institute of Technology and the author of *Undercover: Police Surveillance in America*. His writings have appeared in numerous publications, including the *New York Times*, *Wall Street Journal*, *Washington Post*, and *New Republic*.

The University of Chicago Press, Chicago 60637
The University of Chicago Press, Ltd., London
© 2016 by The University of Chicago
All rights reserved. Published 2016.
Printed in the United States of America

24 23 22 21 20 19 18 17 16 15   1 2 3 4 5

ISBN-13: 978-0-226-28588-7 (cloth)
ISBN-13: 978-0-226-28591-7 (paper)
ISBN-13: 978-0-226-28607-5 (e-book)
DOI: 10.7208/chicago/9780226286075.001.0001

Library of Congress Cataloging-in-Publication Data
Names: Marx, Gary T., author.
Title: Windows into the soul : surveillance and society in an age of high
    technology / Gary T. Marx.
Description: Chicago ; London : The University of Chicago Press, 2016. | Includes
    bibliographical reference and index.
Identifiers: LCCN 201537631 | ISBN 9780226285887 (cloth : alk. paper) | ISBN
    9780226285917 (pbk. : alk. paper) | ISBN 9780226286075 (e-book)
Subjects: LCSH: Electronic surveillance—Social aspects. | Electronic surveillance—
    Moral and ethical aspects. | Technology—Social aspects.
Classification: LCC HM846 .M57 2016 | DDC 303.48/3—dc23 LC record available at
    http://lccn.loc.gov/201503763]

♾ meets the requirements of ANSI/NISO Z39.48-1992 (Permanence of Paper).

It's a remarkable piece of apparatus.

FRANZ KAFKA, "In the Penal Colony"

Contents

Material Available Online at press.uchicago.edu/sites/marx/

Chapter 8 Children: Additional Material

Chapter 9 Voire Early Experience: Additional Material

Chapter 10 Voire Analysis: Additional Material

Chapter 12 Techno-Fallacies of the Information Age: Additional Material

Chapter 13 Ethics Questions: Additional Material

Additional Culture Chapters:

   A Soul Train: Surveillance in Popular Music

   B The New Surveillance in Visual Imagery

Additional appendix B "Your Papers Please": Personal and Professional
   Encounters with Surveillance

Preface

Dear Sir or Madam, will you read my book?
It took me years to write, will you take a look?
. . . .
It's a thousand pages, give or take a few
I'll be writing more in a week or two
THE BEATLES, "Paperback Writer"

In that song the Beatles nail the open-ended, eternally expansive potential of much scholarly inquiry. This book took much longer to complete than I anticipated. As the tortoise's tale reminds us, slow guys sometimes finish well. Rather than writer's block, the long gestation period reflected writer's freedom. Being retired (at least from a formal organization) offered a research grant for life and the delightful absence of pressure to finish. The more time taken to write, the more information and ideas there are to be inspired and/ or challenged by, and the more one can learn. Since history and social life are dynamic and answers often lead to new questions, the job is never finished.

Dispatching the image that some social scientists like to present of the clean, deductive scientific model, I confess that my ideas and questions were not packed neatly in boxes within boxes stacked in rows and columns. Rather like toys thrown in the closet, they were piled high, and when I opened the door, they came tumbling out. The self-filling closet never stayed empty. Writing about a contemporary topic is like working with a jigsaw puzzle to which new pieces are continually added and others subtracted even as the formal structure of a puzzle shows constants.

While it runs contrary to a utilitarian cartographic view of the world, Wynonna Judd got it right when she sang, "When I reach the place I'm going, I will surely know my way." Given enough time, diverse events and strands of intellectual work may come together in unanticipated ways. One then discovers what the inquiry is best about. Particularly when working in a new field, there may be a parallel to a sculptor contemplating a block of stone. The artist knows that something worthwhile lies within, but only immersion in the work can reveal it.

When you are in the groove and the ideas are flowing, there is no thought of stopping until the reality of what you are after is clear or (as in the case of this book) the publisher calls a halt. The original volume was almost twice the length of this one with additional chapters on music, art, advertisements, explanation, policy, and comparative international questions and more notes and references. I wanted the book to serve as both a conceptual mapping and an encyclopedic reference source. The need to significantly shorten the book meant cutting an entire section on culture and other chapters and some notes and references.

The need to cut also meant skimming the surface of many empirical cases, instead of probing them in depth with the concepts. As Winston Churchill (1996) wrote, rather than offering "a scrutiny so minute as to bring an object under an untrue angle of vision," I offer a "sweeping glance" that hopefully helps us see bigger pictures. Ideally, our understanding of the broad landscape should be based on a portrait built up from systematic and deep empirical observations. Other than the fictional case studies (chapters 7–11), I do not offer such in-depth analysis. Given space limitations and the book's goal, my glance instead is based on empirical illustrations of the concepts derived from my observations and from the rich empirical research of others in the references. Since this is primarily a conceptual undertaking rather than a comprehensive empirical study, there is warrant for this illustrative approach, although it may disappoint some readers. I also acknowledge that the plethora of concepts can be overwhelming. Precision can be the enemy of parsimony. Yet classification is central to knowledge, and scientific advances require specification of the minute and policies need to reflect context.

Information Control and Discovery

This inquiry seeks to advance understanding of the social and ethical aspects of personal information control and discovery as a naturally bounded, analytically coherent field, in the tradition of Erving Goffman. This involves studying interaction—whether face-to-face or remote involving agents and subjects of surveillance. A central task of the sociological tradition of symbolic interaction and dramaturgy is to understand how individuals and organizations present themselves through the control and release of personal information, and how others respond to this. Of equal interest are efforts to discover information that is not presented (or to avoid knowing information that is). This approach emphasizes the dynamic, interactive quality of social life and attends to how individuals interpret their own and others' situations. In using the metaphor of dramaturgy Goffman emphasized the presentational actions of the player (the "actor") for the audience rather than the discovery or detection aspects of the audience for the player. This book emphasizes the latter, even as a processual and contingent focus links them. The idea of a front and back stage alerts us to the possibility of selective and distortive presentations and the need for uncovering mechanisms.

I have been concerned with the topic for much of my career (Marx 2012 offers a longer personal statement; see also the University of Chicago Press web site at press.uchicago.edu/sites/marx/). This book continues the interest in questions of social control, self-presentations, and information gathering explored in a 1988 book, *Undercover: Police Surveillance in America*. However it differs from *Undercover* in a number of ways. It emphasizes technology rather than people as the primary direct means of discovery. It looks beyond criminal justice to personal information extraction practices across society. Like a stone dropped into a pond, the technology reverberates across institutions and activities, often moving from its military and law enforcement beginnings to business as usual and then to personal uses. The book considers conceptual and theoretical issues including, but going past, the sociology of social control and surveillance across a range of techniques and explores social processes such as resistance and counterresistance, aspects of popular culture and offers fictional scenarios.

In doing another book on surveillance, I recall a comment about a colleague's latest work, "Yes, it's a good book—it should be, it's the third time he's written it." Since academic books in general are little noted, nor long remembered, a little repetition might be defensible. However the book treats new issues and offers a more encompassing framework.

This book began as a conventional social science inquiry driven by passionate concern over traditional abuses of authority (e.g., COINTEL and Watergate) and the potential for new abuses involving computers. Over time it became less a passionate meditation on the structures and processes of surveillance and a mediation between conflicting elements. It also became a less conventional social science inquiry as I added fiction, music, and visual materials. I did this out of a desire to more fully understand the culture of surveillance as it communicates meaning and to better convey the emotional experience of watching and being watched. I also added material on sex and gender (chap. 9), which in the beginning had not much been on my radar. But it became clear that hints (and more) of sexuality were often found with surveillance, and gender was one of the few sociodemographic variables that correlated with surveillance attitudes and behavior.[1]

As ever more was written on specific surveillance topics and as the headlines reported the latest surveillance opportunity or crisis du jour, I came to see that I did not want to write a current-events book. Given the rapidity of change in the personal data collection business, writing a truly current current-events book is impossible. Since the time I started writing, media attention and public concern have moved from computers to drug testing to video, then on to communication and electronic location monitoring, and more recently to DNA, radio frequency identification chips, social networking sites, drones, cloud computing, big data sets, and wireless intercepts of phone and Internet uses and news events involving the NSA. Further, these various data sources will increasingly be networked into interactive systems of ubiquitous computing and ambient intelligence. New uses of the electromagnetic spectrum to collect as well as to send (whether covertly or overtly) signals to the body (reading brain waves, scents, and other biometrics), drones the size of flies, and the further blurring of the line between the human, the machine, and various environments will probably be next.

During my years of packing and unpacking the closet of accumulated topics, the Internet continually offered new examples and ideas, whether on itself or on other topics. This astoundingly bountiful (but time-sink) resource also served as a brake on and a break from completion.

In addition, the opportunity to publish op-eds slowed down the book's completion. When I encountered current events I felt a strong need to comment on, it was easy to find an immediate audience. This, along with the ease of posting just-published material on a personal web page, relieved the egoistic and strategic pressure to rush into print with a book. Such posting also provides a quick attention fix and feedback for the hungry and otherwise isolated producer.

Why Study That?

Those writing about surveillance technology and social control issues in the 1970s and early 1980s were frequently asked, "Why would you want to study *that*?" The roots of my interest in surveillance are varied. Of course all children have fantasies of being omniscient and omnipotent and imagine being able to transcend the senses and the laws of physics. Most persons can recall the childhood thrill of seeing things that glowed in the dark and envying the powers of superheroes.

Those growing up in the 1940s and 1950s may recall the excitement of looking in the shoe store's fluoroscope machine the first time and seeing the eerie green image of foot bones through shoe and skin. Superman and his x-ray vision offered another example—although it is well to note his principled use of x-ray vision, which was usually turned off.

Growing up in Hollywood during the Cold War, when little boys everywhere wanted to be the heroic sheriff with the white hat in the western movie, or the square-jawed G-man with the fedora watching from the shadows in a comic book, further supported an interest in the topic. Hollywood itself was a propellant toward watching and being watched. The affable and stalwart police officers who led my Boy Scout troop in Los Angeles no doubt contributed to the interest, as did encounters with police in Berkeley and travel experiences in Eastern Europe (Marx 2012).

Other early influences include having a relative who worked closely with the director of the CIA, having a distant English relative who was George Orwell's first publisher, and being raised under the watchful eyes of a stern paternal disciplinarian who stressed the importance of liking what you see when you look in the mirror in the morning. With a strong superego of course comes the potential for guilt and the fear of being discovered (whether because of actions or mere thoughts), in spite of the front one offers to the world. As the work of Franz Kafka and his progeny suggests, conditions of modernity and marginality heighten such feelings and, no doubt, an interest in surveillance.

Then there are professional and political reasons for the interest. As Graham Greene (1971) observes in his autobiography, "Every novelist has something in common with a spy: he watches, he overhears, he seeks motives and analyzes character." This can also hold for the social analyst.[2]

More broadly, as Georg Simmel ([1908] 1950) noted, the secret holds particular fascination. To have insider knowledge and to be able to go beyond the taken-for-granted world can make one feel important and can be a source of power. Surveillance offers a means of assessing one of sociology's (and indeed more broadly science's) first assumptions—that "things are often not as they seem" (Berger 1972). By disposition and training scholars seek to probe deeper and discover things that others don't know. In that regard studying surveillance technology and its fruits is appealing as both means and end. Ironically the method is also the message.

Studying surveillance is a natural topic for sociology, a profession informed by skepticism until there is empirical documentation (and even after that, given what we know of errors, perspectivalism, and the potentially duplicitous nature of self- and organizational presentations). Doubts are also encouraged by awareness of the impact of power on culture and on what is taken to be knowledge. The skepticism involves an interest in the sociology of knowledge and how facts can be socially and technically generated and interpreted. Given its history and organization, American society may have a particular (or at least distinctive) fascination with surveillance—both the need for it and curiosity about its results.

In its uncovering (more than its documentation and verification) capacity surveillance may reveal disjuncture, anomalies, and fraudulent or erroneous claims and beliefs. The surprises of incongruous perspectives noted by Burke (1969) makes life interesting, encourages questioning, and can advance knowledge and the search for resolution, even as it may demoralize and thrust toward cynicism.

When I began writing about surveillance in the 1970s few scholars or practitioners were interested. The topic was seen as something to be left alone. Those in the know (whether on the dark or light side of policing and national security) had a professional interest in not wanting certain topics studied—at least by risk-free outsiders not bound by confidentiality and secrecy agreements or the solidarity of secret cultures. For many scholars the topic was seen as atheoretical, marginal, and even tainted by its proximity to the forces of darkness and dystopia. What is more, reforms in the 1970s such as new FBI policies and passage of the Freedom of Information Act and the 1974 Privacy Protection Act offered grounds for optimism regarding privacy and civil liberties. The study of surveillance was seen as more the province of science fiction writers, the sky-is-falling journalists, and ACLU activists than of serious scholars (at least of the professionally certified kind). Studies of technology and society also had to deal with the ever-present suspicions of technological determinism. Yet whatever the obstacles, the topic has been a crucial one for study because it goes to the very heart of the idea of democracy, the dignity of the person and the kind of society we are becoming or could become.

I spent two decades teaching at MIT—an institution that prides itself on being "data driven and problem solving." This admirable ethos needs to exist alongside that of being "value driven and question raising." The relatively uncritical optimism for technical solutions I saw there stimulated my interest in the worldview that many engineers and scientists bring to social questions. I do not share René Descartes's disquietude about science (in *Discourse on Method*), which he expressed in prayer-like fashion as "Thanks be to God, I did not find myself in a condition which obliged me to make a merchandise of science for the improvement of my fortune." But I did find the dominant ethos at MIT with respect to social questions to be disquieting. At the first faculty meeting I attended in 1973, a distinguished engineering professor said, "We won World War II, we put a man on the moon, and now we will solve the problems of the cities." We are still waiting.

Not long after that, I had the good fortune to meet and learn from historian and philosopher Lewis Mumford (1934). I was moved by the breadth of his knowledge, his independence and vision, and the big questions he raised about technocratic civilization. Whatever their obvious virtues, the modern tools in Pandora's box could also creepingly and creepily undermine important human values, if not subjected to appropriate visibility, integration, analysis, and regulation—and maybe even then. Genies don't usually go back into their bottles.

This book is very much in the spirit—and in the substantive and stylistic shadow—of George Orwell. Yet it departs from Orwell in at least three major ways. First, it seeks empirical evidence for the questions he raised and notes that by many conventional measures, the trend is away from the society he described (e.g., with respect to factors such as literacy, the availability of independent communication tools, human rights, and the vibrancy of civil society).

Second, it notes that forms of control have softened—something Aldous Huxley noted in a 1948 letter to his former student (see chap. 5, pp. 116–17). While coercion and violence remain significant factors in social organization, softer, more manipulative, engineered, connected, and embedded forms of lower visibility have infiltrated our world. These are presumed to offer greater effectiveness and legitimacy than Orwell's social control as a boot on the human face.

Finally, it reveals the fact that the state is no longer the only institution to pose a threat to privacy and liberty. Partly as a result of Orwell, Americans are familiar with the idea of an all-powerful repressive state; less so with the idea of powerful and repressive private groups. In calling attention to Big Brother, Orwell ignored the potential threats from nonstate actors, whether organizations or individuals (as well as the possibility that private interests might capture the state). The private sector has the same technologies as government and in many ways is subject to fewer restrictions—whether in the treatment of workers or consumers. Surveillance awareness is no longer associated only with spies, police, political abuses, and the state.

In order to capture the rich variation and the social and moral complexity of the paradoxes and the contradictions of the topic, we need a comprehensive set of content-neutral concepts. Explanation and evaluation require a common language to identify and measure the fundamental properties and contexts of surveillance.

This book aims to provide a language and a conceptual guide to the understanding of surveillance structures and processes—whether these occur within institutions and are wielded by officials specifically charged with the surveillance function or escape these defined agents and seep into the activities of private actors and, indeed, private life. The initial question should not be Is surveillance good or bad? but rather What concepts do we need to capture the fundamental surveillance structures, processes, goals, and kinds of data, regardless of tool or setting? In the appendix to an early paper on privacy and technology (Marx 1996; http://web.mit.edu/gtmarx/www/privantt .html) I listed almost a hundred questions related to this topic. Raising and organizing the topic in a systematic way provides tools for judging whether and why a given instance may be good or bad.

While my inquiry is driven by the new technologies that so define our age, it involves questions regarding the individual and society that have nothing specific to do with any given technology or crisis. My study reflects a more general interest in the discovery/revelation and concealment/protection of personal information (and the broader fields of the sociology of information control and access) and the forms, functions, and dysfunctions of physical and cultural borders that protect information and means of transcending borders. I touch here on themes such as the public and the private, secrecy, anonymity, confidentiality, accountability, trust and distrust, the social bond, the self and social control, and power and democracy.

The official seal of the Defense Department's defunct Office of Information Awareness was inspired by the familiar Great Seal of the United States that appears on the dollar bill—the all-seeing eye of Providence (symbolic of the Renaissance), surrounded by rays of light on top of an occult pyramid with the motto "Scientia Est Potentia"—"knowledge is power." But the Office of Information Awareness altered the image to show the all-seeing eye gazing at the earth. The agency's mission, as expressed in paradigmatic new surveillance talk, was to "imagine, develop, apply, integrate, demonstrate and transition information technologies, components and prototype, closed-loop, information systems." According to William Safire (2002), its goal was to generate 300 million dossiers on citizens. This mission was also the inspiration of China's Golden Shield program (introduction, p. 3). The Defense Department denied that its aim was to create dossiers on Americans; it was, rather, to develop tools for authorized agencies to obtain information on terrorist networks (http://www.information-retrieval.info/docs/tia-exec-summ _20may2003.pdf; also the informative treatment in Harris 2010).

Whatever the program was, its goal of "achieving total information awareness" using a "virtual, centralized grand database" involving electronic transactions and communication in both the private and public sectors was science fiction. Legal and civil-liberties considerations apart, the technical limitations on merging such an array of public and private databases with very different operating systems and standards are enormous (National Academy of Sciences 2006).

Congress formally defunded the Total Information Awareness program in 2003 over concerns that it could lead to mass surveillance. Its name was changed to the more modest Terrorism Information Awareness Program, and the pyramid logo was dropped from its web page. The eye, however, remains part of the Great Seal of the United States and is still on the dollar bill. The issues that generate concern for us in the twenty-first century, and that preoccupied Huxley and Orwell in the twentieth century, Mill and de Tocqueville in the nineteenth century, Burke and Rousseau in the eighteenth century, and Locke in the seventeenth century endure. The rays of sunlight around the eye can illuminate and warm, but they can also blind and burn.

Acknowledgments

My interest in research on the self and information control was aided and abetted by work with Professor Erving Goffman. While he devoted little attention to technology as such, many of his examples involve technical means of acquiring and protecting information. With aplomb and in a cool, off-handed manner Professor Goffman offered concepts, a method, legitimacy, and fragments of a role model for such pursuits. I am as well grateful to Neil Smelser for an introduction to the joys of conceptualization and the importance of systematically approaching comparative questions and for his friendship over the years and to the late Seymour Martin Lipset for showing how social science could be applied to understanding the supports and threats to democracy.

Academics may be paid less than successful actors, but no matter, since they also get the use of the hall. I have been blessed by access to many halls. The book had its beginnings in the Jensen Lectures delivered at the American Sociological Association and Duke University. I am most grateful to the late Alan Kerckhoff for encouraging me to give those early lectures. The Jensen Lectures were followed by a month in residence as the first Earl and Edna Stice Memorial Lecturer in Social Sciences at the University of Washington with the kind support of Professor Gerald J. Baldasty; GTE lectures at Rose-Hulman Institute of Technology, Salve Regina Rhode Island College, and Northern Kentucky University; the Appel Distinguished Lecture in Law and Technology at Denver University; and the Fortunoff Criminal Justice Lecture at NYU. The National Science Foundation, the Whiting Foundation and the Deutscher Akademischer Austauschdienst provided grants for research and travel.

I owe enormous debts to Larry Nichols for the chance to serve as the A. D.

Carlson Visiting Distinguished Chair in Social Sciences at West Virginia University, to Richard Olsen for the opportunity to serve as the Hixon-Rigs Visiting Professor of Science, Technology and Society at Harvey Mudd College, to Michael Lacey and Ann Sheffield of the Woodrow Wilson International Center for a fellowship there, and to Donatella Dellaporta of the European University Institute for the chance to be a Ferdinand Braudel Fellow in the Florentine springtime.

The lectures, symposia, and conferences associated with the above positions greatly helped the book. The conference at Harvey Mudd "Taking a Look at Surveillance and Society" is described at http://www.hmc.edu/newsandevents/hixon08.html. I also learned from colleagues at other conferences I organized at the University of Colorado and coorganized at Arizona State University and Vanderbilt. I benefited as well from postretirement teaching in North America at Florida State University, the University of California at Berkeley and at Irvine, Northwestern, the University of Washington, the University of Illinois, Eastern Kentucky University, the University of Puerto Rico, and Université Laval in Quebec.

If there is a heaven on earth for academics it surely must be found in the research havens that I have been privileged to be associated with. These included the Center for Advanced Study in the Behavioral Sciences at Stanford and the Rockefeller International Center in Bellagio, both of which I visited several times, the Woodrow Wilson International Center for Scholars in Washington DC, the Max Planck Institute in Freiburg, and the European University Institute in Fiesole. The time I was fortunate to spend in such environments among a broad and giving group of colleagues enriched the book and my soul. As with Greta Garbo in the film *Grand Hotel* ("I just want to be alone") and in life, the scholar too needs to be alone. Yet at its best, scholarship is also communal. It thrives in such places, far removed from the avaricious, bureaucratic, pragmatic, commercial, and political demands of daily academic and American life.

My understanding of the comparative international issues (and of the need for caution in offering sweeping generalizations based on one's own society, discipline, and time period) was enriched from courses I taught at Leuven University, the University of Louvain, and Vrije Universiteit in Brussels; the International Institute for the Sociology of Law in Oñati, Spain; the Technical University of Vienna; Nankai University in the People's Republic of China; and in short courses or a series of lectures in the Netherlands, Germany, France, England, Italy, Portugal, Wales, Chile, Australia, and Japan.

Still, there were times when the search for support from well-known organizations was unsuccessful (names not mentioned to protect their privacy). I know how many qualified applicants there were relative to resources, since the e-mail rejection form letters I received were informative on that point. I wish these organizations well in their future funding endeavors and am sorry we didn't have the chance to work together. Perhaps some other time. To my coauthors, colleagues, research assistants, and students (often serially overlapping roles), thanks for letting me be a mentor and for your help. Academic careers ought to be judged not by citations or grant size, but by the number of one's students who become productive scholars, teachers, and thoughtful citizens.

While it is true that the perception of originality is partly tied to the secreting of one's sources, an author's gratitude to his sources must never be secret. I am profoundly grateful to Professors Stephen Margulis, Craig McEwen, and Jacqueline Ross, and to Susan Messer, Jaclyn Schildkraut, and Erik Carlson, for the extraordinary care and intelligence they brought to every line of this book (including those that fortunately got cut). I am as well most appreciative of the detailed editorial comments or other significant help of David Altheide, Colin Bennett, Fred Conrad, Catarina Frois, Albrecht Funk, Pat Gillham, Glenn Goodwin, Keith Guzik, Kevin Haggerty, Peter Klerks, Jesse Larner, Stephane Leman-Langlois, David Lyon, Glenn Muschert, Val Steeves, Mary Virnoche, and Jay Wachtel.

Many others have critically commented on parts of the manuscript or provided materials, ideas, information, and megaphones: Sheri Alpert, David Armor, Judith Auerbach, Bernard Avishai, Valeria Balestrieri, Ami Benjamin, Didier Bigo, Tom Blomberg, Sissela Bok, James Byrne, Andrew Clement, Simon Cole, Ron Corbett, Mary Culnan, Michael Curry, Simon Davies, Mathew Deflem, Paul de Hert, Howard Erlanger, Amitai Etzioni, Malcolm Feeley, Pedro Ferraz de Abreu, Cyrille Fijnaut, David Flaherty, Chiara Fonio, Peter Fusey, John Gilliom, Jan Goldman, Peter Grabosky, Graham Greenleaf, Serge Gutwirth, Trine Haagensen, John Hagan, Leon Hemple, Mireille Hildebrandt, Dan Hillyard, Bob Hoogenboom, Shengfa Hu, Laura Huey, Martin Inness, Jim Jacobs, Val Jenness, Dick Jessor, David Johnson, Rosabeth Kanter, Ian Kerr, Rolf Kjolseth, Reinhard Kreissl, Kevin Leicht, Richard Leo, Michael Levi, Peggy Levitt, Rene and Renee Levy, J. Robert Lilly, Kevin Macnish, Peter Manning, Emile and Maya Malet, Michael McCann, Dario Mellosi, Lynette Millett, Torin Monahan, Emilio Mordini, Susan and Isaac Moryenztern, Aldon Morris, Ethan Nadelmann, Christina Nippert-Eng, Helen Nissenbaum, Detlef Nogala, Clive Norris, Paul Ponsaers, Henry Pontell, Nicole Rafter, Pris Regan, Nancy Reichman, George Ritzer, Jeff Ross, Marc Rotenberg, Carol and Zick Rubin, James Rule, Fritz Sack, Minas Samatas, Stuart Scheingold, Julia Scher, Chris Schneider, Michael Schober, Manfred Schumpeter, Barry Schwartz, Bob Scott, Dmitri Shalin, Joan Sharpe, Sanford Sherizen, Jim Short,

David Shulman, Susan Silbey, Ida Simpson, Bob Smith, Emily Smith, Jeff Smith, William Staples, Barry Stein, Ken Tunnell, Greg Ungar, Rosamunde Van Brakel, Mary Virnoche, David Wall, Robert Weiss, Lois Weithorn, Chuck Wexler, Chris Williams, James Willis, Dean Wilson, Ann Wood, David Murakami Wood, David Wright, Herbert Yin, Myron Zukewich, Nils Zurawski, and Elia Zureik.

Those so inside their own heads (whom a D. H. Lawrence character called "the scribbling fellows") would be unable to work were they not sustained by the tolerance and support of others in their immediate environment and sometimes reminded to come out and play. In that regard, my love and gratitude to the Marxes large, small, and in-between—to Ruth for the gift of life and how to live it well and for the good; to Nicki, Josh, Ben, Stacey, Cori, Sallie, Nate, Julien, and Simon for receiving what we passed on and for overflowing the cup; and to Phyllis Anne Rakita Marx, who was so vibrant, loving, and beloved and a fellow traveler for decades in the happiness of pursuit, and to Mimi Grace-Marx, who opens windows into my heart and soul.

Brussels 2014

Introduction

During occasions when new industries and technologies are developed, the physical and physiological details usually taken as given can become a matter of concern with consequent clarification of the assumptions and conceptions we have of what individuals are.

ERVING GOFFMAN, *Strategic Interaction*

In the sixteenth century, Queen Elizabeth declared that she did not want "to make windows into men's hearts and secret thoughts."[1] Her actions bolstered liberty and sharpened distinctions between the public and the private that became central to our ideas of the good society and the dignity of the person.[2] Over the next four centuries the sanctity of private thought and expression and the borders between the self and society have in many ways grown stronger. The consequences of this are varied, but on balance overwhelmingly positive.

Yet contemporary social and technical developments have the potential to greatly undermine, and even reverse, this trend. How and why this is happening and how it should be viewed are at the core of this inquiry.

New extractive technologies are central here. Unlike the technologies of industrialization, the tools are not pumps or drills, nor is the extracted substance valued because of its physical properties. The technologies are a broad family of computers, sensors, transmitters, biochemical assays, spectrographs, video lenses, software, and management practices that construct the "new surveillance" and that transcend the senses, space, and time, as well as the traditional borders of the self, the body, and the group. The substance is personal information.

Information is extracted from the ubiquitous flow of distinct data points. The data revealed may have a self-evident factual quality, such as what time a person was at a given location. Or the data may create new organizational identities for the person based on abstract categorizations whose meaning emerges only from combining bits of data about the person and the setting into composites. The composite is then evaluated in relation to broad statistical models (e.g., assignment to risk categories). New versions of the person are in a sense manufactured. The technologies offer possibilities for "windows into the soul" in forms and on a scale previously imagined only in science fiction and in the superhero fantasies of children.

In 2001 in an interview with a university official responsible for an all-purpose student ID card that was used to gain access to buildings, libraries, and meals, and that was linked to a credit account for purchases, I encountered the following case:

The registrar came into his office on a Monday morning and discovered a failed arson attempt. A long burn mark on the carpet led to a Gatorade bottle full of flammable liquid in a closet.

The police requested weekend card access records for the secure building. They next checked the lot number on the Gatorade bottle and determined it had been delivered to a campus convenience store. They then generated a list of recent Gatorade purchases made with the university ID card. Upon matching the records of purchasers of Gatorade with those entering the building, the police got a hit. They confronted the suspect, and he confessed to arson. His motive was to burn up his academic records, as he was failing several classes and didn't want his parents to know.

This high-tech tracking of metaphorical human spoor needs only to be bolstered by a video camera, DNA matching, an implanted location chip, and perhaps eventually odor-detection identification and lie detection based on brain wave analysis for further verification to serve as an ideal example of the "new surveillance." The student might have made the police's job easier had he used a location- and time-communicating cell phone while in the building, or boasted of his exploits on Facebook. Better still, the school might have thought it could have prevented this had it used a more sophisticated admissions model to predict and exclude those expected to fail or who might be of dodgy character.

The prevention of arson and the apprehension of arsonists are admirable goals. Quite separately from these goals, the case of the student is of interest because it suggests how much the means of surveillance have changed. Each small increment may be easily justified and barely noticed. But each new technology, application, and protocol creates a precedent, and the totality reflects more than the sum of its parts, particularly as results are linked. These changes gradually become part of our taken for granted world.

A single change element may engender a "gee whiz" response, particularly in those of a certain age. But what is astounding is the range of tools, the breadth, depth, and integrative potential of the data, the varied settings in which they can be applied, and the ubiquity and rapidity of change.

The topic touches an ever-expanding number of areas. Consider public health and its concerns with epidemics (e.g., AIDS and SARS); management concerns with hiring, work monitoring, productivity, and access to consumers; marketing and media concerns with sales and persuasion; parents' concerns with their children's development and behavior; and the emergent crosscutting areas of prevention, risk assessment, and crisis management—whether involving insurance, mortgages, credit cards, individual health, travel, criminal justice, national security, and entering or leaving secure areas.

When governments with their special powers, resources, and responsibilities draw on and seek to integrate the multiplicity of tools and data, a new level is reached lessening the fiction in traditional science fiction. Consider, for example, China's Golden Shield, a state effort drawing on US surveillance software and hardware.

The Chinese program offers continuous data through networked CCTV cameras, remote monitoring of computers, digital voice recognition technology that identifies phone callers, and a Great Firewall capable of tracking and blocking Internet use. The system uses a photo ID card for identifying location and movement. Facial image and other biometric data, along with information such as residence and work history, are included in scannable electronic chips. When fully implemented, Golden Shield is expected to have data on each of the 1.3 billion people in China.[3] Results from cameras, the Internet, telephones, facial recognition, and GPS monitoring will be brought together into searchable and linkable databases. The technology in this case functions like a one-way mirror, with data flowing from citizens to government.

The metaphor of extraction rooted in the traditional understanding of spying and privacy invasion by a state with coercive power captures much contemporary surveillance behavior. Understanding current realities, however, requires a broader analysis—beyond extraction (and beyond the state). The willing expulsion of data to other individuals, the private sector, and the state needs to be considered. Individuals are often unaware of the consequences of this. Relative to other democracies the United States has on the average weaker protections regarding the interception, repackaging, and selling of personal data that the person "voluntarily" donating it did not agree to and may be unaware of.

Facebook, Twitter, Foursquare, e-mail, and mobile phones used for purposes of self-advertising, sociability, and community change expectations, and there is ambiguity in judging them relative to the actions of a draconian state coercively draining data from its subjects. If you "voluntarily" (whether actively or passively) offer your information (as with social networking sites, facial appearance, location, or the use of an unprotected wireless device) to others who then use it for their own ends, has your autonomy been lessened or your privacy invaded? These tools can be subtly coercive—we come to expect that we can watch or learn about others and are suspicious when we cannot. Why is there nothing about this person on the Internet? Why doesn't he or she have an answering machine, a cell phone, or a Facebook page?

A Maximum Security Society?

The industrial noises broke the solitude, the sharp lights, though unseen, mocked it. A man could no longer be private and withdrawn. The world allows no hermits.
D. H. LAWRENCE, *Lady Chatterly's Lover*

In *Undercover* (1988a) I explored the merging of traditional covert police means with video and other new forms of information collection. In noting significant changes in social control, I asked if we were moving toward becoming a *"maximum security society"*—-a society ever more transparent and porous, as the traditional borders that formerly protected personal information were weakened or obliterated by new technologies, new ways of living, and new threats.[4] Such a society increasingly relies on categorical suspicion, dossiers, actuarial decision making, self-monitoring, and the engineering of control. Surveillance is ubiquitous, and its results are linked in networks of astounding complexity.

The ethos of the maximum security society is reflected in the eleven subsocieties shown below. These efforts at rational control are illustrated throughout the book. They involve varying degrees of generality, and some might be seen as subtypes of others, but each reflects something distinctive.

Components of the Maximum Security Society
1. A hard-engineered society
2. A seductive and soft-engineered society
3. A dossier society
4. An actuarial society
5. A transparent society
6. A self-monitored society
7. A suspicious society
8. A networked society of ambient and ubiquitous sensors in constant communication
9. A safe and secure society with attenuated tolerance for risk
10. A "who are you?" society of protean identities both asserted by, and imposed upon, individuals
11. A "where are you, where have you been, who else is there, and what did you do?" society of mobility and location documentation

In the years since *Undercover* was written these developments have become much more pronounced. Technologies have become available that previously existed only in the dystopic imaginations of science fiction writers. We are an ever-changing surveillance society, however imperfect (imperfect, that is, both in the moral sense and in the sense of the distance we have yet to travel to attain the "ideal" form of a surveillance society).[5]

The September 11, 2001, attacks and the ensuing war on terror drive the development and application of information-hungry technologies and organizations. Beyond the massive Homeland Security Agency, we see the expansion and standardization of global surveillance systems (such as the United States' international effort for biometric passports for travelers). However, this move toward a suspicious, surveillance society also reflects continuity. The wheels that began turning with industrialization gained great momentum during the second half of the twentieth century and continue to accelerate. Issues of personal information and technology are central to modern society and go far beyond questions of government and national security, or the particulars of historical events. These developments are also mired in controversy.

Consider uses in marketing research and sales. The extension and the granularity of information-gathering techniques into the routine activities of shopping, beyond the familiar data gathering associated with credit card purchases and frequent shopper programs, is striking. A humble man who claims to have created the "science of shopping" proudly reports that his company can measure "close to 900 different aspects of shopper-store interaction" (Underhill 1999, 17), and "depending on the size of the store, we may have ten cameras running eight hours a day trained on specific areas—a doorway for example, or a particular shelf of products."

The conflicting claims of surveillance advocates and critics often share imprecision and some common rhetorical excesses. These include failing to differentiate potential capabilities claimed under ideal conditions from actual capabilities and consequences under realistic conditions; degrees and forms of application and implementation and their consequences; and effects across diverse actors, groups, time periods, and places. Public discussion would shed more light and less heat if it were empirically grounded and attended to factors that allow for a more realistic assessment of utopian or dystopian predictions. They would also benefit from a greater awareness of universals in human societies and of the continuities alongside the discontinuities in those societies, since the industrial and agricultural revolutions. The field of surveillance studies wrestles with these issues.

Surveillance Studies

I've got my eyes on you. . . . I've set my spies on you.
                    COLE PORTER

Surveillance studies are fragmented, and scholars often disagree.[6] The field's conceptual and theoretical deficiencies reflect the variety of disciplines and the growth of far-flung literatures.

To understand surveillance abuses and the social causes and consequences of new technologies, we need an inclusive approach and we need ways of talking about personal information that transcend particular academic specializations, contexts, technologies, data properties, specific abuses, and popular language. We need to think about the enduring elements behind our contemporary concerns. Concepts must be better defined and ideas better stated.

The book addresses those concerns by offering a framework that more systematically defines surveillance questions with respect to structure, organization, practice, function, and process.[7] Through actual cases and fiction, it also offers a phenomenology of the topic as it is experienced by both subject and agents. To that end, I suggest that the field be defined around concepts and stories that help capture the following:

1. The structure of relationships between agents of surveillance and those they seek data from and related roles and rules about information
2. Characteristics of the means agents use in data collection
3. The goals of surveillance
4. Characteristics of the data and the locations in which they are collected
5. Social processes surrounding surveillance—the dynamic and interactive aspects
6. Cultural aspects of surveillance—symbols, meaning, subjective experience, and public attitudes
7. Principles for ethical, legal, and policy evaluation and controls

Under such a conceptualization, we can ask empirical questions about surveillance occasions (who was involved, what happened, where and when did it happen, and with what distribution and correlates?), theoretical questions (under what conditions was it done and why?), and ethical and practical questions (is it right or wrong, and what should be done?). These questions can yield dependent variables—factors we try to explain by discovering their prior correlates, as well as factors treated as independent variables whose subsequent consequences we seek to identify. They can in turn contribute to more cumulative and inclusive scholarship and to more conversations across the fragmented fields of surveillance studies. The book looks at both those being looked at (subjects) and those doing the looking (agents).[8] The primary focus is on the practices of organizations relative to individuals and on individuals in relation to each other. The emphasis is on the enduring and changing rules and behavior around personal information, particularly as these reflect new means of data extraction and changing expectations. The book plays less attention to interorganizational surveillance (such as corporate spying and strategic intelligence), where the playing field is likely to be more equal, and which raises some related, but also distinct social, legal, and moral issues when compared to organizations watching and influencing individuals or individuals watching each other. This book focuses on the latter. The book emphasizes work and home as the institutional contexts where surveillance of individuals takes place. Some attention is also given to issues of consumption and citizenship, including domestic and international political surveillance. Since 9/11 and the war on terror, the latter has received the most attention from scholars. Whatever their exceptional elements, wartime, national security, and domestic crisis surveillance form part of a larger set of social practices and developments touching ordinary events and lives, beyond the day's headlines.

Those developments are seen in sports and entertainment events. Mega-events in urban areas such as the Olympics offer showcases for an ever-expanding "surveillance industrial complex" to test and to propagate the new surveillance. Here we see core social processes and forms such as the myth of surveillance, securitization, techno-control, profiling, automatization, monetization, commoditization, privatization, the blurring of public-private organizational borders, global and transborder policing, fortification, restrictions on movement, zones of exclusion, and the normalization and nonexceptionality of new forms of control (Samatas 2014; Ball and Snider 2013; Fussey and Coaffe 2011; Bennett and Haggerty 2011; Graham 2010; Bigo and Tsoukala 2008).

Methods, Data Sources, Genre

The data for this book come from observations, interviews, the academic literature, government reports, periodicals, court records, and popular culture. Using a relatively unstructured but directed and opportunistic format, I talked with more than four hundred people who had been either subjects of surveillance (work-monitored employees, drug-tested athletes, activists, professional gamblers, electronically monitored probationers, and customers) and others who had experienced extreme invasions of privacy.

I also spoke with and listened to practitioners of surveillance (executives; supervisors; accountants; federal, local, and private police; national security agents and intelligence officers; parole officers; casino, campus, and department store security administrators and agents; computer security and access control experts; forensic DNA analysts; drug testers) and manufacturers and merchants of surveillance tools. Finally, I interviewed those involved in creating laws and policies, those developing and providing technology, and publicists, lawyers, lobbyists, and activists on all sides of the issue. While I focused on the United States in my data collection, I also conducted interviews in Europe, Japan, China, and Australia.

To develop the conceptual framework for these data I have used the method of analytic induction (Katz 2004). Here, one starts with empirical cases and extracts broader organizing concepts. One then asks if the categories can encompass the variation offered by other empirical examples. I have drawn on examples gathered over recent decades through interviews and observation, news accounts, trade journals, pro- and antisurveillance commercial web sites (sometimes the same sites!), message boards, and the useful compilations in Smith (1997) and Alderman and Kennedy (1995), material generated for two National Academy of Science panels on privacy and information technology on which I served (National Research Council 1993, 2007), and the reports of many hearings and conferences.

Although this is a work of social science drawing from empirical research, it is not the type of social science that systematically tests ideas with freshly plucked quantitative data. Nor is this book a theoretical statement in the sense that it offers a tight system from which one can logically derive propositions to be tested. Nor does it offer a single, hard-driving argument (a central theme is how hard it is to have a central point about such a varied, complex, and dynamic set of activities). It does, however, offer a soft-driving argument that identifies questions central for explanation, evaluation, and regulation and parses empirical possibilities into categories involving types of behavior and four basic surveillance contexts.

Chapter Organization

The book's organization follows the framework above and focuses on three major strands: social scientific, cultural, and normative. While these are interwoven, chapters 1–6 emphasize the social scientific, chapters 7–11 the cultural, and chapters 12 and 13 ethics and policy. The final chapter combines all three in considering broad implications.

In researching a topic of wide interest the academic author is pulled between writing for a broad audience and one's peers (and for the latter between being the fulsome ethnographer and historian getting all the details because they are there and interesting and the bare-bones theorist who seeks only the structure and generalizations across cases). Esoteric communication is not an appealing brew. But neither is pablum a sustaining breakfast. I have tried to write for both the general reader and the specialist. The more conceptual chapters (1–4), offering definitions, some literature review, and an analysis of means, goals, and data attributes, will probably be of less interest to the general reader. The chapters with abundant descriptive material on social process and culture and on work, interpersonal uses, children, and security (5–11) will hopefully be of interest to the general reader. Chapters 12–14 address speculative and normative questions that might interest both groups of readers.

Part 1 ("Conceptual and Theoretical Issues") asks what surveillance is. More specifically, how does it relate to a family of categories involving privacy and publicity, private and public, secrecy, and borders? What is the new surveillance? And finally, how can we identify the major dimensions and forms so that we can systematically compare surveillance means, goals, and the kinds of data collected?

Part 2 shifts attention from the relatively static or fixed elements of social roles, goals, and organization to social interaction and developments over time. In chapters 5–6, the focus is empirical and emphasizes social processes and surveillance in everyday life and across the life cycle as well as episodes or "occasions" of surveillance. Social processes seen in the development, application, interpretation of, and resistance to the means of surveillance are discussed.

Part 3 emphasizes culture and the imputation of meaning. Cultural analysis asks what images and symbols accompany and even define surveillance. What messages are sent? How is surveillance perceived and experienced, rationalized or rejected? What does culture say about how it should feel to be either watched or a watcher under varying conditions? The images held of a tool are socially constructed, patterned, and partially independent of the qualities of the technology.[9]

Part 3 explores the cultural aspects of surveillance through words seen in composite case studies rather than through music or images (the latter two are treated in chapters that were cut and are available at press.uchicago.edu/sites/marx/). Unlike most social science description, the case studies use fictional narratives to make their basic points. I go beyond conventional social science and enter the realm of the fiction writer in creating social worlds. Yet the accounts are drawn from real world events and bound by standards beyond imagination. The cases involve the work-monitoring program of a high-tech company, the manifesto of a social movement dedicated to protecting children, a clinical report on a peeping Tom, and a speech by Rocky Bottoms, the president of a national surveillance association.

The narratives illustrate four major contexts for surveillance. These are the *three Cs*—contracts, care, and coercion, and a residual free-range form of surveillance apart from an organization, group, or role where information is simply available with no need for a mechanism or motivation to reveal it. While elements of the four contexts are found in any rich setting, the chapter on work emphasizes contracts, that on children highlights care, that on the peeping Tom Voire focuses on publically available data, and Rocky Bottoms underlines coercion by government. These fictions raise issues and reveal complexity in ways that are not possible when relying on a single, documented case study.

Part 4 treats questions of ethics and public policy. Here, the questions are, How should the technologies be judged? What is at stake? What assumptions about technology and society underlie the conclusions individuals reach in thinking about the collection of personal information? What competing values are present, and how can citizens best respond to conflicts between these values? What is most problematic about extractive technologies? What are the major forms of abuse, and how can they be minimized? Under what conditions should individuals be required to provide information about themselves? When should personal information be protected? What policy mechanisms are available, and with what consequences? The concluding chapter considers implications and enduring questions for selves, society, and social theory that transcend any given technology.

With respect to the latest newsworthy surveillance event, those studying the topic are often asked, "Are you for it or against it?" My initial answer is "Sometimes," followed by a request that the interviewer reframe the question. What I am for is understanding it; only then is it appropriate to take a position. A central task for this book, then, is to suggest why *surveillance by itself is neither good nor bad, but context and comportment make it so.* As the indefatigable lion of good cheer who has done so much to create and sustain the surveillance studies field, David Lyon (1994) has observed, it is indeed Janus- (and, perhaps even better, octo-) faced. To support the argument, I have sought concepts that capture the rich empirical variation in surveillance settings and behavior and that feature the complexity of social orders, while nonetheless revealing patterns. As a first step in that process, I define the basic concepts—the purpose of the next chapter.

PART I

Concepts: The Need for a Modest but Persistent Analyticity

Frango ut Patefaciam.

PALEONTOLOGICAL SOCIETY MOTTO

The translation of that phrase—"I break in order to reveal," describes the intention of the next four chapters, which break surveillance into major components and offer varieties of rearrangement. These chapters also do some crosscutting along analytic dimensions to unite seemingly dissimilar phenomena and separate seemingly similar ones—for example, identifying both enemy spies and loving parents as surveillance agents, or making a clear distinction between a drug test categorically applied to transportation workers and to applicants for college loans.

My goals in classification are to define and organize the empirical patterns; to assess what is new about the new surveillance and the extent to which it is new; to specify the variation across time periods, settings, and methods that theory needs to account for; and to offer a systematic way for grounding (and comparing) ethical and policy judgments about particular tactics and practices.

Having identified ways of classifying the phenomena of interest, the analyst can then construct still-broader types by combining and reconfiguring the variables.[1] The social scientist may next seek to generalize across cases by linking concepts in the form of empirically assessable hypotheses and then testing them. As we move from naming, to hypothesizing, to testing, the task becomes more difficult. There is a division of labor by task, skills, and interests of the researcher and time period. The first need is for improved tools of classification. But even without the steps of hypothesizing and testing, the systematic identification of variation can inform citizens and policy makers.

In offering general concepts, I hope to help define the fragmented field of surveillance studies and contribute to the broader field of the sociology of information. Scholars are often so busy tending their small gardens that they miss activity in adjacent fields, let alone plant history. Species diversity with its genius for niche finding need not preclude cross-pollination. Intellectual anarchy and the absence of central direction may have their virtues, given the not-infrequent tilt of authority toward self-perpetuation, parochialism, and corruption. However, as a field matures, there is need for cumulative scholarship and integration. Concept development of the kind suggested here can contribute to this by offering a common language and foundation.[2]

Chapter 1 deals with basic definitions. Chapter 2 identifies the attributes of surveillance tools. Chapter 3 is concerned with the many goals the tools can serve, and chapter 4 identifies the kinds of data they can gather. In these chapters on the *social structures of surveillance,* I have sought, as Erving Goffman advised, to contribute to the development of sociological concepts and to conceptual frameworks appropriate for *both* clothing the children and tenting the congregation.[3]

Defining the Terms of Surveillance Studies

We are at any moment those who separate the connected or connect the separate.
GEORG SIMMEL

Getting to my conceptual planet, country, region, neighborhood, house and room involves a series of permeable, moveable Russian dolls within dolls.
ROBERT K. CONJURETSKY

Whether in academic or popular discussions the term *surveillance* is often used in a vague, imprecise and, seemingly, self-evident fashion. That is also the case for accompanying terms such as *privacy, publicity, secrecy, confidentiality, anonymity, identifiability*, and *borders*, which can simply describe outcomes of surveillance practices or may involve rules designed to ensure or avoid such outcomes. This chapter first considers definitions of these terms. It then turns to a second set of concepts useful for analyzing the organization and structure of surveillance settings which produce such outcomes (e.g., the role played as an agent or subject of surveillance).

Two major forms of studying the topic can be noted: the surveillance essay and the focused empirical inquiry. The surveillance essay grows out of the theoretical traditions of political economy, social control, law and society, and criminology. Such essays tend to draw on and extend the work of Michel Foucault (although he was writing about earlier centuries); and further in the background the ideas of Frederick W. Taylor, Weber, Nietzsche, Marx, Bentham, Rousseau, and Hobbes; and even further back the watchful and potentially wrathful eye of the biblical God of the Old Testament.[1] (The ancient of course can be combined with the most modern; see the warning in a church's parking lot in fig. 1.1.)

The *surveillance essay* seeks to capture the appearance of a new kind of society but without enough specificity to take us beyond very general statements. (See chap. 2, table 2.1). It generally does not begin by offering an inclusive definition of surveillance, nor does it identify components that would systematically permit differentiating the new from the old forms, making comparisons within and across these, or seeing what is universal in human societies.

FIGURE 1.1. Church parking lot: You are not alone.

If the theoretical essays tend to be too broad, the focused empirical inquiries are often too narrowing, divorced from larger questions and too often
unaware of research in nearby fields. Many empirical studies focus on only
one technology, such as databases, work, communication and location monitoring, drug testing, or video (the most frequently written-about forms). This
is often done within a single institutional context such as employment, education, or law enforcement, rather than across contexts. The occasional studies
that are more comparative, looking across technologies or settings, generally
do so with a single disciplinary focus or method. The work of some journalists and text writers is an exception, although their emphasis is usually on
summarizing the literature, rather than extending it.

The numerous strands of theory and research in geographically and ac-
ademically diverse areas indicate a boom, yet there is a lack of integration
(and even awareness) among literatures. They do not adequately build on
each other. There are relatively few middle-range approaches involving systematic empirical inquiry guided by an effort to assess ideas using standard
terms or measures. There is a need for increased communication between
fields, improved definition and operationalization of concepts, and nuanced
abstractions filled with systematic empirical content. There's too much confusion, duplication, and people talking past each other as they impute different

meanings to the same words. There must be some way out of here (as the joker said to the thief). An important first step in overcoming these limitations is to develop better definitions of concepts and a clearer picture of how they connect. We begin with surveillance and the concepts that encircle and cut through it.

Surveillance, Traditional Surveillance, and the New Surveillance

Prepare the table, watch in the watchtower . . . anoint the shield. . . . Go, set a watchman, let him declare what he seeth!

ISAIAH: 21:5, 6

The English noun *surveillance* comes from the French verb *surveillir*. It is related to the Latin term *vigilare* with its hint that something vaguely sinister or threatening lurks beyond the watchtower and town walls. Still, the threat might be successfully warded off by the vigilant. This ancient meaning is reflected in the narrow association many persons still make of surveillance with the activities of police and national security agencies. Yet in contemporary society the term has a far wider meaning. What is surveillance? Dictionary, thesaurus, and popular usage suggest a set of related activities: look, observe, watch, supervise, control, gaze, stare, view, shadow, scrutinize, examine, check out, scan, screen, inspect, survey, glean, scope, monitor, track, follow, tail, bug, spy, eavesdrop, test, guard. While some of these are more inclusive than others and can be logically linked (e.g., moving from looking to monitoring), and while we might tease out subtle and distinctive meanings for each involving a particular sense, activity, or function, they all reflect what the philosopher Ludwig Wittgenstein calls a family of meanings within the broader concept.

At the most general level, surveillance of humans (often, but not necessarily synonymous with human surveillance) can be defined as regard for or attendance to a person or factors presumed to be associated with a person. A central feature is gathering some form of data connectable to an individual (whether uniquely identified or as a member of a category). Gathering is a many-splendored thing.

In his analysis of "the look" Sartre illustrates a basic distinction. He describes a situation in which an observer is listening from behind a closed door while peeking through a keyhole when "all of a sudden I hear footsteps in the hall" (1993). He becomes aware that he himself will now be observed. In both cases he is involved in acts of surveillance, but these are very different forms. In the latter case he simply responds and draws a conclusion from a state of awareness. In the former he has taken the initiative, actively and purposively using his senses.

Surveillance can simply mean the routine, autopilot, semiconscious, and often even instinctual awareness in which our sense receptors are at the ready, constantly receiving inputs from whatever is in perceptual range. Hearing a noise that might or might not be a car's backfire and looking before crossing the street are surveillance examples. Drawing conclusions about the gender, age, appearance, and location of those walking toward us as pedestrians (and the need to appropriately orient ourselves so that we don't collide) can be included, as would overhearing a cell phone or restaurant conversation. A census, an opinion or public health survey, an informer's activities, a pacemaker's readings, a poker player interpreting opponents' expressions, a uranium miner being monitored for radio activity, and a computer mining data from credit card use all fit the definition as well.

Within this broad definition, the degree of self-conscious awareness of the act, intentionality, and effort vary greatly, as well as do subsequent efforts that may include trying to block out or avoid what is taken in, as well as trying to magnify it.

Thus, we can identify one form of surveillance as attentiveness or wakefulness in which an agent, with minimal malice or benign aforethought, consumes data from a subject without directly seeking it. This involves a passive, nonreflective and reactive response to the environment. This can be called *nonstrategic surveillance*. The natural world simply serves up data to the unaided senses.

This contrasts with cases of *strategic surveillance*. Strategic surveillance often involves an adversarial context in which the subject withholds (or at least does not offer) information. Thus, the surveillance may have an inquisitorial, discovery component. In turn, the subject may engage in information protection and other practices designed to shape what an agent discovers. Or the surveillance may involve information that is waiting to be discovered, unveiled, located, created, collected, or collated, or it may involve information that is known but needs to be validated.

Within the strategic form—which to varying degrees ferrets out what is not freely offered—we can distinguish two mechanisms intended to create (or prohibit) conditions of visibility and legibility—material *tools* that enhance (or block) the senses and *rules* about the surveillance itself. While these are independent of each other, they show common linkages, as with rules requiring reporting when there are no available tools for discovery or rules about the conditions of use for tools that are available. A stellar example is the "lantern laws" which prohibited slaves from being out at night unless they carried a lantern (Browne 2015). Here the emphasis is on requiring the subject to make him- or herself visible given the limitations brought by darkness. But note also efforts to alter environments to make them more visible as with the creation of "defensible space": via taking down shrubs or using glass walls (Newman 1972) or less visible à la architecture of bathrooms.

Within this field we can distinguish the *traditional* from the *new surveillance*. *Traditional surveillance* relies on the unaided senses and was characteristic of preindustrial societies. Given these limitations, information tended to stay local and compartmentalized (Locke 2011). Covert and overt watching, hearing (and overhearing), inspections, question asking, and tests and contests fit within the category of traditional surveillance and are found in various forms and degrees in all societies.

With the development of language, numeracy, writing, and more differentiated forms of social organization involving larger political entities, more complex and systematic forms of surveillance appeared based on counting, record keeping, interrogation, informing, infiltration, self-reports, confessions, and the expanded use of tests.

With the emergence of industrial society these forms were supplemented, but hardly displaced, by new surveillance and communication tools that enhanced the senses and cognition. For example, the telescope extended vision. The telegraph and telephone meant conversations could be intercepted far removed from the communicators. Collections of photographs, fingerprints, and other biometric measurements improved the identification of suspects. Forensics offered the ability to match data from different sources. Bureaucratic record keeping sought to rationalize information location, retention, processing, and sharing. Surveillance results became more centralized. New means of measurement and data storage and new statistical techniques improved analysis and meant increased use of prediction relying on behavior modeling.

Yet until digitalization and other advances that began in the last half of the twentieth century, this work was labor intensive, and surveillance results collected in different forms, places, and times were rarely merged. Law enforcement, for example, was still largely inductive, needing to identify a suspect and build an inquiry around that person. Once a suspect was identified, the person's phone could be tapped; a photo, physical measurement, or fingerprint could be compared; data could be gathered using binoculars or discrete tailing; and a polygraph test could be administered. Information from various sources could be combined into a paper dossier.

But the scale, comprehensiveness, speed, and power were modest relative to what was to come. Consider the instantaneous search of vast databases, which can now deductively provide subjects from multiple, integrated data pools, many of which continuously receive real-time information from ubiquitous sensors. The distinction between centralized and decentralized organizational forms breaks down as data flow within and between networks regardless of proximity or the need for a central location or even wire connections.

Dictionary Deficits

One indicator of change from traditional forms of surveillance to the increasingly prominent new ones can be seen in the gap between dictionary definitions and current understandings. To take a prominent example, in the *Concise Oxford Dictionary*, surveillance is defined as "close observation, especially of a suspected person." This definition works well for traditional surveillance (a suspect discreetly followed by police after robbing a bank or an undercover police agent infiltrating a criminal group). However, this historically bounded definition is not adequate for the new forms of surveillance, nor does it capture the more general meaning of surveillance as a fundamental social process across institutions and settings. It also takes attention away from viewing surveillance as a universal process applying to animals as well.

New surveillance technologies are increasingly applied categorically, rather than being "especially" applied to "a suspected person." In broadening the range of suspects (or, better, subjects), the term "a suspected person" takes on a different meaning, implying everyone in a given group. The technologies greatly expand the power of the dragnet.

In a striking innovation, surveillance goes not just to a particular person known beforehand, but to contexts (geographic places and spaces, particular time periods, networks and systems). Various attributes of the disembodied person are attended to, such as consumption and indebtedness patterns, physical remnants, and behavioral aspects such as the way a person walks. These may be categorized into risk and desirability pools.

The dictionary definition also implies a clear distinction between the subject of surveillance and the agent carrying it out. In an age of servants listening behind closed doors, binoculars, and telegraphic interceptions, that separation made sense. The watcher was easily separated from the person watched. Yet with many current uses, classifying role players only as watcher or watched is not possible, and roles may blend and alternate. For example, that is the case for *self-surveillance*, where the individual is both subject and agent (e.g., monitoring one's driving speed to stay within the limit).

The dictionary definition also needs to be expanded to take account of the several forms of *cosurveillance* discussed in the last section of this chapter, in which individuals' self-surveillance is joined by that of other watchers.

Some definitions of surveillance are also lacking because they imply a necessary conflict or oppositional relationship between the subject and agent. However, surveillance through technology may instead serve as a facilitator of sociability, merging or alternating the role of agent and subject. Consider, for example, the social networking and location sites or the video camera in recording memorable social events.

The term "close observation" from the traditional dictionary definition also fails to capture contemporary practices. Surveillance may be carried out from afar, as with satellite images or the remote monitoring of communications and work. Nor need it be "close" as in detailed observation; much initial surveillance involves superficial broad scans looking for patterns of interest to be later pursued in detail.

The dated nature of the definition is further illustrated in its seeming restriction to visual means as implied in "observation." The eyes do contain the vast majority of the body's sense receptors in contrast to the much greater role of smell for canines or hearing for bats.[2] For the Greeks the circle, emblematic of the eye, was the perfect shape. Phonetically speaking (and more), "the ayes have it" and culturally the visual is a master metaphor for understanding— note terms and expressions such as "worldview," "I see," "I get the picture," "that's quite a scene," "as seen in," "eagle eye," "eye-opening," and it can also be literal, as with "seeing is believing." "Foresight" is appreciated, in contrast to "hindsight," which is often treated with sarcasm, or the error resulting from "an oversight," which doesn't mean seeing over, as with hierarchical surveillance, but rather the failure to see. Or consider the presumed "insight" from being able "to see through people." William Holden in the film *Picnic* says, "She saw through me like an x-ray machine." Indeed "seeing through" and "overseeing" are convenient shorthand for the surveillance, even as they need not literally involve the eyes. To "turn a blind eye" is to refuse to acknowledge what the eye provides with the implication that it is accurate. We speak of "the mind's eye" not its ear or nose.

The visual is usually an element of surveillance, even when it is not the initial means of data collection (e.g., events and conversations that are written about by others or transcripts of audiorecordings are seen, as are texts and images based on the conversion of measurements from heat, sound, or movement). Yet for a detective or supervisor to "observe" a distanced, acontextual printout of text or measurements in numerical or graph form is in many ways different from direct observation by that same person (who might in turn be observed) of an identifiable person.

The eye as the major means of direct on-scene surveillance is increasingly joined or replaced by hearing, touching, smelling, and distanced visibility.[3] The use of multiple senses and sources of data, including a variety of remote nonvisual sensors is an important characteristic of much of the new surveillance. In response to changes in communications technology Marshall McLuhan (1962) called attention to the increased importance of the visual relative to the other senses in western culture and society. Recent changes, however, may suggest a slowing down and even reversal of this pattern.[4]

As used here the term *surveillance* is intended to be denotative. As a neutral behavioral term it formally marks off a social activity that is central for understanding society and the borders around persons and groups.

Meaning becomes fuzzier when we consider second-order connotations via the meanings individuals bring to controversial topics. Depending on the observer, terms such as *surveillance, drug testing,* and *video cameras* overflow with both emotional and cognitive connotations. Other terms within the new surveillance umbrella such as *health monitoring* have more uniformly positive imputations. Given the variety of goals and evaluations potentially associated with the term, it is important to approach it in a neutral denotative fashion and then proceed to analyze connotations. Substituting a term such as *scrutiny* avoids the problem but does not flow as easily.

The New Surveillance

Given the breadth of the term *surveillance*, I will not offer a formal definition for the broad category; however, the major interest of the book, the new surveillance, may be defined as *scrutiny of individuals, groups, and contexts through the use of technical means to extract or create information.* In this definition the use of "technical means" to extract and create the information implies the ability to go beyond what is naturally offered to the senses and minds unsupported by technology, or what is voluntarily reported. Many of the examples extend the senses and cognitive abilities by using material artifacts, software, and automated processes, but the technical means for rooting out can also involve sophisticated forms of manipulation, seduction, coercion, deception, infiltrators, informers, and special observational skills.

Including *extract or create* in the definition calls attention to the new surveillance's interest in overcoming the strategic or logistical borders that inhibit access to personal information. These inhibitors may involve willful hiding and deception on the part of subjects or limits of the natural world, senses, and cognitive powers. *Create* also suggests that data reflect the output of a measurement tool. The tool itself reflects a decision about what to focus on.

In using *extract or create* I am also pleased to straddle a fence that too often splinters observers into silly extremes. The use of *contexts* along with *individuals* recognizes that much modern surveillance attends to settings, or patterns of relationships and groups, beyond focusing on a given, previously identified individual. Meaning may reside in cross-classifying discrete sources of data (as with computer matching and profiling) that, when considered separately, are not revealing. Systems as well as persons are of interest. The collection of group data or the aggregation of individual into group data offers parameters against which inferences about individuals are drawn for purposes of classification, prediction, and response.

This definition of the new surveillance excludes the routine, nontechnological surveillance that is a part of everyday life, such as looking before crossing the street or seeking the source of a sudden noise or the smell of smoke. It also excludes the routine attentiveness to, and interaction with, others that is fundamental to being a social being (as with mannerly behavior such as opening the door for another or offering a seat to an elderly person). An observer on a nude beach or police interrogating a cooperative suspect would also be excluded, because in these cases the information is volunteered and the unaided senses are sufficient.

I do not include a verb such as *observe* in the definition, because the nature of the means (or the senses involved) suggests subtypes and issues for analysis and ought not to be foreclosed by a definition (e.g., how do visual, auditory, textual, and other forms of surveillance compare with respect to factors such as intrusiveness or validity?). If such a verb is needed, I prefer *scrutinize, regard,* or *attend to* to *observe,* with its tilt toward the visual.

The proposed definition is also more inclusive than those in most of the surveillance essays and many empirical inquiries. Many contemporary theorists offer a narrower definition tied to the goal of control (e.g., Rule, McAdam, et al. 1983; Giddens 1990; Dandecker 1990; Lyon 2001; Manning 2008; Monahan 2010). Taking a cue from Foucault's earlier, more one-sided, writings, in this body of work control as domination is emphasized (whether explicitly or implicitly) rather than as a more positive direction or neutral discipline.

French and German also lack terms that capture contemporary meanings. The French definition of the verb *surveillir* is "to watch," "keep an eye on," or "supervise."[5] The most common German equivalents, *erwachen* and *überwachen*, imply "to watch over," "control," "inspect," and "supervise." *Wach* is cognate with *wake* and *watch*, and *über*, meaning "over," suggest a power differential.

These definitions bring an important message regarding the power to watch and social position. Yet as Lianos (2001, 2003) observes, the modern role of surveillance as control must be placed in perspective alongside its fundamental importance in enhancing institutional efficiency and services.

Surveillance, particularly as it involves the state and organizations, but also in closer relationships such as the family, commonly involves the more and less powerful and on balance favors the former. Understanding this is of the utmost importance. However, it can be better understood in comparison to settings involving other goals, such as protection and entertainment, and where surveillance is reciprocal or does not only or necessarily flow downward or serves to harm the subject.

Given the nature of social interaction and a resource-rich society with civil liberties, there is appreciable data collection from below as well as from above and also across settings. Indeed, the greater the equality in subject-agent settings, the more likely it is that surveillance will be bilateral. Reciprocal surveillance can also be seen (if less often) in hierarchical settings. Mann, Nolan, and Wellman (2003) refer to watchful vigilance from below as *sousveillance*.

In imaginative norm-breaching and -bending video experiments, Mann, the principal researcher, used a visible webcam to film employees in stores who themselves were using video cameras to watch customers. Demonstrators filming police and workers documenting the inappropriate behavior of superordinates are also illustrative.

As the above discussion suggests, the conventional definition of surveillance as hierarchical watching over or social control is inadequate. One indication of the sense in which surveillance can have a positive meaning is its association with "responsibility" (although toward whom and for what is a different issue). This is clear in looking at words such as *carelessness, ignorance, neglect, negligence*, and *indifference*, all shown in the dictionary as antonyms for the term.

To define the topic in terms of control is too narrow for comparative analysis. The broader definition offered here is based on the generic activity of surveilling (the taking in of data). It does not build in the goal of control or specify directionality. In considering current forms we need to appreciate bidirectionality and horizontal as well as vertical directions (at least eight logical categories for analysis). Control needs to be viewed as only one of many possible goals and/or outcomes of surveillance, and in particular that of care. When this is acknowledged, we are in a position to analyze variation and note factors that may cut across kinds of surveillance. This speaks to the Simmel quote that begins this chapter.

The Extended Family of Related Terms

> If this [dissemination of FBI criminal history records] is done properly, it's not a breach of privacy.
>
> CLARENCE KELLEY, former FBI Director[6]

How do surveillance and *privacy* relate? In popular and academic dialogue surveillance is often wrongly seen to be only the opposite of privacy—the former is seen as bad and the latter good. For example, social psychologist Peter Kelvin (1973) emphasized privacy as a nullification mechanism for surveillance. But Kelvin's assertion needs to be seen as only one of four basic empirical connections between privacy and surveillance. Surveillance is not necessarily the dark side of the social dimension of privacy.[7]

Surveillance implies an *agent* who *accesses* personal data (whether through discovery tools, rules, or physical and logistical settings). Privacy, in contrast, involves a *subject* who can *restrict access* to personal data through related means. But both involve efforts to control information—whether as discovery or protection—and they can be connected in a variety of ways (Marx 2015a).

Surveillance can obviously invade privacy—that's what the fuss is all about (e.g. early in the AIDS epidemic, an employee in a lab testing for AIDS who sold information on positive results to a mortuary). Yet surveillance can also be the means of protecting privacy (biometric identification and audit trails, video cameras that film those with access to sensitive data). And privacy can also protect surveillance (undercover police who use fake IDs and call forwarding to protect their identity) just as it can nullify it (e.g., encryption, whispering, and disguises). Privacy for whom and surveillance of whom and by whom and for what reasons need to be specified.

Depending on how it is used, active surveillance can affect the presence of privacy and/or publicity. As nouns, the latter can be seen as polar ends of a continuum involving rules about withholding and disclosing, and seeking or not seeking, information. Thus, depending on the context and role played, individuals or groups may be required to engage, find it optional to engage, or be prohibited from engaging in these activities, whether as subjects or agents of surveillance and communication.

The rules applying to agents and subjects are in principle independent. When the rules specify that a surveillance agent is not to ask certain questions of (or about) a person and the subject has discretion about what to reveal, we can speak of *privacy norms*. When the rules specify that the subject must reveal the information or the agent must seek it, we can speak of *publicity norms* (or, better perhaps, disclosure norms). With publicity norms there is no right to personal privacy that tells the agent not to seek information, or that gives the subject discretion regarding revelation. Rather there is the reverse—the subject has an obligation to reveal and/or the agent to discover (Marx 2011b analyzes the four types).

Private and Public as Adjectives

The moral expectations surrounding information as a normative phenomenon (whether for protection or revelation and whether based on law, policy, or custom) can be differentiated from the empirical status of the information as known or unknown. To understand this distinction, we need the related terms *private* and *public*—adjectives that can tell us about the status of information. Is information known or unknown; does it have an objective quality; can it be relatively easily measured? For example, in face-to face-encounters one generally knows the gender and face of a stranger, whether this is in the street, an office, or a home. The information is "public," as in readily accessible, and this may be supported by antimask laws and requirements to wear symbolic items of clothing, tattoos, or badges. Absent such rules, the stranger's political or religious beliefs are likely to be invisible and unknown.

Of course, normative expectations of privacy and publicity do not always correspond to how the adjectives *public* and *private* are applied to empirical facts. Thus, the cell phone conversations of politicians and celebrities that have privacy protections may become public. Information subjected to publicity requirements, such as government and corporate reports and disclosure statements, may be withheld, destroyed, or falsified. Information not entitled to privacy protections, such as child or spouse abuse, may be unknown because of the inaccessibility of the home to broader visibility. The distinction here calls for empirical analysis of the variation in the fit between the rules about information and what actually happens to it.

In consideration of the role of borders below, I note that privacy and publicity can be thought of in literal and metaphorical spatial terms involving invisibility and visibility and inaccessibility and accessibility. The privacy offered by a closed door or a wall and that offered by an encrypted e-mail message share information restriction, even as they differ in many other ways. Internet forums are not geographically localized but in their accessibility can be usefully thought of as public places, not unlike the traditional public square, where exchanges with others are possible or where others are visible, as with an uncovered window.

Those who make claims about privacy would be more likely to agree with one another, or at least be clearer in their arguments, if they clarified whether they were talking about respect for the rules protecting privacy or the empirical status of information as known or not known. When decent laws are followed, former FBI director Clarence Kelley can correctly claim that they haven't been breached with respect to privacy. But he cannot claim that as an empirical matter, privacy is not altered when such records are created and circulated.

All concepts are of course limited, if not necessarily always scandalous. Erving Goffman (1971), in writing of "relations in public" and "public life," attends to the elements and possibilities within the immediacy of physical copresence (that is, in the presence of another person). This is the strand of "publicness" as visibility. It suggests the "public" as known to at least one other person rather than to any rules about the status of information (that it must be revealed or concealed) or to a legally defined place (such as private golf course). So he/we can paradoxically speak of "public order in private places" (Goffman 1971, XIV).

Such visceral immediacy sets up a nice comparative issue as a cousin of the distanced immediacy we have come to know—love and hate—through the Internet, cell phone, and webcam. It also alerts us to the neglected theme of private order and disorder (one form being privacy violations) in public places. Erving Goffman captures the former with his felicitous phrase *civil inattention*. For example, when passing another person we do not know on the street, some minimal glance is necessary in order not to collide and perhaps to acknowledge the other's presence.[8] The other is "available" for a more indelicate personal border crossing, but it does not occur. When it does occur, whether as a result of staring, leering, or inappropriate speech, gestures, or touch, we have an instance of *uncivil attention* (Gardner 1995).

Confidentiality and Secrecy

Surveillance takes place in the context of rules, expectations, and practices regarding publicity and privacy. *Privacy* and *publicity* and *secrecy* and *confidentiality* are inherently social terms. The terms would be irrelevant to Robinson Crusoe when he thought he was alone on the island. They are social in implying an "other" from whom information is withheld or to whom it is communicated and who may, or may not, be under equivalent expectations to reveal and conceal. This section examines the interrelationships of rules regarding secrecy and confidentiality and helps clarify their meaning.

Confidentiality refers to rules about how discovered information is to be treated. It necessitates at least two parties and calls attention to social interaction and the rules and expectations that enshroud it. For confidentiality to be honored as a practical matter, a second party must have obtained the information. For example, once a doctor appropriately has personal information about a patient, the information is no longer "private" from the doctor. We can't speak of the doctor's invading the privacy of the patient through routine data collection (assuming other unrelated borders are honored). We can however speak of a violation of the rules of confidentiality if the doctor wrongly shares the information or does not adequately protect it.

The information can be viewed as a shared secret, even though the prohibition on revelation (except under approved conditions) applies only to the surveillance agent (the doctor). This contrasts with settings where secrecy and revelation are reciprocal obligations, as with nondisclosure clauses in some contractual relations or court settlements.[9] When the interests of the parties overlap, the information is more likely to remain secret.[10]

Some analysts draw a distinction between secrecy and privacy. *Privacy* is used to mean shielding legitimate, nonstigmatizing information, while *secrecy* "implies the concealment of something which is negatively valued by the excluded audience and, in some instances, by the perpetrator as well" (Warren and Laslett 1977).[11] This definition of secrecy slaps a negative value on protected information. Such information may also be positively valued or neutral. A broader definition that does not start with the negative is needed.

To be sure, the nature and properties of any piece of information suggest an important set of variables (considered in detail in chap. 4). As noted, this inquiry is particularly concerned with personal information, as against that about organizations or the physical world. The kind of information withheld by, revealed by, or taken from an individual is significant. Is it stigmatizing, morally disvalued, disadvantageous; morally and socially neutral; or prestige enhancing, morally valued, and advantageous? The organization and dynamics of information control (whether to discover or communicate/publicize information or to block these) of course will differ depending on the kind of information.

The motives and related goals for protecting, discovering, and communicating personal information are certainly important. Thus, it is useful to differentiate information that others do not know according to the degree of intentionality found with the withholding and the relative importance the individual places on controlling the information. When the nonrevelation of the secret is associated with "something to hide" (either as stigma or nonstigmatizing information that would disadvantage), we see greater intentionality than in situations where the unavailability or withholding of information flows from a sense of propriety or natural conditions such as limits on the senses.

By convention, the term *secrecy* often refers to organizational data, while *privacy* refers to the data of individuals. Since organizations do not generally have "rights" in the same sense that individuals do, *secrecy* is a better term here than *privacy*. This may involve *legitimate organizational secrets,* as with patent details and strategic plans, or *illegitimate organizational secrets,* as with false reporting and cover-ups. The rules around organizational information, as with those around personal information, vary from mandatory disclosures to closures with a large discretionary middle area.

However, apart from legal meanings, many of the information-control processes are the same regardless of whether we are dealing with organizations or individuals. What is fundamental is the issue of information control. There is no compelling reason to call the protection of negative information secrecy and its opposite privacy. Whether as noun, adjective, or verb, the meanings of *secret* and *secrecy* overlap those of *private* and *privacy*. When personal privacy is viewed as a right, it calls attention to the subject's ability to control the release of information. This does not mean it cannot be shared, but that the individual has a choice. The Fifth Amendment, for example, does not prohibit individuals from offering information or confessing, it simply prohibits this from being coercively obtained.

In contrast, the rules applying to legitimate secrecy prohibit or limit the subject from releasing information. This is often accompanied by sanctions for violation. In principle, individuals and organizations don't have a choice about divulging information deemed to be secret by formal rules. Thus, the broader terms *protected* and *unprotected information* can be used to include both privacy and secrecy and their opposites,[12] whether this refers to the rules about the information or its current empirical status.

Types of Privacy

Privacy, like the weather, is much discussed, little understood, and not easy to control. Like its family member *surveillance,* it is a multidimensional concept with fluid and often ill-defined, contested, and negotiated contours, dependent on the context and culture. The scholarly effort to define privacy is a growth industry. Yet as welcome as deductive conceptual efforts regarding the meaning of privacy are, they must be approached deftly lest they end in reification and nominalism gone wild. I prefer to begin with empirical topics that are intellectually and socially compelling and to inductively generate concepts from them.

For our purposes, the central factors are the rules and conditions affecting data outputs from and inputs to the person. These rules and conditions encounter and may create or overcome borders around the person—whether natural or cultural. As noted, I use the term *data* or *information* to broadly refer to various sensory phenomena that may cross the borders of the person (whether leaving or entering) or otherwise be associated with the person.

The concerns of this book are primarily with informational privacy, a form early identified by Westin (1967). I don't wish to enter the debate over what privacy "really" is in some essentialist presocial sense. But I will note how a sociology-of-information approach connects to themes in the literature. Within informational privacy we find the conditions of anonymity and pseudoanonymity, often referred to as being necessary for another type of privacy involving seclusion and being left alone. Personal borders are obviously more difficult to cross if an individual cannot be reached via name or location. The conditions around revelation or protection of various aspects of identity are central to our topic.

Informational privacy encompasses physical privacy. The latter can refer to insulation resulting from natural conditions such as walls, darkness, distance, skin, clothes, and facial expression. These can block or limit outputs and inputs. Bodily privacy is one form of this, and its borders can be crossed by implanting something such as a chip or birth control device or removing something, such as tissue, fluid, or a bullet.[13]

A related and taken-for-granted form is aesthetic privacy (Rule, McAdam, et al. 1983), which refers to the separation, usually by a physical barrier of bedroom or bathroom, of activities involving one's "private parts" and unguarded moments. Alderman and Kennedy (1995) discuss a number of such cases in which the shock of discovering a violation surfaces norms of which we are hardly aware because they are so rarely violated. Clothes and manners also sustain aesthetic privacy. The concern over full-body airport scans also illustrates a violation or breach of such norms.

Informational privacy can be considered as it ties to institutional setting (e.g., financial, educational, health, welfare, employment, criminal justice, national security, voting, census); places and times; the kind of data involved, such as about religion or health, apart from the setting; participant roles (communications privacy as involving two-party, one-party, or no-party consent); and aspects of technology, such as wire or wireless, phone, computer, radio, or TV. Considerations of setting, data type, and means are central to legislation and regulation and rich in anomalies and cross-cultural differences.

In emphasizing informational privacy, several other commonly considered forms such as decisional (Decew 1997) or proprietary (Allen 2007) privacy are slighted.[14] Breaches of these forms primarily involve application or use of private information, rather than information discovery. Although it is distinct, informational privacy shares with the other forms the key factor of control over access to the person or at least the person's data. These may be connected. Thus, if individuals can control their personal information—whether not having to reveal their purchase of birth control pills (when this was illegal) or keeping paparazzi from taking pictures—then they need not worry about that information's being used.

Borders

When you are heading for the border Lord
You're bound to cross the line.
KRIS KRISTOFFERSON, "Border Lord"

Much of human history can be read as a struggle involving the access to and symbolism implied by various kinds of spatial and metaphorical borders. The intersection and blurring of the borders of personal information and technology under conditions of modernization and globalization are central to the topic.[15] When surveillance and communication technology are controversial, it is often because of the crossing, or the failure to cross, a personal border, or because border definitions conflict.

Various borders may protect information: physical blockages such as walls, a purse, or skin; kinds of places or organizations as culturally defined, such as a home, a church, or a public park; kinds of role relationships, such as professional and familial; and various temporal forms, such as time after working hours, leisure time, holidays, and amnesty periods.

Various images can be applied. We can think of borders around the person as being like a bubble, clear, frosted, or opaque and hermetically sealed or permeable—and for the last, whether permitting outputs, inputs, or both. With the piercing abilities of the new surveillance, speaking of the *borderless person* (or even *organization* or *nation*) may become less of an oxymoron.

The idea of borders suggests a circumscribed entity (in this case, the person) separate from its environment. Yet borders to varying degrees permit exchanges or, as they say, "flows." This quality alerts us to the important and neglected issue regarding the directionality of border crossings. Borders, like roads, are navigable in several directions.

Technologies that cross personal borders can be differentiated based on the direction of the crossing and data flow. These issues tie to sociology-of-information questions regarding norms about concealing and revealing information. Violations may occur in failing to collect or offer information. Consider an agent's failure to collect vital information from expectant mothers about drug use (Etzioni 1999) or the arrest history of persons working with children or not checking (as of 2015) gun purchasers against the more than one million persons on the DSH watch list of potential terrorist threats. Examples of the latter would be a subject's failure to reveal such as a house seller concealing a leaky roof or a person with a sexually transmitted disease not informing a partner of this. Most academics and activists emphasize the involuntary collecting of personal information by agents while generally giving little attention to the failure to surveil or of subjects to 'fess up.

However, considerations of privacy need to focus on more than only taking from the person or failing to do so or the failure to reveal. Crossing a personal border to impose upon the person is of equal importance in considerations of liberty and in the generation of a broad and logical conceptual framework. Consider, for example, smells sent through a heating or air-conditioning system intended to affect moods or telephone solicitations, spam and regular junk mail or the bombarding of messages in some supermarkets over the PA system or written on the floor, shopping carts, and neon signs. Or consider individuals who offer information inappropriately, as with public nudity, loud music, or revelation of intimate life details to strangers.

Surveillance and Communication

The function of borders as either containing those within or rejecting those outside (or both) is being changed by new surveillance and communication technologies. The spread of sensors and their weaving into data networks especially calls attention to the connections between undifferentiated and differentiated forms of communication and surveillance. These technologies may be mass or individually based and involve extraction or imposition functions.

In most considerations of individual privacy, the emphasis is on the extent to which the individual can, in principle and in actuality, control data from flowing outward, such as that involving telephone or computer communication, credit card activity, social networks, beliefs and feelings, location, facial appearance, or biometric data such as DNA, voice print, heat, and scent. When such outputs are available, the individual is a transmitter of data, and something is taken from or willingly leaves the person.[16] This transmission may happen in an active or passive fashion and with or without the individual's knowledge and consent.

Much less attention is directed to the individual's control over information and stimuli flowing inward, such as sound, sight, smell, touch, taste, and factors affecting the ability to act (the hard engineering in or out of behavior potentials) and even "cookies" placed on one's computer by web sites visited. Here the individual is a potential recipient of information and related inputs, opportunities, and restrictions from outside. These in a sense enter rather than leave the person, or at least the person's environment.[17]

While we are often happy magnets for such exterior inputs, much energy also goes into constructing and sustaining barriers to unwanted communication forms, such as advertisements (the TV mute button, DVR), spam, telemarketing, and junk mail ("do not contact" lists, call restriction devices), outside noise (headsets), and wearing hats, dark glasses, and even masks in public. Such inputs also extend to the unwanted communication from loud cell phone users in public places. In such cases we see the desire to be left alone and for "space" and distance, or at least insulation from others.

The same technology may of course offer outputs and inputs.[18] What surveillance takes from the individual can be joined with a reverse flow of communication imposed upon the individual. The telescreeen in George Orwell's novel *1984* illustrates this. It transmitted the person's image and words to Big Brother, while simultaneously broadcasting propaganda.

Foucault (1977) observed the move away from the spectacle of irregular public executions as control mechanisms intended to instill fear in the audience to softer punishment hidden and controlled within institutions. The systematic use of supposedly scientific knowledge and less visible surveillance were thought to be more effective and humane. Yet with developments in mass communication and the strengthening of the First Amendment, public access to information is strong and may be getting stronger. We see not only the few watching the many, but the many watching the few, sharing the same logic of visibility intended to bring deterrence and accountability. The news entertains and also brings morality tales and symbolic meanings (Altheide 2002; Andrejevic 2007; Doyle 2003; Leman-Langlois 2002; Mathiesen 1997). Entertainment in the form of sitcoms, music videos, and video games brings the news and morality tales.

In the year 1984 Jim Rule observed that with the development of computing, mass surveillance became possible alongside mass communication. In its indiscriminate sweep, the mass surveillance of generalized computer matching (in which two or more entire databases are compared absent reason for specific suspicion) is equivalent to the indiscriminate mass transmission of a TV or radio signal.

Beyond being mass (broadly) directed, as with TV ads or video cameras on roads, communication and surveillance may be focused with varying degrees of specificity on individual subjects of interest, as with targeted marketing and court-ordered wiretaps. This distinction (mass or individual focus) is considered in the next chapter. Here let us simply note some links and some blurring between the two.

We increasingly see tools such as video and computer technologies that combine surveillance and communication functions or blur the line between them. With this comes a move from mass to more individualized communication determined by characteristics of the recipient. Moreover, developments in the surveillance of consumption have been a major boost to targeted forms of communication.

Individualized (targeted or segmented) marketing communication often occurs as a result of some form of surveillance. Calls to an 800 number, visits to a web page, or consumption behavior can lead to spam or targeted solicitations via telephone and mail. Law enforcement also uses mass communications such as advertisements and mailed solicitations to identify potential offenders (those who respond), who may then become subjects of stings and other forms of surveillance.

Contemporary television and webcam transmissions also combine or blur the line between surveillance and communication. Consider live helicopter videos of car chases, as with O. J. Simpson, or investigative TV programs that use infiltration and stings to uncover consumer fraud and sexual predation. In these cases, the surveillance function is seen as a means for the collection of evidence, as an aide to apprehension of violators, and as an affirmation of cultural beliefs about what happens to them. This line blurring is also seen with home cable TV systems that beyond offering entertainment can monitor viewer behavior for billing, marketing, and security. In the case of the latter they can monitor for fire, gases, functioning of electrical and other systems, unauthorized entry or motion, and internal images of the home when an alarm is triggered.

The same tool of course may serve different functions for various groups. Webcam transmissions such as those in bars or on beaches that offer images of swimmers and weather conditions also serve as means of communication and control. Automobile radios deliver music and emergency messages (the latter even if the radio is turned off), and electronic location and engine monitoring devices can control driving behavior while also offering safety warnings. Multifunction handheld devices that offer radio and television service can receive and transmit personal messages and images, while also offering records of location and communication usage.

In summary, communication and surveillance may be mass (broadly) directed, as with TV ads and video cameras in a public square. Or they may be

individually focused with varying degrees of specificity on subjects of interest, as with marketing to particular demographic groups and air travel profiling. Technical and social developments have strengthened both forms, the
linkages between them, and their merging.

Surveillance Structures

Most of the concepts discussed thus far refer to conditions or outcomes that
are seen to be "produced" as a result of surveillance actions. Such concepts
often are relevant to judgments about surveillance behavior (whether they
represent goals or merely associated conditions). But they tell us little about
how that behavior is produced. To understand that requires attention to the
structure of surveillance behavior.

Structures that are fixed at one point in time (as with a photograph) can be
differentiated from processes that involve interaction and developments over
time (as with a video). In the following discussion concepts are treated as if
they were static, while in chapters 5 and 6 the emphasis is on process.

What are the kinds of role available to be played? Three basic categories
are the agent, subject, and audience. These may be distinct or overlap. We
can identify the *surveillance agent,* or inspector, in Jeremy Bentham's words.
Related terms are *watcher, observer, seeker, auditor, tester, monitor, surveyor,*
and, from Dashiell Hammett, "the op."

The role may consist of either the *sponsoring agent* behind the actions or
the *collecting agent* who actually does the work. These roles may be distinct
or combined. The person (or entity) about whom information is sought or
reported is the *surveillance subject.*[19] All persons of course play both roles,
although hardly in the same form or degree. Roles changes depending on the
context and over the life cycle.[20] The roles are sometimes blurred and may
overlap or be simultaneously present, even for the same person in the same
setting.[21]

The agent and subject are to varying degrees intertwined in a data production dance. But for whom and under what conditions? Data are converted to
information and standardized formats so that they *are* communicable and
useful after being collected. This alerts us to the question of who the audience
is. The *audience* (or data recipients) may be managers, merchants, guards,
parents, or other agents or may be less differentiated, as are consumers of the
mass media and more focused publics. When the results are restricted (remain "private"), we have secrecy on the part of the agent; when the results are
more widely known, we have publicity or visibility (and to varying degrees
the subject's privacy may be lost).

Within the surveillance agent category, the surveillance function may be central to the role, as with police, private detectives, spies, work supervisors, investigative reporters, and some scientists—whether in public health or social inquiry. Or it may simply be a peripheral part of a broader role whose main responsibilities and goals are elsewhere. Illustrative of this are checkout clerks who are trained to look for shoplifters, or dentists who are encouraged (or required) to report suspected child abuse when seeing bruises on the face. Or in another form, under appropriate conditions, any member of a group (in addition to a specific organizational role) may be expected to act as a surveillance agent as an act of good citizenship.

Beyond the sponsor and data collector noted above, the agent role can be separated into the *initial* and often the *secondary user* (and beyond—not to mention a more passive audience which merely becomes aware of the information). These distinctions are rich with empirical and ethical implications. Accountability issues are less pronounced when these are joined than when they are separated (as they increasingly are) in the case of surveillance for hire and secondary users. Such users may legitimately obtain personal information through contracting with the data collector (e.g., to carry out drug tests or purchase consumer preference lists). Or they may obtain it because the collector violates confidentiality, or because an outsider illegitimately obtains it (through wiretaps, hacking, or corrupting those with the information).

When the sponsor, data collector, and user are within the same organization, we see primary use. But when data collected for one purpose migrates elsewhere, we see the important "secondary use" and data-flow issues. Here the data are likely to be used without an individual's permission for unrelated purposes. The United States, relative to Europe, has a much freer market in personal information. Large organizations warehouse and sell vast amounts of very personal information, without the consent and with no immediate benefit to the subject and with little expectation that the individual has any personal or proprietary rights with respect to this.

Many contemporary concerns over surveillance involve the practices of large organizations as the impact reaches to employees, clients, or the public. *Organizational surveillance* is distinct from the *nonorganizational surveillance* carried out by individuals. As Jim Rule (1974) has noted, modern organizations are the driving force in the instrumental collection of personal data. As organizations increasingly use personal data for what David Lyon (2003) calls social sorting, the implications for many aspects of life are profound.

At the organizational level, formal surveillance involves a constituency. This term is used broadly to refer to those with some rule-defined relationship or potential connection to the organization. The connection may be one of formal membership or of mere contact, as through renting a video or showing a passport at a border.

Organizations have varying degrees of internal and external surveillance. Erving Goffman (1961) has richly described many kinds of employee or inmate monitoring, within "total institutions." His examples fit within the category of *internal constituency surveillance.* Here individuals "belong" to the organization in a double sense. First they belong as members. With a loose analogy to property, they also in a sense are "belongings" of the organization, to be treated as objects often managed through deep surveillance.

External constituency surveillance is present when those who are watched have some patterned contact with the organization (e.g., as customers, patients, malefactors or citizens subject to laws of the state). Those observed do not "belong" to the organization the way an employee or inmate does. Credit card companies and banks, for example, monitor client transactions and also seek potential clients by mining and combining databases.

The control activities of a government agency charged with enforcing health and safety regulations is another example. In this case the organization is responsible for seeing that categories of persons subject to its rules are in compliance, even though they are not members of the organization (e.g., pharmaceutical or manufacturing organizations). The same compliance function can be seen with nongovernmental organizations that audit or grant ratings, licenses, and certifications.

In the case of *external nonconstituency surveillance,* organizations monitor their broader environment, including other organizations and social trends. The rapidly growing field of business intelligence seeks information about competitors, social conditions, and trends that may affect an organization. One variant of this is industrial espionage. Organizational planning (whether by government or the private sector) also requires such data, although this is usually treated in the aggregate instead of in personally identifiable form.

Nonorganizational surveillance, in which an individual watches another individual or an organization (whether for protection, strategic, or prurient reasons) apart from an organizational role, is another major form. It may involve *role relationship surveillance,* as with family members (parents and children, the suspicious spouse) or friends looking out for and at each other (e.g., monitoring location through a cell phone). Or it can *involve non-role-relationship surveillance*—as with the free-floating activities of the voyeur whose watching is unconnected to a legitimate role (chap. 9 on Tom Voire).

Agent-initiated surveillance, which is particularly characteristic of compliance checks, such as an inspection of a truck or a boat, can be differentiated from *subject-initiated surveillance.* In the latter, the individual makes a claim or seeks help and essentially invites, or at least agrees to, scrutiny. Examples include submitting one's transcript, undergoing osteoporosis screening, or applying for a job requiring an extensive background investigation. Consider also the "How am I driving?" signs on vehicles that offer a toll free number for observers to report (these contrast with the third-party-initiated drop-a-dime programs). Gamblers, too, can exercise self-exclusion if they are concerned over their lack of self-control by requesting that their names be placed on a list of persons banned from casinos.[22]

The federally funded Watch Your Car program fits here. Vehicle owners attach a decal to their cars inviting police to pull them (the cars) over late at night to be sure the cars are not stolen. To the extent that this "coproduction" of social order becomes more widely established, it is easy to imagine individuals wearing miniature video, audio, location, and biological monitors sending data outward to protective and other sources. They could also serve to send data to the individual (e.g., warnings for drivers about traffic diversions), or, as is the case with implanted health monitors, this could also involve various kinds of physiological inputs, such as stimulating the heart or releasing chemicals into the body (e.g., in an effort to lower serotonin levels).

The self-restraint and voluntary compliance favored in liberal democratic theory receives a new dimension here. The line between public and private order maintenance becomes hazier. The border between self and other may also be blurred in the sense that a continuous transmission link can exist between sender and receiver, as with brain waves or scents.

The agent and subject merge with *self-surveillance* when individuals watch themselves. Appealing to morality, offering role models (particularly in the case of consumer behavior), or communicating reminders and creating uncertainty about whether or not surveillance is operating,[23] has the goal of creating deterrence through awareness, prevention, and certain kinds of consumption (e.g., for underarm deodorant—don't leave home without it). Self-surveillance receives strong support from the engineering of environments for visibility and documentation. In the driving example note road signs telling drivers their speed.

Self-surveillance may be for the benefit of the subject who initiates it rather than some external agent. As chapter 6 will note, drug-testing tools are available to individuals as well as to organizations to help defeat the latter's tests. In addition, the availability of products that permit individuals to self-test for alcohol and drug level, pregnancy, menopause, AIDS, and genetic patterns can be viewed as a form of empowerment.[24] When individuals can genuinely choose to be surveilled and can control the results, they have far fewer concerns with conventional privacy invasions.

Still, self-monitoring can be intertwined with an external surveillance agent in the form of parallel or *cosurveillance.* This is the case, for example, with remote health monitoring (e.g., of a heart pacemaker), in which both the monitored person and a health agency simultaneously receive signals about the subject.

In the above case, cosurveillance is *nonreciprocal,* with personal data going from the watched to the watcher (e.g., employers, merchants, doctors, teachers, parents), and tends to reflect power and resource differences. In contrast, *reciprocal surveillance* is by definition bidirectional, as with social networking sites. Other examples include deterrence and compliance inspections in national security contexts or the filming of guards and prisoners.[25] Consider also the suspicious society's surveillance rotunda (significantly expanded since 9/11), in which authorities seek information from citizens as general members of a group. In this context, individuals are encouraged to watch each other and report suspicious behavior and objects, whether in public or in specific settings such as work and schools. Such programs expanded significantly after 9/11.

But reciprocal need not mean equal. Surveillance that is reciprocal may be *asymmetrical* or *symmetrical.* In a democratic society citizens and government engage in reciprocal but distinct forms of mutual surveillance. Citizens can watch government through requirements for open hearings and meetings, freedom of information requests, and conflict-of-interest and other disclosure statements. However, unlike government, citizens cannot legally wiretap, carry out Fourth Amendment searches, or see census or tax returns. Citizens can obtain some information from the public records that corporations must file. And the corporation may require citizens to provide personal information in return for goods and services, but it does not offer equivalent information about those within its organization. Patients reveal a great deal to doctors but, beyond seeing framed diplomas and licenses, generally are not offered the doctor's personal information.

In bounded settings such as a protest demonstration, there may be greater equivalence with respect to particular means. For example, police and demonstrators may videotape each other—an illustration of symmetrical reciprocated surveillance. This is seen in many settings of organizational conflict in which the contending parties are roughly equivalent. Games such as poker involve this, as do some contractual agreements and treaties (e.g., the mutual deterrence of nuclear arms sought through reciprocal watching).

Symmetrical forms may be present even in the absence of formal agreements. Spies or (more neutrally) intelligence agents, whether working for competing countries, companies, or athletic teams, are often mirror images of each other and stay within some broad, rarely stated (but widely understood) expectations about how far to go, although in contrast to games such as poker, these are not part of the formal rules. They offensively seek to discover their opponent's information and defensively to protect their own.

Yet on balance asymmetry in formal surveillance and information rights within hierarchical organizations and other stratified settings remains. This asymmetry is not always easy to see, because it can be embedded in the physical and cultural environment.[26] At the same time, mutual surveillance, particularly in face-to-face settings, is common. This may reflect the rights of those in lower-status positions, but more frequently it is simply an accompaniment and accomplishment of their being sensory beings.

The distinctions in this section make clear how varied the patterns are when we approach the topic inductively from the empirical ground up. Taking just the role played (subject or agent), self- or cosurveillance, reciprocal or nonreciprocal, symmetrical or asymmetrical, and the audience size (and whether the results stay private or become more broadly public) yields many outcomes to be accounted for, and that expands greatly when the other concepts listed below are considered.

This Chapter's Concepts

A. Basic Terms

Surveillance
Nonstrategic surveillance
Strategic surveillance
Traditional surveillance
New surveillance
Self-surveillance
Cosurveillance
Sousveillance
Privacy
Publicity
Privacy norms
Publicity norms
Informational, aesthetic, decisional, proprietary privacy
Civil Inattention
Uncivil Attention
Confidentiality
Secrecy
Legitimate organizational secrets

Illegitimate organizational secrets
Protected information
Unprotected information

B. Surveillance Structures

Surveillance agent—sponsor, collector, initial and secondary users
Surveillance subject
Surveillance audience
Organizational surveillance
External constituency surveillance
Internal constituency surveillance
External nonconstituency surveillance
Nonorganizational surveillance
Role relationship surveillance
Non-role-relationship surveillance
Agent-initiated surveillance
Subject-initiated surveillance
Self-surveillance
Cosurveillance
Nonreciprocal surveillance
Reciprocal surveillance
Asymmetrical surveillance
Symmetrical surveillance

This chapter has discussed general concepts that define the sociology of surveillance and of personal information. Chapter 2 identifies dimensions that can be used to characterize any act of surveillance, but with a particular interest in ways of conceptualizing what is new.

So What's New?
Classifying Surveillance Means for Change and Continuity

There's something happening here.
What it is ain't exactly clear.
STEPHEN STILLS

From our general definition of concepts, the next three chapters turn to a more detailed consideration of the basic surveillance components of means, goals, and data characteristics. As noted, using a common group of attributes permits researchers to make more differentiated and precise comparisons between cases, identify change and continuity, and reach explanatory and normative conclusions. We begin with a brief historical review and then a narrative discussion of the new surveillance. The final section articulates a set of dimensions for characterizing any surveillance tool.

A Brief History: Six Centuries in Two Pages

In the fifteenth century, religious surveillance in Europe was a powerful and dominant form. It built on the watchful and potentially wrathful eye of the biblical God. This involved the search for heretics, devils, and witches, as well as the more routine policing of religious consciousness, ritual, and religiously based rules such as those involving adultery and wedlock. It also allowed officials to keep basic records of births, marriages, baptisms, and deaths. Given the intertwining of the state and religion, political and religious surveillance could be indistinguishable. Over the next several centuries these became less closely bound, as the state took over some of the record keeping of the church, individuals gained new rights, and religious surveillance gradually declined.

In the sixteenth and seventeenth centuries, with the appearance and growth of the embryonic nation-state, which had new needs as well as a heightened capacity to gather and use information, political surveillance became more sophisticated and increasingly important. Secularism, a scientific worldview, and protections for religious dissent slowly spread. As new borders between the state and religion (and civil society more generally) developed, religious and other forms of personal expression came to be seen as matters of individual liberty. Yet new possibilities for suspicion of political loyalty appeared, along with new fears of being watched.[1] Wider domestic political surveillance is a natural corollary of the centralization of power and the increased heterogeneity, scale, and mobility associated with the emerging modern society. Concerns over possible links between internal and external security become more evident.

Over the next several centuries we see a gradual move to a broadly "policed" society in which agents of the state, industry, and commerce come to exercise control over ever wider social and geographical areas. In building on the work of Weber, Nietzsche, Marx, Bentham, and Hobbes, many scholars have elaborated on these developments.[2]

Foucault (1977) is of particular importance in calling attention to the expansion of social control surveillance. His model suggests an octopus with ever more powerful and penetrating information tentacles. Foucault offers an eloquent description of institutional changes in processing, organizing, and responding to persons that became increasingly visible toward the end of the eighteenth century. In the case of criminal justice, he observes that rather than inflicting indiscriminate punishment on the body of offenders as a generic class in a very public fashion, the emphasis was on a less visible categorizing of the individual and motivating future behavior.

The creation of categories of person permits different treatment that can be publicly justified as being fair, since equivalent cases are treated in the same way and the results can be scientifically sanctified. Individuals are believed to be better understood, located, controlled, manipulated, and changed when they are inspected, sorted, and compared to each other through empirical measurement of their presumed characteristics and predispositions. Those deemed threats, risks, or in need of help are identified for appropriate response. The categorization of the individual relative to others was intended to create "the docile person," who is amenable to the goals of the organization, behaves in a disciplined way, and exercises self-control, aware of being under surveillance.

The standards for judgment reflect a process of "normalization" by which persons are assessed. This can involve an evaluation of how well the individual complies with rules or a coding of the individual with respect to an array of physiological, social, and psychological measurements as a guide to more differentiated responses. These evaluation systems initially were seen as means of controlling or managing the individual, but later categorizations identified individuals for favorable selection and treatment.

Relative to earlier time periods, this system requires attention to the characteristics of the unique individual and the creation of detailed personal records. The individual becomes a distinctive object to be scrutinized, understood, and improved upon through measurements offered by the newly emerging sciences of the person. But at the same time the person is deindividualized in being assigned to generic categories of classification.

To elaborate further on this system, setting the standards and measuring persons is the province of imperial experts whose organizational power and resources permit them to define what knowledge is, assess subjects, and use the results to further the goals of the institution. The creation of presumably rational (and therefore easier to rationalize) "disciplinary regimes" drawing on a variety of social and cultural means is intended to mold and manipulate individuals toward the organization's ends.

Many in Foucault's tradition make a latent (and sometimes explicit) assumption that what serves the organization generally does not serve the individual, although the individual may not realize that. Whether or not (or better, *when*) that is correct is a question meriting empirical inquiry.

Overall, in this line of thinking, the trend is a gradual and continuing expansion, systematization, and scientification of the means of observation, measurement, detection, record keeping, analysis, and communication. The development of identity cards and passports is one example of this (Caplan and Torpey 2001; Groebiner, Kyburz, and Peck, 2007). The ethos Foucault identified went beyond the prison and the hospital to other enclosed spaces, such as the factory and school, and became ever more important for governance throughout society, wherever there was a perceived need to categorize and organize subjects. Included in this ethos was a move away from the direct use of force, in part because it was less necessary as a control vehicle. In the case of work, authority shifted from the family and local guild to the factory.

For the state, in addition to enhanced categorization of criminals and deviants as well as information gathering and infiltration because of fear of revolution, this system of assessment involved the creation of specialized intelligence units and an expanded census, improved record keeping, police registers and dossiers, identity documents (including those based on crude biometrics such as the shape of the head), and inspections. Personal information came to be collected not only for taxation, conscription, law enforcement, and border control (both immigration and emigration) uses, but also to determine citizenship and eligibility for democratic participation and to improve social planning and public health. And as a corollary, the line blurred between direct political surveillance and a governance or administration that was more modern and in some ways more benign even as it also contained the seeds of twentieth-century totalitarianism.

In the nineteenth and twentieth centuries, with the growth of bureaucracy and the regulated and welfare states, the content of surveillance expanded yet again to detailed personal information in order to determine conformity with an ever-increasing number of laws and regulations and eligibility for various welfare and intervention programs from social security to the protection of children and animals. A state concerned with controlling its borders and bureaucratically organized around the certification of identity, experience, and competence depends on the collection of personal information. Risk assessment, prediction, prevention, and rational planning also require such information.[3] A society with heightened aspirations for individual and social perfection that seeks to be safe and secure under the banner of challenged concepts such as "zero tolerance" must also be data avaricious.

Government uses of data in turn have been supplemented (and, on any quantitative scale, probably overtaken) by contemporary employment, consumer, and medical surveillance. The contemporary commercial state is inconceivable without the massive collection of personal data.

So where does this highly selective and compressed historical summary leave us? The surveillance essays noted in the previous chapter suggest the appearance of a new kind of society and set of practices, but they lack the specificity to take us beyond very general statements. The surveillance essay authors use different names to describe the new societies they envision and its fundamental processes. Below I give a representative (although hardly exhaustive) list of their concepts, starting with Jeremy Bentham's panopticon (Bentham 1995).

Surveillance Essays That Name the New Society and Some Key Aspects of It
  (a Representative, Although Hardly Exhaustive, List)

the panopticon (Bentham 1843)
disciplinary society, the gaze, and biopower (Foucault 1977, 1988)
surveillance society, the new surveillance, and maximum security society
    (Marx 1985, 1988, 2002)
net widening (S. Cohen 1985)
dossier society (Laudon 1986b)
dataveillance (Clarke 1988)
superpanopticon (Poster 1990)
society of control (Deleuze 1990)
l'anamorphose de l'état-nation (Palidda 1992)
panoptic sort (Gandy 1993)

minimum security society (Blomberg 1987)

synopticon (Mathiesen 1997)

securitization (Waever 1995)

telematic society (Bogard 1996)

techno-policing (Nogala 1995)

transparent society (Brin 1998)

liquid modernity (Bauman 2000)

information empire (Hardt and Negri 2000)

surveillant assemblage (Haggerty and Ericson 2000)

postpanopticon (Boyne 2000)

glass cage (Gabriel 2004)

ban-opticon (Bigo 2006a)

high policing (Brodeur and Leman-Langlois 2006)

ubiquitous computing (Greenfield 2006)

überveillance (Michael, Fusco, and Michael 2008)

safe society (Lyon 2007)

ambient intelligence (Wright et al. 2010)

thick and thin surveillance (Torpey 2007)

cryptopicon (Vaidhyanathan 2011)

In general, in offering broad theoretical accounts, these grand (and *grande)* narratives draw on newsworthy accounts and secondary empirical data, often sweeping across contexts, countries, and technologies. Theoretical essays offering such concepts are a necessary first step. They convey an intuitive sense that something significant is happening. But too often they fail to disentangle the multiple dimensions that make up their ideal type and to explore distributions, correlations and interrelations. Generally, this work does not begin by offering an inclusive definition of surveillance, nor does it identify components that would systematically permit differentiating the new from the old forms, making comparisons within and across these, or seeing what is universal across human societies.

Consider, for example, Torpey's (2007) differentiation of *thin* from *thick* surveillance. The former monitors movement and transactions (e.g., as with cell phones or credit cards) but generally without constraining mobility, while the latter refers to confinement to delineated and frequently fortified spaces. While thin surveillance is universal, the thicker forms disproportionately affect lower-status and marginal groups, such as the institutionalized. The piling on and mutual reinforcement of surveillance forms can engender what Lemert (1951) termed secondary deviance and additional inequitable restrictions, data collection, and new procedural violations (Lyon 2003; Newburn and Hayman 2001; Patillo, Weiman, and Western 2004; Neyland 2006).

Torpey's distinction usefully captures some aspects of the interaction and social distribution of kinds of surveillance. "Starter datum" can, in the vocabulary of statisticians, generate breeder documents that become central for life chances (for jobs, credit, rentals, and the like). The expansion and tightening of stigmatic social control tentacles can reach new heights—or lows, depending on one's perspective. This is particularly the case in total institutions and in their reproduction beyond physical walls as a result of electronic location and behavior monitoring and vetting as a requirement for access to goods and services. The new technologies have major implications for social stratification, both reenforcing and undermining traditional patterns.

Yet the distinction between thin and thick surveillance also collapses dimensions that should be separately studied, such as types of access (e.g., physical access involving combinations of entering and leaving vs. digital access to opportunities for communication or service) and the scale or comprehensiveness of surveillance (e.g., its intensity and extensity as seen in the number of areas of life considered, the degree of probing, and the integration of data).

Conclusions, whether explanatory or evaluative, must identify broad, ideal types as well as the dimensions by which the richness of the empirical world can be disaggregated. We need these specific dimensions in order to take systematic account of the variation whose causes, processes, and consequences we seek to understand.

As the twentieth century drew to a close and the new surveillance became more apparent, the seventeen themes below were often seen in scholarly discussions. This book is an effort to wrestle with, specify, and extend ideas 1–9 and to raise questions via qualifying statements about 10–17. As Erving Goffman (1981) sagely put it in one of the last things he wrote, "There are already enough inflated pronouncements in the world; our job is to dissect such activity, not increase the supply."

Surveillance Essay Themes

1. Surveillance is about the exercise of power.
2. Knowledge is central to the exercise of power.
3. The technical ability to know and use knowledge has undergone profound quantitative and qualitative changes since industrialization and has accelerated since the mid-1950s.
4. Data collection vastly expands in breadth and depth continuously (or at least routinely if episodically), covering and recovering ever more areas of life, often giving meaning to what previously was meaningless.
5. The internal and external network connectivity of various forms of knowledge increases, enhancing the power of the center but not requiring it to be directly on the scene, crossing national borders at will.

6. The classification of subjects becomes ever more precise and differentiated.

7. The surveillance of subordinates (especially the suspected) spills beyond the organization and specific cause to the decentralized, categorical examination of routine activities.

8. Data collection is ever more embedded and automated as it becomes a part of the activity itself (e.g., using credit cards, communicating, driving, setting room temperature) rather than being imposed upon it or in its association with an identifying symbol attached to a person or object.

9. Control is softer and less visible, presented as being in the interest of its subjects, who cooperate in providing information about and in controlling themselves and others.

10. Surveillance subjects are passive, indifferent, or welcoming, and they provide personal data as a result of ignorance, manipulation, deception, or seduction.

11. A bright line separates controllers from the controlled and the guilty from the innocent.

12. Surveillance is bad and privacy is good.

13. The power of the state and organizations (national and international) grows ever greater, and this is matched by lessened visibility and accountability and the weakening of those controlled.

14. Surveillance phenomena are treated in a general fashion as if they were unidimensional with a failure to differentiate components such as the means, data collected, users, goals, settings, and point of view of the observer and the actor.

15. The engine driving this is global capitalism under the sway of neoliberalism.

16. Things work as planned.

17. If we are not careful (and, even if we are, perhaps), dystopia is just around the corner, or at best a few blocks away.

Defining the New Surveillance

You touch nothing, nothing touches you.
OUTDATED UNDERWORLD FOLK WISDOM

The term *surveillance* comes from Latin and French. In Latin *vigilare* means "to keep watch." The prefix *sur* in Latin refers to below. Here we see the power differential that is central to many forms as "Sur-veillance" can mean keeping watch on those below. But viewed from French *sur* can also imply "super" (greater in quality, amount, or degree) as in *surcharge*. One might think of the new surveillance as involving supercharged, superwatching technologies that probe and analyze more rapidly, deeply, widely, and inexpensively. *Superwatching* conveys an important strand but is awkward. In spite of its unplanned nature, this linguistic joining of multiple meanings helps to capture the contemporary topic—both its enhanced technical power and its frequently being a factor in power relations.

The new information-extractive technologies go beyond everyday observations routinely made with the senses. Consistent with the dictionary's definition of *extract*, they "remove or take out, especially by effort or force anything firmly rooted." However the "effort" is increasingly soft, unobtrusive, and manipulative rather than directly forceful. Apart from overcoming firm roots, the tactics also create new information by connecting unconnected data.

While not "firmly rooted" in a conventional way, much personal information has traditionally been unavailable for several reasons. First, the physical world has its limitations (e.g., the inability to see in the dark or through solid barriers or hear far away). There have also been logistical and practical limitations—for example, the difficulty of searching through vast amounts of data, combining widely dispersed or differently formatted records, or searching everyone and everything entering and leaving a location. Thus, if individuals did not wish to reveal personal information they traditionally had considerable room to protect or disguise it. New technologies overcome many of these limitations, even as they may offer new means of protection and evasion.

In the Olmstead case in 1928 Justice Louis Brandeis wrote, "Discovery and invention have made it possible for the government, by means far more effective than stretching upon the rack, to obtain disclosure in court of what is whispered in the closet. The progress of science in furnishing the government with means of espionage is not likely to stop with wiretapping." His haunting words apply even more clearly today as the line between science and science fiction is continually redrawn. Not only are new "means of espionage" widely available to government, but they are also available to nongovernmental organizations and private individuals.

New technologies for collecting personal information are constantly appearing, and they transcend the less effective and efficient old means as well as their greater physical and liberty-enhancing protections. The new technologies probe more deeply, widely, and softly than traditional methods, transcending the barriers—both natural (distance, darkness, skin, time, microscopic size) and constructed (walls, sealed envelopes, incompatible formats)—that historically protected personal information.

In short, the boundaries that have defined and given integrity to social systems, groups, and the self are increasingly permeable. The power of governmental and private organizations to compel disclosure (whether based on technology, law, circumstance, seduction, or deception), and to aggregate, analyze, and distribute personal information is a defining attribute of our time. We are becoming a transparent society of record and of records, such that documentation of our history, current identity, location, and physiological and psychological states and behavior is increasingly complete. With predictive profiles, there are even claims to be able to know individual futures. Information collection often occurs invisibly, automatically and remotely—being built into routine activities. Awareness and genuine consent on the part of the subject may be lacking. Data collection is likely to occur gently with a velvet glove rather than a mailed fist (although that might be unseen inside the glove).

The amount of personal information collected has vastly increased in recent decades. New technologies have the potential to reveal and analyze the unseen, unknown, forgotten, withheld, and unconnected. Like the discovery of the atom or the unconscious, these technologies surface bits of reality that were previously hidden, or did not contain informational clues. People are in a sense turned inside out.

To be alive and a social being is to automatically give off "signals of constant information" as Paul Simon sings in "Boy in the Bubble." These can be as heat, pressure, motion, brain waves, perspiration, breath, cells, sound, olifacteurs, microbes, waste matter, or garbage, as well as more familiar forms such as communication and visible behavior.

The widely quoted defense of personal borders offered by William Pitt (1763) to the House of Lords in the eighteenth century needs revision for the twenty-first century to read:

> The richest person may, in his summer cottage,
> no longer bid defiance to all the forces of the Crown.
> It may be strong; its roof may not shake; the wind may
> not blow through it; the storm may not enter;
> But no matter—with the glories that are, neither
> the King of England, nor his force, have any
> need to physically cross the threshold of that glorious tenement
> to know what occurs within.

The King no longer has to come to the data. The data come to him. Cottages, castles, and fortresses ain't what they used to be. Remote data increasingly flow into computers directly from natural actions such as head and eye shifts, speech, movement, and body functioning and through previously protective borders. Increasingly, too, the flow is more rapid, efficient, and comprehensive than in the days of manual collection and entering of data. The computer is no longer only the passive recipient of time-lagged data about which the subject is likely to be aware.

The signs, markers, emanations, tracks, traces, remnants, deposits, debris, and residuals that accompany being in the world and interacting with others are given new meanings by technology. Through a value-added, transformational, mosaic process, machines (often with only a little help from their friends) may find significance in surfacing and/or combining heretofore-meaningless data into personal information.

This surfacing is aided by an automatic, labor-saving process of *prohesion* identified by Keith Guzik (2016). With prohesion, dispersed data (e.g., records in different agencies pertaining to a subject) become more *cohesive* and data may become more *adhesive* in their attachment for purposes of identification/location to the person or objects such as a car, a tool, or an animal.

The world is awash in new kinds of data which previously had no meaning or whose meaning was hidden and unknown, absent their being combined with other data and transformed via measurements and tests into something claimed to be meaningful (if occasionally lacking in transparency with respect to the inner working of the means and evidence of validity, which makes some tests more akin to magic than to science). Consider, for example, the analysis of abandoned DNA (Joh 2006), saliva or scent, or elaborate profiles based on a mosaic of distinct variables in which the constructed whole is greater than the sum of the individual parts.

A central feature of much new surveillance is the conversion to digital form of what is gathered. This makes it communicable and comparable on a previously unimaginable scale. Many of the raw data have no direct meaning. Thus, meaning must be added by interpretive programs generated (if often not adequately reviewed) by humans and often accompanied by the illusion (and dream of many computer scientists) that the meaning is inherent in the data and not partly an artifact of the means used. New methods such as dataveillance (Clarke 1988) and data mining are used for locating or supplying meaning to what had simply been data.

The indicators used to make meaning are often inferential, circumstantial, and future oriented, being several orders removed from the direct observation of actual behavior (e.g., counting how many units are processed or directly observing illegal behavior, or seeing a person actually swim). Meanings, for example, can be generated by comparing an individual against a large database in order to make predictions, the assumption being that indirect measures (often in combination) serve as a shorthand-proxy for the outcome of interest (e.g., identifying lawbreakers, national security threats, absenteeism, drug use, health, loyalty, honesty, and a variety of other "tested" potentials).

TABLE 2.1. Surveillance dimensions

Dimension	Traditional surveillance	The new surveillance
Senses	Unaided senses	Extends senses, new kinds of sensing
Visibility (literally or known about) collection of data, who does it, where, when, and on whose behalf)	Visible	Less visible or invisible
Consent	Lower proportion involuntary	Higher proportion involuntary
Cost	Expensive per-unit data	Inexpensive per-unit data
Location of data collectors or analyzers	On scene	Remote
Fixity of data collection	Stationary (one location)	Stationary, roams
Ethos	Harder (more coercive)	Softer (less coercive)
Integration	Data collection as separate activity	Data collection folded into routine activity
Data collector	Animate (human, animal)	Machine
Operation	Manual	Automated
Time lag between data collection and action based on it	Yes	No, can be immediate
Attached to person or object	No	Can be
Where data resides	With the collector, stays local	With third parties, often migrates
Timing	Single point or intermittent	Continuous, omnipresent
Time period	Present	Past, present, future
Data availability	Frequent time lags	Real-time availability
Technology availability	Disproportionately available to elites	More democratized, some forms widely available
Focus of data collection	Individual	Individual, categories of interest, objects
Comprehensiveness	Single measure	Multiple measures
Context	Contextual	Acontextual
Depth	Less intensive	More intensive
Breadth	Less extensive	More extensive
Ratio of surveillant to self-knowledge	Higher (what the surveillant knows, the subject more likely knows as well)	Lower (surveillant more likely knows things subject doesn't)
Identifiability of subject of surveillance	Emphasis on known individuals	Emphasis also on anonymous individuals, masses
Emphasis	Individuals	Individuals, networks, systems

TABLE 2.1. (*continued*)

Dimension	Traditional surveillance	The new surveillance
Data appearance	Direct representation	Realistic, abstracted, indirect, simulated
Form	Single media (narrative or numerical)	Multiple media
Who collects data	Specialists	Specialists, role dispersal, self-monitoring
Where collected	Enclosed, bounded space	Bounded or open
Ease of data analysis	More difficult to organize, store, retrieve, analyze	Easier to organize, store, retrieve, analyze
Extent of data merging	Discrete, noncombinable	Easy to combine because digitized
Ease of data communication	More difficult to send, receive	Easier to send, receive
Documentation, record keeping, searching	Requires additional steps, less routine	Inherent in the process or routinely done
Basis of judgments	The unique individual	The individual in relation to statistical averages and aggregate categories

Beyond the increased amount of information is the increased merging of previously compartmentalized information (whether based on form, place, time period, or organization). In relatively unrestrained fashion, new (and old) organizations are combining and selling traditional and innovative forms of personal information, as well as using them in their internal management. Haggerty and Ericson (2000) refer to this connectivity as the *surveillant assemblage.*

Another trend is the local and international marketing of data, as well as of techniques to gather it. While some of this spills over into the marketing of self-monitoring devices, in general the ratio of what individuals know about themselves (or are capable of knowing) to what outsiders and experts can know about them appears to have shifted away from the individual—even though, in absolute terms, individuals have ever more self-information.

For most of history, personal reputation in small-scale environments was sufficient to validate an individual's claims. One could assume that under cover of darkness, physical barriers, distance, or time, one's secrets were safe, since surveillance had to rely on the unaided senses or relatively crude tools such as telescopes. One might also assume that visual evidence such as a photograph had greater validity than is the case today, with more easily manipulated digital images (although as soon as the camera appeared, so did deceptive uses—Tagg 1988).

But now there is less certainty than ever about whether a conversation or behavior is being secretly audio- or videotaped; whether supposedly confidential personal records are being remotely accessed by faceless voyeurs, enemies, and merchants; whether darkness has been pierced by night-vision cameras; or whether the physical remnants we invariably leave—olifacteurs or DNA from skin or hair, or the way we walk—have come within a data collector's net. Even something as banal as the idle comments one makes while on hold during a call to a business may be recorded and analyzed. The simple act of deleting a communication from a computer and seeing it "disappear" is no guarantee that a backup copy has not been made or that it could not be retrieved.

The social implications of these changes are little understood. As noted, to better understand them, researchers need to approach these realities in a systematic way, making comparative statements across time periods, techniques, contexts, and cultures. The broad descriptions in the surveillance essays, news accounts, and fictional stories of later chapters suggest profound change. We will better understand the changes when we identify the dimensions of the topic and locate contemporary practices within a more general framework by which any act of strategic surveillance can be categorized.

Dimensions of Surveillance

Is the new surveillance really so new? The answer partly depends on where and how one looks. It is possible to argue that it isn't that new, and even if it is in principle, the gap between its supposed potential and actual implementation is large. Information boundaries and discovery and protection actions are found in all societies and, beyond that, in all living systems (Beniger 1986). Enduring elements are present whether spies are watching from a mountain top, a Civil War balloon, or a satellite.[4]

In considering whether something is new—and if so, what is new about it and whether there is difference or similarity, rupture or continuity, qualitative or merely quantitative change—it is necessary to specify the level of abstraction. Viewed very abstractly, qualitative social change is rare given the constants (both common needs and resource restrictions) and the influence of tradition in human societies. The new surveillance of necessity builds on and shares elements with traditional forms. Some elements of the form emerge out of the universality of the surveillance function and of human potentials, others out of the power of tradition (numbers were used for identification before digitalization).

However, I don't think we gain a great deal by noting that trial by ordeal, torture, the polygraph, and DNA analysis are all means of gathering information and assessing truth claims. Nor are we helped much by seeing that at some level intercepting a cellular telephone message is equivalent to one group reading another's smoke signals. If one wishes to understand a given form in its context and its relation to the culture and social structure in question, to ask about continuity and change, to analyze variation across settings and to reach normative conclusions, we need more precise concepts. Without a language for analyzing change we cannot understand the profound experience of shock (and often affront and invasion or sense of security) many individuals feel in the face of the new surveillance.

The definition of the new surveillance offered in the previous chapter (scrutiny of individuals, groups, and contexts through the use of technical means) separates it from previous forms and more closely reflects the contemporary situation. Yet the very breadth of big definitional tents must be approached cautiously. Broad concepts may "shroud a galaxy of connotations" (Smelser 1959, 2) and fail to capture the richness and internal variation of the topic.

At the most general level the definition of the new surveillance above captures some common elements in the enormously varied contemporary tactics. Thus, my definition would include

A parent regarding a baby on a video monitor during commercials or through a day care center webcast

A database for employers that lists persons who have filed workers' compensation claims against which to compare job applicants

An employer that makes providing Facebook passwords and provision of a DNA sample mandatory for employees

A supervisor monitoring employee's location and e-mail and phone communication and using software that reveals the number of keystrokes and patterns of computer use

Smart homes with Smart Meters (as part of the Smart Grid infrastructure) which can minutely (literally, as in minute by minute) monitor and remotely control electrical uses for "smart appliances" or lower your thermostat

Computer matching and data merging and mining

An Internet search company that provides lists of topics searched and IP addresses to advertisers and government

Uninvited cookies that track web page behavior

Google's contested collection and retention of Internet Wi-Fi signals as part of its Street View Camera cars

A conventional imaging or thermal sensing device aimed at a person or the exterior of a house from across the street, from a drone, or from a satellite thousands of miles away (including to measure the body temperature of passengers departing from international airports to determine whether they carry swine flu)

Video monitors in a department store scanning customers and matching their images to those of suspected shoplifters and charting movement through the store

A hidden camera in an ATM

Analyzing hair to determine drug use

A self-test for level of alcohol

The polygraph or technology that monitors brain waves to determine truthfulness

Intelligent transportation systems

Tracking location and travel through signals a cell phone responds to (pings) (including police use of simulated cell phone towers to intercept communications data)

Still, to note that these are all instances of the new surveillance and contrast with traditional surveillance does not get us very far. Such general terms as *new* and *traditional* can mask differences found within the same family of technologies and elements that may be shared or absent across specific forms.[5] As ideal type concepts, traditional surveillance and the new surveillance are useful as intellectual shorthand. But to go beyond the obvious contrast between the servant listening behind the door as traditional surveillance and satellite photographs as the new surveillance, their basic elements must be identified.

Another challenge is that descriptive terms are often emotionally laden. Many persons have strong feelings of support for or aversion to terms such as *drug testing* or *video surveillance* that can distort analysis. The social analyst needs frameworks for locating variation that go beyond popular language, even if some call it jargon. Moreover, the broad distinction between the new and traditional surveillance requires dimensions by which any act can be categorized. Of course, Occam's razor must be applied deftly. The proliferation of categories must have an end other than itself. One must avoid the danger of making distinctions that only a social scientist could love, or of offering material only appreciated in a presentation to a hairsplitter's convention. But what is life without risk? The point, overall, is that we can dissect the descriptive examples of the new surveillance more abstractly and analytically through a conceptual language that brings parsimony and unity to the vast array of both old and new surveillance tools and behaviors.

A Framework for Thinking about Change

Table 2.1 suggests a number of dimensions for categorizing the instruments used for surveillance. In broad outline, this table also highlights differences between the new and traditional surveillance. The traditional means (*left column*) have certainly not disappeared. They have however been supplemented by the new forms, which tend to fall on the right side of the table. However, in addition, the dimensions are useful in contrasting surveillance means independent of that traditional/new distinction. By reducing the size of the angels or increasing the size of the pin, categories can further proliferate. But these distinctions capture major sources of variation in the means per se.

A variety of other dimensions run across these. Consider, for example, the distinction between inherent, unalterable properties of a technology (such as that infrared devices go beyond the unaided senses or that a recording device requires a power source) and those attributes that policy can affect. An example of the latter is whether or not a device comes with an on-off switch for making a recording. In this case classification depends on the policy and its being honored. The distinction is important because, given its fundamental properties, a technology may make a given use more likely. Thus, the miniaturization offered by the video lens means that it is easy to hide relative to the traditional bulky 35 mm camera. But a policy announcing that a hidden video camera is in use would lead to its being classified as visible, at least in the sense that its operation is known about.

Still what is physically "inherent" in a material tool may reflect the prior directions of law or policy and not some unalterably deterministic emanation from the tool. Thus governments set certain standards for equipment they purchase, including requirements that will facilitate (or at least not block) tapping. RFID chips can be made with a passive or an active technology (that is, an external scanner may be required to "read" them or they may automatically generate signals). The requirements for 9-1-1 emergency phones offers another example (Phillips 2005).

For simplicity I have arranged the categories largely in a series of discrete either/or possibilities (e.g., visible or invisible, gathered by a human or a machine). But there may be continuous gradations between the extreme values (e.g., between visible and invisible). Some dimensions—for example, the dimension of comprehensiveness—appear to involve mutually exclusive values (e.g., single vs. multiple measures), but many do not (e.g., the hybrid case of a guard dog wearing a tiny video camera).[6]

I don't claim that the values on the right side of the table cleanly and fully characterize every instance of contemporary surveillance that has appeared since the development of the microchip and advances in microbiology, artificial intelligence, electronics, communications, and geographic information systems. Nor do the values on the left side perfectly apply to every instance of the old surveillance prior to this. Social life is much too messy for such claims. There is some crossing-over of values (e.g., informers, a traditional form, have low visibility, while drug testing, a new form, is discontinuous). In short, new and old surveillance are ideal types whose virtue of breadth often comes with the vice of combining elements that vary significantly when looked at less abstractly. But if the categories are useful in analyzing big variation (or more useful than the descriptive ad hoc naming we presently have), they have done their job.

Relative to traditional surveillance, the new surveillance extends the senses by directly enhancing an ability that is present, such as seeing or hearing. But it could also be seen to bring new kinds of sensing to the fore, experienced only indirectly and inferentially (e.g., perception of heat from an image of infrared radiation, not from touch, or the presence of dangerous radiation revealed by a Geiger counter, or the simulation of processes that do not literally describe an actual occurrence).[7]

The new surveillance not only reveals the hidden; it often is of low visibility or is invisible. It is more likely to be involuntary. The data collection of the new surveillance is often integrated into routine activity or may be a byproduct of it (rather than being the main goal). It is more likely to be softly elicited than harshly coerced. It is also more likely to be automated, involving machines, than (or in addition to) manual, involving humans. It is relatively inexpensive per unit of data collected, and it is often mediated through remote means rather than on scene, with data residing with third parties and beyond. Data are available in real time, and data collection can be continuous and offer information on the past, present, and future (à la statistical predictions). The subject of data collection goes beyond the individual suspect to categories of interest, and the individual as a subject of data collection may also become the object of automated intervention.

We are moving toward a society of ubiquitous computing with ever more networked sensors in places, objects, and persons (Greenfield 2006; Waldo, Lin, and Millett 2007; Wright et al. 2010). Time, space, and separate activities are increasingly woven together and accessible in automated systems. Only

FIGURE 2.1. The fail-safe, risk-averse, self-monitoring, soft, maximum-security society. (Dana Fradon/ The New Yorker Collection/The Cartoon Bank.)

a short interval may exist between the discovery of the information and the taking of action (such as the triggering of an alarm or the granting or denial of some form of access).

In addition to all of that, the new surveillance is more comprehensive, often involving multiple measures, as the cartoon "Joe's Drive-Thru Testing Center" indicates (fig. 2.1). It is more intensive and extensive. An anonymous individual, a mass, or an aggregate is more likely to be an object of surveillance than it was in the past. The emphasis is expanded beyond the individual to systems and networks. The data often go beyond direct representation to simulation, and from narrative or numerical form to also include video and audio records. As noted, the monitoring of specialists is often accompanied (or replaced) by self-monitoring. It is easy to combine visual, auditory, text, and numerical data and to send and receive these. It is relatively easier to organize, store, retrieve, and analyze data. And, in general, traditional surveillance is the reverse of all the above.

No Change or Maybe Change

In contrast to table 2.1, table 2.2 considers dimensions that are also useful for contrasting forms of surveillance, but for these, the evidence of change is less clear or lacking. I am thus hesitant to claim these as being more characteristic of the new or traditional forms. Some of the dimensions in table 2.2 appear not to have changed significantly over recent centuries or even the

TABLE 2.2. Surveillance dimensions not showing clear historical trend

Invasiveness	Less invasive	More invasive
Reliability and validity	Lower	Higher
Honesty	Deceptive	Nondeceptive
Knowledge that tactic is used	More likely to be known	Less likely to be known
Specific knowledge of where and when used	More likely to be known	Less likely to be known
Basis	Tool	Rule (both)
Active surveillance supported by	Subject	Agent (both)
Emphasis on	Subject's body; Subject's behavior	Subject's soul; Person, objects, environments posing threat to subject

Note: More or less, table columns refer to new compared to old.

past fifty years, such as the extent of deception and the ability to neutralize a technique.

The table also lists factors for which I might make the case for a change over time, but for which I might also make the case that on balance no significant change occurred or that conflicting trends could be seen. For example, the new surveillance is both more and less invasive (partly depending on what is meant by invasive, whether physically or psychologically). Absent the specification of indicators and empirical measurement, it is difficult to say whether change has occurred and in which direction. While, as noted, the greater invasiveness of many tactics is obvious, one trend is toward less traditionally invasive, softer techniques (e.g., drug testing from a strand of hair rather than from a urine sample). Also, given the potential for sophisticated neutralization, the current techniques with their greater power are not necessarily more valid, since adversaries can draw from the same wells of innovation, generating a moving equilibrium. In some ways the greater power and precision of the new techniques may offer less certainty, given the tendency for enhanced information to lead to new questions. And because the tactic is frequently mediated by physical and social distance (with resultant acontextuality and lessened accountability), validity and usefulness can be undermined.

Lists imply an egalitarianism among concepts that is often unwarranted. The dimensions in these tables are hardly of equal significance, something that depends on who is doing the signifying. They can be clustered or ranked in various ways. For example, among those on the new surveillance side with the clearest social implications are the ability to extend the senses, aggregate data, keep a low visibility, obtain involuntary compliance, collect data from remote locations, and decrease cost. All the dimensions, however, help capture the major sources of variation in the tools. But why is the tool used to begin with? That question suggests another major source of contextual variation involving the goals of surveillance, the topic of the next chapter.

So What's Old? Classifying Goals for Continuity and Change

They got a building down New York City, it's called Whitehall Street, where you walk in, you get injected, inspected, detected, infected, neglected and selected.
ARLO GUTHRIE, "Alice's Restaurant"

Mr. Marks, you are under arrest . . . for the future murder of Sarah Marks that was to take place today.
CAPTAIN ANDERTON, *Minority Report*

The previous chapter uses changes in the means of surveillance over the last century to define the new surveillance and develop a conceptual framework for examining its varied methods. Relative to the profound changes in means, surveillance goals as broadly defined (e.g., control, nurture, protect, discover rule violations and violators, verify identity and eligibility, maintain a competitive advantage, sell, entertain) have not fundamentally changed. Most groups have some common functional needs which can be met in a variety of ways. Figure 3.1 illustrates this in showing a popular control technique before the security camera. However the specific contents and meanings of goals (e.g., the kind of rule enforced or eligibility verified or control imposed) has changed, and the priority among goals has changed as well (e.g., the increased prominence of prevention and decreased attention to inner-belief conformity).

An examination of surveillance goals provides a central tool for the contextual analysis of ethics and policy. Attention to the appropriateness of goals and of means for a given setting illustrates a central idea of the book—that surveillance must in general be judged according to the legitimate expectations of the institution or organization in question. To articulate a surveillance goal and to apply a surveillance tool brings questions of empirical and ethical judgment. That is, how well does the tactic achieve both immediate and broader goals appropriate for the context? How does it compare to other means for achieving the goal or to doing nothing? Is the goal desirable and, if so, by what standard? The clarity and consequences of publicly stated goals are central to understanding surveillance, even as we ask whether the stated goals are the real goals.

"Sorry - our security camera broke"

FIGURE 3.1. The means (structure) changes but not the end (functions). (N. Hobart, by kind permission of *The Spectator*.)

The immediate goal of the collecting agent, such as capturing an image, taking a sample, or matching two databases, contrasts with the reasons why the sponsoring agent wants this done. The latter usually involves pragmatic justifications that reflect the instrumental rationality that Max Weber (1978) identified as central to the organization of modern society. This involves means-ends relations and the continual search for improved methods.

In considering goals, we ask a "why" question of the agent—"Why is the surveillance carried out or the information sought?" The answers of interest are in the form of "We do this in order to accomplish that." Such responses are more specific and immediately linked to the activity than is the question-begging answer, "because it is the right thing to do." Or the answer may be to a different question: "Because it is less expensive and more reliable than the alternatives."

We should also ask if there are less visible goals, including sending a public message, obtaining insurance or a government contract, or avoiding legal liability. Attention must be paid to linkages among goals, other levels of causation, and unintended consequences that may later become goals.

Difficulties in Studying Goals

The stories people (or organizations) offer to explain and justify their actions are the data for inferences about goals. Whether the tellers believe the accounts they offer and whether those accounts are empirically supported are important but different questions. Even when individuals and organizations prevaricate or are ill informed, what they offer is still data for analysis.

It is easier to identify and classify surveillance means than goals, because the properties of interest for the former are more likely to be self-evident and quantifiable (e.g., the need for a power source). In the previous chapter the focus was on readily identifiable, objective empirical attributes of a single technology, based on the point of view of the outside observer, using criteria that can be applied across observers (e.g., visibility). With goals the focus is on subjective, often obscure, varied, and changeable points of view of multiple internal actors at different locations.

Determining goals can be difficult for many reasons. Varied organizations using the same means may have different goals (e.g., public police in principle concerned with due process and justice as against private police concerned with protecting the interests of their employer). Within an organization a given technique may simultaneously serve multiple goals and users.

In addition, as will be noted in chapter 5, a goal's multiplicity may be sequential and have a "career." Goals may change or receive different emphases over time (e.g., the social security number started as simply a tax collection and benefits device in the 1930s and became increasingly important as a generalized, unique identifier through the 1990s).

Unintended but desirable consequences may become confounded with the original goal and themselves become goals (e.g., the airlines' use of a picture ID introduced for security reasons has become important in combating credit card fraud). The same may be the case for socially undesirable consequences that benefit the agent. Thus, the admirable goal of disease identification and prevention may lead to discrimination and exclusion, as surveillance results prove useful for other goals such as cost-effectiveness and profit.

Another complication is that there may be a lack of consensus on the relative importance of various goals. Parts of the same organization may have different and competing goals, or at least different priorities regarding the use of the information gathered (e.g., the intelligence vs. operational units of a national security or police agency). And individuals within the same organizational unit may have different goals, depending on the role played and the motivation of the player. Simply obtaining the information is usually the proximal goal for the data collection agent. This is nicely captured by surveillance expert Harry Caul (Gene Hackman) in *The Conversation*, who tries to convince himself that he is just a neutral technician. Much as satirist Tom Lehrer sings about Werner Von Braun sending rockets up but not caring where they come down, Hackman says, "All I want is a nice fat tape. I don't care what they use it for." Of course, he does care, and his angst sets up the tension of the story. However, for sponsors and various data consumers, the goal is in the use.

Those playing the same role can also have varied motivations. Contrast the ambitious go-getter committed to organizational goals with the noncommitted ritualist who rigidly follows organizational rules but is indifferent to the goals. As Merton (1956) notes for such a person, the means become the end. Complicating matters further, some employees have private goals (e.g., police who secretly sell criminal justice data to insurance companies).

Goals may also be elusive. Individuals may be unclear about the goals either because they are uninformed and just following orders or because goals are not well defined or prioritized (whether intentionally or unintentionally). Lack of clarity can offer flexibility and deniability. There may also be different interpretations of what a goal means.

Goals may be hidden, and the ostensible goals may not be the real goals. For example, the real goal of a company that advertised it could help persons with bad credit records was to create lists to sell of persons with bad records. The reason some firms request phone numbers from credit card users is not to ensure the security of the guaranteed transaction, but for marketing purposes. An unstated goal for some drug testing (and the hoarding of results) may be to offer grounds for firing workers at a later date should that be desired and no other grounds are available. Some companies have been rumored to use the results of drug tests to fire persons before they become eligible for pensions or other benefits. Or results from employment medical tests can reveal that a woman is pregnant and may prevent her from being hired.[1]

But just because the waters are filled with sharks does not mean one should never go swimming. There is no magic methodology for determining and assessing goals other than to ask and observe. However, awareness of the complexity and difficulty in determining goals can moderate the claims made.

Foucault's Goal: Unsafe Smiles?

I speak of peace while covert enmity
Under the smile of safety wounds the world.
SHAKESPEARE, *Henry IV, Part 2*

In our increasingly engineered societies we daily live out some of Foucault's truth. The historical changes he observed in *Discipline and Punish* (1977) are central for the analysis of contemporary goals, even if in that book he does not go beyond 1836 (no examples of computer dossiers or biometric analysis bolster his case). Of course, the failure to directly experience a topic one writes about need not be disqualifying; George Orwell never rode in an airplane and H. G. Welles didn't know from space travel. All stories are limited and partial.

Foucault's empirical documentation is illustrative rather than systematic and tends to exclude important surveillance topics beyond the control of superordinates in hierarchical organizations. His tone and examples give a subversive, even conspiratorial twist to the hallowed ideals of the Renaissance and the Enlightenment regarding the consequences of seeking truth and social betterment. Rather than ensuring freedom and universal benefits, knowledge serves the more powerful. However, he does not offer an adequate theory of why hierarchy is necessarily undesirable.

With respect to the categories for the structural analysis of surveillance noted in chapter 1 (pp. 33–39), Foucault focuses on the watchers who are directly carrying out internal constituency, nonreciprocated, rule-based, organizational surveillance of individuals on behalf of the organization's goals. The hope behind such watching is that subjects' fear of possible discovery will lead to self-surveillance and that rational analysis will improve outcomes desired by agents. The social significance of these forms is clear.

Yet other forms neglected by Foucault—for example, organizational surveillance for more benign ends, interorganizational surveillance, and the nonorganizational surveillance by individuals of each other—also need consideration. His analysis, as with that of many contemporary observers, does not give sufficient attention to the multiplicity and fluidity of surveillance goals and the conflicts between them. Surveillance may serve parallel or shared goals of the individual as well as the organization. It may be initiated by the individual and used against an organization. It may focus on rule-based standards involving kinds of behavior, or it may involve social, psychological, and physiological characteristics used to classify persons—whether to favor or disfavor them.

Foucault, and many of those uncritically under his spell, collapse or reduce the more general process or activity of surveillance to just one context—the organizational—and to one goal, which is control, a term often used interchangeably with domination and repression. As argued in chapter 1, it is more useful to start with understanding generic forms (whether structures or processes) and then to divide these into various species. In chapter 1, the species involved contexts and structures; in chapter 2, they were means; and in this chapter, the focus is goals.

The Multiplicity of Surveillance Goals

Using an inductive method, sifting hundreds of examples to answer the question "What is use of the surveillance tool intended to accomplish?" I identified twelve concepts within which the variation noted can be organized.[2]

Goals for Collecting Personal Information

A. Compliance
   Behavioral rules
   Certification standards
   Subjective rules (correct inner attitudes and feelings)
B. Verification
C. Discovery
D. Documentation
E. Prevention and protection
F. Strategic advantage (influence)
G. Profit
H. Symbolism
I. Publicity
J. Organizational functioning (or governance, administration, or management)
K. Curiosity
L. Self-knowledge

I added categories until any new example fitted within the existing categories. I do not argue that any given application will necessarily fit into only one category (although one may be dominant), that goals should only be studied statically, or that observers would all necessarily agree on how to categorize what agents say about goals. For example, the point of view of the respondent may differ from that of the analyst; that is, a respondent might categorize surveillance of children as being for protection, while an analyst might code it as a form of control.

In the previous chapter, means were conceptualized as bimodal dimensions with values at the ends of a continuum. In contrast, here each goal is an end point (although it could be treated as bimodal if scored as present or absent). The goals may occur together (e.g., compliance and documentation), and some are broader than others. For example, the goals of organizational functioning and documentation are perhaps the broadest and most content neutral of those in the list, potentially touching most of the others.

Some natural clusters of goals and temporal patterns tend to be associated with specific contexts. Yet there may also be tension between goals (e.g., to

prevent via an intervention vs. to merely document). Goals A–J are disproportionately associated with organizations, while K and L are more likely to
involve individuals acting in a personal rather than an organizational capacity (although individuals may also seek many of the previous goals, such as
documentation, influence, and prevention). Let us briefly consider each goal.

Compliance Surveillance

Ten percent of the people are honest. Ten percent are dishonest. All we're trying to do is
to keep the other 80 percent from jumping the fence.
VIDEO SURVEILLANCE SPECIALIST

The central features of compliance or standards-based surveillance are rules
and a surveillance agent with authority (or power, influence) over a subject.
The agent is charged with assessing the subject's conformity. This may be used
to reward employees for their contribution to the work product or to negatively sanction them for not meeting contractual obligations.

Compliance systems of social control have greatly increased over the last
century and a half (Reiss 1984). In tandem, social complexity and the rules it
calls forth have proliferated within an ethos of equality in rule enforcement.
Relative to preindustrial society, violation of many of the rules of modern
society does not involve easily identifiable infractions or a complaint by a
harmed individual. Thus, anticipatory specialists actively seek to locate and
define transgressions rather than responding to those that become known
after the fact. As an example, contrast the multivolume IRS code with the
simpler tax system of an agrarian society.

As governments and organizations extend their jurisdiction and the matters they are concerned with, they promulgate ever more rules encompassing
larger pools of persons. Individuals increasingly are subject to surveillance as
a condition of eligibility for or membership in an organization or community,
not because there is a particular reason for them to be a suspect. Modern
ideas of the universality of the law and the standardized treatment associated
with bureaucratic rules vastly expand expectations for rule enforcement. In
principle the mandate for inspection applies independently of social status or
any particularized suspicion. Merely to be within a population the rule applies to (when evidence of conformity is not manifest) makes the individual a
potential subject for scrutiny. This creates new industries for meddling (Edgley and Brissett 1999) and new incentives to disobey.

Compliance surveillance may apply to entire populations or to subcat-
egories. The norms may be proscriptive ("Don't bring weapons to school") or

prescriptive ("Carry a driver's license"), and a clear moral justification may or may not be present ("Don't steal from the company" vs. "Do not wear sandals to work"). The norm may involve overt behavioral rules ("Wear clothes"), eligibility ("You must be a citizen in order to vote"), or appropriate inner attitudes and feelings ("You must take a loyalty oath").

Based on these distinctions I identify three kinds of compliance surveillance involving (1) behavioral norms, (2) certification, and (3) norms about beliefs and feelings.

Behavioral compliance. The central questions for behavioral compliance are "Are the rules followed?" and "Is what is done consistent with the standards?" Compliance may involve norms such as driving within the speed limit, not using illegal drugs, wearing a hard hat, or following the work protocol for handling telephone service center calls. An emphasis on "right behavior" gives individuals ample room for subversive attitudes and feelings (several of the types shown in table 6:3).

Certification. The second form, certification compliance, asks, "What kind of a person is this?" It can involve standards related to various kinds of eligibility. Here it is not so much what the individual is doing, but what the person has done or is believed capable of doing or being in the future or "is" in some existential sense involving beliefs about a person's character. It involves essence more than a given strip of behavior. This form determines "who" the person is as defined by prior experience (college attendance, criminal convictions), a skill or ability (something one knows how to do, such as swim, type, program a computer, or speak a foreign language), or a condition (such as whether one is the carrier of a disease potential or what one's gender or ethnic background is). It can refer to a "state of being"—for example, being over eighteen or having a blood alcohol level below .05. A historical example of this type of surveillance can be seen in the "spotters" employed by white establishments in the South to be sure that African-Americans did not attempt to enter sections of theaters or train cars reserved for whites (Dollard 1957; Myrdal 1944).

Certification may also involve a complex social construction, such as being a person of good character or mentally healthy. Such compliance inspections apply a "kinds of person" standard (e.g., commercial pilots must meet certain health standards; national security agents must be loyal citizens; bonded carriers must be trustworthy). The reason for such surveillance is generally better understood and less controversial than with some of the other goals, even as the measurement means are likely to be subject to controversy.

Licensing is a form of certification. There is often a quid pro quo, as the individual in effect strikes a deal with controllers. That is, in return for agreeing to be under surveillance and offering (in whatever form) personal information relevant to the rules, the state or other organizations may certify that the individual is in conformity with the standards and thus is eligible for benefits or privileges and can do things the nonlicensed cannot do. Licensing is a generalized means of communicating trust and a form of contract.

We also see a myriad of organizational forms of certification involving health and safety requirements. Some forms are relational, such as the requirement still in certain states that people seeking a marriage license pass a blood test. The stated justification is that individuals desiring children are encouraged to be aware of the compatibility of their blood types. Perhaps in the near future with better tests and predictive models, a license will also be required to have or keep a child.

Inner compliance. The third form involves assessing attitudes, beliefs, feelings, and attachments. Because such matters are interior to the individual, they require the individual's voluntary revelation or they must be inferred by indirect means such as informers or presumed "truth"-determining technologies whose validity may be challenged. The question here is "Do you truly believe?" and the emphasis is on feelings, as well as content.

During the religiously dominated centuries before the Renaissance, inner compliance was of much greater significance. Locally, eccentric beliefs may have been tolerated (Le Roy Ladurie 1979). But for beliefs perceived to threaten the status quo seriously, the inquisitorial response was severe. These means were moderated over later centuries. Modern democratic societies, drawing on a Greek instead of a Christian tradition, emphasize behavioral rather than belief conformity. This reduces conflict in heterogeneous societies and the need for surveillance of the inner person. Since the means for assessing overt behavior are, in general, more reliable and valid, an emphasis on behavior fits with due process expectations of fairness.

In contemporary society, common standards are to be met in the public sphere, while what goes on within the private sphere of the home and one's thoughts has become less subject to external authority and discovery (with mixed consequences, to be sure, as with child and spouse abuse). Increased rights of the individual and the separation of these public and private realms mean greater tolerance for diverse beliefs and an emphasis on right behavior more than right attitudes. This societal value is aided by efforts to engineer or structure environments in a "hard" fashion such that the individuals' attitudes or preferences cannot affect their behavior.

In spite of the historical shift, the emphasis on "right attitudes and feelings" and undiluted loyalty remain within some religious and political sects, within contemporary authoritarian societies (which may have witch hunts, loyalty oaths, and denunciations)—forms not unknown in democracies, particularly during crisis periods. Beyond material technologies for determining right attitudes, the confession, group critiques, informers, and ritual oaths and affirmations are prominent here.

Even during noncrisis periods efforts to reach the inner person characteristic of early nineteenth-century reform efforts such as the Quaker prison are present in some forms of contemporary psychotherapy, cult reprogramming, substance abuse, and political reeducation programs, as well as programming in some criminal justice settings.

Overall, contemporary organizations seek to nurture and reward commitment. To do that, they must be able to measure it. Inner compliance is likely to receive greater emphasis in certain occupations such as policing and national security where the costs of disloyalty are seen to be great. The development of new technologies that claim to reveal the inner person more accurately, such as those that read brain wave patterns, may lead to increased emphasis on feeling and thinking "correctly."

Verification: Will the Real Anastasia Please Stand Up

> In God we trust. All others we polygraph.
> POLYGRAPHER'S MOTTO

Erving Goffman has called attention to a near-universal expectation that individuals are to be who (and what) they claim to be. Of course, in a world where individuals are not personally known, where interaction is not face-to-face, where the claims subjects put forth are not immediately validated and/ or where temptations for violation are present, it is prudent to verify. Even under opposite conditions, persons change, and looks can be deceiving. Verification of what can be called the *authenticity presumption* (or at least *hope*) is a primary form of compliance, but it has distinctive features.

The individual makes a claim, and in a latent, or not so latent, contract, essentially agrees to be looked at, over, under, or through, often as a condition for gaining a benefit. The price of admittance is scrutiny by a gate keeper to verify that eligibility standards are met. The goal here is to assess a claim that is put forth in asking, "Are you telling the truth?"

A major form of verification is to control access to resources and places. This can involve verifying that a particular identity is eligible. A subsequent social process may involve authenticating that an eligibility token or symbol is valid and appropriately represents or "belongs" to the person offering it.

One form of verification is based on things the individual has, such as documents (ticket, passport, driver's license) or keys and badges in which possession is taken as an indirect indicator of eligibility. A second form involves things the person knows, such as a password or secret hand signal. A third form of verification involves transference, in which a trusted party vouches for the individual. And a fourth form involves automated biometric means, such as fingerprints, handprints, retinal and iris patterns, scent, and DNA, in which the material the individual offers is compared to that in a file believed to represent the "real" individual. Or it may involve a combination of performance and biometrics—comparing handwriting or speaking and walking patterns to those of the genuine individual.

The verification of biography is yet a fifth form. This may occur by checking and/or matching computer databases for claims made, such as whether one graduated from a given college; has a certain income, employment status, and record; owes back taxes; has an arrest record; or belongs (or belonged) to prohibited organizations. It may involve record checks or physical tests to verify claims on a health or life insurance application. Birth and death records may be examined to determine family background. Intensive background investigations such as those for high-level government jobs and law enforcement may involve interviews with teachers, employers, and neighbors going back decades.[3]

For claims not verifiable by records, artifacts, or other individuals, the person's account may be indirectly assessed through inferences from physiological and psychological measurements such as pulse, eye movements, voice, sweat, and even stomach flutters and brain waves.[4] Contemporary variants are in some ways logically equivalent to ancient truth-assessing mechanisms such as walking on coals and dunking. Unlike the traditional forms, however, these claim scientific rather than mystical justification.

Discovery

And thus do we of wisdom and of reach,
With windlasses and with assays of bias,
By indirections find directions out.
POLONIUS IN *HAMLET*

In the lines from Hamlet, the suspicious Polonius boasts of his ability to ferret out his son's activities in France. This is an example of *scented discovery*. Agents have an inkling that something of interest is present, but they don't know details. The ever-expanding net of contemporary scrutinizing seeks to provide tools to locate scents, tremors, and hints that call forth more focused and intensive inquiry.

Discovery, rather than starting with a general rule or with a person who makes a claim about being in conformity, starts with a problem that generates a search for a person and/or details. It is *suspicion driven* and also can be *prevention driven*, meaning there is a sense that something might be amiss or predictive of future trouble. The hint may involve red flags, tips, or evidence that a standard has not been met. Discovery can have either a *generalized* or a *particularized* focus. Polonius's focus on a given subject contrasts with random trolling or periodic compliance investigations, such as the annual (if unannounced) use of the polygraph or drug tests for all public safety officials.

Information that serves to mobilize inquiry is present, but agents are uncertain who is responsible, where the person is, what is planned, or what happened.[5] The question might be "Who stole the cookies from the cookie jar?" Agents know that the cookies were stolen and seek to find out who is responsible. Or a person may come under suspicion, but agents are not sure where, when, or what kind of cookies were (or will be) involved, or if the theft might involve something else (bagels? gluten-free biscuits?). The question is not "Is there compliance?" but, rather, "What kind of noncompliance is there?" A related logic applies in the case of mysterious illnesses, as public health officials seek to learn the nature of the problem.

The discovery effort may be narrowed to particular kinds of person, activities, or places believed to be associated with what is of interest. When the FBI learned that scuba gear might be involved in terrorist attacks, it sought to identify anyone who had recently taken diving lessons (Moss and Fessen 2002). Knowing that in general some of those visiting or attached to embassies might be spies or turncoats, countries commonly take surveillance photos of those entering the embassies of adversaries (Mendez, Mendez, and Henderson 2003).

A common problem is trying to determine the core identity (chap. 4) of a person for whom the investigator has some seemingly unique identifier, but whose name and/or location is not known. Consider the case in a small English town where authorities had the DNA from a murderer but did not know whose it was. In a broad, "round up the usual [or in this case 'the most likely'] suspects, Louie" sweep à la the film *Casablanca*, all males in the village were asked to submit to DNA analysis. While this was not legally required at the time, the social pressure was great, and to refuse made one a suspect (in fact the culprit was caught through an informer, not DNA). A request that everyone in a unit where a theft has occurred undergo a polygraph is a related example.

When used to match parents to children in paternity, custody, and adoption cases DNA serves to verify claims put forth, but with those suffering from amnesia the aim is to discover what kind of claim should be put forth. Inquiries that seek to locate carriers of contagious diseases (such as AIDS) by discovering contact patterns are another example. Here the question is not "Who?" but "Who else?"

The preventive area of risk prediction—focused on standard(s) or states one might potentially deviate from—looks to discover future behavior and conditions, not current rule violations or health. This involves statistical models based on probabilities of what kind of an employee, customer, citizen, or patient a person is likely to become. But the discovery goal is the same—determining who is most likely to behave in a particular way or be in a situation of interest to those using the tool.

Documentation as Record Keeping: Dossiers and Docility

> Hey, just the facts, Jack.
> POLICE SERGEANT, *L.A. Confidential*

Documentation includes many of the other goals. A common form involves using a document to validate a claim the individual puts forth—for example, proof of legal age when entering a bar. But here I refer to documentation in a broader sense, as memorializing or the creation of a reviewable record. The emphasis is on documentation of activity. For example, there may be video and audio recording of the interaction as well as the audit trail left from an officer's data entry into a computer to check car registration, driver's license, and warrants. Such documentation of activity often moves beyond documentation of the subject's data and involves the procedures and behavior of the agent and the interaction of subject and agent, as with video cams worn by police.

One characteristic of contemporary life is a trend toward ever more recording of personal information. In the nineteenth century, documentary records tended to be extrinsic to the behavior in question. They consisted largely of after-the-fact written accounts of second- and third-party observers, such as police, informers, inspectors, teachers, and doctors, as well registries by agents of the church or state regarding marriage, birth, death, and property ownership. Now, however, surveillance as documentation is increasingly being built into unfolding activities (even if much of it is never used). Current techniques are often passively and automatically triggered by the subject and remotely available in real time, rather than requiring an agent on the scene to take a separate step to directly record a reviewable account. Consider the generation of records inherent in routine activities such as using credit cards, cell and landline phones, ATMs, and home or work computers, or by merely being in the presence of a video camera.

These automated processes may only require that the machinery work, not that a human agent be available to record what happened. Nor is the co-operation of the subject necessarily needed, as with traditional forms of work monitoring, such as punching a time card, signing in, or, for a police officer, turning a key in a call box.[6] Other technical developments have created new economical ways to easily document the calling cards humans involuntarily and unwittingly leave apart from such engineered data collection examples. Such exudations can involve a scent, visual image, voice, fingerprints, heat, motion, or the DNA in a strand of hair or a saliva-sealed envelope—all simply waiting to be read. Goffman (1969) offers examples of this sociocultural and physical leakage.

An external telltale facilitator may link a person to an activity, substance, or object. Such material identifiers may be buried within objects the individual encounters, such as "smart dust" on a door knob (which leaves residue on the person who touched it), a distinctive mark on a photocopy, markers in fertilizer and other materials that can be used for explosives, gunpowder residue on the hand, radioactive markings or hidden chips on diamonds or expensive parts, unique identifiers on currency, or the exploding dye used as a deterrent to bank robbery.

The ability to record or memorialize sound, visual images, movement, heat, odors, location, and electronic communication (local and networked computers, telephones, beepers, television, etc.), appliance and vehicle usage via an EDR (event data recorder) and the great advances in forensic science involving DNA and fingerprinting have vastly increased the appetite for creating records in stone that live forever and can be forever merged.

As noted, it is not only that more information is subject to surveillance, but the ratio of recorded to unrecorded surveillance is probably shifting. The scale changes are monumental. Consider, for example, the shift from paying with cash to using a credit card in terms of the record generated, or the proliferation of various documenting sensors or video cameras compared to previous, largely unrecorded observations by human observers. One large Las Vegas Hotel alone has fifteen hundred continuously recording video cameras.

For any surveillance activity, a digitalized documentary record that can be easily memorialized, communicated, enhanced, joined with other data, and carefully and repeatedly analyzed by others offers many advantages. For one, machine-recorded information is often assumed to be more valid and less subject to dispute than the account of a human observer, although as noted throughout the book, such assumptions must be critically analyzed. Such analysis requires a standard of accessible and reasonably clear measurements to resolve conflicts of the "she said, he said" variety. Even if the measurements don't meet a clarion standard, machine-recorded information may at least lessen decisions based on the relative power and status of the disputants and unreflective cultural tilts.

Other advantages to record keeping include the Boy Scout goal to "be prepared" and the organizational goal to "cover your tail." Documentation makes analysis possible, offers an insurance policy, and can be a hedge against uncertainty given the open-ended and unpredictable quality of the future. Analyzing records across cases permits the identification of trends and unanticipated developments and patterns. An accurate record can support claims of due diligence and due process on the agent's part.

Records also permit interpretations and judgments regarding disputes about performance or what happened in an incident. Perhaps surprisingly, in conflict or competition settings such as those involving police and interrogated suspects or persons in custody, sports teams, or brokers and clients, both sides may welcome the documentation (Leo and Richman 2007). Video cameras on police cars or worn by police have a more mixed reception. Beyond the issues of validity and interpretation (should seeing mean believing?), there are concerns about increasing police passivity, spillover (as with filming bystanders), and the confidentiality of communication with police. However, a camera experiment in Rialto, California, saw cameras associated with a reduction of both complaints against police and police use of force (Stoss 2013).

In addition, records (when available to the parties in a dispute) may serve as a way of keeping authorities accountable and protecting parties against fraudulent claims. Yet, to use records in these ways, parties must establish some transparency and rules (e.g., time, date, and location information and perhaps video recordings of computer use as well as access logs and rules about destruction of the record). Absent that, records may be laundered and destroy accountability while pretending the opposite. When there is the expectation that records will be made, their absence can serve as a warning signal that something may be amiss.

The imbalance and lack of reciprocity in the ability to make, see, and communicate or share records generally follows the contours of unequal organization-individual relations and is a major cause of current controversy. Yet there is variation in the degree of one-sidedness, and some ironic undercutting tendencies are present (considered in chap. 6). The absence of, or gaps in, a record may bite back and embarrass agents, but so may the record. When illegal surveillance is discovered, and if its documentary fruits are not destroyed, the tool recoils.

President Nixon's covert recording of his White House conversations is illustrative. He was damaged by what was on the tape, as well as by what was absent. That said in spite of his opinion that "the country doesn't give much of a shit about it [bugging]." However, he was triply petarded—by the Watergate burglars caught red-handed, the famous 18½ minute gap in the Watergate tape, and the incriminating material that *remained* on the tapes. In this context, with the documentation, plausible deniability is implausible, and the absence of documentation is suspicious.

Strategic advantage (influence)

I find the information age to be a healthy thing. The more you know about somebody else, the better off everybody is.

OWNER OF A DATABASE COMPANY

The broad category of strategic advantage or influence also touches many other goals. Any kind of purposive action can be seen as strategic. But here I initially refer more specifically to situations of conflict and competition in which the goal is to obtain information which is unavailable (whether by intention or the natural structure of the situation). For both organizations and individuals, strategic surveillance can involve efforts to influence a subject's rule conformity, anticipate future moves, or inform countermoves. That is obviously the case with the planning and covert activities of law enforcement and more broadly efforts to increase conformity with norms.

But strategic influence goes beyond rule enforcement per se. Consider targeted appeals based on knowledge about the person (or the person's type) that comes from web or credit card uses. For market research, the goal is to identify those thought most likely to become potential customers, clients, donors, or advocates of political positions and to find the best way of approaching them with respect to the content and form of a solicitation. Categorization of people may aid organizational efficiency by suggesting whom to ignore or exclude as well.

Covert communication intercepts may be used to guide interaction with the subject and create an advantage in that interaction. Thus, in bargaining and negotiating situations, the parties may seek to learn about the expectations and plans of their rivals. Consider the bugging of corporate offices or phones and spying in labor-management negotiations.

The personal information gathered by private detectives (e.g., in divorce and custody and other legal disputes) also fits here (Shulman 2007). This information may be used in calculating how to respond in a conflict situation, addressing what is introduced as evidence, what is released to the media, or what is otherwise used as a negotiating resource (in a logical equivalent to blackmail). A nice example can be seen in collectors of DNA going through the trash in search of evidence in family disputes to answer the question, "who is my daddy?"[7]

Classic spy operations such as Ultra during World War II, in which the British broke the German codes, offer well-known examples of seeking advantage for one side in a conflict. Intelligence agencies (whether foreign, domestic, public, or private) are also interested in knowing the personal habits of opponents or competitors. A classic spy tactic is generating a dossier on the drinking, gambling, financial, sexual, and other interests of an individual it would like to recruit or influence. Through both covert and open sources, national intelligence agencies also may serve their country's economic interests (or that of particular organizations or sectors).[8]

Less well known are the many examples of surveillance in sports. Long before the 2007 "Spygate" (O'Leary 2012) case in which the New England Patriots were disciplined for videotaping the opposing team's signals and using a prohibited radio frequency to communicate with their quarterback, there was the October 1951 playoff game between the New York Giants and the Brooklyn Dodgers. With two runners on base and trailing 4–2 in the bottom of the ninth inning, Bobby Thomson hit the most famous home run in history off of Ralph Branca to defeat the Dodgers. Only later was it claimed that a Giants' coach with binoculars in the bleachers had observed the catcher's signal to the pitcher and was able to inform Thomson of what pitch to expect (Prager 2008). Covert video- and audiotaping in criminal justice settings is also illustrative of surveillance for strategic advantage—whether used to intervene, locate a fugitive, obtain a guilty plea, or provide courtroom evidence.

The spy examples fall into in a gray area with respect to legitimacy (particularly among friendly nations),[9] but blackmail is the classic illegitimate case. The blackmailer may encounter discrediting information or take active steps to create it. In return for keeping information confidential, the subject may in varying degrees agree to the blackmailer's demands.

Forewarning can also be the objective. Consider the anticipatory goal of university and other fund-raisers who are provided Internet-generated intelligence files on the fat felines they solicit. As a development officer reported, "This helps me know a little bit about the person I'm meeting with. There are three forbidden topics: sex, religion and politics. I can't mention them, but if the prospect brings them up, I have to know how to answer."

Another example of the strategic use of surveillance lies in fraudulently obtaining and using someone else's personal information. The goal is to influence gatekeepers to accept the fake ID, credentials, or passwords (or those that are legitimate but not for this user). This differs from the types discussed above because the person who is influenced is not the person whose data have been gathered. Rather, the information is used to deceive a resource-bearing organization.

The thief seeks to con an organization into providing advantages to which he or she is not entitled—whether through use of a credit card or a telephone calling card—or to help a fugitive create a new identity. As more societal business occurs remotely and instantaneously without the traditional forms of face-to-face identity validation, the appropriation of another's identity and/or creation of false records is increasingly seen as a social problem, although systematic data on extensiveness are difficult to obtain. Estimates of identity fraud vary depending on how it is defined, a factor not unrelated to the interests of the definers (Cole and Pontell 2006; McNally and Newman 2008). Yet identity fraud clearly has markedly increased in an absolute sense.

Finally mention can be made of an important goal within discovery—the search for sociability and connectivity using the Internet and social media (although there is greater blurring and fluidity with respect to the roles of agent, subject, and audience than with other goals). These need not involve strategic gains as in the conflict and competitive settings discussed above. But social media are a way of pursuing a person's interests, even if this often involves sharing with others. In these cases there is discovery (but not as in the discovery goal above to find what is hidden), and it is not used in conflict settings, but rather the goal is one of communality.

Prevention and Protection

It's about prevention. Just having this test in your house is a deterrent.
ADVERTISEMENT FOR A "FAMILY" DRUG TEST KIT

Intervention is part of the broader rationality associated with modern society. Once we are freed from the idea that events reflect a divine plan, it makes sense to (and indeed is irresponsible not to) take anticipatory actions to prevent untoward outcomes. Surveillance is often framed in protective terms. The protection of human and material assets is an important goal of work surveillance (Ball 2010). Clients and customers encounter announcements such as "For your protection, this area is under video surveillance" or "For your protection, please enter your social security number." Identifying from whose point of view and how these terms are defined is a central task for analysis—what is being prevented, who is being protected, and are subjects in agreement with agents about the answers?

While prevention often seeks to identify, stop, or exclude potential rule violators, it also uses personal information apart from compliance concerns. Consider, for example, efforts to prevent illness, errors, and accidents and to create conditions favoring an organization's goals. These efforts can involve looking for early warning signs of a potential, or emerging, problem in order to fix or lessen it—whether by eliminating the individual from the system (exclusion, segregation), deterring unwanted behavior, or altering the individual or the system.

Public health surveillance systems such as those of the Centers for Disease Control and the World Health Organization are among the most developed and sophisticated of preventive tab-keeping institutions. They use surveillance to avoid or contain epidemics and contagious diseases by monitoring individuals and environmental conditions (Fairchild et al. 2007).

The many forms of health screening for ostensibly well people have the goal of identifying signs of illness (e.g., chest x-rays are illustrative). Health rule certification requirements seek to protect individuals from illness (e.g., the school requirement that students must offer proof of vaccination is for the inspected individual as well as other students). The radiation level detection devices applied to workers in nuclear power plant and x-ray settings seek early warning signs, as do general health screens. The regular monitoring of diabetic or heart patients is intended to prevent the disease from reaching critical thresholds.

Another form of prevention/protection surveillance is the electronic location monitoring of abusing former spouses, intended to encourage self-regulation, based on the idea that the abuser will fear being caught, or to send an alarm that notifies police and the protected person, should the abuser approach the protected person. Banks and credit card companies that monitor unrelated financial activities of their customers offer another example. By reducing or eliminating a customer's credit line or calling in a loan, banks seek to reduce the likelihood that an individual will default on a loan, enter bankruptcy, or be unable to make monthly payments. Such actions are taken even though the monitored transactions may not involve the monitoring financial institution and the subject's behavior does not involve violations. Credit lines may be increased and new loans offered as a result of such monitoring as well.

A considerable amount of surveillance is intended to be benign and is so viewed by both agents and subjects. The reviewing of student and worker records may involve compliance checks as well as paternalistic protection for the early identification of problems. The monitoring of blood and sperm donors for HIV; of patients in intensive care, assisted living, and nursing homes; of police looking for drunks to take to a shelter to protect them from freezing or becoming crime victims; of bodyguards and those they guard; and of parents looking out for dependent children and aged relatives is in each case an example of preventive and protective surveillance.

The distinction noted above between *generalized* and *particularized* surveillance applies here. Thus, lifeguards offer a general protection for those within their territory—in principle, watching all persons in the water to be sure they are not struggling and are staying within appropriate boundaries. Another example is the efforts of good Samaritans who use a geographic information system (GIS) to locate and provide help to undocumented immigrants crossing the US-Mexican border (Walsh 2010). In contrast, bodyguards (or in contemporary parlance "personal protection agents"), special assistants, personal secretaries, chauffeurs, valets, caregivers, and public relations agents focus on protecting and aiding persons whose identity is known.

The emphasis may be on watching the subject to be protected or on attending to others and the environment that may pose a threat.[10] In public settings the Secret Service creates a human border, as well as other borders, between the protected and the environment, watches the crowd, and also pays prior visits to those on a watch list of persons deemed to be potential threats, reminding them that they are being more carefully watched. Lifeguards watch swimmers and also watch for conditions that would endanger them, such as other raucous swimmers, water quality, tide changes, and sharks.

Profit

And you will have a window in your head.
Not even your future will be a mystery
anymore. Your mind will be punched in a card
and shut away in a little drawer.
When they want you to buy something,
they will call you. . . .
WENDELL BERRY (1971)

Financial gain drives much surveillance. This is most explicit in the case of collecting agents who are in business to do surveillance for others. The goal for private investigators and the large information or data-warehousing and analysis industry is simply profit. They are hired guns whose goal is to sell data (and related services) apart from the ends of the purchasers. New data, public record information, and data already gathered for other purposes are collected, repackaged, and sold. The amount of such information for sale is astounding.

In the United States, even for many primary data collectors and users whose surveillance has other goals, a secondary goal is to sell the information they gather after they use it. The extent of this varies by sector—legal restrictions on health, educational, cable TV, and video rental data are much stronger than for most other sectors. In the United States while banks generally limit their sale of customers' data, to a significant extent this is more for good customer relations than because of stringent legal requirements.

The mass media in pursuit of selling advertising offers personal information as entertainment, and often the more personal, private, intimate, sensitive, or embarrassing the entertainment, the better from the standpoint of garnering a large audience. The worldwide popularity of Big Brother kinds of TV programs is noteworthy. However, the initial and driving goal of the personal information gathering and revelation regarding the TV shows' participants in these cases is profit, or persuasion using surveillance as free entertainment to reach those of interest. The entertainment is the hook that draws the potential consumers in, or the sugar that makes the medicine go down. The concept of the audience for surveillance was mentioned in chapter 1 and is central to surveillance as entertainment, publicity, symbolism, and curiosity, which is considered below.

Publicity

My philosophy is, when in doubt, let it out.
CLARENCE PAGE, reporter

The Warren and Brandeis (1890) law review article that helped create modern tort notions of privacy was partly a response to the authors' indignation over unwelcome photos of society parties that began appearing in newspapers following the development of higher-speed film. The fact that it was no longer necessary to pose for an extended period meant photographers could snap and run, essentially eliminating the previous de facto requirement of consent imposed by technical inefficiency. As with contemporary paparazzi, the photographer's goal (or of the organization buying the images) was to bring lifestyle information to a curious, voyeuristic, mass audience living vicariously.

In bringing the news, surveillance may communicate indignation over misbehavior. In explaining his view of reporting negative information about public figures such as Jesse Jackson, Clarence Page (2001) further states, "I am very concerned about leadership in general and about the quality of black leadership. . . . I feel obliged to be more aggressive because I feel a special responsibility to African-Americans and in Jesse Jackson's constituency to hold him accountable. Like a sort of consumer advocate."

Such publicity is a major goal for a variety of surveillance agents who seek to use the mass media to advance their concerns. This overlaps the goal of strategic advantage, whether by serving some abstract principle, harming the public image of an opponent, or enhancing one's own image. Investigative reporters, political parties, and social reformers frequently use the tactics in pursuing the public interest as they define it. For them the broad goal of collecting personal information is to publicize it, for commercial, political, or personal ends.[11] Turning up dirt and smearing opponents during election campaigns are sadly familiar. Business competitors may spy on rivals in the hope of discrediting them as well as strategically outfoxing them. The "outing" of well-known persons as homosexuals or as adulterers is another example.

A form of *faux* (or at least unofficial) *compliance surveillance* can be seen when an independent, essentially self-appointed agent without official authority, such as a journalist, private detective or activist, takes on the task of scrutinizing and even setting up a subject.[12] Erving Goffman (1974) notes one form of this called "vital tests," in which unsuspecting people are given a contrived opportunity to test their character or organizational loyalty. Note the freelance, vigilante-like tactics of some TV programs that offer opportunities for misbehavior and then report on them. While the information collected may be turned over to authorities, the central purpose is to inform, embarrass, or entertain with programs that advertisers will pay for.

Government and business groups, political parties, and social movements may seek damaging personal information to be leaked to the press in order to embarrass their opponents. Consider examples such as General Motors' hiring private detectives to investigate Ralph Nader and to generate events that could be used to discredit him, the Watergate-era break-in at antiwar activist Daniel Ellsberg's psychiatrist's office to find information that could be used to embarrass him, the COINTEL dirty-tricks campaign to damage the public image of 1960s protest groups, and the FBI's wiretapping of Martin Luther King's indiscretions (Garrow 1986; Cunningham 2004).

Another goal of publicity-related surveillance may be to influence or prevent certain behaviors. In Florida, a retired police officer created an organization to secretly videotape police abuses. Some antiprostitution groups post photos and license plate numbers on the Internet of persons in red-light areas at night; some police departments make available to the media photos and names of persons arrested in such areas; some antiabortion groups post images and names of those entering abortion clinics; and a number of web sites feature cell phone pictures of men behaving badly. The goal is to embarrass and shame people and hence serve as deterrence or retribution and perhaps also as a form of nonjuridical punishment via stigmatization. This use can also be seen in interpersonal relations, where angry ex-lovers reveal intimate details on the internet and elsewhere about their former partners.

Publicity-related surveillance is also important to social science and medical research. A basic goal is to develop knowledge as its own end and to communicate this to others with common interests who may then apply or extend it. However, what is publicized is general information about categories of person rather than a specific individual. The audiences for research and those for viewing celebrities cavorting in the nude may seem unrelated, but they share curiosity, if about different aspects of the world.

Symbolism

A tactic may have an intended symbolic meaning, beyond whatever instrumental goal the data are presumed to serve.[13] The surveillance theater speaks not only to subjects, but may also be intended to tell us about agents. This goal relates to publicity, since its realization requires an audience. But it differs from the publicity in the previous goal because it makes a statement about the agent rather than about the subject. Consider that in 1978 President Regan and seventy-eight of his top White House aides took a widely publicized voluntary drug test. Some drug testing serves as a public advertisement for the organization. Note the sign in large letters that confronts one at the main entrance to a national hardware chain:

THIS STORE TESTS ALL APPLICANTS FOR JOBS FOR DRUGS. IF YOU USE DRUGS DON'T EVEN THINK OF APPLYING.

Since almost everyone who comes through this entrance is a customer, not a prospective employee, it would be more appropriate to display this sign at the personnel office and in a form handed to applicants. Here, the organization is engaged in a public relations campaign to demonstrate that it is a good corporate citizen. A similar interpretation would apply to the Texas high school in which all students "voluntarily" submitted to drug testing and all passed. This became an annual event proudly reported in the media. According to a spokesperson, the goal was to show the community what kind of a school "we are." Note as well a Los Angeles county leader who said, "It's [voluntary testing] like putting a flag on your lapel for July 4 weekend saying you are a good American."

The head of the stringent World Anti-Doping Agency says that when Olympic athletes tested positive, "it added luster to the Olympic brand," because it demonstrated the seriousness of the International Olympic Committee in policing the use of banned drugs (Sokolove 2008). The same might be said of negative findings if they are publicized as well. Then the agency can claim it is not only serious but successful.

Rigid ideologies that demand unwavering commitment lend themselves particularly well to symbolic expressions. Political or religious loyalty oaths and commitment-affirming behavior have an equivalent communicative quality, particularly in times of panics and perceived crisis. The goal goes beyond the instrumental one of having a certain type of person in the work force; it shows that "we are doing our part" in the war on drugs, communism, or heresy. For example, during the Hollywood loyalty oath conflict, the entertainment industry's surveillance and blacklisting sought to demonstrate that the "reds" had been driven out of the industry (Navasky 1980).

Two final goals—self-knowledge and curiosity—involve individuals rather than organizations initiating the search for personal information.

Self-knowledge

The unexamined life is not worth living.
SOCRATES

Were Socrates alive today, he would find ample resources for such examination and a less punitive state response. Of course, much depends on *who* wants the examination. A major category of personal information collection is initiated with the goal of increasing the individual's self- knowledge, whether for instrumental reasons or mere curiosity. Since the subject is in a sense also the sponsoring (and often the actual) agent, this is less controversial than many forms of surveillance.[14] A cornucopia of professional testers, assayers, and counselors is available to help individuals in their self-assessments.

Consider the vast array of home medical testing devices (e.g., for blood pressure, temperature, weight, hormonal levels, or pregnancy). The self-administered tests available through the mass media and direct marketing ("How good is your sex life?" or "What's your tolerance for financial risk?") are mainstays of popular culture. Note also tools for genealogy and the efforts of adopted persons to locate their birth parents.

In contrast to most organizational users, here the subject decides what is to be scrutinized and how (and if) results are to be used and communi-

84

cated. Holding apart issues of validity, data gathering with the goal of self-knowledge provides a strand of the democratization of surveillance and can even be a way to counter the claims of experts.

Curiosity

Here's looking at you, kid.
HUMPHREY BOGART, *Casablanca*

The curiosity here refers to an interest in other people rather than one's self, as described above. Sociologist Georg Simmel ([1908] 1950) writes of the lure of the secret. While he was dealing more with secrets as they affect group boundaries, curiosity about unknown or unseen aspects of others' lives may be a human universal. It is certainly a central aspect of our mass-media-saturated society, providing the market for a vast array of publications from the hush-hush tabloids to *People* magazine and its variants to the reality TV programs.

The motive for media professionals who gather such information is of course to sell it for publication. But in the case of personal surveillance propelled by inquisitiveness, the motive is noninstrumental. The agent collects information for its own recreational or educational purposes rather than as a means to some other end. Consider hobbyists such as ham radio operators who may legally listen to others' conversations but are prohibited from recording or making use of them, or telescope users in high-rise buildings or the inquisitive homeowner peeking out of a window to observe neighbors' activities and visitors.

The secret collection of personal information (whether via looking through telescopes; using video cameras or secret audio recorders; overhearing phone messages; listening through closed doors; reading another's diary, letters, medical records, e-mail, or documents left on office copiers and printers; or web browsing) are frequently ends in themselves. Prurient entertainment interest fuels much of this, but goes much beyond it to vicarious curiosity. The use lies within the imagination or psyche of the lurker. If the surveillance remains hidden, unlike with many information games in which there is conflict or competition, it may not have a zero-sum quality, meaning that one party's gain must not of necessity be another party's loss. The curious case of voyeur Tom I. Voire is considered in chapters 9–10.

The attraction is in both the secret power of watching (perhaps enhanced by the fear of possible discovery) and the deliciousness of knowing secrets (both what one knows and the fact that the subject and others may not even know that there is a secret).[15] "If everyone minded their own business" as the Duchess recommended in *Alice in Wonderland*, life would be less interesting.

Challenging Goals and Analyzing Variation

Thus far we have discussed goals as ideal types, as if they were easily definable and stood alone, or could be cleanly disentangled, if found together. In the world defined by public relations efforts on behalf of controversial surveillance, such single-goal clarity is not surprising. But as we turn to the world of observed behavior, clean analytic lines often become muddied, and multiple goal settings are common.

Certainly there are settings where an agent has a single clear goal. For example, surveillance as entertainment is unitary. For much voyeurism/ recreational/sport surveillance, the activity is its own end. The point of the watching is the watching—although when done in secret there may be other satisfactions, such as the challenge of being able to pull it off or having secret knowledge. A single well-defined goal can also be seen when an agent views a legitimating token as a means of entry or exit. If possession of the "right" sign is sufficient and no other check is made, nor a record kept, then compliance is the only goal.

Organizations and individuals also vary in the singularity, relative importance, and frequency given to particular surveillance goals. Thus, public health institutions emphasize prevention, welfare agencies focus on verification, and police have the goals of compliance and discovery. Goals of influence, self-knowledge, and curiosity are more important to individuals than many of the other goals involving organizational functioning.

Some intellectual capital is waiting to be gathered from a broad analysis of the consequences of surveillance goal variation in diverse settings—whether across or within organizations and institutions, and on the part of individuals. Moreover, a distinction between single- and multiple-goal contexts with respect to a given tool is needed.

Goals may of course be pursued with various kinds of personal information. We next turn to such variations and consider what terms such as *personal, public, private, sensitive,* and *intimate information* mean.

4

The Stuff of Surveillance:
Varieties of Personal Information

For it is a serious thing to have been watched.
We all radiate something curiously intimate when we believe ourselves to be alone.

E. M. FORSTER (1905), *Where Angels Fear to Tread*

"You ought to have some papers to show who you are," the police officer advised me.
"I do not need any paper. I know who I am," I said.
"Maybe so. Other people are also interested in knowing who you are."

B. TRAVEN (1934), *The Death Ship*

Thus far we have examined structure, means, and goals for surveillance. We turn now to the related but independent question of types of data collected. Such data are honeycombed with attributes and tacit expectations that can be systematically compared. What are the major kinds of data that surveillance may gather? How do the characteristics of these data affect explanation, evaluation, manners, policy, and law? When we speak of surveillance, just what is it that is surveilled? What cultural expectations and attitudes accompany different kinds of data?

A central argument of the book is that understanding and evaluating surveillance require attention to the setting. For example, political beliefs revealed in a campaign ad differ from those revealed to a friend, to a feigned friend serving as an informer, or via a wiretap or in a coercive or duplicitous interrogation.

In spite of the contextual and situational variation, some conceptual value lies in studying the objective attributes and meanings imputed to types of data—holding constant aspects of the setting—such as role relationships, norms, and goals. The questions below illustrate the "kinds of data" issue:

How does being seen but not heard differ from the reverse or from a narrative account?[1]

What changes when a video of a psychiatric interview shown to a medical class involves an anonymous as against a named patient or a disguised face but not voice?

Do you view a traffic camera on a public road that only notes license plate numbers differently from one that also notes speed, tracks the vehicle, and captures an image of the driver or others? What about the fifteen or more kinds of data likely stored in the car's event data recorder attached to the engine?

Why do some film stars refuse to do nude scenes, necessitating the use of a stand-in?

When purchasing something with cash, why does it seem inappropriate for a merchant to ask for a home phone number?

Why should information about my hobbies be requested when I seek a warranty for my toaster?

Why is access to a phone number likely to be viewed differently than to a street address, a post office box, or an email address?

How should we compare videotaping of travelers at an international border with searching and even copying the contents of their computer?

What should those seeking political office be required to reveal (e.g., conflicts of interest, mental and physical health, or experiences with sex, drugs, and rock and roll)? What questions should an interviewer be permitted or expected to ask the candidate?

In my junior high school, student athletic performance was assessed and the top 10 percent received athletic letters and their scores were posted. What assumptions underlie contemporary cases in which schools have been prohibited from publicly listing the names of honor students?

At the federal level, why is a warrant required to wiretap or bug communications, but not required for undercover conversations or for videotaping?

On an airplane trip, does it matter if a stranger sitting next to you is silent or instead asks for (or reveals) personal information? What tacit organizing principles are embedded with respect to the information asked for (or offered) by strangers (and others)?

Untangling the knots presented by these questions requires making distinctions. Concepts such as public and private, impersonal and personal, nonsensitive and sensitive, nonintimate and intimate, anonymous and pseudoanonymous, and unique and core identity (see fig. 41) swirl around the examples.

Some data have an either/or quality (as in a rule defining information as public or private or in the status of information as either known or not known), some kinds exist along a continuum (as in the move from full anonymity to full identity), some present options that are mutually exclusive (information that is nonintimate cannot at the same time be intimate), and some kinds can be distinct in some cases but can also overlap in others (sensitive information may be intimate but need not be, while what is intimate may,

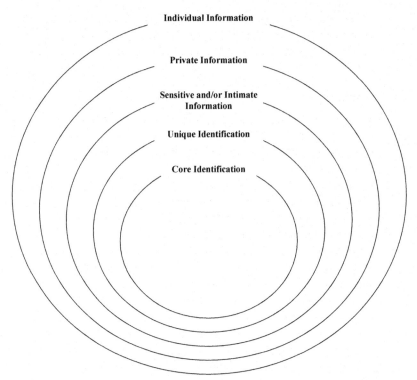

Individual Information

Private Information

Sensitive and/or Intimate
Information

Unique Identification

Core Identification

FIGURE 4.1. Concentric circles of information.

but need not be, sensitive). Finally, some kinds of information build on each other—for example, one kind may by definition be a necessary (or at least an inclusive) condition for another (thus, all the examples are about types of personal information in the sense of being attachable to a person). Yet many indeterminate steps exist between having such information and knowing the full identity of the person in question (see, e.g., fig. 4.1).

The verbal vagueness of terms related to privacy and personal information and the multiplicity of meanings also contribute to the difficulty of clear understanding. The term *individual information* (the outermost circle in fig. 4.1), for example, can refer to basic facts about an individual (address, height, weight, age), but it can also refer to something more directly tied to private identity, as in the expression "That's very personal." Nevertheless, in my conception, individual information is the broadest category, the canopy of branches at the top of a tree, with various lower and crosscutting branches. For some purposes, the topic of individual information can also be presented as a series of concentric circles (and within, some circles that partially overlap).

TABLE 4.1. Person and information types

	Accessibility	
Connection to individual	Public	Private
Personal	A. Scent, DNA, facial image, voice, gait	B. Religious beliefs, sexual preference, health status
Impersonal	C. Height, first language, right-handed	D. Blood type, car mileage

This chapter is organized around visual representations of the variety of personal information, and it explores how the elements of personal information are related to rules and behavior. Table 4.1 combines the dimensions of information accessibility and the personal into four broad types. Figure 4.2 is built around the most socially contentious of the four types seen in table 4.1 (in cell B: that which is both private and personal). This figure adds categorizations involving the presence or absence of intimacy and sensitivity as attributes. As noted, figure 4.1 models the concentric circles of information, thus presenting several ways that the personal and private data in figure 4.2 can be linked to the individual—for example, to someone about whom almost nothing is known (only membership in a general category, if that), to a uniquely identified person or to a person whose unique identity further involves information on biological heritage and legal name (called *core identity*). Thus, the ties of personal data to identity can vary from unknown (fully anonymous) to various kinds of being "known." Table 4.2 is concerned with specific content and describes kinds of information that may be gathered.

Behaviors and judgments about information attachable to the person and the appropriateness of its collection, protection, or revelation are socially and culturally patterned. The patterning is based partly on the characteristics attributed to, or more deeply emanating from, the information. Calling attention to those characteristics is a central point of this chapter. Table 4.3, building on the other tables and figures, identifies crosscutting dimensions that can unite seemingly diverse, or separate seemingly similar, forms and content. This kind of analysis permits systematic comparisons as well as conclusions about how the information gathered is likely to be viewed.[2]

Private and Public

Let us begin by considering the two dimensions that make up table 4.1 and also inform the other figures and tables. Whether information is seen as private or public and whether it is seen as personal or impersonal are central de-

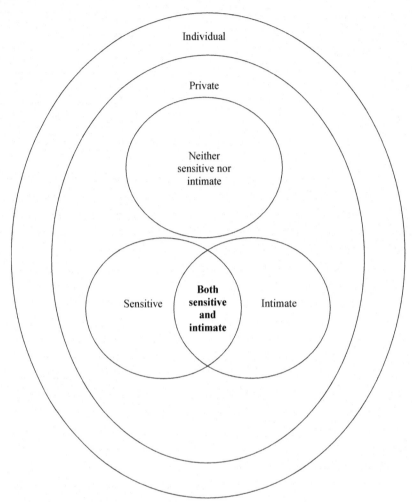

FIGURE 4.2. Sensitive and intimate information.

terminants of surveillance agent behavior seeking to discover, of subject behavior seeking to protect, and of judgments.[3] But what does "private" mean?
In chapter 1, we identified two meanings of *public* and *private* involving rules
and the actual state of knowledge—that is, whether known or not known. A
key factor there is the extent to which the properties of the information make
it relatively available or unavailable to others. How accessible is the information, absent rules or tools regarding discovery? In addition consider the
agent's competence, resources, and social location and the behavior of the
subject in offering or concealing data.

TABLE 4.2. Types of descriptive information connectable to individuals

1. Individual [the who question]
   Ancestry
   Legal name
   Alphanumeric
   Biometric (natural, environmental)
   Password
   Aliases, nicknames
   Performance

2. Shared [the typification-profiling question]
   Gender
   Race/ethnicity/religion
   Age
   Education
   Occupation
   Employment
   Wealth
   DNA (most)
   General physical characteristics (blood type, height, skin and hair color)
   and appearance
   Health status
   Organizational memberships
   Folk characterizations by reputation—liar, cheat, brave, strong, weak, ad-
   dictive personality

3. Geographic/locational [the where, where from/where to and how to
   "reach" the person questions]
   A. Fixed
      Residence, residence history
      Telephone number (land line)
      Mail address
      Cable TV
   B. Mobile
      E-mail address
      Cell phone
      Vehicle and personal locators
      Wireless computing
      Satellites
      Travel records

(continued)

TABLE 4.2. (*continued*)

4. Temporal [the when, how long, and what sequences question]
   Date and time of activity

5. Networks and relationships [the who else question]
   Family members, married or divorced
   Others the individual interacts or communicates with, roommates, friends, associates, others copresent (contiguous) at a given location (including in cyberspace) or activity including neighbors

6. Objects [the which one and whose is it question]
   Vehicles
   Weapons
   Animals
   Communications device
   Contraband
   Land, buildings, and businesses

7. Behavioral [the what happened/is happening question]
   A. Communication
      Fact of using a given means (computer, phone, cable TV, diary, notes, or library) to create, send, or receive information (mail covers, subscription lists, pen registers, e-mail headers, cell phone, GPS)
      Content of that communication
   B. Economic behavior—buying (including consumption patterns and preferences), selling, banking, credit card transactions
   C. Work monitoring
   D. Employment history
   E. Norm- and conflict-related behavior—bankruptcies, tax liens, small claims, and civil judgments, criminal records, suits filed

8. Beliefs, attitudes, emotions [the inner or backstage and presumed "real" person question]
9. Measurement characterizations (past, present, predictions, potentials) [the kind of person, predict your future question]

   Opinions of others, reputation
   Credit ratings and limits
   Insurance ratings
   SAT and college acceptability scores
   Intelligence tests
   Civil service scores
   Drug tests

Truth telling (honesty tests, lie detection—verbal and nonverbal)
Psychological inventories, tests, and profiles
Occupational placement and performance tests
Medical (HIV, genetic, cholesterol, etc.)

10. Media references (yearbooks, newsletters, newspapers, TV, Internet)
[the what was said about the person and who said it question]

TABLE 4.3. Dimensions of individual information

Dimension for classifying attributes of individual information		
1. Accessible	No (private)	Yes (public)
2. Personal	Yes	No (impersonal)
3. Intimate	Yes	No
4. Sensitive	Yes	No
5. Unique identification	Yes (distinctive but shared)	No (anonymous)
	Core	Noncore
6. Locatable	Yes	No
7. Stigmatizable (reflection on character of subject)	Yes	No
8. Prestige enhancing	No	Yes
9. Reveals deception (on part of subject)	Yes	No
10. Strategic disadvantage to subject	Yes	No
11 Multiple kinds of data (extensive and intensive)	Yes	No
12. Documentary (reusable) record	Yes	No
13. Attached to or part of person	Yes	No
14. Biological	Yes	No
15. "Naturalistic" (reflects reality in obvious way, face validity)	No (artifactual)	Yes
16. Information is predictive rather than reflecting empirically documentable past and present	Yes	No
17. Enduring shelf life	Yes	No (transitory)
18. Alterable	Yes	No
19. Individual alone or radiates to others	Yes (e.g., olifacteurs)	Radiate (e.g., communication taps

However, for the average person in the immediate environment of others, factors such as appearance, gender, age, skin color, voice, and gait are public and available for the taking. That is also the case for public record information such as phone number and address in a telephone book and for the thousands of databases providing information online—from conviction records to owners of exotic pets—for a price. With special training and tools, a great deal can be learned about anyone by anyone, and specialists such as medical practitioners, salespersons, psychologists, market researchers, and detectives can learn even more. Such practitioners are skilled in finding direction by indirection and meaning in what is not revealed, beyond what is.

The "public" information above contrasts with that which is "private" in not being easily known, absent being volunteered or involuntarily extracted or collected (often seen as "none of your business" data). Much personal information is simply de facto private for logistical reasons. Consider thoughts, directed communications, possessions in pockets or containers, activities in the dark or behind closed doors, forgotten (or unseen and unrecoverable) pasts, and plans for the future.

Personal and Impersonal

The second dimension or axis of table 4.1 is whether information is personal or impersonal in form and the degree to which it is one or the other. Information may be more or less personal or impersonal as well as more or less private or public.

How does personal connect to private? *Personal* is often used as a synonym for *private,* reflecting the fact that personal information is frequently unavailable, but there can be elements of the personal in the public and of the impersonal in the private (chaps. 9, 10).

Personal has a number of other meanings apart from the conventionally understood public-private aspect.[4] For example, any datum attached to a corporeal individual (e.g., being identified as a citizen or owner of an SUV) is "personal" in the sense that it corresponds to a person and assigns a category. Yet knowledge about the kind of car one drives when millions of people drive a similar car is a most pale form of "personal" information, although driving a Prius or a red convertible may carry symbolic meaning.[5]

Property

Information about ownership, as with the term *personal property*, needs consideration. Knowledge about the kind of television set an individual owns is personal in one sense but impersonal in another. There are "private" personal possessions, as in "mine," which are not personal in the selfhood sense of intimate or sensitive information considered below or of being unique. Nor, as current digital rights management controversies illustrate, need they come with decisional rights (e.g., a software-based product that cannot be altered or copied; Cohen 2012).

However, there can be spillover between personal and impersonal, and between public and private in the context of property ownership. Consider a manufacturer who builds a product such as a computer program that it can remotely inspect or make inoperable, or that self-destructs if used in ways prohibited by the maker. Many persons would consider this a personal violation, even if the inspected content were impersonal in being technical and nonsubstantive.

However, a property control definition of the personal has obvious limitations, because personal elements remain even after control is relinquished and even as others have a right or are given permission to access, use, and even "own" another's information. Yet the fact of control by a person other than the subject does not then make it that person's "personal information" in the sense implied here.[6]

With the new technologies, the private and control/ownership issue is often unclear. The lines between mine and not mine, self and other, and copy and original are grayer. We see the peculiar connection between simulation and dissimulation, which need not be opposite (both are distortions of something, if in different ways).

Consider Henrietta Lacks (Skloot 2010). The cells removed from her cervix without her permission became the HeLa immortal cell line widely used in biomedical research. This "remnants" issue can also be seen with technologies for reading brain waves and olifacteurs. Are these personal property (or even private) after leaving the body? What would we say of a commercial photographer who owns photos of a subject? What if the subject is dead and the photos were recovered from the trash, as in a California case involving historic police mug shots marketed on note cards (Rosen, 2011)?

Arbitrary symbols can be invested with personal meaning. As examples, consider the personal possessiveness many persons feel toward "their" phone numbers and the customer resistance sometimes seen to changes in telephone area codes. The act of paying for phone service (and paying for an unlisted number) seems to imply control over your assigned number. Yet as legislation and regulations generally imply, the phone number is rented from and "belongs" to the phone company (at least that is the case for landlines). The question of formal ownership is distinct from the conditions of use and whether the number can be released if the phone company so chooses (e.g., via caller ID and related services).[7]

Some "personal" remnants go beyond information about the person. Consider the intangible essence of the other that remains for those who purchase (often for outrageous sums) the costumes and shoes of movies stars or the original manuscripts and letters of famous individuals. Our ever-expanding celebrity culture (and DNA analysis) has given new impetus to collecting the hair of the famous and infamous. Of course trace elements of the personal may be rejected as well. Consider a tuxedo ad suggesting that it is uninviting to wear a tuxedo someone else has rented or be assigned a hotel room where a smoker has stayed. These are unwanted border crossings that impose on, rather than take from, the person.

Sensitive Information

A central theme of Erving Goffman's work is that the individual, playing a role and angling for advantage, presents a self to the outside world that may be at odds with what the individual actually feels, believes, or "is" in some objective sense. The tolerance associated with civil society supports this, as do inertia and the difficulties of discovery. Through manners and laws, for many purposes, modern society acknowledges the legitimacy of the hidden person behind the mask, regardless of whether the hidden information is sensitive, stigmatizing, or strategically advantageous to others.

The sensitivity of information is a dimension that intersects with the personal and impersonal in multiple, complex ways. The term *sensitive* has a legal and bureaucratic meaning with respect to restrictions on information access. It can refer both to methods of collection and to content. Terms such as *confidential, secret, top secret,* and other, more restrictive terms that it might be illegal even to name are common within government security agencies. Much sensitive government information is not intimate— involving secret expenditures, specifications, findings, and plans. Some of course does involve intimate information, as with the identity of spies and intelligence files on life habits of persons of interest, as well as personnel files of employees.

Sensitive organizational information has its informal counterparts in primary groups and interpersonal relations and, at the extreme, may include information that an individual would prefer never to reveal to anyone. Part of freedom of thought, belief, imagination, and personal autonomy lies in one's sense of having a protected zone between the public face offered to others and the backstage regions of the self and the group. There is a special poignancy when the gap between public face and inner realities and unseen offstage behavior is pronounced, whether for the individual or the group. Whatever the content or communal goals, the outing of others is indeed strong medicine. Not only is a border crossed, but the crossing may show that the subject is a liar and hypocrite. This is the authenticity assumption referred to earlier.

With regard to the personal/impersonal dimension we might gain some conceptual leverage and empirical knowledge by studying the size of the gap between what others know and what the subject knows to be true. The size and correlates of that gap surface the tangled connection between the number of persons who have access to certain information and the extent and form of its being intimate, sensitive, or something else. Certainly to the extent that information is widely known, it may appear less personal. For example, a straight-appearing person in broadcasting he is gay has one less intimate secret.

The kind of behavior, role and emotions involved also matter. Consider those gainfully employed in the pornography business. They are paid to go public. Is there a difference between impersonal and personal sex, or is the latter an oxymoron? Does the indiscriminate revelation of intimate activities with multiple partners make the behavior impersonal and less or not intimate? How is knowing about people different from knowing them? Do elements of the personal remain when the performers use pseudonyms, wear masks (as was the case when such behavior was illegal), or are not psychologically involved in the behavior?

What if those performing in fact genuinely care about each other, even meeting off camera? Does the meaning of intimacy change depending on where they express carnality? Is a prostitute who goes through the motions, knowing that she is faking it, preserving her intimate feelings? What of the convincing sex scene in the film *Don't Look Now* (1973) involving Donald Sutherland and Julie Christie? Apparently the off-screen partner of actress Julie Christie didn't see it as impersonal and broke off the relationship—even though the film actors were simply playing an occupational role they were paid to perform. Contrast this with the Rock Hudson–Julie Andrews love scene in *Darling Lili* (1970), in which observers could clearly see that the actors were distanced from the roles they played. And what can, or should, we say about nakedness and bodily contact in the form of a pelvic exam where there also presumably is emotional distance from the contact? The fact that it occurred and the results are private, but is it in some ways personal and intimate?

Round in Circles

And Adam knew Eve his wife.

GENESIS 4:1

Rather than the linear-boxes approach of table 4.1 above, let us shape shift to concentric circles. Figure 4.2 elaborates on cell B of table 4.1—information that is personal and private (as in not immediately available). Having particular relevance to public policy, this is the most socially contentious of the types.

The outermost circle refers to information about an individual (which in a loose sense is "personal"), while the next refers to that which is personal and private, and the innermost circles to that which is either (or both) sensitive and intimate or neither.

Thus, the inclusive, outermost circle includes any datum or category that can be attached to a person and is distinct from information that applies to aggregates such as states, regions, organizations, or groups (whether in the world or only statistically). The individual need not be personally known, or even known by name and location, by those gathering or attaching the data. Individuals need not be aware of the data linked to their persons.

Such individual information varies from that which is relatively impersonal with minimal implications for an individual's uniqueness, such as being labeled as living in a flood zone or owning a four-door car, to that which is more personal, such as health status, sexual preference, religious beliefs, facial image, address, legal name, and ancestry. The latter information has clearer implications for selfhood and life chances, and for distinctly reflecting the individual. Individual information may be provided by, or taken directly from, the person (e.g., through remote health sensors or a black box documenting driving behavior). Alternately, it can be imposed onto persons (e.g., in the form of statistical risk categories determining credit or insurance).

The next circle refers to private information in the sense that it is not immediately available. Absent special circumstances to compel disclosure, as with the use of a social security number for tax purposes or a subpoena or warrant for a search, such information is defined by discretionary norms regarding revelation. An unlisted phone or credit card number and nonobvious or nonvisible biographical and biological details are examples. As the case of "private [body] parts" suggests, such information retains its moral, if not its existential, status as private, even when revealed, as with physical information at a nude beach. We can refer to information about the person that is not known by others and whose communication the individual can control as existentially private.

Intimate

Within the private circle (attachable and relatively unknown) are other forms that refer to information which can be either, both, or neither intimate or sensitive. In Latin *intimus* means "inmost," suggesting outer protective layers or borders, whether physical or cultural. Used as a verb, the word *intimate* means "to hint" or "suggest," implying that the information is less likely to be known; it may even lose something of its intimate quality the more widely known it becomes. As an adjective, it can suggest something close to the person, cherished, comfortable, not widely available to others, as well as knowledge that is detailed and thorough. It can be the touchstone for assessments of authenticity and may have enormous implications for the individual's life chances and self-image.

Intimacy is also an attribute of the primary group in which individuals have their "closest" attachments, are presumed to be most "themselves," behave with the least formality, wear the fewest masks, and expect that others will effectively patrol the borders of confidentiality. Some "very personal" attitudes, conditions, and behaviors take their significance from the fact that they are a currency of intimacy—selectively revealed, only to those we trust and feel close to. In the biblical sense, to know someone meant to have carnal knowledge. Thousands of years later, the Beatles reversed the order when they sang, "To know, know, know her / Is to love, love, love her / And I do."

Within the intimate "circle," individuals can communicate both restricted content and trust. Such personal information is not usually willingly offered to outsiders, excluding the behavior of exhibitionists, those lacking in manners, and the refreshing honesty of small children.

The point is not that the information or behavior classified as intimate is necessarily personal in the sense of uniquely defining the individual; nor is it necessarily stigmatizing or disadvantaging. Still, having control over access affirms a sense of self-respect and sustains the value of intimacy and intimate relationships. Persons who prematurely reveal their hole cards or private parts are likely to do poorly at both cards and love.

In contrast, certain forms of information or behavior are intimate because they do not involve others. E. M. Forster (1961) nailed it when he wrote that being alone communicates something "curiously intimate" (p. 96). Here we see the intimate but without sensitivity in its formal policy or legal meaning. Solitude or apartness can mean protection from intrusions and imply a sense of security, of being able to let one's guard down and be "one's self," and lessened self-consciousness."[8] Humphrey Bogart's wry observation about the House Un-American Activities Committee—that "they will nail anyone who

ever scratched his ass during the national anthem"—argues for the importance of moments apart, even during occasions of national solemnity. This
apartness from others, whether based on a cranially protected (at least before
brain wave technology) freedom of thought and imagination, walled enclosures (bathroom activities), or manners can sustain respect for personhood,
beyond any strategic advantage or avoidance of stigmatization.[9]

Consider also respecting the intimate during moments of vulnerability
and embarrassment observable in public—for example, the expressions of
sadness and anguish in a sudden tragedy, as with a mother who has just lost a
child in a car accident. We respect the individual's horror and grief by looking
away, not by publishing news photo of the person's anguish.

Sensitive

Information can be thought of as sensitive in the sense of strategic, or useful
for an opponent in a conflict situation involving negotiation, or capable of
making an individual vulnerable to harm through victimization (e.g., credit
card and banking information). This need not be intimate information. Sensitive information could include plans to change jobs or partners, as well as
that which can be used for wrongful discrimination. It can also involve information on vulnerable groups such as children. Once sensitive information is
widely known, it qualitatively changes, even though its status as defined by
law or policy remains.

The European Union's data protection directive requires special safeguards for "sensitive data"—that on race and ethnicity; political, philosophical, and religious beliefs; health; and sexual life. Even if not legally required, a
"Don't ask" policy can serve as protection. In the United States, given goals of
affirmative action, information collection on race/ethnicity is more common.

On the other hand, information may be intimate without being sensitive
in that it can strategically disadvantage a subject or an organization if it is
known. Bathroom activities within a stall or behind a closed door are seen as
intimate but do not generally involve sensitive information in the sense considered above. Finally, much (most?) private information is neither intimate
nor sensitive; it is simply logistically and socially unavailable to others.

Who Are You? Unique and Core Identity

What this taught me was that, contrary to what I'd believed, a passport is not a document that tells us who we are but a document that shows what other people think of us.
ORHAN PAMUK[10]

A final piece in the analysis of personal versus private information involves the various connections between types of data that can be linked to the individual. These links occur with varying degrees of specificity from disconnected anonymous to attributes tied to a unique core identity. Figure 4.1 first separates cases where there is a direct link to a unique individual from those where there is no such link (or only the weakest of links to a category). For the weakest links (the kinds of information in the outermost circle), there may be a tie to a general category—English speaker or full or partial anonymity.

Where a unique identity is present, a separation can still be made between an individual who is distinctly identifiable by a number or other identifying symbol and the biological individual identifiable by his or her core identity as defined by parents and place and time of birth. The kind of information that reveals a unique identity may include numbers or letters—as with the code on an airline reservation—but does not reveal the individual's core identity. Core identity is represented by the inner circle of the figure 4.1 and traces back to biological parents, time and place of birth, and legal name (descriptive elements shown in table 4.2 and analytic elements in table 4.3)

Types of Information Connectable to Persons

Getting to know you
Getting to know all about you
HART LORENZ AND RICHARD ROGERS

What are the major forms of surveillance data gathered and connected to individuals? Stated as questions, ten forms are noted:

Who is this individual in core identity?
What profiles and categories apply to this person?
Who is this person connected with?
Where is this person geographically and how can she/he be reached?
When does the behavior of interest occur and with what sequencing? (temporal)
Which one, whose is it, who has used or touched it? (objects such as a computer or weapon)
How does this person behave and/or spend his/her time?
What does the person really believe and feel? (inner or backstage "real" person)
How does this individual measure up (or down)?
What is in the public media about the person?

A concern with aspects of these questions runs throughout the book. Of the many kinds of information that can be connected to individuals, the "who" and "where" questions are particularly important and are emphasized in the discussion. The ability to identify, categorize, and locate are fundamental to the other forms of data and actions that may subsequently be taken. The next section explores aspects of identity involving the "who" question.

Unique and Core Identity

The categories considered above, in tables 4.1 and figure 4.1 and 4.2, are general concepts. These can be further broken down, as shown in table 4.2. Each person has various identity pegs. With enough information, these pegs link to a unique and even core identity ("only you," as the song says). They are attached to what Goffman (1966) refers to as an "embodied" individual, who is usually assumed to be alive, or if not, previously was.

Knowing someone's unique identity answers the basic question raised by the children's television program *Sesame Street*, "Whoo . . . is it?" The question assumes the point of view of an outside observer trying to be honest, because individuals may prevaricate, have fluid identities, or in rare cases not know "who" they are.[11] It is from this identity that many other sources of information about the person can be found, and it is to this identity that still other sources of information can be attached.

Traditionally, unique identity tended to be synonymous with core identity based on biological ancestry and family embedment. Excluding physically joined twins, each individual is unique in being the offspring of particular biological parents, with birth at a particular place and time. Parents and place of birth of course may be shared. Yet even for identical twins, if we add time of birth to the equation, the laws of physics and biology generate a distinctive core identity in the conjunction of parents, place, and time of birth. Unknown sperm and egg donors, eggs from distinct women, gestational carriers, abandonment, and adoption may muddy these bases for core identity.

For most persons and throughout most of history, discovering identity was not an issue. In small-scale societies, where there was little geographic or social mobility and people were rooted in very local networks of family and kin, individuals tended to be personally known. Physical and cultural appearance and location were generally sufficient to answer the "Who is it?" question. Names and titles may have offered information about status, family, gender, occupation, or residence. Names popular in one time period that go out of fashion also may offer unwitting clues to approximate age.

With large-scale societies and the increased mobility associated with urbanization and industrialization, core identity came to be determined by fuller names and reliance on proxy forms such as a birth certificate, passport, national identity card, and driver's license (Caplan and Torpey 2001). Yet, given the limitations of paper documents, identification is increasingly supplemented by forms more directly connected to the person.

With the expansion of biometric technology, a variety of indicators presumed to be unique (and, at least initially, harder to fake) are increasingly used. For example, beyond improved fingerprinting, we see identification efforts based on DNA, voice, retina, iris, wrist veins, hand geometry, facial appearance, scent, and even gait.

Yet these need a unique identity to be linked to a core identity. Police files are filled with DNA and fingerprint "John Doe" data that are not connected to a person's core identity. With data from multiple events, because of matching, police may know that the same person is responsible for crimes but not know who the person is.

The question "Who is it?" may be answered in a variety of other ways that need not trace back to a biologically defined ancestral core or legal name. For many contemporary settings, what matters is determining the presence of attributes warranting a certain kind of treatment (admittance to a theater because one has a ticket) or continuity of identity (verifying that this is the same person who took the first part of the exam), or an individual's location, not who the person "really" is as conventionally defined. How much and what kinds of "Who is it?" information are necessary in various contexts is at the center of many current controversies. This brings us to issues of anonymity and pseudoanonymity.

Pseudonyms

Among pseudonymous forms are the alias, pen name, nom de plume, nom de guerre, and alphanumeric indicators on secret Swiss bank accounts, ID cards and auto licenses and testing for AIDS. While names can be held in common, letters and numbers are sufficient as unique identifiers. As buffering devices, pseudonyms offer a compromise in which literal identity or location is protected while the need for some degree of identification, whether involving eligibility or continuity of identity (that is, ensuring that the same person is involved when there are repeated interactions), is still met.

In many settings anonymity is implied, as with barter and cash purchases, and presence in public places. In other settings some information and continuity of identity (apart from literally knowing core identity) is required. Many contexts require that the individual have some general characteristics warranting inclusion or exclusion, degrees of access, or a particular kind of treatment

Eligibility certificates (or tokens) offer a way of showing that one is entitled to a given service without requiring that the user be otherwise identified. Tickets for the theater or ski lift or stamps on the hand at concerts are familiar. Smart cards for copying and electronic toll-collection tools (e.g., E-ZPass) have become widespread. These permit access but need not lead to further identification (although a video camera or other sensors may reveal more).[12]

Other forms of shared, but not uniquely personal, information can be gleaned from appearance, artifacts, and knowledge or skill demonstrations. Uniforms, badges, group tattoos, crosses, scarlet letters—these define place in a category, but not core identity.

The possession of knowledge may do the same (e.g., knowing a secret hand signal, PIN or account number, code, or the "color of the day" used by police departments to permit officers in civilian clothes to let uniformed officers know they are also police). Demonstrating a skill, such as passing a swim test in order to be in the deep end, is a form of identity certification.

Anonyms

Among the dictionary meanings of anonymity are "unknown name," "unknown authorship," and "without character, featureless, impersonal." When no aspects of identity are available (being uncollected, altered, or severed), we have true anonymity. Yet the traditional meanings of the term are somewhat undercut by contemporary behavior and technologies. Haggerty and Ericson (2000, 619) note "the progressive 'disappearance of disappearance'" as once-discrete surveillance systems are joined. Genuine anonymity appears to be less common than in the past, even though remote interactions have greatly increased. But this trend is matched by an increase in pseudoanonymity and the expansion of insulating layers between core identity and some distanced blurry facsimile. A variety of forwarding and blocking services offer ways to protect identity such as by stripping identifying header information from an e-mail.

Whatever the intention of the actor wishing to remain unrecognized, "anonymous" persons may leave clues about aspects of themselves (apart from name and location) given meaning by the new surveillance—whether face and vehicle recognition technology or seepage of a DNA sample onto a glass or a licked envelope.

FIGURE 4.3. Where does spit in Britain go and how long does it stay? Answer: the national DNA database and forever. (Photo by Tamara Polajnar.)

Where You Are? Location

An important component of personal information is location. Location answers the "where" question, although it may also have implications for the "who" question and serve as an alternative to it. Location may involve a fixed or mobile address—that is, a hard-wired phone line versus a cell phone, e-mail connection, or implanted chip—may come with varying degrees of personal information, and need not involve a core identity.[13] With "reachability" through electronic means, the sender may be unaware of the geographic location of the recipient. Even with caller ID, the recipient of a call from a cell phone may know the number of a caller but not where the caller is; with call forwarding, the sender will know the phone number called but not necessarily where the called person is.[14]

Portable electronic addresses stand in a different relationship to the person from that of a fixed geographic address, as with most residences and workplaces, landline phones, and post office boxes. The latter involve a kind of tether from which persons usually venture forth and return, and they can permit face-to-face encounters and discrete tracking. A trailer or camper bus can be either fixed or mobile.

Distance-mediated and remote forms of cyberspace interaction are ever more common, and the ability to reach and be reached is central for many activities. This potential to locate persons through their postal and conventional phone addresses is now matched by the ability to locate mobile cell phone and computer users and to know who they (or whoever is using "their" machine) has contact with and when.[15] Knowing location is increasingly important—beyond whatever it additionally offers, such as validated information about a place's climate or that which is merely inferential for such social characteristics, as with Harlem or Beverly Hills. It may reveal network connections, and, with individuals who are truthful, it may reveal their activities or whether they are otherwise meeting expectations.

For many purposes, being able to "reach" someone becomes as or more important than knowing "where" the person literally is geographically. The "locator" number for bureaucratic records is a related factor, but it connects to the file, not to the person.

Thus, the "where" question need not be linked with the "who" question. The ability to communicate (especially remotely) may not require knowing who it "really" is, only that the person be accessible and assessable. Conversely, with blocking mechanisms location may be unavailable even as identity is, something generally unavailable with conventional landlines.

As noted, access or its denial are dimensions of privacy and publicity. Knowing location may permit taking various forms of action, such as communicating, granting or denying access, rewarding, delivering, picking up, or apprehending.[16]

Such action can occur remotely, directly, or in sequence. Consider a New York City cable provider's means of penalizing thieves of its cable TV signals: It used a roving truck with a remote sensor to identify homes illicitly using its services. It then sent a signal that made reception impossible. The core identity of the violators was not known. However, when the thieves brought the equipment they were illegally using in to be repaired, they faced arrest.

Fugitives offer a nice example of knowing the "who" but not the "where." Even if both name and location are known, an individual may still be unreachable. For example, the United States knew that fugitive financer Robert Vesco was in Cuba, but officials were unable to arrest him there.

Nor need the specific identity be known in order to take broad actions based on categorical or group-inferred attributes. The slogan of Claritas, a large data-gathering corporation, is "You are where you live." Where you live can determine appeals and advertisements, environmental engineering, prices (such as for insurance), and membership in statistical pools of presumed desirable customers and unwanted ones who don't pay their bills.

Claritas offers its customers "segmentation, market research, customer logistics and site selection," which essentially amounts to selling location information. In reducing the several hundred thousand census blocks to a limited number of geodemographic types, it is assumed that "people with similar lifestyles tend to live near one another." One of its' "products," PRIZM, "describes every U.S. neighborhood in terms of 62 distinct life style types, called clusters," while its MicroVision "defines 48 lifestyle types called segments" (www.claritas.com).

Such characterizations combine census, zip code, survey, and purchase data—meaning that you are what you consume. For many marketing purposes, there is no need to know core identity if fixed or mobile location is known. The ability to locate people has received a very large boost with the appearance of the federally mandated 911E (emergency location) system. This is a response to the rapid spread of cell phones not tied to a fixed residence. While, absent extenuating circumstances, the service provider cannot legally reveal this information, nothing prevents individuals from agreeing to release it in return for consumer rewards.

Ongoing location information has a very special status in that it can permit someone to identify and monitor or track movement over time, as well as identify social networks.[17] As with monitoring of Internet behavior in order to deliver relevant advertisements, ongoing location information can sequentially join two forms of personal border crossing—both taking from and imposing upon. It would be useful to map the ecology and consequences of location rules as new means of communication become more salient and are changed by globalization. Does a geographically fixed address bring greater accountability, security, and justice but less creativity and risk taking (of both positive and negative kinds)? How do varying degrees of registration and restriction on domestic mobility and communication relate to liberty? Apart from whether or not the location is physically anchored, what are the consequences of having multiple addresses or of being able to change an address at will? The topic involves a rich, underdeveloped area of the sociology of remote control and interaction and protean social and geographic identities.[18]

A central point of this chapter is to illustrate how the objective attributes of information (the "kinds of data" question) matter even in the face of variations involving structure, organization, law, means, and goals. The next section further develops this argument, and I develop it in more detail elsewhere.[19]

A Note on Form

This chapter argues that the components of surveillance data can be analyzed and compared apart from each other and from the collection means. But the kind of data gathered and the means used may also overlap. Some tools always mean a particular kind of data. A visual tool can include a video, a photograph, or a sketch. While the discussion in this chapter has emphasized ways of classifying content, the intertwining of form and content can also be analyzed.

The kind of data initially collected obviously depends on the tool used to gather it (audio devices record sound). But the link between the tool and the resulting data may be subsequently disconnected in the presentation of results. In other words, the sense used in data gathering need not be that involved in subsequent communication. Thus, a purloined document can be read out loud. Rather than showing a video or playing an audiotape, an agent can offer a written narrative or a transcript. A video of a conversation without audio could be supplemented by a lip reader's transcription or a simulated recording.[20] Conversely, written accounts of an observer can be converted to visual images, as with a sketch of a suspect or a video reconstruction of a traffic accident for court presentation.[21] Important issues involve the appropriateness of the fit between the collection tool and the form of presentation and questions of interpretation.

Many new forms of surveillance involve a conversion process in the move from data collection to presentation (beyond the substitutions noted above). Thus, physical DNA material or olfactory molecules are converted to numerical indicators, which are then represented visually and via statistical probability. With thermal imaging, the amount of heat shown in color diagrams is sometimes suggestive of objects. The polygraph converts physical responses to numbers and then to images in the form of charts. Satellite images convert varying degrees of light to computer code, which is then offered as photographs. Information can thus be easily communicated as against the raw, unconverted data. Consider a photo image enhanced by simulation, or a score based on multiple indicators that claims to predict recidivism. But as noted, what the conversion means may be disputed.

Assessing Surveillance Data

How do the kind and form of data relate to assessments of surveillance? Table 4.3 recasts key categories from the prior figures and tables into variables that can be coded yes or no (even though many involve continua) and adds some others with implications for evaluation. Arraying the variables this way can help disentangle the empirical elements of the surveillance mélange. Identifying properties of the data via the numbered items in the table can provide dependent variables to be explained and can help ground judgements.

When judgments about surveillance are made, the kind of data involved can be a factor. Thus, when surveillance is questioned (or at least seen to require control policies), whether based on the role it plays or the means, conditions, or goals of data collection, additional concerns are more likely when the values shown in the center column of table 4.3 apply to the kind of information. Conversely, the values on the right side of the table 4.3 make it less likely that surveillance behavior will be questioned.

The variables in table 4.3 can be combined in a variety of ways—for example, that stigmatizing information is more likely to be private, and anonymous information to be public. The table can also be used to explore the patterning of rules about information with respect to revelation, discretion, and withholding.

The variables might also be ranked relative to each other; that is, the potential for a negative critique regarding the surveillance seems much greater for some items (e.g., if it offers the potential to unfairly discredit or diminish a person, as with items number 7–10) than for others (e.g., whether the information is from multiple or single sources, as with item number 11). But the brambles are never far away—single-source information can be wrong, while validation may be increased with multiple measures. Yet multiple sources of information may be seen as more invasive because they give a fuller picture of the person.

But for now, let us simply note that the variables have an additive effect, and the more (both in terms of the greater the number and the greater the degree) the values in the center column are present, the more likely it is that surveillance will be seen as needing to be controlled.

The intensity of the negative judgments is likely to be greater to the extent that a core identity and a locatable person are involved and when information is personal, private, intimate, sensitive, stigmatizing, strategically valuable, extensive, biological, artifactual, or predictive,[22] reveals deception,[23] is attached to the person, and involves an enduring and unalterable documentary record. Settings, of course, will vary, and these qualities of the data may have contradictory impacts. As a result the values noted earlier won't all be present in any given case. Moreover, under some conditions, those attributes may support favorable assessments, and it is their absence that will be associated with criticism, even when means and ends are appropriate. Thus, being unable to identify and locate a subject can be a sign of failure and wasted resources. The lack of extensive data may mean less confidence in results. Naturalistic forms may be seen as too invasive.[24]

Some Explanations

It is one thing to list characteristics likely to be associated with attitudes toward surveillance. Proof and explanation of those attitudes are a different matter. The assertions drawn from table 4.3 are hypotheses to be empirically assessed. If this patterning of indignation (or conversely acceptance) of the stuff of surveillance is accurate, what might account for it? Does a common thread or threads traverse these? I believe the answer is yes, as follows.

Tools with an invasive potential that break the natural borders protecting private information maintain a taint, no matter how lofty the goal of the surveillance. In the absence of appropriate regulation, they are likely to be negatively viewed.

For information that is not naturally known, norms tend to protect against revealing it if it reflects negatively on a person's moral status and legitimate strategic concerns—for example, their safety and the expectation that they will not face unreasonable discrimination in employment, banking, or insurance. The policy debate revolves around when it is legitimate to reveal and conceal (e.g., criminal records after a sentence has been served, unpopular or risky but legal lifestyles, contraceptive decisions for teenagers, genetic data given to employers or insurers, or credit card data passed to third parties). That debate also concerns the extent to which the information put forth may be authenticated, often with the ironic additional crossing of personal borders to gather still more personal information.

The greater the distance between the data in some presumed natural form and their "artifactuality" as conditioned by a measurement device, the stronger is the need to explain how the tool works and to validate non-self-evident claims. Contrast a claim about deception based on a polygraph exam with a videotape of a shoplifter. The seeming realism and directness of visual and audio data make them easier to understand and believe than more disembodied data appearing from unseen and generally poorly understood tests, measurements, and algorithms.[25]

Another factor affecting indignation or acceptance can be the extent to which the information is unique, characterizing only one locatable person or a small number of persons. This is one version of the idea of "safety in numbers," holding apart the potentially negative aspects of anonymity.[26]

Beyond any characteristics of the surveillance tool used or its immediate instrumental consequences are norms that sustain respect for the person by protecting zones of intimacy, whether they involve insulated conversations and the behavior of friends, actions taken when alone, or the physical borders of the body. A factor here is scale or scope: the wider or greater the form or circle of intimate contacts involved, the more likely it will be that restrictions are present. As an example, contrast the lesser standard for searching an individual person than for a wiretap warrant that involves repetitive monitoring (at least initially) of communication that can involve a great many persons in the subject's circle. Over time, greater restrictions seem likely to appear where there is a tar brush effect—that is, where surveilling one person leads inevitably to include many others who may not be proper subjects for personal border crossing. Beyond information picked up from a family member's innocuous calls if a phone is tapped, consider how DNA reveals some information about families as well as the subject.

Guarding the indiscriminate crossing of informational borders can offer protection to the innocent, and both symbolically and practically, it can sustain individual autonomy and liberty. In addition, allowing backstage behavior to remain backstage can create spaces where individuality and associational activities independent of a strong state or organizations can flourish.

This chapter has analyzed the substance and nature of personal data that can be collected through surveillance, and it suggests a framework for more systematic analysis of the topic and how we evaluate it. Knowledge of the kind of data gathered can contribute to a fuller understanding of the ecology of surveillance. When the dimensions noted here are joined with other dimensions for characterizing surveillance, such as the structure of the situation and the nature of surveillance means and goals (chaps. 1–3), we have a framework for systematic analysis and comparisons of particular applications, as well as across time periods, societies, institutions, organizations, and cultures. In considering definitions and structures, however, the analysis thus far has been rather static. But reality is a fast-moving target, barely containable within the stagnant borders of circles or tables. In focusing on social processes, the next unit takes account of this.

PART 2

Social Processes

Like a moving train, much surveillance is dynamic—and as with a train in the terminal, its components can be analyzed when uncoupled. In other words, surveillance can be approached as static or as an ongoing series of events involving interaction and strategic calculations. The classifications suggested thus far tilt toward fixity. To the unwary, categories such as visible or invisible and public or private may distort in implying rigid and timeless dichotomies. In freezing examples within the same category, we necessarily ignore overlaps and interstitial zones and may miss connections between forms.

The approach in the previous chapters represent *structural analysis.* Like a single snapshot it is static, permitting comparisons at that moment but not revealing what was there before, or what will come after. We stop the world and act as if it could be contained within the fixed concept. For many purposes this is necessary. But attention to the fluidity of interactions, linkages between them, and changes in the realities the concepts capture is also required.

The chapters in this unit offer a *process analysis* involving observations over time. Such analysis views behavior in systemic terms. It calls attention to the interdependence (and a degree of open mindedness) among the parts of any social system—whether the immediate elements in a specific surveillance situation, the influence of factors in the broader society, or the historical antecedents and development over time of a tactic. Process analysis is necessary to capture issues of contingency and trajectory. Speaking analogically, in contrast to the still photograph of a river, process concepts are like a videotape of that river as it roils downstream, twists and turns in response to impediments and bends, and perhaps is stopped by a dam, only to be released again. Social process concepts reflect the interweaving and continuous flow of activity streams. Prior factors (themselves conditioned by more distant factors) condition surveillance, which in turn shapes subsequent developments.

Some processes are abstract, cumulative, and aggregative, involving many cases. We can see them only by drawing diverse occurrences together over time. We view a given strand—for example, visibility or consent—over extended time periods, whether decades or (for the bold scholar) centuries in search of trends and changes.

Chapter 5 considers four aspects of social process: the *softening of surveillance*, meaning it becomes less visible and directly coercive, often being engineered into an activity; *patterns of expansion and contraction*, such as the tendency of a given means to quietly expand to new users and goals beyond those initially envisioned; *changes in surveillance* as social relationships change; and *stages of behavior* in the application of a tactic. Chapter 5 explores one of these stages—that of data collection—in greater depth. Chapter 6 does the same, analyzing the efforts of subjects to neutralize or block surveillance and in less depth (because of the need to cut) of agents to counter such efforts.

But before that, a paragraph on the penultimate grandmother of all social process topics and one that socially and ethically arches over the other topics in this chapter (in particular, the life histories and fate of surveillance efforts—pp. 129-39). I refer to the "what's the impact?" question. Questions about consequences can never be fully contained. This is because modem societies are like the rushing river with multiple, evolving forces and currents in perpetual motion across centillions of interactions and places.

For analysis to be possible, we identify levels and act as if they had end points. For example, in considering impacts and outcomes of surveillance four categories of increasing generality are the careers of a given tool, of a given (often newsworthy) application of the tool and the strips that make this up, of full programs such as those studied by Tunnell (2004), Guzik (2016), and Shuilenburg (2016), and of impacts on and across civilizations over centuries.

Even granted the often arbitrary nature of the cutoff point, understanding outcomes requires consideration of the interactions of variables such as the nature of the problem/goals, the characteristics of the tool and objects/data, the relevant actors (subjects, agents, plus) and interests, and the context and its broader setting involving history, social structure, roles and culture.

The inherent conflicts, contradiction, and ironies amid the dynamism and fluidity of social life, where individuals and groups act and interact facing events and environments only partly of their choosing and comprehension, mean that uncertainty is always our copilot. Projects will be surprise filled and rarely fully meet (or continue to meet) their objectives, and the greater the scale of the surveillance project, the truer that will be. A more systematic empirical rendering of the relevant variables calls for a very large research project. For now, my aim is more modest—to give a sense of some of the most salient social processes.

5

Social Processes in Surveillance

Civilization is a movement and not a condition, a voyage and not a harbor.
ARNOLD TOYNBEE

Just because they don't use a cattle prod doesn't mean it ain't happening.
JEFF FOXWORTHY

This chapter's four sections are organized around several locations for and kinds of surveillance processes. Social processes are visible only over time, and in spite of their fluid and less than fully predictable nature, patterns across multiple occurrences and settings can be identified. The first three sections consider cultural, organizational, and behavioral processes that transcend any direct use. The first section examines the trend toward the softening of surveillance. Here, the tools for surveillance are viewed as cultural and physical objects, and the unit for analysis is ideas. The theme of surveillance softening is used to illustrate an idea that drives the development and spread of many techniques. The second section treats the processes of change in behavior in agent-subject surveillance interaction over the life cycle of individuals, relationships, and "careers" in organizations. The third section deals with the life history or career of the techniques themselves over time—in particular, their patterns of diffusion and contraction.

The fourth section of the chapter suggests a way to organize evolving steps in any given application of a surveillance tool. There, seven stages of development (called *surveillance strips*) are identified—from the initial decision to apply a tactic to the fate of the data. Taken together, these strips constitute the *surveillance occasion.* This temporally bounded concept encompasses the major emergent components of a given real world application.

Other surveillance social processes such as monetization, commoditization, securitization, hard engineering and automating of control, privatization and public-private border blurring, globalization, and the myth of surveillance are illustrated in the narratives in part 3.

Patterns of Surveillance Softening

Some men will rob you with a gun.
And some with a fountain pen.
WOODY GUTHRIE

In chapter 2 dimensions for differentiating the new from the old surveillance
were suggested in a rather static and didactic fashion. When viewed dynami-
cally, many of the dimensions identify not only a move from the traditional
to the new (e.g., the senses to technology, single to multiple measures), but
also the continuing intensification of the new surveillance attributes, as with
speed, power, and lessened visibility.

Contemporary surveillance means share with many other modern technologies a seemingly linear tendency to become more powerful, automated,
versatile, reliable, self-contained, and also easier to use, cheaper, smaller,
safer, and faster over time. As the many examples considered make clear, surveillance tools continue to increase in intensity and extensity, in flexibility
and adaptability, in analytical, integrative and communicative power, and in
their ability to reveal the unseen and give meaning to the unrecognized.

These changes reflect a developmental process fraught with moral ambiguity involving the continual *softening of surveillance*. In the epigraph that
opens this chapter comedian Jeff Foxworthy is referring to women's influence
on men.[1] The observation, however, can be generalized to many contemporary forms of social control apart from gender.

The current softening (feminization?) of surveillance (and its frequent
corollary, control) involves, if not a marriage, at least a tense cohabitation of
science and technology with the ideals of the modern democratic state that
appeared with the French and American revolutions. Central to these defining ideals is respect for the dignity of the person, as this involves consent and
choice rather than coercion, punishment, or tradition as motives for conformity. Supposedly more scientifically and pragmatically based conditioning,
rewards, and engineering offer alternative resources for gaining conformity.[2]

This softening, even as it appeared in 1949, was captured in a letter Aldous
Huxley wrote to George Orwell after the publication of *1984*:

Within the next generation I believe that the world's rulers will discover that
infant conditioning and narco-hypnosis are more efficient as instruments of
government, than clubs and prisons, and that the lust for power can be just as
completely satisfied by suggesting people into loving their servitude as by flog-
ging and kicking them into obedience. In other words, I feel that the nightmare of *Nineteen Eighty-Four* is destined to modulate into the nightmare of a

world having more resemblance to that which I imagined in *Brave New World*. The change will be brought about as a result of a felt need for efficiency [and as viewed 60 years later, we can add seduction and fear]. (Huxley 1969)

If Huxley was off with respect to some particular technologies such as narco-hypnosis, and if he missed problems such as scarcity and a degraded environment, the statement is terribly current in the broader process it notes.[3] The changes then and now reflect continual discovery and invention—better science, new materials, and new ways of constructing and measuring and learning from past experience that makes control less visible and easier to accept as just the way things are. The research supportive of soft control offers new possibilities, even as it responds to newly perceived needs. Of course the harsh controls of the iron fist and the jackboot have not disappeared, but their ratio to the soft controls, particularly as applied domestically, has altered.

These soft controls emerged in the context of the scale, heterogeneity, and rapidity of change that came with urbanization and industrialization, which brought unprecedented new needs for maintaining domestic order. Simultaneously, new ideas of rights, citizenship, and government based on respect for the dignity of the person appeared, which limited the unleashing of technologies of control. The received wisdom and brutal techniques of preindustrial society have continued to lose legitimacy and when present are more likely to be hidden.

The contrasts between hard and soft control, coercion and deception, force and manipulation, threat and seduction, punishment and reward, and prevention and after-the-fact detection—are profound indeed. In a society valuing the dignity and liberty of the individual, voluntarism, and consensus, the harder forms are seen as less desirable and primitive, even if they are perhaps more honest.

The new soft surveillance has several aspects: minimal visibility and invasiveness as well as passive, often automated data collection. The means may be disguised, as when sensors and cameras are hidden in everyday objects, whether the proverbial nanny cam in the teddy bear or the reporting eyes and unseen tools of guards at Disneyland in Mickey Mouse costumes—a lovely example observed by Shearing and Stenning (1992). The trend is toward techniques that do not require consent or even awareness. They gather what is involuntarily radiated, unwittingly left behind, or silently and effortlessly made available by breaking borders that traditionally protected information. Where the subject's cooperation for data collection is necessary but is not legally mandated, it is increasingly sought through soft, technical seduction and communication techniques involving various kinds of persuasion and reward.

The digital camera is the poster child for mechanical soft surveillance, given its capacity, speed, sophistication, flexibility, infrared and search capability, integration with other data sources, low cost, and potential to be hidden or disguised. Digital technology cuts the camera loose from the darkroom and other limits of the traditional analog camera. Images can be endlessly recorded from an enormous number of sources and remotely searched from anywhere with an Internet connection. Consider also the very remotely gathered images from satellites such as Google's Street View or the tiny lens for facial scanning technology.

The various forms of biochemical analysis offer further examples.[4] A vacuum-like device is available that can draw the breath away from a person suspected of drunk driving without the need to ask permission. DNA may be involuntarily taken from a drinking glass or a discarded cigarette or dental floss. Or consider the development of nonelectrical sensors for analyzing saliva (Dreifus 2005). Whatever can be revealed from the analysis of blood is also potentially found (although in smaller quantities) in saliva—not only DNA and evidence of disease, but also of drugs and pregnancy.

To take blood, the body's protective armor must be pierced. But expectorating occurs easily and frequently and is more "natural" than puncturing a vein. Vials for delivering spit to a lab are sold over the counter. Nor does saliva collection involve the unwanted observation that can be required for a urine drug sample. Saliva samples can be easily and endlessly taken without bodily invasion or embarrassment. Keeping a permanent cumulative record of the data may make possible the early identification and presumably prevention of problems.

When a saliva sample is sought for medical diagnostic purposes or as an aspect of work monitoring, the subject's knowledge and permission are required. In some work contexts involving hazardous materials, the identification of early-stage pregnant employees is important (although finding alternatives to the use of hazardous materials can avoid this form of inquiry).

However, knowledge and permission are slightly less voluntary in Sheffield, England, where the transit authority, as part of an antispitting campaign, distributed three thousand DNA swab kits to transportation staff. Posters proclaim "Spit It Out" and warn persons who spit that "you can be traced—and prosecuted. Even if we don't know what you look like. And your records will be on the national DNA data base. Forever." For those of another era, this is reminiscent of the grammar school teachers who threatened to add notes about misbehavior to "your permanent record."

DNA can be voluntarily (as well as involuntarily, with the shedding of hair) offered and quickly and painlessly gathered using a mouth swab. This approach contrasts with more traditional "hard" police methods, such as legally sanctified and even compelled arrest, a custodial interrogation, a search, and a subpoena or traffic stop, which seek involuntary compliance via coercion and threat.

A case in Truro, Massachusetts, offers an example of increased reliance on "softer" means for collecting personal information involving both technology and communication. At the end of 2004 police politely asked all male residents to provide a DNA sample to match with DNA material found at the scene of an unsolved murder. Residents were approached in a nonthreatening manner (even as their license plate numbers were recorded) and asked to help solve the crime (Belluck 2005).[5]

The automated analysis of urine (considered below and in the story of the Omniscient Organization [chap. 7]) is another example of the softening of techniques. A diagnostic test (routinely used in some Japanese employment contexts) requires that an employee who enters a stall be identified through a personal access card. This permits a comprehensive record of the employee's flushed offerings over time, as automated analysis occurs with each use, and may help in the early diagnosis of illness.[6]

Smart machines can "smell" contraband, eliminating the need for a warrant or asking the sniffed for permission to invade their olfactory space or "see" through their clothes and luggage. Dogs may be trained to do the same (Marks 2009). As mentioned above, breath can now be "drawn" by vacuum to test for drunkenness of pulled-over drivers. Research is also being done with the goal of using human odor to identify specific persons, illness (both mental and physical), and even early pregnancy.[7]

Thermal imaging technology applied from outside can offer a rough picture of a building's interior based on heat patterns, with no need for a person to enter the space, unless to plant a hidden transmitting device. Night vision technology illuminates what darkness traditionally protected (and the technology is itself protected, unlike an illuminated spotlight). The National Security Administration's satellites engage in warrantless remote monitoring of electronic communication to, from, and sometimes within the United States. Classified government programs are said to permit the remote reading of some computers and their transmissions without the need to directly install a bugging device.

Beyond the traditional reading of visual clues offered by facial expression, some technology manufacturers and researchers claim that the covert analysis of heat patterns around the eyes and tremors in the voice offer windows into feelings and truth telling. Similar claims are hyped about reading brain wave patterns as keys to truth telling. Reading brain wave patterns requires attaching sensors to the head and thus an informed, and in polite society at least, willing subject. With current technology, efforts to remotely gather brain waves could fry the brain.[8]

Some other techniques are designed to be less directly invasive and less dependent (if at all) on subject cooperation—for example, computers that scan dispersed personal records for cases of interest, obviating, at least initially, any direct review by a human. Similarly, x-ray and scent machines "search" persons and goods for contraband without touching them, alerting a human viewer only if there is something worthy of attention given the parameters that excite the machine. Even then, programs for backscatter image machines are available to mask genital areas, which would otherwise be revealed by a scan.[9] Consider also the move to chromosomal tests rather than direct observation for determining the sex of athletes.[10] And the use of hair rather than urine for a drug test involves a less intimate form of data collection, though other factors such as cost favor the use of urine tests. Still, urine tests become less invasive through the use of a heat strip to measure the sample's temperature in lieu of having a direct observer present. Inkless fingerprints (euphemistically called Touch Signature) can be taken without the stained thumb symbolic of the arrested person (Murray 2000).

Communication devices, vehicles, wallet cards, and consumer items may have RFID (radio frequency identification) chips embedded in them. These chips can be read from up to thirty feet away by unseen sensors. As yet, we have little legislation requiring that subjects be informed. Righteous social scientists are often at the forefront in calling attention to the above developments and warning of potential abuses and unwanted consequences. Yet they are enthusiasts in using the tools in their own work, as the following fictitious example suggests.

An illustration of the soft prying-out of information can be seen in selections from a fictitious paper (but inspired by real events, as they say) presented by the equally fictitious Paul F. Lasers-Field and Vance Picard at a social science symposium concerned with new unobtrusive research techniques that permit access to the most sensitive personal information without disquieting the subject. As with the narratives in chapters 7–10, this one is fiction but is also true (or could almost be true). Many of the new social research surveillance techniques they advocate, including the use of "paradata," are described in Conrad and Schrober (2008) and have found new favor among market researchers.

The Soft Interview of the Future: New Wine, New Bottles?*

PAUL F. LASERS-FIELD, PH.D., AND
VANCE PICARD THE BUREAU

Fight ignorance! Fill out a questionnaire.
American Sociological Society

In this paper I report on an exciting exploratory project we have just completed. This large, interdisciplinary National Séance Foundation (NSF) effort involved a collaborative relationship between police and national security[11] investigators, social scientists, and industry.

The result is a prototype for acquiring data in those difficult situations where the subject/suspect is uncooperative or unaware of the information needed or where the direct approach seems unseemly or potentially biasing. This project is another of the fruits from the tree so presciently planted by the Social Science Research Council half a century ago in its call for the creation of improved federal means for generating and using personal data.

This project grew out of my own prior work on improving methods of data collection in contexts of minimal or no cooperation, where an agent has reason to suspect at least some dishonesty, regardless of whether subjects are survey respondents or interrogated suspects. We are also very interested in applying the latest amazing new tools to elicit information of which the subject is unaware. As we now know, only a tiny fraction of brain activity is conscious, and even cooperative subjects can't decipher their own brain's electrical frequencies.

Whether the researcher comes up empty because people don't know what we need to find out or because they are uncooperative, it's all the same. We have made great progress in developing tools to overcome these limitations. Our project uses the tools to identify, in the hope of preventing, problems related to (1) drug use, (2) political extremism, (3) crime, and (4) inappropriate sexual behavior. It also aims to help consumers get the information they need and want and to give something back to our generous private-sector sponsors.

Given the sensitive nature of the topics we need to know about and the difficulty of obtaining adequate and valid data on them, the researchers developed unobtrusive methods based on the pioneering work of Webb et al. (2000). These sought to minimize, or even hide, the role of the human agent. Such methods can enhance the face-to-face interview by probing beneath the deceptive veneer of the seemingly "authentic intentionality" found when one must rely exclusively on the subject's words. The methodology draws from recent communications research on the ease of conversational deception and on the limits of any survey that gives the respondent space for impression management, beyond the strong role played by the unconscious.

With our approach, then, a mostly noninvasive multimodal approach (NIMMA) exploiting all channels of communication is used. This includes methods such as PEP, fMRI, EEG, EKG, BPMS, eye tracking, and Wmatrix (Person et al. 2008) and some additional means still under beta test such as ZOWIE, WAMIE, and BMOC©. Validity and completeness of response were greatly enhanced by access to unobtrusive measures and comparisons to data from beyond the interview situation. New meaning is found through creating a mosaic of previously meaningless, unseen, unconnected, and unused data. In short, the scientist who relies entirely on words is a rather unscientific, profligate, one-trick *ancien* pony who needs to get with the program.

How does our method work? The interview and related detection occur in an ambient-intelligence, pastel living room matched to the social and psychological characteristics of the subject (i.e., age, education, gender, lifestyle). Specifics of room conditions are inspired by the clustering of respondents into types pioneered by marketing research. One size hardly fits all. The rooms can be internally rearranged to accommodate sixty-eight distinct types of respondent. Respondent characteristics are determined by a preliminary research encounter, including an electronically measured handwriting sample, a Google search, a search of commercially available public records, and, under carefully controlled conditions, restricted databases regarding sensitive behavior.

Subjects are videotaped as they approach our office and researchers (aka surveillance agents) draw inferences from various aspects of their gait, posture and dress. The elevator records the subject's image and any words. Over soft music, a subliminal voice repeats "be truthful and cooperative."

Once settled in the study room, the subject is told that in order to accurately capture his/her experiences and opinions, a variety of "state of the art" technologies are being used. However, the subject is not told that the chair seat (drawing on the pioneering work of Dr. Sigmund O'Scopey) measures the smallest moves, body temperature, and electrodermal response, or that facial expression, eye patterns, voice microtremors, and language usage are recorded and that the calming scent of pine is delivered through the air duct system. Nor is there notice that the timing of responses and word use patterns (whether oral or written) are analyzed for evidence of lying and psychological characteristics.[12] Some inferences, too, are made about the respondent based on answers to questions unrelated to the topics of direct interest (indirect personality assessments to determine latent racism and sexism). The internal consistency of responses is analyzed, and answers are compared to data found through cross-checking a variety of databases.

We originally planned to covertly read brain wave emission, but the Human Suspects Review Committee rejected this idea out of fear of harming subjects and garnering bad publicity. While we believe research will soon show that if used remotely "the MRI doesn't lie," the evidence to back this up is not yet here and there are still some health concerns about this technology. The goal of our research is to help people, not to hurt them. We believe that the brain doesn't lie, even if it whispers too softly for now.

The room is slightly warmer than most rooms.[13] Subjects are provided with a full complement of free beverages and encouraged to use the adjacent restrooms during or at the conclusion of the two-hour interview, which they have private access to with a unique ID number. The softly lit toilet environment provides a heated seat and soft music to relax the sphincter muscles. Subjects are not told that a variety of automated biochemical urine and olfactory assays are performed on their voluntary offerings. The method is guided by the principle that "what doesn't stay in the body doesn't belong to the body" and by the goals of knowledge advancement and social amelioration. Anything that might be discovered regarding drug use and/or sexual behavior is kept strictly confidential. Anonymity is guaranteed, as a number is substituted for each subject's name.

Our research project used both the CAPI (computer assisted personal interview) and the SAPI (self-administered personal interview), along with a traditional interviewer. This approach reduces costs, as we need fewer interviewers, and also enhances standardization. Above all, our techniques bring increased control to the survey situation for *all* parties. When interviewers are used, they too must be watched and recorded to prevent them from making up or telegraphing answers.

All the data from the interview part of the study are available in real time via a password-protected web page to professional observers at the cooperating research agencies. To reduce generative performance anxiety, respondents are not told about the remote observation. The interviewer wears a tiny earpiece device that permits feedback and suggestions from the remote observers. Case agents with backgrounds in either law enforcement or psychology in another room monitor all data flows and quietly inform the interviewer if the respondent is deceptive, frustrated, stressed, fatigued, or unclear about the question.

We also offer feedback to subjects. Based on research on peer influence, before asking about controversial behaviors, participants are given fictitious feedback that a majority of other interviewees had "acknowledged" engaging in the behavior of interest. This has the impact of increasing honesty in what subjects will tell us.

Respondents are encouraged to learn more about themselves by volunteering (and most do, given the rewards we offer) to let us apply our cutting-edge neuroscience tools capable of discovering real hidden meanings beyond the clumsy old-school devices that track skin, respiratory, muscle, and facial responses or the plethysmograph used for phallometric assessment. During our interviews, subjects wear a fabric cap with EEG (electroencephalograph) sensors and an eye-tracking device while being exposed to web sites or video images that are appropriate (e.g., featuring desirable consumer products from our sponsors and/or altruistic behavior) or inappropriate (e.g., featuring dangerous consumer products such as drugs and/ or antisocial behavior). By computing deep subconscious responses to such stimuli, we can measure attention, emotion, and memory far better than we can by asking people questions. And we eliminate the worry about the lying or uninformed subject, or contagion effects from focus groups. As this technology evolves, it will hopefully permit us to brandwash in the good stuff and brainwash out the bad.

Respondents are promised confidentiality. Only those agents who need to know their identity and data for a valid social purpose will have them. However, in order to benefit from generous frequent shopper rewards and to maximize choice, subjects are given the opportunity to waive this protection. A large percentage do, particularly those of lower economic status. Funds for this project were provided by leading marketing researchers and helping agencies who are eager to identify customers and clients in need of their goods and services.

NOTE

*A paper presented to the annual Conference on New E-Methods (CONEM), Ann Arbor, 2015.

"What? Run That by Me Again": Manipulation or Consent?

The engineering of consent is the very essence of the democratic process, the freedom to persuade and suggest.

                    E. L. BERNAYS, 1947

Apart from covert collection of information, language, as Orwell illustrates, can be a soft form of control both in the terms it offers and in disingenuous communication that seeks to make it appear that individuals are voluntarily providing their information. The statements below reflect verbal manipulation, if not always dissimulation, in implying consent and that the choice the individual is presumed to be making is meaningful.

The ubiquitous building signs that read, "In entering here, you have agreed to be searched."

A message from the Social Security Administration to potential recipients: "While it is voluntary for you to furnish this information, we may not be able to pay benefits to your spouse unless you give us the information."

A Canadian airport announcement: "Notice: Security measures are being taken to observe and inspect persons. No passengers are obliged to submit to a search of persons or goods if they choose not to board our aircraft."

A personnel manager in a one-industry town: "We don't require anyone to take a drug test, only those who choose to work here."

A life insurance executive on discounts for wearers of health-tracking devices: "You do not have to send us any [health] data you are not comfortable with. The trade-off is you won't get points for that."

A federal appeals court decision, 2006: Those on welfare can avoid unannounced searches of their homes including drawers, medicine cabinets, and trash (usually in search of evidence that an adult male lives there) by giving up their welfare benefits (Liptak 2007).

A phone company executive in defense of unblockable caller ID: "When you choose to make a phone call, you are choosing to release your phone number."

A customer service representative assisting new phone or electrical service customers: "Your account information is confidential and is protected by law. May I have your permission to access your account?" (*"No, I'll just sit in the dark and shiver"*).

A note on the Department of Homeland Security's web page asking for personal information from those seeking its public information: "Furnishing this information is voluntary; however, failure to provide this information may prevent the individual from receiving the information requested."

On the New York subway system, automatic sensing machines now supplement random searches of riders by officers. Potential riders need not submit, but then they may not use the subway.

A surveillance hardware company's web page: "By using our site, you consent to our privacy policy."

What is noteworthy in all these examples is the eclipse of logic through the verbal jujitsu that implies the subject is taking voluntary action in the full meaning of the term, when failure to comply has serious consequences (e.g., being denied a job or a benefit, or appearing suspect in another's eyes). To be meaningful, choice implies genuine alternatives, and refusal costs are not wildly exorbitant. Absent that, we have trickery, double-talk, and the frequently spoiled fruit of inequitable relationships. We also have the laws that wink at the bypass of constitutional protections in the face of ambiguous behavior that can be labeled "consent." Ian Kerr (Kerr et al. 2009) and his colleagues show how subtle consent-gathering schemes in the absence of adequate laws skew individual decision-making while preserving the illusion of free choice,

Not by Trickery Alone

In observing cleverly applied technologies and end runs around consent, it is easy to miss the extent to which the public willingly offers personal information. Subjects are increasingly complicit in volunteering information in return for rewards or convenience. We gladly, if often barely consciously, give up information in return for the ease of buying, traveling, and communicating and the seductions of discounts and frequent flyer and other reward programs. This behavior can be viewed as the highest form of American civilization, as free market players willingly enter into mutually beneficial exchanges. The seller makes a choice and receives fair value in return for self-revelation. Personal information is converted to a commodity, and any rights associated with it are welcomingly waived in return for a benefit. No waiver, no benefit—you choose, isn't that fair?[14] Individuals are bought off, but in these cases, they are bought off for their communication, not their silence. The agent's desire for personal information can be seen as a kind of bribery or, worse, as inequitable seduction exploiting human weakness, need, or interest.

Here, there is a clear distinction between subjects who offer or market their information and the agents who purchase it. The latter are usually the more motivated of the parties, and they initiate the exchange. This contrasts with an economic model in which one party is both the subject of, and the agent for, collecting the information and takes the initiative to create a market for it. An example is the reality webcam providers who invite customers to view them for a fee or otherwise play with surveillance (D. Bell 2009; Koskela 2012). Celebrities who cooperate with paparazzi and online gossip web sites by providing personal information in return for payment or publicity also merge to a degree the roles of subject and agent.

Issues of subject consent have a different meaning in these forms relative to the behavior of mass marketers. Consent as a moral or policy issue applies more clearly to the audiences whose perceptual borders may be unwillingly crossed by narcissistic purveyors of information on themselves. The self-promoting seek to create a demand for the information they already have and want to supply. In contrast, companies that market personal data, such as Choice-Point, need not only to generate demand, but also to find ways of obtaining the data on others they will sell when it is not public.

In many settings, volunteering information, sacrificing a bit of one's self for the common good, particularly in times of crisis, is hardly controversial. Such efforts draw on the higher civic traditions of democratic participation, self-help, and community. Whether such volunteering results from rewards, convenience, fear, or the desire to avoid being shamed or appearing as a bad or uncooperative person with something to hide, it reverses the presumption of innocence and may involve a waiving of taken-for-granted rights to protect personal information.

Surveillance agents often use tools that don't require active subject cooperation. They justify their data collection by claiming that subjects "volunteer" their data by walking or driving on public streets; entering a shopping mall; failing to hide their faces, wear gloves, and encrypt their communication; or choosing to use a phone, computer, or credit card. In the case of the Lasers-Field survey described above, they offer data by wiggling in their chairs, sweating, speaking at a given speed, giving off heat, having voice tremors, and using particular words.

This *blame the subject* approach for any lack of privacy within what is in one sense "public" is equivalent to the *blame the victim* approach to crime. The implied-consent logic of this *caveat subjectus* view cries out for a cartoon entitled, "Where will it end?" Beyond the paper shredder that has become routine in many homes, the cartoon would show a citizen driven to protect privacy by always wearing gloves, a mask, and perfume; having a closely shaved head; talking in code and encrypting all communications; using only cash; insulating home, office, and packages in thermal-image-resistant tin foil; and only using restrooms certified to be monitor free. Given the continuing move to passive means for gathering personal information, perhaps a new Miranda-like warning will eventually appear: "Whatever you radiate or leave behind can and will be used against you in a court of law, at work or in the marketplace."

The historical softening of surveillance considered thus far involves a process of change seen in the tools themselves as they have evolved in recent centuries. Another aspect of this process looks not at changes in technique, but at changes in meaning and expectations as social relationships develop. The key factor here is not so much the passage of time but the kind of relationship present between agent and subject.

Changing Patterns of Surveillance in Social Relationships over Time

Next we consider changes in the agent and subject roles in different contexts such as organizations, friendships, and the human life cycle over time. Some life-cycle changes involve biological processes such as aging, while others involve kinds of social relations, as in the case of strangers who become friends or the reverse.

Chapter 8 (pp. 000–00) deals with transitions in childhood from complete dependence to gradual independence, with various conflict bumps along the way. The borders for both parents and children in the move from infant to toddler to tween to teen to adult are often unclear and involve radical changes in surveillance expectations and behavior.

As the child reaches adulthood and leaves home, surveillance declines significantly. The pattern may eventually be reversed as the adult child looks after elderly parents. This relationship can even be formalized with the grant of a power of attorney. Technologies with equivalent functions are used for dependent parents—implants and attachments for monitoring physiology and location, systems for toilet control, locked doors, and video transmissions from nursing homes via the Internet. Warning signals are also present, as with panic buttons or devices that trigger an alarm if the refrigerator *is not* opened for a period of time or an exit door *is* opened.

Relative to the family, in the more formal setting of the organization, surveillance shows greater temporal constancy. The pattern for applying bureaucratic rules for compliance surveillance is essentially flat over time (unless of course the rules or roles change). In principle, being with an organization for many years has little bearing on drug testing, access controls, or work monitoring (although mobility within the organization may). Once the rules are in place, they continue to be applied, given bureaucratic assumptions regarding universal (as both rational and fair) enforcement.

That said, individuals generally undergo more intense scrutiny when applying for a job than once they are hired, and the scrutiny may diminish somewhat once they have passed some probationary status, achieved a secure position through tenure or civil-service protection, or moved up. Beyond changes in organizational status, the creation of trust, familiarity, and routinization may lead to lessened vigilance in spite of the rules—for example, the guard who violates the rules by waving through seemingly familiar persons or vehicles without checking ID each time. But in broad outline, this more constant pattern of formal surveillance contrasts with the cycles seen between parents and children and among friends.

In the case of the more equal relationships of strangers who become friends, we see another pattern. Efforts to learn about the other are initially inhibited by limits on the sharing of personal information and by the protection of manners. The presentation of official, normatively expected public fronts and greater wariness or reserve in communicating to those who are not well known are also factors. It is both prudent and normative for people who have just met and might establish closer relationships (whether business or personal) to engage in mutual surveillance. An example is investigating the backgrounds of potential business or social partners. The new technologies make this very easy to do, and advertisements imply that it is irresponsible and risky not to do this.

Yet as persons get to know each other and trust builds, formal surveillance applied to ascertain authenticity or compliance declines or disappears. If it continues and is discovered, it is likely to hurt the relationship because of the distrust it communicates. A symbolic indicator of the trust we hold for others is the risk taken in *not* checking what they say and do. Intimacy involves the sharing of private information and feeling free and comfortable enough to express thoughts, feelings, and behavior, even if they are at odds with conventional expectations or could be used to harm the individual.

The vulnerability that comes with the potential for revelation of secrets is an important element of friendship and trust. This implicitly says to the other, "I trust you to behave honorably with respect to my confidences, and I believe what you say, and I will not pollute our relationship by secretly surveilling you to obtain confirmation of that trust." Doing so would hollow out the bond of the relationship.[15] An Italian proverb, "To trust is good; to distrust is better," does not apply here. While surveillance that communicates distrust shrinks as a relationship deepens, that involving caring and protection (such as being sure someone got home safely) is likely to increase. And so we see changes in kind rather than in amount of surveillance as relationships develop and deepen.

Life Histories of Surveillance Tools:
Patterns of Expansion and Contraction

Among the most exciting and inspirational of questions for students of technology and society are those involving creativity, discovery, and invention. The development of the computer chip, microsensors, wireless technology, and new energy sources and materials were necessary conditions for much of the new surveillance.

But these offer potentials only. In and of themselves they do not determine specific form—a factor significantly affected by the payer of the piper. Why were resources put into developing this rather than something else? Why did it develop in a specific fashion?[16] Important here can be perceived need, often related to a crisis or very newsworthy precipitating events such as IRA violence in Britain or 9/11 in the United States.

Even with sponsorship and the enormous number of home labs and workshops, patent offices are overrun with stillborn inventions. A large literature deals with the move from new knowledge to application in usable tools, and from there to their career or fate. Technologies that "work" may not be adopted, or they may be adopted only years later.

The emphasis in this section is on growth and decline, not conception. What happens once a tool is available to be used? What factors are associated with patterns of its adoption or rejection? What factors are associated with the broad career of a tactic?

Diffusion of New Tools

The softening discussed in this chapter supports the expansion of surveillance, since data gathering can increasingly be presented as less intrusive and invasive and often as a matter of choice and benefit to subjects. The research tradition on the diffusion of innovation can be applied to new data collection tools (Strang and Soule 1998). By doing so, a natural history or career approach can chart patterns and the pace of adoption. How much time elapses between the availability of a tactic and its acceptance, and between acceptance and efforts to control it via law and policy; or between its adoption by adversaries who, in a process noted by Simmel, come to mirror image each other.[17] What are the institutional, organizational, and national correlates of these processes? The diffusion of computer-based communication and surveillance technology is noteworthy for the rapidity of adoption—a process much faster even than the relatively rapid spread of the telegraph and automobile.

As the benefits of a tactic are realized and it becomes familiar, it may move beyond the initial purposes and sectors it was developed for. Experience is gained with the technique and precedent established. What was initially seen as a shocking intrusion may come to be seen as business as usual (for the social scientist this translates to the idea of normalization or routinization). Higher-status organizations with greater resources may be the initial adopters, followed by those looking to them for leadership and wanting to appear up to date.

Economies of scale reduce the per-unit cost. Entrepreneurs and interest groups push the case for adoption. Organizations that might not apply a new technology on their own may be tempted to do so by governments bearing gifts. Such sponsorship was central to the British Home Office's provision of funds for public webcams and the Justice Department's sponsorship of undercover operations. Or an organization may be compelled to adopt as a result of new laws or the practices and demands of other organizations in their environment. For example, drug testing greatly expanded following an executive order by President Reagan that applied to federal contractors.[18] Insurance companies may require particular forms of surveillance as a condition of receiving coverage. In competitive and conflict settings, a tool may be adopted as a counter to what rivals are doing.[19]

There are some predictable if not invariant patterns in this diffusion. For example, initial applications are likely to reflect power and other resource

FIGURE 5.1. Surveillance creep. (© Chris Slane, used with permission.)

differences between agents and subjects. A common pattern involves initial
tests and eventual use on animals (whether cows or pets); moving then to
colonies and enemies in war; prisoners, and those under judicial supervision;
later, to those on welfare, the ill, and the dependent, such as children; and
then, sometimes more broadly, throughout the society. Figure 5.1 captures
this process.

With regard to diffusion across institutions, the typical pattern is that tactics are initially developed for, and adopted by, government for law enforcement and defense purposes, after which they spread to manufacturers and
commercial users and then to interpersonal uses involving friends, family,
and others. Many of the tactics first seen in maximum security prisons or
in total institutions (Goffman 1961a) have radiated outward to noncustodial
settings and activities, reflecting a trend toward the maximum security society. Video surveillance cameras, once restricted to prisons and high-security
areas, are found in offices, shopping malls, and the perimeters and interiors
of homes, not to mention beaches, bars, and churches.

The Internet, developed by the Department of Defense, is a well-known
example of a tool that moved from military applications to you. Drug testing
has moved from the military to criminal justice; then to special categories of
workers, such as those in transportation and public safety, as well as to athletes; then to the workforce at large; and eventually to some schools and even
families, in which parents test their children regularly or for particular occasions such as prom night. Global positioning satellite data, which was once
restricted to the military, is now used by real estate agents showing property,

market researchers, cell phone users, drivers, and hikers. In one contrasting pattern, however, RFID chips that developed out of private-sector efforts to improve supply chains moved from industry to the military.

As the tools spread from the center to the periphery of society and become easier to use and less expensive, as with audio and video recording, some egalitarian turning, or at least balancing, of the tables may occur. Subjects may become agents, and transparency ceases to be a one-way street, as subjects can make covert recordings of sexual harassment or protesters can videotape police. Even when tactics are restricted by law or policy to officials, black and gray and do-it-yourself markets will exist for simpler forms.[20]

Patterns of diffusion with respect to means of neutralizing surveillance tools (chap. 6) can also be observed. Thus, means of sending fake telecommunications signals (such as of telephone number or location) or of debugging may move from government to private-sector and personal uses.

The surveillance appetite may become insatiable as both a tool and a bureaucratic end in itself. In spite of some economic and logical countertendencies, there are strong inclinations to over- rather than to undercollect. Given an ethos of suspiciousness about wily adversaries, awareness of past mistakes, and the search for greater certainty, not to mention the need to cover your posterior (aka CYA), more information can stimulate the desire forevermore. This is particularly the case with the dynamic growth of database forms of surveillance.

Valid results may depend on obtaining personal information not directly related to any particular goal. Thus, to avoid confounding effects, those who do drug testing must ask the subject about medications taken, such as for epilepsy, that would otherwise remain private.

Another example of the tendency to overcollect relates to data mining, which requires large amounts of data. Even with simple searches, a standardized format offers the temptation to integrate and merge data and expand the amount and kind of data gathered. Consider the case of the National Consumer Telecom Exchange, which began in 1998 as a way for telephone companies to exchange information on questionable accounts. By 2002, it had morphed into the much larger National Consumer Telecom and Utilities Exchange, which now goes beyond phone service to include the exchange of consumer data on basic utilities, cable, satellite, wireless and Internet services. Expansion can also be seen in the increased integration and geographic and temporal reach of data organizations for screening tenants, such as the National Tenant Rating Bureau (aka—in their words—the Deadbeat Database), a service of the Landlord Protection Agency.[21]

Pressure for expanded use of a tactic or technology may also come from the need to locate the identity of an unknown person by comparisons to known persons in a database. Thus, fingerprints, DNA, and photos—even if unique, hard to fake, and gathered under ideal circumstances—are of little use for identification if there is no population base to match them against. The decision to adopt biometric means of identification bootlegs in the need for a database of the relevant population, including those not under surveillance.[22]

New Goals and Subjects

But even as tactics diffuse and as the supplementary surveillance contingent on those tactics grows, changes in goals and subjects occur. The prescient French scholar Jacques Ellul (1964), called attention to the role of technology in perpetuating itself. Winner (1977) suggests the term *function creep* to refer to new *uses* for a tool or policy. The case of DNA databases offers a nice example (Williams and Johnson 2008; Dahl and Sætnan 2009).

Changes can also be seen with respect to new *users of a tool*. The term *surveillance creep* may be applied to changes in agents and subjects, as well as goals. It can also refer to the expansion of surveillance once a precedent is established.

The concept of creep implies a slow pace and brings a slightly conspiratorial tone of sneakiness, or at least a danger of being overlooked because it is gradual. It needs to be supplemented by *surveillance gallop*—as may be the case with the spread of GPS tracking and perhaps drones. Surveillance gallop is more characteristic of sudden crises or special events such as the Olympics. A key issue is whether responses to exceptional times and events create precedents and interest-group pressure which normalizes the expansion or whether there is a contraction.

Creep and gallop involve a horizontal dimension of adoption across new agents, subjects and goals. In contrast *surveillance seep* suggests a vertical dimension wherein the initial agent applies the tool to penetrate the capillaries of the initial subject in ever greater depth, as with electronic monitoring.[23] Concepts for the speed and direction of change offer a way to more systematically understand the dynamics.

As a tactic with control goals saturates society, other goals may appear, such as communication, entertainment, play, and self-help. Consider the interesting case of video cameras introduced into churches as control and documentation means. Later, cameras were used to deliver church services to those unable to attend. In seeking new markets, technology entrepreneurs may contribute to a surveillance culture involving not only security and fear, but also convenience, efficiency, fashion, fun, and reward.

Note the driver's license, which has gone far beyond driver certification to have a broader identification and security function, as have the social security number[24] and IRS files. The latter, intended to be used only for tax purposes, are now required for a mortgage, a college loan, and for some jobs. Credit cards originally for credit purchases now must be shown to check into many hotels, even if one is paying with cash. Bar-coded student photo ID cards, initially only for university business such as library use, have morphed into all-purpose building access, debit, and credit cards. Curry, Phillips, and Regan (2004) document the "creeping legibility" of persons and places in emergency response systems, drawing on new uses for directories.

Consider also the move from using toll road tickets to determine the fee a driver owes to using the same information to issue speeding tickets to drivers who arrive at the place exited too quickly (a case of same subject and tool, new goal). In a related move, note the expanding use of photo-radar systems (both fixed and mobile) for issuing tickets. And systems developed to monitor traffic, such as the first cameras in Tiananmen Square, may come to be used to control dissent.

The open-ended systems of audio, video, and location capture can be endlessly expansive, depending on an agent's goals. In work environments, cameras introduced to monitor for security purposes may come to be used internally to control employees. Mike McCahill's (2002) study of British malls reports the appearance of new goals involving employee productivity and compliance monitoring (e.g., appropriate greeting of customers and service quality), far removed from the crime control goals used to explain the introduction of the technology.

The FBI's records of criminal histories, created as a crime-fighting tool, are now most frequently used to investigate job applicants, not crime. The polygraph, introduced as means of lie detection with respect to a specific criminal incident, expanded to broader uses for presumed character assessment. A 1996 National Directory of New Hires intended as a means for states to track parents who failed to pay child support has been extended to also track other unpaid debts, such as student loans. Drug tests have come to be used as an eligibility tool for access to student loans, public housing, and welfare assistance, a goal far removed from the beginning uses in crime control, work, and sports settings.

The military, promising that DNA taken from its personnel would only be used for identification in the event of death, faces pressure to use it for identification in criminal investigations around military bases. DNA data overall offer a vista to observe creeping surveillance. Mandatory DNA fingerprinting is now required in some states for violent offenders. One can imagine this moving to nonviolent criminals, then to anyone having contact with the criminal justice system, and finally to everyone.

In the latter case, to infer from previous patterns, this might initially be voluntary and only for purposes of identification—for example, as protection for missing children and for amnesia or Alzheimer's victims. Success with that could lead to a numerically expressed national DNA standard for all Americans, which could find its way onto all the documents that make up a person's "data image" in distant computers. This could serve to authenticate identity in everything from using a computer to entering a building, driving a car, or watching television.

We are also likely to see new uses that go beyond the limited number of DNA strands used for identification. For example, information on one's complete genetic makeup may someday become available. Among potential uses related to prevention and risk reduction are required therapy or the denial of certain types of employment or insurance or even the right to have children for those whose genetic makeup (it will be claimed) indicates they are prone to particular illnesses or forms of antisocial behavior. As chapter 13, on ethics, argues, questions about the process of surveillance creep and possible latent goals should be a central part of any public policy discussion of surveillance before it is introduced.

Surveillance Contraction

While I could list many other areas of potential expansion, there is surveillance contraction and even disappearance as well. It is not just that the camel's nose is pushed back from under the tent; occasionally the camel is banned from the campground. Contraction most commonly occurs following concerns over costs, the appearance of better methods, compelling evidence that the tactic doesn't work or has undesirable consequences, perception that a crisis or need has passed, a well-publicized scandal, restrictive legislation, and/or political mobilization against a tactic. Concern over liability and negative publicity are also inhibiting factors.

Just as national security surveillance expands during periods of crisis, contraction occurs during more relaxed periods and reforms in response to scandals. Whether there is a reversion to the previous state of liberty (or an expansion of liberty) has rarely been systematically studied. We do know, however, that in democratic societies, many of the greatly expanded government powers in wartime disappear or are weakened as peace returns. Following 9/11, for example, the Patriot Act significantly increased government surveillance powers. Congress subsequently weakened some provisions, and it was replaced in 2015 with further limitations by the Freedom Act, although surveillance was in some ways strengthened a few months later after attacks in Paris and San Bernardino.[25]

And here, too, there are other examples: In 1968 Congress passed the Omnibus Crime Control Bill, which established criminal penalties for unauthorized wiretapping. This resulted in a change in behavior on the part of many private detectives, who came to engage largely in the debugging business rather than also in the bugging business (at least publicly).[26]

Following the Watergate scandal and revelations about the FBI's COINTEL program, policies were changed, and until the post-9/11 period, the number of domestic national security investigations dropped from thousands to fewer than fifty a year.

After expanding for many decades, the use of the polygraph was severely curtailed by Congress in 1985, as doubts about its validity became more widespread. This contrasts with the situation in Europe, where the polygraph was never widely used, although other forms generally unappreciated in the United States, such as handwriting analysis (graphology) as a clue to character, are very prominent in France.

Regime changes in countries such as South Africa, Spain, Portugal, East Germany, Italy, and Greece have brought democratic reforms abolishing or limiting many previous surveillance practices (Samatas 2004; Clavell and Ouziel 2014; Fonio and Agnoletto 2014; Machado and Frois 2014; Svenonius, Bjorklund, and Waszkiewicz 2014).[27] These need to be contrasted with the pronounced post–World War II democratic changes seen in Japan and Germany (Sorensen 1993; Elster 2006). Reverses are of course possible as well.[28]

Thus, if we treat a given tool such as drug testing or the polygraph as the unit of analysis, we can follow its career development over an extended time period, including its diffusion, contraction, and broad life history. In the next section the focus shifts and becomes the phases that can be observed within a bounded time frame defined by a given application.[29] There the emphasis will be on the flow of activities naturally occurring (or potentially occurring) within a series of events, moving from initiation to some end point. The emphasis in this short section is on actual *patterns of application.*

Surveillance Occasions and Strips

Any application of surveillance by an organization occurs against background conditions involving design, technical standards, requirements, and laws and policies. This involves problem determination, agenda setting, instrument design, proposed solutions, and identification of agents and conditions for use.[30] Technical developments and the struggles of interest groups over rules, resources, and meaning create the conditions for specific applications.

Phillips (2005) in studying the 9-1-1 system offers a model for research at this level. [31] He notes how actors using different rhetorical, economic, and legal resources generate the field within which the surveillance occurs. However the strategic actions of contemporary agents and subjects are powerfully shaped by broader, often unseen, factors as well.

An important strand of research from the science and technology studies field looks further back at how historical, cultural, social, political, legal, and natural factors define, enable, restrict, or prohibit the appearance of specific forms and the institutionalization of technical innovations. Innovations emerge out of multiple planned and unplanned actions, rather than being given in the nature of the technology, being rigidly determined by a causal factor such as a capitalist, or more recent neoliberal political economy, or a great inventor or entrepreneur.

Beyond any given use at a particular place and time, these reflect broad social currents that, in the case of surveillance, occur on a global scale.

There is more than one way to get here from there. Practices such as x-ray screening at airports or Smart Meters that come (or will come) to be seen as routine and inevitable are contingent and emergent. New tools grow out of interaction, tinkering, translations, and chance factors at various levels. (reflective of this position: Sewell 1995; Pickering 1995, 2005; DeLanda 2006). This involves, and results in, an extensive network of actors and activities assembled in the generation and use of the tool.

This discussion picks up at that point. A major area for the study of social process involves the behavioral sequences present as a tool is applied (e.g., the move from collecting data to acting on results). Here I cut into the train of events at the point at which a problem has been defined, and surveillance as well as the appropriate agent has been identified as the solution (or an aspect of the solution). It is in the application phases that surveillance is most likely to be controversial and challenged.[32]

As noted, "surveillance," is a general concept that encompasses a series of actions that are temporally and behaviorally distinct, even as they may be sequentially (and often causally) linked. A given action under the surveillance umbrella may be contingent upon events that preceded it (whether interaction or further in the historical background) and will have implications for subsequent events. The shifting borders of before, during, and after time frames can be identified for surveillance behavior.

Once the surveillance tool has been defined and is in use, the analyst may identify discrete units of action; each implicitly answers a different question and involves a distinct goal. Seven kinds of activity that follow each other in logical order are listed here:

Seven Surveillance Strips
1. Tool selection
2. Subject selection
3. Data collection[33]
4. Data processing/analysis [raw data] numerical/narrative
5. Data interpretation
6. Data uses/action
7. Data fate

Viewed individually, each can be called a *surveillance strip*. The strips (or stages) are temporally, conceptually, empirically, and often spatially distinct. They can involve different roles and actors. In most cases agents are aware of the stage that concerns them.[34]

Each strip is an episode or chapter that combines with others to form full surveillance stories. We can better explain and evaluate a surveillance story when these elements are differentiated. Not unlike the frames in comic books, they illustrate the emergent character of "surveillance" as a multi-faceted concept—not only one with various dimensions but also one that is more fully seen when followed over time. Unlike the frames in comic books, these frames are not intended to be entertaining, and the patterns are more like the fluid, jumpy sequences of cyberspace explorations than the rigid frame ordering of the comic book. Nevertheless, when linked, the frames tell the story of "what happened." When viewed sequentially in their totality, these elements constitute *surveillance occasions*, or cases.[35]

A surveillance occasion begins when an agent is charged with the task of gathering information. Following that, the seven phases begin.[36] These distinctions offer a way to order the basic behaviors occurring within the family of direct surveillance actions.[37]

Sometimes the stages, or strips, occur almost simultaneously, as when a smoke and heat detector sets off an alarm, activates a ceiling sprinkler, and notifies the fire department; or when a motion sensor is triggered, sending a message to a central computer, sounding an alarm, and locking doors; or a retinal pattern is matched to a given identity and a computer unlocks. A human pressing a panic button to send for help is the functional equivalent. But for a goodly proportion of applications, such as drug testing or data mining, the activities and stages involve a division of labor, with agent roles played by various actors over longer time periods, and as the chain lengthens, the room for errors, incompetence, and monkey business expands.

The stages may develop in a serial fashion, as one stage logically leads to the next (e.g., from data collection to analysis), or they may stop early on, as when a tool and subject are identified but no data are collected, or the data are not analyzed or applied. Looking across many cases suggests a variety of ideal type career patterns (with different stopping and turning points). However, once data have been gathered, questions regarding the data's fate, including rules about deleting and forgetting, preserving, and sharing, must be asked.

Each stage of the surveillance occasion warrants extensive analysis. Given space limitations, the next chapter generally deals only with the interactions found in the data collection process. The activities at this stage bear heavily on questions of fairness and validity and engage assumptions made about subject passivity noted earlier. I hope future work can fill out the other stages and identify the correlates of patterns in an equivalent fashion.

6

A Tack in the Shoe and Taking the Shoe Off:
Resistance and Counters to Resistance

Every time they build a better mousetrap, the mice get smarter.
WALTER MATTHAU, *Fortune Cookie*

It may well be doubted whether human ingenuity can construct an enigma of the kind
which human ingenuity may not, by proper application, resolve.
EDGAR ALLEN POE, "The Gold Bug"

Peter Weir: I know you better than you know yourself.
Truman: You never had a camera in my head.
THE TRUMAN SHOW

How do people resist surveillance efforts, how do surveillance agents act to overcome these efforts, and what new forms of resistance develop in response? This chapter addresses these questions. The chapter's title refers to efforts to defeat the polygraph by stepping on a tack hidden in one's shoe and efforts to defeat such resistance by requiring that shoes be removed. A tack in the shoe is an example of an individual instrumental *neutralization* technique. The requirement to remove shoes is a *counterneutralization* technique. Given the spiraling nature of the surveillance process, *counter-counterneutralization* techniques ad nauseam can also be observed.

This chapter offers concepts to help order the array of behaviors and attitudes in opposition to, or in support of, surveillance. The resistance responses of subjects of surveillance are a form of behavioral neutralization.[1]

The previous chapter presented surveillance as a dynamic process. Studying the stages of surveillance occasions offers a way of capturing temporal developments. Thus, *anti-* and *prosurveillance* actions can be studied at any point in the surveillance process (e.g., creation, adoption, data collection, analysis and interpretation, application, data fate, and the fate of the tactic itself). The emphasis in this chapter however is primarily at the stage of data collection (although actions taken at this stage may often reverberate to a later stage, as with adding a substance to a urine sample that distorts the analysis).[2]

The Limits of Surveillance

Fatta la legge, trovato l'inganno
ITALIAN PROVERB

The advantages of technological and other strategic surveillance developments are often short-lived and contain ironic vulnerabilities, and that is also true for new developments to counter surveillance. The logistical and economic limits on total monitoring, competing values, the interpretive and contextual nature of many human situations, system complexity and interconnectedness, and agent vulnerability to being compromised provide ample room for resistance.[3] Particularly in liberal democratic societies there is space for resistance, irony, and surprises. Indeed the relative openness of the society as well as legal and civil-society protections are intended to limit the agent's power.

It is not just that society has space and demand for both surveillance and neutralization, but that the *same* organization can benefit from providing services for both, however unpatriotic this may appear to those in the maelstrom. Some businesses do provide an indiscriminate panoply of offensive and defensive means and services (e.g., for drug testing and drug detoxifying, radar detectors and radar guns, bugging and debugging). As they say, business is business, even if some of it is best preceded by the adjective *monkey*.

The progenitor of contemporary surveillance practices lies in the nineteenth century's physically based, centralized, and hierarchical organizations. They were inspired by a mechanical spirit of rationality and with a clear distinction between surveillance agents and subjects. Yet many current forms are tied to neither a physical locale nor face-to-face presence, involve horizontal rather than vertical ties, and share, merge, or blur the roles of watcher and watched. As Dupont (2008) observes, the "rock and mortar architecture of the prison" is distinct from the structure of the Internet built on wire and bits. The latter can serve as a form of "invisible barbed wire" (Morozov 2013), but, with its open and connecting architecture, can also offer a buffer against the control efforts of the more powerful and can also be turned against them. Horizontal networks that are independent of a central source may distribute rather than concentrate power (Lessig 1999). These changes radically break with the forms of surveillance of interest to Bentham and Foucault and those anticipating dystopia by next winter. The changes bring new possibilities for resistance.

As the introduction to this book argues, the rhetoric must be separated from the capability, and the potential of a technology for harm or good must be kept distinct from its realization. Just because something negative or positive *could* happen does not mean that it *will*. In short, little consideration has been given by prognosticators to how the expected outcomes will actually be produced or to causal factors.[4] A major factor working against dystopic outcomes is resistance by subjects. Anticipated resistance and fear of bad public relations can modulate practices, and if surveillance is applied, resistance can limit its effectiveness. Furthermore, control systems are rarely as effective and efficient as their advocates claim, and they often have a variety of unintended consequences.[5] And a gap frequently exists between the seemingly conforming behavior that is picked up by surveillance and less visible attitudes, emotions and hidden contravening behavior.

Other limits on the efficacy of the new surveillance result from the fact that new technologies rarely enter passive environments in which agents completely dominate subjects. Instead, they become enmeshed in complex, preexisting systems. They are as likely to be altered as to alter. Professional associations, oversight organizations, and political and social movements can also act as constraining factors, as can the new markets that control technologies inadvertently create for countertechnologies.

A free press and free market and the ease of Internet communication make an extensive "how to do it literature" available for those who wish to resist surveillance. Early print examples on the underground best seller's list— *The Anarchist's Cookbook, Steal This Urine Test,* and *The Paper Trip*—have many current imitators. A Google search for "beat drug testing" and "antipolygraph" returns thousands of sites. There are guides for using cell phones to film police. And one can easily find numerous spyware stores and catalogues for surveillance and neutralization technologies, though it may be difficult for the would-be resister to tell what tools actually work (most with web sites proudly reporting their privacy policy). The fact that it is often difficult to tell which purpose the tool has shrouds and softens the cultural tilt toward spying. Self-defense and the right to know are, after all, important values.

A strand of Christianity associates the "mark of the beast" with RFID chips and calls on Christians to resist (Dice and Albrecht 2006). Resistance is also a central theme in much contemporary science fiction and film (Kammere 2004). But resistance can also be seen at work (Dalton 1959; Burawoy 1979; Gabriel 1999), in prison (Sykes 1971), in the family, or in efforts to create a carceral society, as with the former East Germany (Pfaff 2000).

All this is to say that the individual is often more than a passive and compliant reed buffeted about by the imposing winds of more powerful persons and institutions, or dependent only on protest organizations for ideas about resistance. Humans are wonderfully inventive at finding ways to beat control systems and avoid observation. And on the other side of the equation, most surveillance systems have inherent contradictions, ambiguities, gaps, blind spots, and limitations, whether structural or cultural, and if they do not, they are likely to be connected to systems that do.

As Goffman (1961) notes in his study of the underlife of organizations, challenges abound when individuals feel that surveillance and the controls associated with it are wrong. This holds even in the most extreme cases, such as the maximum security prison (Rhodes 2004). Behavioral techniques of neutralization are a major means for mounting such challenges.

Given the limits of surveillance we have noted, this chapter argues against the imminent collapse of the sky as envisioned by some of my friends in universities, social movements, and the media, as well as the arrival of utopia as envisioned by some entrepreneurs and agents. Empirical inquiry and attention to recurring processes can cool heated rhetoric—whether it prophesizes doom or salvation.

Making Some Sense of Techniques of Neutralization

In order to make sense of the forms of resistance this chapter takes an analytic approach and looks across specific applications rather than descriptively considering all the ways one can respond to a given means such as drug testing, the polygraph, or red-light cameras.[6] While organizing the empirical in that way may help those who want to resist a given tool, it does little to increase our understanding. My analytic approach looks across specific applications to identify twelve general techniques of neutralization and responses to them. These are inductively drawn from observation and interviews.

The *individual, strategic* focus of interest here contrasts with the sheer contrariness to authority that Foucault (1977) writes about—that is, "a certain decisive will not to be governed."[7] It also differs from the everyday forms of resistance noted by Scott (1985), such as "foot dragging, dissimulation, false compliance, pilfering, feigned ignorance, slander, arson, sabotage."[8] Foucault's and Scott's forms of symbolic and/or noninstrumental behaviors express indignation and rebellion. Yet the contumacious are not necessarily strategic.[9]

The generality of the neutralization types suggested here permits us to see the common aspects of resistance in varied phenomena such as a citizen concerned with protecting personal privacy, a criminal seeking to avoid detection, and a control agent protecting his or her information. In spite of the obvious moral differences across motives and groups, there are behavioral similarities and equivalent structures, contingencies, and processes in the moves to protect and discover personal information.

The resistance actions an individual takes to defeat a given application are often covert in order to maximize effectiveness and/or avoid suspicion and sanctioning. Moreover, the goal is to defeat a given application, not to abolish it. Direct resistance or avoidance of this kind contrasts with a broad strategic response such as challenging a law or encouraging a boycott.

The decentralizing aspects of computing, in which individuals send and receive information without the need for a directing authority, suggests a form that is intermediate between individual and group protest—for example, the virtual advocacy networks for surveillance practices identified by Introna and Gibbons (2009). The decentralized organization of computing (Martin, van Brakel, and Bernhard 2009) also illustrates how much resistance to, and support for, surveillance goes beyond the more easily seen subject-agent relationships.

The spread of the new surveillance has been accompanied by organized political and legal challenges from established civil-liberties, consumer, and worker organizations as well as by new organizations.[10] For these challenges the emphasis is on stopping or regulating a broad strategy or a particular tactic within it, not stopping application of the tactic in a given case. And the politics of surveillance can also involve one level of government resisting another.[11]

Solitary individual responses are also distinct from the efforts of advocacy groups to educate the public, create awareness, and offer alternative sources of data and interpretation (whether directed at a particular case or tactic or more broadly). Consider the collective public outreach cultural activities of guerilla theater groups (e.g., the New York Surveillance Players, the Glass Bead Collective), satirical and critical offerings on the Internet, newsgroups documenting surveillance (e.g., the eyewitness video project), and artists, treated in the two deleted culture chapters (press.chicago.edu/sites/marx/).[12]

Twelve Easy Moves

> Let 'em flutter me. I know how to pass a polygraph.
> W. CASEY, former CIA head

The number of *repertories of surveillance neutralization* and *counterneutralization* is limited, even though the specifics and settings for surveillance vary greatly.[13] This limit reflects the directive power of culture as well as commonalities in the nature and structure of surveillance contexts and resources.

The strategic actions of both watchers and watched can be thought of as moves in a game, although unlike traditional games, this one may not allow a good time to be had by all, and the rules may not be equally binding on all players. In this game, childhood prepares individuals to play both roles, and some of the excitement of the challenge, contest, and chase may remain. The game has a double reiterative quality—involving both the same old limited tactics and the dynamism of reciprocal innovations.

Twelve types of neutralization moves are shown in table 6.1: (1) discovering, (2) avoiding, (3) piggybacking, (4) switching, (5) distorting, (6) blocking, (7) masking, (8) breaking, (9) refusing, (10) explaining, (11) cooperating, and (12) countersurveillance. These moves emphasize visible behavior, although the analyst can draw some inferences about presumed motives of subjects. Table 6:2 illustrates these by examples from work settings.

Each move can be seen as a rib within a broad umbrella of resistance or noncompliance. Thus the refusal move in its extreme form literally involves saying "no," as when the surveillance is overtly rejected or ignored—whether out of principle or strategic calculation that it will fail. Most of the other moves involve a more subtle and partial refusal to fully cooperate, even as cooperation may be feigned.

Each move also refers to a distinct empirical element. In most cases, however, they are not mutually exclusive and can be systematically related. Several types may be simultaneously present, as when a person wearing gloves to

TABLE 6.1. Twelve neutralization moves

Neutralization technique	Action
Discovering	Find out if surveillance is in operation, and if it is, where, by whom, and how
Avoiding	Choose locations, times periods, and means not subject to surveillance
Piggybacking	Accompany or be attached to an eligible or qualifying object
Switching	Transferring an authentic result to someone or something it does not apply to
Distorting	Altering input such that a technically valid result appears but the inference drawn from it is invalid
Blocking	Eliminating or making data inaccessible
Masking	Blocking but with deception regarding factors such as identity and location
Breaking	Rendering the surveillance device inoperable
Refusing	ignoring the surveillance and what it is meant to deter
Explaining	Accounting for an unfavorable result by reframing it in an acceptable way or offering alternative data and the claims of rival experts, making rights and procedural violations claims
Cooperating	Making collusive moves with agents
Countersurveillance	Reversing roles, so that subjects apply the tactics to agents; taking advantage of the double-edged potential of tools

TABLE 6.2. Neutralization moves: workplace

Neutralization technique	Action
Discovering	Use bug detectors
Avoiding	Choose employer that doesn't monitor electronic communication
Piggybacking	Walk into restricted facility behind person with access
Switching	Substitute clean urine sample
Distorting	Hold down computer keys to appear productive
Blocking	Encrypt communication
Masking	Use another person's ID and password
Breaking	Add battery acid to a urine sample
Refusing	Don't file reports about dating another employee
Explaining	"I didn't know there was marijuana in the brownies"
Cooperating	Get advance warning of drug test from supervisor
Countersurveilling	Audiorecord a supervisor's harassing statements

block fingerprints also masks the true prints by leaving items containing another's fingerprints. The moves may also be temporally and logically linked, as when discovery that one is watched leads to avoidance of places where the watching occurs.

Neutralization may be direct or indirect. Subjects may seek to affect the data they offer by or that is taken from them, their identity or location, or the conditions under which data collection occurs. It may also directly engage the instruments of data collection and analysis and attempt to hamper or distort their operation. As to further variations, it may involve neutralization with regard to the subject's body or materials from it or aspects of the surveillance tool itself.[14] Let's move now to the specifics of each kind of move.

1. DISCOVERING MOVES

In the context of discovering, an important distinction exists between surveillance that the subject knows about, whether because of its material properties and/or publicity (as in fair warning and deterrence), and surveillance that the subject previously does not know about, either that it is being done at all or what its specific details are.

Discovery moves are referred to as surveillance detection in the intelligence trade. The initial goal of the subject is to find out whether surveillance is in operation and, if it is, where, by whom, and how. Such discovery is aided by a thriving private security industry that routinely sweeps offices, homes, and vehicles for listening devices and also sells do-it-yourself antibugging and other devices—for example, pocket bug and tape recorder detectors, and small flashlight-like devices for finding hidden video cameras. Whether the product delivers on the advertising hype or these are made for "your catalogue suckers" (as a character said in the film *The Conversation*) is a question for research.

In the name of discovery (whether done by the subject or by their agent) everyday objects may be examined to see if they are other than what they appear—for example, does a towel dispenser, book, or teddy bear hide a video lens? The tip of a fingernail touched against a mirror which appears to directly touch the image of the nail suggests a two-way mirror. The red and green (call-carrying) wires on a home telephone can be inspected to be sure that they are not attached to the yellow and black wires (generally a bad sign). Door handles, documents, and drawers may be examined under ultraviolet light to see if they have been coated with fluorescent dust. Access keypads to a safe or to a telecommunications device may be inspected to see if they have been coated with a waxy film that will reveal what keys were touched to gain access.

"Vital tests" (Goffman 1974, 97–99) may be applied to uncover potential surveillance. For example, a criminal may test a would-be partner by requiring that an act of violence, theft, or drug use occur before a drug deal is completed. Joe Pistone, an FBI agent who successfully infiltrated several New York Mafia families, reports that "to become a made man, you have to make your bones"—that is, kill someone. Pistone was given such a contract, but the subject disappeared, so his cover was protected (Pistone 2006, 92). The film *Battle of Algiers* offers a riveting example when a potential recruit to the Algerian independence movement is suddenly handed a gun on the street and told to kill a nearby policeman (the recruit himself is a police infiltrator). A similar incident occurs in Clint Eastwood's *In the Line of Fire*. Or, more benignly, a prostitute may require that a client's request for services be put in writing (or even audio- or videotaped) before agreeing to anything, thus permitting a defense of entrapment should the client turn out to have an additional motive.

Further examples are for a newcomer to establish credibility by having a trusted person vouch for her/him, using back channels to gain access to protected records that would reveal the surveillance and using freedom of information acts to determine the identity of informers.

Once they've discovered a surveillance source, subjects and others may publicize it. The CB radios of truckers traditionally gave warnings of where the "smokeys" with speed traps were. Now, in many regions, ordinary drivers with Internet access can learn where hidden cameras are. Folklore abounds with suggestions about how to identify unmarked police vehicles.[15]

In Britain, in the interest of defending clients, criminal defense attorneys have created a database with the names of those known to be government informers. In the United States, certain web sites claim to disclose the identity of informers and undercover officers. Wikileaks and related anonymous postings may reveal names and operational procedures.

In an ironic turning of the tables, the very technologies used for control can also be also be used to discover a neutralization strategy. Consider the practice of empirical testing to discover thresholds and vulnerabilities. A tool designed to combat drug use may serve instead to protect it through direct engagement with what Moore and Haggerty (2001, 390) call "the particularities of an observational regime." Facing a urine drug test, employees can first experiment at home, testing themselves with a variety of readily available products of the kind used in the official test. The timing and amount of drug usage may then be calibrated to meet the threshold for passing the test. The subject's pretest may reveal whether the tactic identifies a given drug and, if so, if it can be defeated via flushing the system or adding adulterants.

2. AVOIDING MOVES

Avoidance and subsequent moves may follow the discovery that surveillance is present. Generally, subjects may assume that because surveillance might be present, avoidance is a prudent response. Avoidance moves are passive rather than active and involve selectivity and withdrawal. For example, when avoiding, the subject makes no effort to directly engage, or tamper with, the surveillance.

From one view, when discovery leads to self-regulated avoidance of the behavior of interest to the agent, surveillance has met its goal of deterrence. Mission accomplished. Consider drivers who slow down when their anti-radar "fuzz buster" warns them, or drug users who cease drug use (at least temporarily) because of concern over employment testing. The answer to the question "Do you know the one sure-fire way to beat the breathalyzer?"—"Don't drink"—also reflects this.

But given motivation to continue the behavior, avoidance as cessation is often short lived. Rather, the subject engages in displacement of the behavior to times, spaces, and means in which the identified surveillance is presumed to be absent or irrelevant.[16] Consider the hushed conversations in saunas or baths seen in films on organized crime, where a wire would be difficult to hide (or might give a shock). Frequent changes in place, identification, appearance, timing, and mode of operation are means to avoid creating a predictable and therefore more easily identifiable and observable pattern of behavior.

Subjects can avoid certain settings (e.g., supermarkets with frequent-shopper cards) or switch technologies (e.g., making calls from a pay phone, as the calls cannot be traced to a particular telephone subscriber). Or the subject may take routes that minimize the chance of being seen on a video camera. In New York and several European cities, web sites permit viewers to map routes with the fewest cameras. Other web sites provide information on the location of speed and red-light cameras or lists of companies that drug test their employees.[17] Employees may have the option of choosing less monitored work environments or a drug test less likely to reveal the kind of drug they use.

Avoidance may also occur within a given setting. Consider, for example, shoplifters who operate within the interstitial areas of surveillance relying on camera blind spots—whether those that are "natural" as a result of the building's architecture or are created as a result of a shield offered by another person or a display; thieves who know that not all goods or library books are electronically tagged and apply the "five-finger discount" only to untagged items; or thieves who lift an electronically tagged item above the sensor's portals or drop it from a window. Paying with cash or bartering rather than using a credit card or check avoids easy identification. As pretend jewel thief FBI agent Joe Pistone (2004, 34) wrote, "There is nothing as clean as dirty money."

A concern over the loss or theft of items such as laptops and smaller communications devices has led some companies to require that employees upload data files to central computers rather than having them remain on a portable or local device. Some companies provide employees with "clean" laptops for foreign travel, with only the minimal information needed for business trips. Beyond theft, a factor here is the ability of customs officials to access and copy confidential and proprietary material.

Those of a passive-aggressive disposition who want the job and yet resent being tested may secretly stick it to the organization by smoking marijuana shortly before their test (assuming they haven't smoked for some time), knowing that marijuana residue must be in the body several hours before a urine test can discover it. The individual may be impaired but will pass the test, because what is measured is the presence of drug metabolites, not the ability to perform. However, someone who is not impaired, having smoked several days before on a weekend, would fail the test.

A union contract may require some notice about the timing and conditions of a pending drug test. Contracts may limit the frequency of tests (absent cause) and require that once tested, an employee can't be tested again until all other employees have been. College athletes in many sports may use prohibited steroids off season, expecting not to face testing. Social systems also often leak, and the date of a supposed random or surprise test or search may be anticipated, permitting abstinence or more active neutralization measures.

Security consultants advise clients with sensitive information not to use an unsecured telephone, fax, or Internet connection unless they would not mind seeing their communications in the newspaper the next day and never to use cordless microphones for presentations in private meetings. Moreover, cell phones and GPS devices should be turned off when not in use. Fax machines should be frequently checked for security and turned off after hours. Originals should not be left on copy machines.[18] Caution is advised even in face-to-face conversations, unless the room has been recently swept for bugs and the person the potential subject is talking to can be checked for electronic signals suggesting transmission or recording. Even after that, the truly cautious are on the lookout for lurking lip-readers and would never bring a cell phone into a meeting for fear that it could unwittingly transmit.[19] Nor would they talk in a car or other enclosed space.

Beyond presuming security only in face-to-face meetings and dealing only with those who are known or vouched for,[20] subjects may favor certain physical or social locations for secret conversations, such as an open field, a boat, a church, or even another country.[21]

The protection (and revelation) of personal information has a spatial, social, and temporal geography. Avoidance via location can involve architectural and natural physical features that preclude visibility and other forms of data collection. The classic case here opens *1984* as the protagonist Winston enters his apartment and crouches down in order to be beyond the range of the not quite all-seeing telescreen. Or it can involve culturally protected places such as safety zones, safe havens, and sanctuaries (e.g., churches or medieval cities where "city air makes one free"). Norms of "Don't ask, don't tell" and "Ignore" may be stronger in border, frontier, and interstitial areas and ports, or in vice and skid row areas of cities ("What happens in Vegas, stays in Vegas"). Moreover, protected relationships, as with spouses, medical, religious, or legal specialists, may be worked in favor of avoidance, although there are limits here when imminent danger or serious crimes are involved.

Time periods must also be part of any map of avoidance responses. Thus, some actions of interest to agents may occur late at night or on weekends, when fewer observers are present. And subjects may take advantage of the fact that agents can be more tolerant and loosen their control during periods of celebration such as New Year's Eve, Mardi Gras, Halloween, or following major sports victories. Or subjects separate activities presumptive of violations in time and place (such as directly exchanging contraband for cash or staggering the time and/or location of the exchange). A different aspect of timing lies in the move to faster-growing marijuana strains planted in national forests, which limits the time authorities have for discovery.

With the introduction of federally mandated computer record checks, we have a nice example of avoidance via displacement to means less available for surveillance. Computer record matching has made it more difficult for those on welfare to avoid discovery if they obtain extra income from a job, workmen's compensation, retirement, or assistance in another state. However, this tightening has led to an increase in under-the-table cash and exchange forms of payment for work (Gilliom 2001).

Another form of avoidance is staying under the radar by meeting exclusion requirements. For example, banks do not need to report deposits under $10,000 to the federal government. Those wishing to stash cash may avoid banks altogether, may make multiple smaller deposits in their own names, may use aliases, or may use others to make deposits. Such actions can in turn be criminalized, generating still new forms of avoidance.

Related logic can be seen in avoiding the identifying criteria for surveillance profiles. For example, the person who wants to avoid suspicion would not pay for a one-way airline ticket with cash at the last minute or use the kinds of cars and routes believed to be associated with drug carriers. As awareness of profile criteria spreads, evasive behavior often appears.

Changing locations or running away is a central neutralization component, even as it may conflict with the need to find coconspirators and gain familiarity with an environment. Graffiti writers and gamblers with their portable tools float across venues. Some con artists and prostitutes frequently move to new cities to avoid control attention. Those hiding affairs are advised to vary their locales and, given Google street-level pictures, not to meet in predictable places such as the "no tell motel."[22]

Individuals may avoid certain medical tests or genetic analyses because they do not want results on their insurance and other records, or to have these linked to the health records of family members. And many people are unaware of the protections against using genetic predisposition data for employment or health insurer decisions (e.g., the 2008 Genetic Information Nondiscrimination Act and the Americans with Disabilities Act). Even those who do know about the protections, however, may forgo testing because of concerns over areas not covered by law, loopholes, lack of enforcement of the law, the inability to protect confidentiality, and concern over being denied life insurance.

An avoidance alternative is to have medical tests done privately and pseudonymously, or with self-testing kits. The same logic rests with hiring a private polygrapher and releasing results or agreeing to take an official polygraph only if the results from the private test are favorable.

The discovery and avoidance moves just discussed are rather passive. The rest of the moves discussed below would probably be appreciated by poet-philosopher Wendell Berry, who advised, "Every day do something that won't compute. . . . Be like the fox who makes more tracks than necessary, some in the wrong direction. Practice resurrection" (1971).

3. PIGGYBACKING MOVES

Here, subjects directly face surveillance rather than avoid it but evade control or protect information by attaching themselves or the information to a legitimate subject or object. An important context for this move is entrance and exit controls. For example, a subject can sometimes thwart systems requiring an access card by walking or, in the case of a parking structure, driving quickly behind a person with legitimate access. The fact that the door or gate must remain open long enough to permit the legitimate entry may offer a window for others. This nicely illustrates the ironic vulnerability of control systems in which there is a necessary link between what is included and what is excluded. The need to open creates the possibility for illegitimate as well as legitimate entrance and egress.

Minimization rules for wiretapping require that monitors click off when conversations do not appear to involve matters pertinent to the warrant. One trick reportedly used by organized crime patriarchs is to have a female companion telephone another female and talk about children or cooking, prompting the listening agent to stop listening, and in turn prompting the female conversants to pass the phone to a male companion who engages in a brief conversation relevant to the warrant.

Steganography, which permits hiding information in images and documents, is available and easy to use on the Internet. With such tools, conventionally communicated computer information can bootleg other information that is only available to those with the appropriate software. The viewer without the software sees only what is immediately visible and will have no reason to suspect that anything has been added.

4. SWITCHING MOVES

In settings involving testing, certification, and validation, a subject can transfer an authentic result to someone or something to which it does not apply. While accurate in what it purports to show, the accuracy is misplaced. Consider test substitution in a large classroom where one person pretends to be another. Assuming the test taker did not cheat, the results are valid in assessing him or her but not the person they purport to represent. Or consider the common *stand-in* tactic of those barely of age purchasing alcohol or cigarettes for those underage.

A common form of switching involves *certification transference*: A subject uses a ticket, entry card, license, computing password, or entitlement or identity marker belonging to someone else. South Africa provides an unusual example where welfare payments can be obtained from ATMs. The recipient enters the correct information into the computer and offers a thumbprint for verification. One enterprising family collected welfare payments long after an elderly relative had died by cutting off her thumb and continuing to use it as certification. Similarly, in a urine drug test if the sample generation is, as they say, "unsupervised" (not directly observed by an agent), a subject can purchase "clean" urine in powdered form from a non-drug-user and substitute it, as occurred in a memorable scene when a student was drug tested by his parents in the film *American Beauty*.[23]

But switching may occur even with an observer present. Consider the enterprising athlete who used a catheter to insert his girlfriend's drug-free urine into his own system and then passed it back under the watchful eye of an observer. He was discovered only because, although the sample showed no sign of drug use, it did indicate he was pregnant. Likewise, consider the reusable $150 Whizzinator, available in five different flesh colors and described in marketing material as an "easy to conceal, easy to use urinating device using a very realistic prosthetic penis and synthetic urine."[24] A female version is also available.

A Canadian doctor accused of rape used switching moves to try to fool authorities when they sought his DNA for a match. The first time, he turned his back to an observer and substituted another's blood sample. Doubts led to a second test, in which the observer directly watched him draw a sample from his arm. However, this time he had inserted a plastic vial with another's blood under his skin. A final sample taken from his mouth established his guilt.

As a condition of sentencing, those arrested for drunk driving may agree to have a breathalyzer attached to their car's ignition. The alcohol ignition interlock prevents a car from starting until the driver blows into a funnel-like device that analyzes the alcohol content of the driver's breath. For the car to start the interlock must indicate a blood alcohol level below the cutoff point. When first developed, the interlock could be tricked by having a friend breathe into the device or, in a temporal switch, by using air from a balloon filled before the drinking. The individual may also start the car and then begin drinking. Avoidance by using a different car is another option.

5. DISTORTING MOVES

Distorting moves manipulate the surveillance collection process such that, while test or inspection results are technically valid, the inferences drawn from them about performance, behavior, or attributes are invalid. In other words, the technical data do not mean what they appear to say. Distorting moves contrast with switching moves, because with switching, the socially misleading inference involves a fallacious identity. In contrast, an example of distortion is moving a magnet over the meter for home electrical service, which could create a false reading of the amount of power actually used.[25] Or consider a tactic used by some data entry clerks who were judged by the number of keystrokes they entered. At the end of the day some workers simply held down one key for a few minutes. This generated the impression of greater productivity than was actually the case. The employer had an accurate record of the number of keystrokes, but given the way they were produced, the measure was not valid for assessing performance. GPS devices are generally very accurate in transmitting their location, but if they are detachable, the person or object they are presumed to locate may be elsewhere. That was the case in Boston with a snowplow driver hired by the state to clear the road. He was observed stashing the device in the snow while he went off to do a private plowing job.

In order to "beat the box," the antipolygraph literature provides tips for distinguishing ambiguous "control" questions from "relevant" (incriminating) ones. To distort the test when answering control questions, the literature suggests "sphincter clinching" (but with a relaxed buttocks), varying patterns of breathing, and biting "down slowly on the side of your tongue hard enough to produce moderate pain, but don't cut your tongue" (Maschke and Scalabrini 2005, 149). As noted, stepping on the tack is also a distorting move.

Efforts to defeat drug tests via distortion may involve adding to the sample substances such as bleach, vinegar, and drain cleaner, or taking medications or eating foods thought to confound the tests. Evidence of such tactics can be made to disappear, as diuretics are used to flush the system. "Purifying commodities" with names such as Urine Luck (say it slowly), THC Terminator

Drink, Fast Flush, Whizzies, and Klear may be used in the hope that they will purge the body of drug metabolites. Along with such products, large doses of vitamin B-2 are recommended to avoid production of suspicious colorless urine. That successful efforts are common can be inferred from contrasting the annual number of failed employment drug tests (about 1–2 percent a year) with the much larger percentage of the adult population engaged in casual drug use.

6. BLOCKING MOVES

Blocking and masking, the next two forms, call explicit attention to the communicative aspects of surveillance. Agents desire to read the signals given off by their subjects. Blocking eliminates or makes inaccessible what is of interest to agents, whether involving routine activities such as closing curtains and doors or using codes. If subjects cannot physically or otherwise block or eliminate access to the communication, they may try to render it (or aspects of it, such as the identity, appearance, location, or behavior of the communicator) unusable.

A "photo flash deflector" fluid that blocks the photographing of a license plate became available soon after automated video systems for monitoring red light and other violations appeared. When cars have the deflector, the violation is noted but not the identity of the violator. Rear-mounted license plates are also potentially blocking, as they are much more difficult for newer police radar to detect, as are darker cars and cars with dark front-end bug covers. Radar and laser jammers, which use white noise to create a blank reading, are available in many states. A unit that combines a radar detector with a jammer is also available.

A related form that blocks discovery as well as immediate data collection is a laser shield. With this device, a beam of infrared light locates the electronic sensors used by a digital camera and then aims a bright light at the camera, rendering any pictures taken unusable. This is an antipaparazzi device that has also been used for crowd control.[26]

A means of stopping eavesdropping via the traditional telephone was to turn the dial and hold it in place by inserting a pencil, effectively blocking the microphone within the phone. Playing loud music, whispering, or running a blender accomplishes the same goal (covering the lips with one's hands is equivalent in face-to-face conversations). Caller ID in most states can now be stopped by line or per-call blocking. Those making credit card phone calls in public places such as airports are advised to shield the numbers entered to prevent theft of access codes by lurkers—including those using binoculars

from a distance. And those who want to block surveillance can also exploit
dead spaces where radio transmission is poor or blocked (in some underground settings, tall buildings, elevators, or mountains) or where a video
camera's direct sight line is blocked.

Commercial services using 900 numbers can forward calls and then immediately erase the source of the call as a way of blocking telephone number
identification systems. Anonymous remailers, who forward computer messages stripped of their sender's address, also stop identification. And disposable identities, pseudonyms, and anonyms (chap. 4) offer means of preventing the aggregation of information from different sources and can protect
identity and location. Another example of blocking involved adding certain
chemicals to cocaine, converting it to a black, odorless substance and making
it undetectable to drug-sniffing dogs and routine chemical tests. Until agents
discovered this tactic, "black cocaine" was smuggled in as toner, and the disguising chemicals were later separated out with a solvent (Branigin 1999).

A form of implicit blocking (and avoidance) can be seen when the limitations on the senses and the given "natural" properties of a surveillance
method result in a default blocking of identification without the need to take
protective action. Consider the anonymous phone call that was possible after
electronic switching eliminated the need to rely on an operator to make a
call.[27] Such switching became widespread toward the middle of the twentieth
century. The anonymity lasted until the advent of digital telephony and caller
ID in the 1990s.

Moves and countermoves around the electronic tagging of consumer
goods, persons, and documents also involve blocking. For example, if all goes
according to the agent's plans, when identification documents or electronic
keys pass through (or touch) sensors, the information is recorded as doors
open or close. Or, in the case of tagged consumer items or library books that
are not demagnetized, the sending of a signal may trigger an alarm and block
movement.

However, a metallic shield around the tagged item may prevent it from
sending signals. Such shields can take many forms—a large shopping bag
bearing a familiar store logo with a second aluminum or duct-tape-lined bag
within it, or metal-lined girdles and undergarments to block signals. More
inclusive is the Faraday cage, a metal or a metallic mesh enclosure that blocks
electronic transmissions. There is even a portable version available for travelers.[28] Neodymium paint may also inhibit transmissions. But a signal may not
even be sent if a subject desensitizes it using a portable, commercially available device. Or a subject can remove the electronic tag from merchandise or
the spine of a book. Those under judicial supervision may also remove their

electronic location monitors.[29] Another type of shield can be seen in commercial products such as X-ray absorbing underwear that claim to obscure the most private parts of the human body from airport scanners.

The physical principles and responses go far beyond criminals. Anyone can purchase a variety of RFID-blocking cardholders, wallets, and passport sleeves to thwart the transmitting of data from a credit or other card to a nearby reader. Even simpler is the piece of tinfoil to be wrapped around a document that the advocacy group epic.org gave away as an RFID "foiling" kit. This giveaway combined the political with the practical—raising awareness of the radiating culprits in wallets as well as protecting personal information that could be taken without the knowledge of the person, as hidden devices can read contact-less cards with RFID from up to about thirty feet away.

Subjects may block identity by simply removing identifying marks— whether cutting labels out, removing serial numbers on autos and appliances, surgically altering fingerprints, or simply wearing gloves. Unmarked police cars, plainclothes police, and covered or removed badge numbers and name tags are further examples.[30]

Another form of blocking involves wearing a veil or loose-fitting, buttoned-up clothes. In response to the phenomena of covert "up skirt and down blouse" videotaping, one policewoman reports always wearing pants to the mall. Another woman I interviewed who was secretly videotaped in her home said, "I sometimes take a shower with my clothes on." Generic ski or Halloween masks worn by bank robbers and the helmets with visors or masks worn in some protest demonstrations, whether by police or demonstrators,[31] are other examples of blocking identity.

Do-it-yourselfers can build a ring of battery-powered infrared lights attached to a headband. This is said to produce a bright white spot where the face should be when seen on a monitor. It might save energy just to wear a mask. Either way, however, such blocking devices call attention to the wearer as atypical.

Situations in which those watching are unaware that specific blocking has occurred, as with children and others writing in invisible ink, can be contrasted with those where the fact of blocking is obvious.[32] The encryption of communication using widely available programs such as PGP (Pretty Good Privacy) lets the interceptor know something is being communicated. Encrypted communications are easy to intercept, but meaningless without decryption. Commonly used e-mail programs offer encryption, but most people do not use it, being unaware of it or feeling it isn't needed. Online commercial transactions are likely to be automatically encrypted and call for no action from the consumer.

In contrast to the real-time blocking of information via encryption is destruction after the fact. Disposable cell phones that can be obtained without identification are one example. An advertisement for Spy Paper reports that it "looks and feels like high-quality notepad paper yet dissolves completely in a matter of seconds when it comes into contact with water." If a store is sold out or the subject happens to be in the Mojave Desert without water, he or she always has the option of the pen whose ink disappears after several days.

Along these lines, since data may remain on a hard drive even after the delete command is given, a "wiper program" can ensure they are eliminated. Hard drives, too, can be reformatted before being retired to block access to data. In extreme cases the drive may be literally sanded. Subjects can destroy "piano roll" faxes, as these contain records of what has been received. And paper shredding is another example of blocking, as is destruction by fire or chemical. In elevated security settings, information may be shredded and cross shredded, then burned at a very high temperature so that not even ashes are left.

7. MASKING MOVES

Masking is a form of blocking in which the original information is shielded, but it adds deception with respect to the identity, status, and/or location/ locatability of the person or material of surveillance interest. Masking shares with one form of blocking the goal of eliminating genuine identifying marks (e.g., by removing serial numbers or wearing a generic mask),[33] but it differs in the sense that it replaces what is blocked with information intended to mislead, such as a disguise or fake serial numbers.

Blocking without masking may call attention to itself (e.g., a car with no license plate, a weapon with the serial number removed, an anonymous e-mail), while masking need not (e.g., altered numbers, a pseudonymous e-mail address). As a result of masking, the surveillance mechanism operates as intended, but the information collected is misleading or useless and the agent may not even recognize this.[34]

Efforts to disguise identity, whether with wigs, dyed hair, elevator shoes, padded clothing, plastic surgery[35], or fake documents, belong in this category and again contrast with generic giveaway forms such as a mask. The film *Personal Record*, in which a woman wears a wig and uses fake documents to create a seemingly untraceable paper trail in committing a crime of revenge, is a nice example.[36] A related example resonating with twenty-first-century sensibilities, or fantasies, is in *Minority Report* (2002), when Tom Cruise (after an eye implant has been inserted) is identified by a store's retinal scanner and welcomed as Mr. Yakamoto.

The old movie trick of disguising one's voice over the telephone using a handkerchief to block identity is well known. But one can also purchase voice-changing devices, whether involving material objects that cover the mouthpiece or distorting software that creates a robotic voice, converts an adult voice to a child's, or reverses male and female voices.

Monahan (2015) notes responses such as fractal face paint and hair styles, resin masks, reflective underwear, and antisurveillance camouflage that permit hiding in plain sight while in public. Masking can additionally be seen in giving a false social security number, name, or phone number. Remote computer entries using another's identification and password (whether to send or take information) are other examples. The computer security system accurately records transactions and the use of a particular entry code from a given machine, but it cannot determine whether the entrant is the person or organization it technically appears to be, absent additional means such as biometric identification and video recording.

Dupont (2008) considers the distributed masking moves made possible by the architecture of the Internet, which relies on multiple nodes for communication. Free computer masking tools such as TOR (The Onion Router) and Freenet encrypt a part of the user's hard drive. When the user goes to the Internet, communication moves through nodes of a "trust network" before it goes to the open, potentially surveilled part of the Internet. Anonymity results from the complex paths taken as data enter and leave the encrypted network, because the specific machine used and the identity presumed to be linked to it (whether as registrant or actual user) cannot be traced back (there is nothing to erase, unlike with the telephone call-forwarding services).

In their counterneutralization efforts, agents concerned with controlling access through identity verification or authentication must determine first whether the identity, authentication, access code, or document is valid and, if so, whether the user is authorized. For those trying to avoid observation, a free program called BugMeNot (BMN) meets the first requirement but not the second. It offers access to its database of several hundred thousand web site accounts. These are "real" accounts, but the user may not be the person the web site thinks it is. The account's usernames and passwords have been created based on fallacious information. The data left by those using BMN are thus not of much help to the agent's site in creating profiles or in using matching techniques to send unsolicited information to the user. Users can also obtain fake e-mail addresses that disappear after a day.

A related form, Mailinator, offers users an anonymous e-mail address that they can use temporarily to receive information or file a web site form, while not revealing their true e-mail address. These moves parallel the destruction of information after the fact, as with wiper programs noted above. The disposable address prevents an inbox from overflowing with spam.

TrackMeNot protects browsing behavior by drowning a user's genuine search within a sea of randomly generated queries.[37] That is, it creates artificial noise that makes it harder to locate the genuine signal. As a result, profiling and/or sending out unrequested information (or otherwise using knowledge of what a user searched for) become more difficult.

8. BREAKING MOVES

The goal of breaking moves is to render the surveillance device inoperable. However, as with blocking moves, agents (at some point) are likely to discover this. Breaking moves are the crudest form of neutralization. Examples include disabling electrical and phone lines; immobilizing a video camera by aiming a laser pointer at it, spray painting the lens, attaching tape or stickers to it (or to a webcam lens), or simply smashing it or the natural progression to shooting down a drone trespassing in the curtilage over one's property;[38] erasing or confounding computer data with a magnet; or trying to disable a drug-testing device by submitting a sample with hydrochloric or battery acid. Similarly, a male guard dog may be neutralized with a tranquilizer dart, mace, poisoned food, or female dog in heat.

When radar location detection devices were first attached to police cars to allow supervisors to track their officers, some officers in Boston responded by smashing the device with their clubs. More subtly, they defeated the system by driving beyond city limits and entering at a different point. Leaving the system in this way caused the monitor to lose track of the police car.

Subjects can also functionally break a system by flooding it, a move characteristic of collective protest. Harassing calls intended to tie up phone lines or filing endless bureaucratic forms are traditional means of protest against organizations. Kiss (2009) identifies *overwhelming* as a text-messaging protest tool used at the 2004 Republican National Committee meeting in New York. Police monitoring the thousands of messages did not have the resources to put the data to immediate strategic use.

9. REFUSING MOVES: NON SERVIAM

To varying degrees the responses discussed thus far are all forms of refusal by subjects to cooperate under the terms desired by agents. A more pronounced form of refusal is to "just say no" and to ignore the surveillance or even throw it back at the, agent as in figure 6.1.[39] *Refusal* is a broad term that can in-

HEY BOSS. I'M NOT SURE OUR COVERT
SURVEILLANCE IS REAL COVERT ANY MORE.

FIGURE 6.1. Covert surveillance usually has a shelf life and can self-destruct when action is taken based on the results.

volve omission or commission.[40] It may be legitimate, as with choices to opt in or opt out of a survey, or illegitimate, given the rules of the system. It may mean literally ignoring a request for information—as with those who refuse to register for the draft. Or it can involve the literal and symbolic destroying of documents, such as the South African "passbooks" previously required of nonwhites, the shredding of national identity cards by protesters in Japan, or the destroying of machines by the British "Luddites" praised by Lord Byron (1816)—"And down with all kings but King Ludd!"[41]

The act of watching another can involve bidirectional data flows, not simply the power imbalance noted by those in the panoptic tradition. Bruce Schneier (2003, 2015) writes of "surveillance theater," in which agents (even if they are unseen) perform a communicative act, often rich in symbolism. Yet, while surveillance agents send messages, they also receive them. The mind and behavior of the subject are not automatically captured by the more powerful agent. An alternative image is "participatory theater," in which the roles of performer and audience shift. Subjects may find it hard to avoid surveillance, but they can have an effect on what is taken in by the agent, as with the performance in figure 6:1. As moral witnesses they are unwittingly provided a stage, as with protest groups performing for the camera and the six o'clock news. As Yar (2003) observes this reverses "the uni-directionality of the gaze, such that the 'guardians of the spectacle' are themselves turned into the objects of moral judgment." The classic example is the martyr seeking social control, not avoiding it.

In some settings information seekers or customers (even when they pay with cash or a credit card) are routinely asked for their phone numbers or e-mail addresses. In response, individuals can refuse to give the requested information, report that they don't have phones or e-mail, or offer to sell or trade the information. This is an assertion of autonomy. It can also prevent agent access to the rich array of personal and census tract data that can be linked to phone numbers and e-mail addresses and correlated with bar-coded purchases.

Refusal can be specific to certain kinds of information. Thus, there is no legal necessity for providing the social security number for private-sector uses; the Privacy Act of 1974 restricts the mandatory collection of social security numbers to a limited number of governmental purposes. Individuals have a vast space in which to just say no to such requests.

As part of the employment process at a large state university, I was asked to sign a form swearing that I was a loyal citizen and supported the laws of the state and country. I also was asked if I had ever belonged to various suspect political groups. While I had not and had not even heard of most of them, the question seemed inconsistent with the First Amendment, which I had just indicated I supported with respect to the laws of the state. With more curiosity than trepidation, I ignored the second question and waited. But as with so much on bureaucratic forms, nothing ever happened.

Requests to participate in public opinion surveys, whether over the phone, in person, or by computer or mail, may be refused. Indeed, considerable evidence indicates that refusal rates for surveys have been increasing.[42] With respect to unwanted phone requests, whether for interviews or sales pitches, one response is to say, "This isn't a good time for me to talk, but if you give me your home phone number I will call you back late tonight."

Refusal may involve feigned participation, meaning that expectations about how the subject is to participate are violated. Consider reporting that one cannot produce a urine sample in spite of repeated efforts, or showing up for a hair drug test with a shaved head. Or, if faced with a surprise drug test, the individual may feign sickness and leave work or fail to report for drug testing if done off site. A person may fill out a form but "forget" to sign it, write illegibly, or withhold permission to access other records.

Offering false information (masking) can also be seen as a subtype of refusal. This can involve checking the wrong column for income or indicating a preference for golf when one's preference is really for cooking. According to some research, 30 percent or more of web site visitors admit providing incorrect information. Changing the spelling of one's name or middle initial permits tracking the solicitation networks through which names are sold because if one receives assorted junk mailing with the same misspelling, the recipient then has an idea who might be distributing their name to mass mailing lists. Misspellings might also serve as a form of resistance that impedes database matching.

Even when participation as a subject is mandatory, if individuals know that surveillance is selective (rather than categorical), they may refuse on the assumption that the chance of being identified is small and the risk worth the gain. Drug smugglers flood borders with many couriers carrying small amounts, knowing that most will get through. In the *sacrificial lamb* approach, smugglers may plan to have a truck carrying drugs stopped as a diversion, knowing the resources focused there are less likely to be applied to trucks just behind.[43]

Many of those who violate rules via refusal do so in the hope that it will not be seen or, if seen, will be ignored. Less common is overt refusal, which denies the legality or legitimacy of the surveillance or makes a narrower claim that it should not apply to the kind of person the subject is.

Such refusal is explicitly political and a direct challenge to the practice ("Just Say Yes"). It need not imply an admission that the subject engages in actions the inquiry seeks to locate.[44] It can instead involve an effort to assert a right. A court's ruling on the legality of the questioned practice may be sought. In such cases, then, instead of deterring, data collection efforts can inspire refusal in those who hope to gain a broader public and legal hearing. As is the case with some civil disobedience, the subject may view refusal as a principled response called forth by conscience, apart from the likelihood that a legal challenge will be successful. This form of refusal can involve opposition to the technique, the goal(s) it seeks, or both.

The First Amendment may be invoked in refusing to answer questions about political activity. Drug tests have been challenged (generally unsuccessfully) as violations of the Fourth Amendment. Those already employed and beyond a probationary period in general have greater legal protections with respect to drug testing and other invasive forms of inquiry than those seeking employment. Federal employees also in general have stronger protections. A few local jurisdictions prohibit on-the-job drug testing in all but critical jobs. Some work contracts may also limit testing. More narrowly, test exemption may be sought because drug use is defined as medically required (e.g., in states where medical use of marijuana is legal) or as religious expression. The collection of bodily emanations may be viewed as a violation of one's religious tenets. And some may refuse to offer DNA samples because of concerns about use.[45]

10. EXPLAINING MOVES

One could say that Henry Ford II was not an adherent of explanatory moves. When he was arrested for drunk driving in Santa Barbara, he supposedly said, "Never complain, never explain." However, an alternative is to account for an unfavorable result by explaining in order to cast doubt upon a tactic, whether broadly or on a particular result, by offering an alternative to official views. Reframing is a common rhetorical tactic.

The fact that many tactics involve inferences offers room for a subject to account for why the inference is wrong. For example, subjects who *piss hot* (a term for a failed drug test in some military and urban circles) may report eating food or taking medications that produce positive results on a drug test. Or they may claim that the test is accurate, but they were unaware that the brownies they ate were baked with marijuana or that they inadvertently drank from a drug-spiked soda.[46] Then there is contamination. Consider the case of a tennis player who convinced a review panel that his positive test for cocaine resulted from kissing a woman in a nightclub (Goetz 2009).

When questioned about a polygraph finding suggesting deception, subjects are advised to have explanations such as "All I can think of is that I've always felt guilty when I'm accused of something. When I was a kid, if my Dad asked me if I had done something bad or a teacher accused me of copying someone else's homework, even if I hadn't, I'd get upset, and I just knew I looked guilty to them." Or "I recently heard that an old childhood friend of mine had died of a drug overdose. . . . I couldn't help thinking of him when you asked me about drug use" (Maschke and Scalabrini 2005, 152–153).

Some alcoholics are said to wear a medical alert medallion for a condition with symptoms similar to drunkenness. Thus, the subject does not question the indicators police use, but rather, the source of the indicators, here redefined as illness. Or doubt may be cast on the machine's validity. In an apocryphal Russian story, a family coming back from a picnic is stopped by police and the driver fails a Breathalyzer test. He protests: "That's impossible, I haven't been drinking. Your machine must be broken. Please try it on my wife." She also fails the test. The man gets even more insistent that the machine is broken and says, "Please try it on my young daughter." She is tested and also fails. At which point the police officer, doubting his own machine, lets the man go. The man later remarks to his wife, "That was really a good idea to let little Anya drink with us."

11. COOPERATING MOVES

Surveillance efforts can be neutralized or undermined if agents come to co-operate or collude with subjects. One of the findings from research on white-collar crime is the frequency of insider perpetration and cooperation with violators beyond the organization. In his pioneering work on white-collar crime, Sutherland (1949) noted that to train a person to be an accountant was to train a potential thief. With their knowledge of and access to control systems, agents are ideally situated to serve a market for illicit services.[47] Or those in positions of power may do this for personal reasons, as in the early days of computerized records, when a police chief simply erased the record of his son's drunk-driving arrest.

In contrast, subjects may secretly cooperate with agents in pursuit of orga-nizational goals. In law enforcement settings, given the varied and dispersed activities to be controlled and legal and policy restrictions, police often need the cooperation of those they are charged with controlling (e.g., Sykes 1971). This can result in *nonenforcement*, as controllers exchange a resource they have for some form of cooperation from the controlled (Marx 1981).

Collusive moves seem particularly characteristic of control systems where agents are poorly motivated or indifferent and feel fatigued and under-rewarded. They also characterize situations where agents come from the same social milieu as their subjects and identify with them. Such factors can lead to the routinization of surveillance, lessened attention, and taking action only when it can't be avoided. Trying to motivate and control first-line surveil-lance agents in low-visibility field settings is a major issue for organizations. McCahill (2002) observes the hesitancy of some mall guards to follow up on minor infractions involving people they know. Tunnell (2004) notes how minimum wage drug testers may be less than vigilant as they settle into their routine work. Smith (2015) offers an ethnographic study of the complexities and challenges of the "reality inspectors" who monitor CCTV.

Beyond empathy, the sharing of goals can support cooperative moves. Thus, an athletic coach may indirectly communicate that a drug test is com-ing. Collusive moves may also be ideologically motivated. Some of the wel-fare workers studied by Gilliom (2001) bent rules and looked the other way in the face of a system they saw as unreasonable. Information from the counter-surveillance moves discussed next may be used to coerce agent cooperation.

12. COUNTERSURVEILLANCE MOVES

Test your government not your urine
> FOUNDER OF A POWDERED URINE COMPANY

Mr. Gallagher, are you that smart?
> WILFORD BRIMLEY TO PAUL NEWMAN IN *ABSENCE OF MALICE*

While there is certainly no equivalence, many surveillance tools are inexpensive, easy to use, and widely available and as such can offer some counterweight to the factors that otherwise favor the more powerful and sustain inequality. Thus, technologies are often appropriated in creative ways that transcend the initial, intended uses (Eglash 2004). This can include redirecting these technologies.

Countersurveillance moves are of a different order from any of those listed above. Those engaged in countersurveillance may use the same tools as agents, and they may do so to record the behavior of agents or their interaction with subjects. Countersurveillance can be a form of discovery, and its results can inform other moves, whether defensively or to coerce cooperation. Here, there is role reversal, as subjects become agents and the watchers become the watched.

Incriminating results may be used to compromise those doing the initial surveillance. Rather than agents flipping a subject, the subject flips the surveillance agent. Agents may be seduced, blackmailed, coerced, or otherwise manipulated by those they watch. Paul Newman offers a stellar example in the film *Absence of Malice* (1981) when he turns the tables on the federal agents who were wrongly investigating him.

If countermeasures uncover questionable practices, which are then publicized, it may lead to their moderation or cessation. Knowing that targets of surveillance may respond in kind and that their documentary record may challenge official accounts can be a factor that limits or inhibits agent behavior.

Dean Wilson and Tanya Serisier (2010) use the term *video activist* to refer to those using video as a tactical tool. Groups such as I-Witness Video (http://iwitnessvideo.info/) and other citizen monitoring groups offer an alternative to official accounts. As with Steve Mann's advocacy of *sousveillance* (see chap. 1, p. 25), these can offer undersight as oversight. Brin (1998) develops the argument for sharing surveillance technology as an accountability device. Video and audio recording, with their miniaturized, remote, battery-operated qualities, are equal opportunity tools and lend themselves well to reciprocated surveillance compared to a tool such as a satellite.[48] Those who use countersurveillance means may offer a view that differs from the view of official sources.

Rodney King's case is well known and was an accidental result of a bystander's possessing a video camera. But such efforts can be made strategically as well. Consider a Jewish Defense League informant (and later defendant) who secretly recorded highly incriminating conversations with his police handler. These came out in court after the police officer committed perjury by denying that he had threatened the informant and then, to his great surprise, heard his tape-recorded threats played back (Dershowitz, Silverglate, Baker 1976). Similarly, independent videographers at the 2004 Republican National Convention in New York City offered documentary evidence which conflicted with police testimony that those arrested had ignored clear warnings to disperse. This contributed to 400 charges against protesters being dismissed or dropped (Dwyer 2005; M. Farrell 2004).

Protesters at that same convention used TXTmob, a cell phone text message broadcast system, as *defensive surveillance* to coordinate protest and avoid arrest. Police location and activity (such as blockades) were documented, and unobstructed escape routes were identified. The developers of this system drew on a predator-prey metaphor in contrasting "stereoscopic and peripheral vision. If surveillance is the predator's gaze (both eyes straight forward), defensive surveillance is the vision of the prey (an eye on each side of the head), like a gazelle that maintains a watchful eye on the lions lying in the tall grass, ready to flee to distant velds at the slightest rustle of the reeds" (Institute for Applied Autonomy 2006, 172).

Agents and subjects alike can make use of the structures and processes within surveillance organizations. Thus, those directly carrying out the surveillance activities are themselves monitored, but they also may use their position to advantage. McCahill (2002, 145) reports a mall guard knowing from his visits to the video control room "where all the blind spots are for when you want to stop and talk." Guards track their supervisors and "take it easy while the operations manager and security manager are off the site." But in some cases, agents may not oppose countersurveillance moves such as videotaping because they feel this can protect them against false accusations (Newburn and Hayman 2001).

Huey (2009) emphasizes a different meaning of countersurveillance in exploring how activists use freedom-of-information laws to learn about government actions. Those studied tended not to see their actions as antisurveillance, and they viewed the term *surveillance* negatively, through its association with covert behavior. Instead, they saw themselves as invoking democratic principles of accountability and transparency. According to Huey's subjects, covert surveillance is to be stopped by political changes, not by mimicking it or by using more powerful technologies.[49]

In summary, the neutralization moves of subjects in all their forms are part of a dynamic system that includes and anticipates the behavior of agents. We turn next to agent counterneutralization moves in response.

Taking off the Shoe: Some Forms of Resistance to the Resistance

The observer, suspecting that what he might have treated as an unwitting move is actually or possibly an obfuscation or misrepresentation, suspecting that what appears to be ingenious in fact could be shot through and through with a gamesman's manipulation and design, suspecting this, he can attempt to crack, pierce, penetrate, and otherwise get behind the apparent facts in order to uncover the real ones. The observer performs an uncovering move.

ERVING GOFFMAN, *Strategic Interaction*

The twelve moves above illustrate how human ingenuity often trumps the machine. In conflict settings the flexible and creative human spirit has some advantages over "dumb" machines with a limited number of programmed responses (at least the first time around). Yet machines can be quick learners, and such responses provoke countermoves as Goffman suggests above.

Neutralization is a dynamic adversarial social dance involving strategic moves, countermoves, and counter-countermoves. It has the quality of an endless chess game mixing old and new moves. Agents respond to subjects' neutralization efforts with their own innovations, which subjects then respond to, and so on. When inequality is not too pronounced, the advantages from technological and other strategic advances are often short lived.

The cat and the mouse continually learn from each other and adjust their behavior in the face of new offensive and defensive means. For example, a trainer of drug testers uses Abby Hoffman and Jonathan Silvers's (1987) book on how to beat drug tests "to find games people play to avoid detection. I use it heavily when doing training to show students what their clients learn from the 'underground.'"

Four broad counters to neutralization can be noted: technological enhancements, the creation of uncertainty through deception and randomization, the use of multiple means, and the creation of new rules and penalties. These strategies can occur independently, but they may overlap, as when a new means is used randomly, supplements a prior means, and is accompanied by penalties for attempting to neutralize.

A common response to neutralization efforts reflects the traditional engineering model of *enhanced technical control* going beyond the initial efforts. Consistent with the new surveillance argument, many counterneutralization technologies have as well become more powerful, penetrating, stronger, broader in reach, and "smarter." Softer techniques are designed to intentionally bypass the subject's knowledge and consent and overcome the natural limits of the senses and the supports the physical environment offers in protecting information. Consider efforts to increase visibility by requiring students to wear uniforms without pockets and transparent backpacks: these are equivalent to efforts to create defensible space (Jeffery 1971; Newman 1972; Crowe 2000; Welsh and Farrington 2009). There has also been defensive hardening of surveillance tools (e.g., armored video cameras that are difficult to destroy).

There are "adulteration detection kits" to test for temperature and distorting and masking substances in the context of drug testing. Some electronic tagging systems now use sound waves to trip an alarm in order to defeat metal-lined shopping bags. For the polygraph, piezoelectric sensor pads placed on the seat or armrests of the polygraph chair or under the subject's feet are marketed as a means of identifying physical countermeasures.

From the subject's perspective, neutralization and strategic advantage are aided by two factors: agents cannot continually scrutinize everyone all the time, and some agent patterns are predictable. Randomization, repetition, and deception are used to overcome these by creating deterrence or the occasional surprise discovery.

When surveillance appears at unpredictable times and places and in unpredictable forms, uncertainty is created and inspections cannot be as easily gamed. Consider the in-depth search of air travelers or those at borders based not on suspicion, but on a table of random numbers. Using multiple means when it is economically viable makes sense, since a single measure may be spoofed or fail to operate properly. Multiple measures provide a backup and may enhance validity. Current means of home-monitoring of those under judicial supervision can involve video inspection, telemetric alcohol tests, and GPS location. Comparing an individual's voice, retinal, fingerprint, facial, or DNA patterns to those in a database, along with requiring the possession of passwords, documents, or typing patterns offers greater security of access.

When agents cannot defeat neutralization via any of the prior strategies, they may adopt new use *rules and penalties* to persuade subjects, control information about tactics, and criminalize activities and artifacts associated with neutralization. Design standards for instruments may be mandated.

Thus, it is difficult to prevent motivated individuals from purchasing radar

detectors and jammers or from using neutralization means before a drug test
or to stop those under judicial supervision from removing electronic monitoring devices or using another car without an ignition interlock. Yet *criminalization moves* may make such behavior less likely for some persons. Some
states have laws prohibiting the production, distribution, and use of products
intended to falsify drug tests.[50] As a result, manufacturers or merchants who
provide materials used for neutralization may be sanctioned, refuse to sell or
ship to jurisdictions where a product is banned, or add disclaimers.[51] Some
workplaces bar employees from the blocking response of encrypting their
private e-mail and phone communications. The US government has tried to
ban forms of encryption that it did not control and encouraged organizations
to voluntarily adopt a government-provided encryption standard.

Individual and Group Resistance

What are the connections between the individual strategic forms considered
in these chapters and nonstrategic expressions of protest where the goal is
to make a statement and express feelings, rather than to directly stop the
surveillance? Are they alternatives or complementary? Are individual acts
of neutralization intended to advance personal goals also "political" in some
broader sense? Or, in that they may primarily be a means of letting off steam
rather than directly challenging policies, do they ironically support the
status quo?[52]

If we differentiate attitudes from behavior and accepting from resisting
responses (and ignore ambivalence and fluidity), we have a picture that includes four types of response for any given tool (table 6.3). Included in this

TABLE 6.3. Attitudinal and behavioral responses

1. True conformists	Persons who attitudinally and behaviorally accept the surveillance
2. Intimidated (or at least lacking resources or will for neutralization) conformists	Persons who attitudinally reject but behaviorally accept the surveillance
3. Reluctant rebels	Persons who attitudinally accept but behaviorally reject the surveillance (e.g., under peer pressure)
4. Rebels:	
a. True rebels	Persons who attitudinally reject the surveillance and overtly try to neutralize it
b. Closet rebels	Persons who attitudinally reject the surveillance and covertly try to neutralize it

picture could be a measure—termed *neutralization slack*—which captures the size of the gap between the availability of resistance means and their use and offers a way to empirically document variation. Chapter 14 discusses the related concept of *surveillance slack*—a variable reflecting the size of the gap between the availability of a surveillance tool and the extent of its utilization. The two measures intertwine, and they also probably move in the same direction.[53]

Among factors contributing to neutralization slack (where the desire to neutralize is present) may be intimidation and a non-risk-taking orientation. The gap can also reflect deference to authority, politeness, a conflict-avoidance orientation, fear of sanctioning or denial of service, lack of knowledge or resources for neutralization, and exaggerated beliefs about the power of surveillance.

Table 6.3 refers to subjects of surveillance. A related table could be created for surveillance agents as well, to show the variety of their attitudinal and behavioral responses—varying from *loyal agents*, who believe in what they do and do it conscientiously; to *ritualists*, who do not believe in what they are doing but need the work; to *closet rebels*, who perform with indifference and even covert cooperation with subjects.[54] A surveillance agent as *true rebel* is rare and will probably be out of a job if discovered.

Cultures of Surveillance

This chapter has focused on classifying and illustrating the *behavior* of subjects and agents. Yet both neutralization and the efforts of surveillance agents occur within a sea of *beliefs* and justifications constituting the culture of surveillance. For subjects, misguided beliefs about the efficacy of their actions (e.g., rubbing lemon juice on one's face to make it invisible, defeating a hair drug test by shampoo, rubbing fingers with sandpaper to mask prints) illustrate *the myth of neutralization* propagated via folklore and vendors.

The corollary for agents is *the myth of surveillance,*—rhetorical excesses involving perceptions of need (whether consumption or fear based) and undocumented assertions regarding the power and efficacy of the technique. Just what works (and how that is defined) and under what conditions and with what consequences is insufficiently subjected to peer-reviewed scientific inquiry (e.g., the polygraph and voice stress analysis, drug testing and many sophisticated data mining, matching ,profiling, searching and inspection techniques).

Beyond efficacy, the culture of surveillance offers justifications for both supporting and opposing surveillance-related behavior (see chapter 13 on ethics). Culture further instructs in how to think and feel about watching and being watched—whether messages are offered formally or informally, directly or indirectly. The next four chapters are concerned with how the culture of surveillance is represented and communicated through fictional scenarios involving work, children, a voyeur and a police/national security agent.

PART 3

Culture and Contexts

It's too bad for us "literary" enthusiasts, but it's the truth nevertheless—pictures tell any story more effectively than words.

W. MARSTON MOULTON, creator of Wonder Woman and pioneer inventor of the polygraph

Every joke is a small revolution.

GEORGE ORWELL

The two prior units on structure and process relied on language in presenting facts and argument. In contrast, the emphasis in this unit is on satirical stories. Stories along with images and music are one component of the culture of surveillance that so infuses our minds and everyday life. The symbolic materials and meanings of culture are social fabrications (though not necessarily social deceptions). They speak to (and may be intended to create or manipulate) needs, aspirations, and fears. Culture communicates meaning and can express (as well as shape) the shared concerns of a given time period and place. Surveillance technology is not simply applied; it is also *experienced* by agents, subjects, and audiences who define, judge, and have feelings about being watched or a watcher. Our ideas and feelings about surveillance are somewhat independent of the technology per se.

In the original version of the book I divided the cultural materials into two units. The first dealt with stories that can be told about surveillance. The second unit was to deal with surveillance in popular culture and had chapters on lyrics and cartoons, illustrations, advertisements, and art.[1] Unfortunately these chapters were cut because of space limitations, although some images were salvaged to illustrate some of the book's themes.

This unit offers fictional stories as case studies. These involve surveillance used by an employer, parent, voyeur, and government. Each raises distinct issues. Rather than offering new empirical research or taking a piecemeal approach, I have chosen to base my case studies on imagined but realistic accounts drawing from the empirical material at hand. Thus, the narrative chapters in part 3 are in one sense fiction, as was the case with the National Séance Foundation research described in chapter 5.

I chose this approach partly out of resource constraints, but even more because no real world case study would be likely to contain all the elements that are worthy of consideration. For example, a single case involving voyeurism and victims of surveillance would be unlikely to demonstrate the range of tools available to the voyeur. And a case study of any one technology in isolation from other tools and contexts may not seem particularly striking. Also, we can make comparisons to earlier technologies (e.g., before people tapped into computers, they tapped phones, and before that, they intercepted telegraph messages, and before that, they secretly read others' mail), but this numbs the novelty, as what is noteworthy about the new surveillance is its totality and rapid speed (both in diffusion and in operation). Tom Voire (chaps. 9 and 10) for example, is the agent or subject of the enormous number of new (and old) surveillance techniques that were available early in the twenty-first century (particularly in a longer, earlier version available at press.uchicago .edu/sites/marx/). Rocky Bottom's border-blurring career (chap. 11) illustrates many current social processes and links between the public and private that a focus on a given case or tool would miss.

For my integrative, synthetic, comparative, and issue-raising purposes, the quasi-fictional piling-on of techniques offers a convenient way to engage the breadth of the issues and to solder the discrete multiple empirical strands into a sculpture. As with other artistic renderings, these fiction chapters convey the subjective sense of being a watcher and of being watched, including the emotional wallop that persons may feel when they discover they are the subject of surveillance, as well as the powerful attraction exerted by secret knowledge.

These accounts do not reflect an unrestrained dystopian imagination under the influence of some formally banned hallucinogenic at 3 a.m. Unlike the imaginative darkness of much science fiction, these stories are reality based. As with the "dark scenarios" illustrating potential problems with ambient intelligence or ubiquitous computing (Wright et al. 2010), these fantasies involve a technology check and a plausibility check. The former asks whether the technologies in the stories are realistic, given current and emerging knowledge and technique. The latter asks whether equivalent incidents have actually occurred or are likely to occur. I intend the speculation represented in these chapters to have a realistic quality absent in much science fiction involving technologies that might someday be developed and things that might happen if such development were to occur.

Some science-focused readers may dismiss these chapters as fabrications. Language offers multiple meanings to words such as *fabricate*, which means both "to construct" and "to concoct," and "to forge, shape, and invent." Some constructions are clearly false, as in disingenuous fabrications; others are accounts forged out of actual events that, while fabricated, are authentic in the color, feel, descriptions, and issues they provide.[2]

An account or construction may be fiction in multiple ways. One involves lies, deception, hoax, fraud, and distortion, in which a person claims that something happened, but it did not in fact happen. When caught, scientists and journalists get a bad name for passing off fiction as fact.

In contrast, conventional fiction acknowledges that it is imaginary and makes no necessary claim to direct correspondence to a particular empirical entity. An intermediate case is the roman à clef, which involves real persons under invented names, taking varying degrees of liberty with actual occurrences.

Another type of fiction well known to the social scientist is the ideal type, as suggested by Max Weber (Weber 1958). This ideal type makes a greater claim as to its reality, even if in its pure form it cannot be literally found.[3] It is a synthetic mental construct emerging from the empirical, yet going beyond it to distill the central features of the phenomena in its purest form.

My goal in these chapters is to capture the essence of several types of context and their associated behaviors and rationales. As noted, these include settings where the 3 Cs—contracts, care, or coercion—are a central factor or (apart from any of these per se) where personal information is easily available. These settings and behaviors are illustrated through ideal-type case studies of a work organization, a social movement to protect children, a voyeur, and a surveillance entrepreneur whose career and modes merge the lines between government and the private sector.

The Omniscient Organization (chap. 7), Parents Insist on Surveillance Help Inc. (chap. 8), Tom I. Voire (chaps. 9 and 10), and Rocky Bottoms (chap. 11) are fiction because they are not "embodied." Nor are they copies. They represent a composite of the empirical and seek to capture essential objective and subjective features of watching and being watched. The question is not whether it really happened this way, but whether it happens this way or is the trend, and whether the accounts are useful in capturing the central features of the phenomena and in permitting contrasts to other forms.

While the scenarios offered are fiction, they are to be judged by a standard of verisimilitude that need not burden the novel. A composite account might be true even if it could not be empirically accurate. While the events in these chapters did not occur together at the imaginary times and places described, they could happen. They may be fiction, but they are not quite science fiction. The line between fiction and reality can be fluid, and these chapters represent intentional genre blurring. The complexity of the situation made me do it. While I have taken some leeway, most of the substance and many direct quotes are from my observations, interviews, and reading.

Fiction can help us avoid what Mark Twain (1984) referred to as the "impressive incomprehensibility" of many scientific and legal treatises. Thus, fiction informed by reality can supplement our conventional approaches. And perhaps by sparking thought, it can help shape emerging social worlds. What terms would we now use if Orwell had not written *1984*, and would awareness be as acute?

These chapters are both docudrama and mockudrama, and, as mockudrama, they embody the qualities of satire. The author who does not clearly make this claim risks having the work degenerate into propaganda. Even so, in these chapters, I have felt the tension between my scholarly need for accuracy, balance, fairness, logic, and depth and the requisites of provocative satire and fiction. Education needn't be entertaining, but neither should the solemnity of the academy preclude its being entertaining.

In writing fiction and stooping to satire, an author risks being taken too seriously or not seriously enough. Satire can succeed in being convincing but fail in not being seen as satire. The danger for a social scientist in mixing fact and fiction is that some readers will assume that the situations described are real in the literal sense, rather than being real in the ideal-typical sense of representations of things in, or potentially in, the world. At the other extreme, some readers will dismiss it all precisely because it isn't "real" as in literal.[4]

My feelings were mixed when some readers, seeing earlier versions of the pieces included in these chapters (Marx 1987, 1990) wrote and wanted to know where they could purchase the control technologies to regulate bathroom behavior and sought the address of the nonexistent Omniscient Organization described in chapter 7.

A few years after that, in a moment of aging indiscretion, I had the temerity to offer thirty-seven moral mandates for aspiring social scientists (Marx 1997). I urged greater attention to writing and argued for new ways of communicating. I also suggested that researchers should have more fun. Drawing again from Weber (1958), I argued for social inquiry as a vacation as well as a vocation. Life is short, and the stuff many of us study is depressing and tragic. Humor not only alleviates stress, it affords unique insights by pointing out cultural contradictions (Murray Davis 1993). Having a store of information built up from studying the topic of surveillance for several decades, I didn't have to do any new research. I simply thought about the topics, and the fictional cases in the following chapters flowed out.

Satirical fiction can offer additional advantages as a way of knowing and communicating about the social world. As important as traditional system-atic data and theory are, they usually lose the nonspecialist reader. Ernest Hemingway advises the writer to show rather than to tell. But the scholar should not be forced to choose. The affectivity of art, whether in the form of narrative writing, visual images, or music, may enhance the effective compre-hension of the topic. We understand some things noncognitively, and passion can fuel the effort to cognitively understand.

Satire is a marvelous device for communicating about the ironic and para-doxical aspects of social reality. I think our legal and social methods courses would do well to train students in writing reality-grounded fiction and in the uses of irony, parables, satire, and humor.[5] Quantitative analysis includes the well-established fictional tradition of using simulated data. It is more than time to develop an equivalent tradition for qualitative work.

Work: The Omniscient Organization
Measures Everything That Moves

I measure everything that moves.
BANK OF AMERICA EXECUTIVE

Nothing is accidental. Everything has a purpose.
SCIEXPLAN INC. EXECUTIVE ON THE DESIGN OF
DOMINION-SWANN

The new surveillance and conflicts over it are prominent in many work environments. For example, the executive quoted above uses two hundred criteria to assess workers in his credit card division. He also measures a lot that
doesn't move. Such environments are one of the four major surveillance contexts I emphasize in this book. Organizational work settings involve rational
means-ends applications and are based on formal, impersonal, quasi-public,
hierarchical, vertical, and nonreciprocal surveillance among parties who
have some shared interests and some conflicting ones. These rest on contractual relations that typically are supported by coercion from the law and the
unequal power and resources of the parties in the background.

Many issues that surround surveillance at work are illustrated in manufacturing an excerpt from the fictitious Dominion-Swann (DS) Industries'
Employee Handbook.[1] DS is a $1 billion diversified company involved in
manufacturing electrical components for automobiles. The handbook was
prepared by the corporate director of personnel, in consultation with the human resource management firm SciexPlan Inc. and the environmental design
firm Enviro-Con. The handbook reflects an ideal-type Brave (or Cowardly?)
New World workplace. While no such company exists in our real world, the
statement provides a composite of behavior and ideas that can be seen in
many work settings, if rarely taken to this extreme or found all together.[2] The
Dilbert cartoon (fig. 7.1) suggesting the parallels between the workplace and
the prison is illustrative. The satiric handbook statement illustrates many of
the techno-fallacies discussed in chapter 12.

FIGURE 7.1. Omniscient organizations and prisons. (DILBERT © 1995 Scott Adams. Used by permission of UNIVERSAL UCLICK. All rights reserved.)

Dominion-Swann's New Workplace: Hope for Industry through Technology

We are a technology-based company that respects our employees, whose knowledge is the core of the technological enterprise. We value honesty, informed consent, and unfettered scientific inquiry. Our employees, in turn, understand company strategy. They are free to suggest ways to improve our performance. We offer handsome rewards for high productivity and vigorous participation in the life of our company. Committed to science, we believe in careful experimentation and in learning from experience. We also believe in learning from history and our globalized world. As the man said, "We must hang together, or we will surely hang apart." We all must sacrifice for the common good to keep our company strong.

At DS five principles underlie our work support restructuring and current environment:

1. Make the company a home to employees. Break down artificial and alienating barriers between work and home. Dissolve, through company initiative, feelings of isolation. Great companies are made by great people; all employee behavior and self-development counts.

2. Hire people who will make a continuing contribution. Bring in healthy people who are likely to stay healthy so they can be on the job without frequent absences and therefore make a successful contribution. To help us in the hiring process we try to get to know prospective employees in depth. By getting to know our employees, we have a good idea about their future success and productivity. This allow us to build our company with competent and motivated employees (and exclude those better suited to work elsewhere).

3. Use technology-based management solutions, as they are preferable to old-style supervision and persuasion. Machines are not only less expensive, but fairer and more reliable than human managers. Employees want to do the right thing; the

company wants nothing but this and will give employees all the needed technical assistance. Employees accept performance evaluation from an impartial system more readily than from a potentially biased traditional superior and appreciate technical solutions that channel behavior in a constructive direction.

4. Create accountability through visibility and uncertainty about when you will be monitored. Loyal employees enjoy the loyalty of others. They welcome audits, reasonable monitoring, and helpful suggestions based on documentary proof of their activities, whether of location, business conversations, output, or lifestyle. Once identified, good behavior can be rewarded; inappropriate behavior can be improved. When expectations are clear and easily measured, self-control—the best control—takes over.

5. Create (or in a sense re-create) the protective womb of the company town and store that were so important to early US industrialization and economic growth. But create this world without the traditional geographic limitations or coercion. Our clean information technologies offer (a) online shopping (with great discounts provided to valuable employees as a result of DS buying power and commercial savvy, deducted automatically from paychecks so employees no longer need worry about credit cards, identity theft, or high interest rates), (b) health monitoring, (c) day care scheduling and monitoring, and (d) voting guides and recommendations that create the right political and economic environment to advance employer-employee shared values in a winning political environment.

These principles have yielded an evolving program that continues to benefit from the participation and suggestions of our employees. The personnel office will be pleased to discuss any aspect of community performance or breaches of company policy in detail with employees. Our program in brief:

ENTRY-LEVEL SCREENING

As a matter of course and for mutual benefit, potential employees are screened and tested. We want to avoid hiring people whose predictive profile—including medications, smoking, obesity, debt, high-risk sports, and family crises—suggests that they will be unhappy here and could undermine our community's productivity in the future. We test for thirty-nine different behavioral, cognitive, and cultural traits. We have algorithms that strongly predict the best fit between you and the requisites of the job. We continue to track and crunch data once you are hired to gain insight into your current life situation and to help with placements, promotions, and transfers.

Because we are such an attractive employer, job applicants volunteer to undergo extensive medical and psychological examinations and to provide the company with detailed personal information and records, including background information about the health, lifestyle, and employment of parents, spouses, siblings, and close friends. Company associates seek permission to make discreet searches of various databases, including those related to education, credit, bankruptcy and mortgage default, auto accidents, driver's license suspensions, insurance, health, worker's compensation, military service, rental history, arrest records, and criminal activity. We also use a resume verification service. We continue throughout the course of employment to search widely, if less frequently or intensively, than when you were first hired. When using DS-provided smartphones and tablets, employees provide us with their log-on names and passwords for all their electronic communication—whether at or away from work. This is for your and our protection. We treat this information with the utmost respect and privacy. As a valued employee of this company you are a part of us and we are a part of you. We need to be sure that the positive image and high regard of our company is maintained in order for us and for you to be successful.

When we identify an employee we'd like to hire who has a major deficiency precluding employment, we say, "Let's work together to solve the problem." That's the kind of company we are. Take the case of Ms. Mildred Schmalts now working as a valued systems analyst and volunteering as a peer-to-peer weight counselor. When she applied for employment her height/weight ratios did not meet our standards (like many other companies, and as is our legal right, we will not hire obese employees). Yet we knew she could do the job well—today—but we were concerned about what our predictive model said about her future performance and health. She gladly accepted our offer of employment contingent on her losing fifty pounds and was pleased (and surprised) by our offer to pay for her weight loss program. Or consider the opportunity we gave Mr. Frankie Machine, part-time drummer and now a trusted member of our security team and a volunteer in a substance abuse program. He states, "I was a daily dope smoker before I started working here. I'm glad the test showed positive. It was a wake up call. The company gave me a choice—break the habit with our help and we will give you a job. I did and they did."

The company opposes racial and sexual discrimination. And DS does not concern itself with the political ideology or activities of potential employees. Thus, it will not check databases containing the names of union organizers or those active in controversial political causes (whether on the right or the left). Should the company's inquiry unwittingly turn up such information, it is ignored.

Since our community is made up of people, not machines, we have found it useful to compare physiological, psychological, social, and demographic factors of applicants against the profiles of our best employees. Much of this analysis has been standardized. It is run by SciexPlan's expert systems, INDUCT and DEDUCT.

COMMUNITY HEALTH

We want employees who are willing to spend their lives with the company, and we care about their long-term health. Thus, the company administers monthly pulmonary tests to support the zero-tolerance smoking policy. Zero tolerance means lower health insurance premiums and improved quality of life for all employees.

In cooperation with Standar-Hardwick, one of the United States' most advanced makers of medical equipment and a valued customer, we've developed an automated health monitor. These new machines, used in a private stall and activated by employee thumbprint, permit biweekly urine analysis and a variety of other tests (blood pressure, pulse, temperature, weight) without having to go to a health facility. This program has received international attention: at times, it has been hailed; at times, severely criticized. People at DS often express surprise at the fuss. Regular monitoring of urine means early warning against diabetes and other potentially catastrophic diseases; it also reveals early pregnancy. In sum, this program allows us to keep a drug-free, safe environment without subjecting people to the indignities of random testing or the presence of an observer.

THE QUALITY ENVIRONMENT

Drawing on SciexPlan's research, our company believes that the physical environment is key to wellness and productivity. Fragrant aromas such as evergreen may reduce stress; the smell of lemon and jasmine can have a rejuvenating effect. Thus, these scents are introduced to all work spaces through the air-conditioning and heating systems. Scents are changed seasonally.

Music is not only enjoyable; it can also affect productivity Thus, we continually experiment with the impact of different styles of music on an office's or plant's aggregate output. Since psychologists have taught us that the most serious threat to safety and productivity is stress, we use subliminal messages in music, such as "Safety pays," "Work rapidly but carefully," and "This company cares." Personal computers deliver visual subliminals such as "My world is calm" or "We're all on the same team." In some units, to help you locate how well you and your team are doing, timely notices appear comparing your output with that of other individuals or teams.

At the start of each month, employees are advised of message content. Those who don't want a message on their computers may request that none be transmitted—no questions asked (but of necessity a record gets generated so the transmission can be blocked). However, it must be said that on the whole, employees who participate in the program feel noticeably more positive about their work. For home use, employees may also borrow subliminal tapes that help improve memory, reduce stress, improve self-confidence, and aid in weight loss. On the advice of SciexPlan's dietitians, the company cafeteria and dining room serve only fresh, wholesome food prepared without salt or cholesterol-producing substances. However because we believe in balance and know how popular they are, sugar- and caffeine-based high-energy snacks and beverages are available during breaks, at no cost to employees. The company market will also arrange for delivery of groceries and prepared food to your home. There is no need to pay out of pocket. We keep the tab and deduct it from your paycheck, offering rebates for healthy purchases.

WORK MONITORING

Monitoring system performance is our business. The same technologies we use to make engine components that run at peak efficiency can keep our company running efficiently too. That is the double excitement of the information revolution.

At DS, we access more than two hundred criteria to assess productivity of plant employees and data entry personnel. These criteria include such things as keystroke activity, the number of errors and corrections made, the pressure on the assembly tool, the speed of work, and time away from the job. Reasonable productivity standards have been established. We are proud to say that with a younger workforce, these standards keep going up, and the incentive pay of employees who exceed standards is rising proportionately.

Our work units are divided into teams, and we have learned that the best motivator is the high standards of one's peers. Teams, not individuals, earn prizes and bonuses. Winning teams have the satisfaction of knowing they are doing more than their share. Thus, computer screens abound with productivity updates, encouraging employees to note where their teams stand and how productive individuals have been for the hour, week, and month. Computers send congratulatory messages such as "You are working 10 percent faster than the norm" or concern messages such as "You are lowering the team average."

COMMUNITY MORALE

Any community must take reasonable precautions to protect itself from dishonesty. Just as we inspect the briefcases and purses of visitors entering and exiting our R&D division, we reserve the right to call up and inspect without notice all data files and observe work in progress currently displayed on employees' screens. One random search discovered a disloyal employee who was using the company computer to send out a resume to a different employer. Another search uncovered an employee who was running a football pool. We use software that blocks inappropriate numbers such as dial-a-joke. Like all of our competitors, we monitor all phone and e-mail activity for your protection (e.g., a documentary record protects you and us from false claims).

Video and audio surveillance too protect employees from intruders in hallways, parking lots, lounges, and work areas. Vigilance is invaluable in protecting our community from illegal behavior or actions that violate our safety and high commitment to excellence. All employees, including managers, check in and out of various workstations—including the parking lot, main entrance, elevator, floors, office, and even the bathroom—by means of an all-purpose (credit card, health data, communications and entry) tool. In one case, this careful surveillance saved the life of an employee who had a heart attack in the parking lot: when he failed to check into the next workstation after five minutes, security personnel were sent to investigate. This device can be worn around the neck or carried in a pocket. Because we know our employees are unique and because we value each person's right to choose, the design on the tool comes in a variety of colors and can be personalized to your specifications. To save time and insure against loss or theft of ID, we also offer the much heralded ImplaDerm © chip. You have a choice (it's your arm, after all), but to show our appreciation, we offer a $1,000 incentive and free maintenance to those who are fully ready to embrace the twenty-first century. Our dermatologist will also remove unwanted tattoos during the same appointment.

BEYOND ISOLATION

Our program takes advantage of the most advanced telecommunications equipment to bind employees to one another and to the company. Thus, DS vehicles are equipped with onboard computers using satellite transponders that enable a tracking service and additional two-way communication. This technology keeps inventories down and helps prevent hijacking, car theft, and improper use of vehicles. Drivers save time, since engines are checked electronically. They also drive more safely, and vehicles are better maintained, since speed, gear shifts, and idling time are continuously monitored.

Instant communication is vital in today's international economy. The global market does not function only from 9 to 5. Periodic disruptions to vacations or sleep are a small price to pay for the tremendous gains to be won in worldwide competition. DS employees share in these gains. Whether stationary or ambulatory, employees must be constantly reachable—company provided communications devices must never be turned off.

Great companies have always unleashed the power of new technology for social well-being, even in the face of criticism. During the first Industrial Revolution, such beloved novelists as Charles Dickens sincerely opposed the strictures of mass production. In time, however, most of the employees who benefited from the wealth created by new factories and machines came to take progress for granted and preferred the modem factory to traditional craft methods. Today we are living through a second Revolution, driven by the computer and the humane insights from social science research. Advanced work support technology is democratic, effective, and antihierarchical. DS's balance sheet and the long waiting list of prospective employees indicate how the new program has helped everybody win. If the journalist Lincoln Steffens were here, he might well say, "I have been over into the future and it works." No small part of that is because of the early use to which we put big data ("little things mean a lot") in our pathbreaking human analytics algorithm programs. At DS the correlation is king!

Mr. Porter Square III, Dominion-Swan's Director of Talent Acquisition and Assessment from Human Resources: responds to questions we often hear:

Why do you measure and monitor so much?

We generally have little choice, whether as a result of the law, insurers, or our competition. To receive government contracts we must drug test and do extensive (and continuing) background checks. To be insured we must meet security requirements (including video, secure entries, and the licensing and bonding of many categories of employee).

Careful documentation of company activities helps show that we fully comply with laws and government regulations, and it helps us avoid costly fines and litigation (e.g., over negligent hiring) and challenges from stockholders over putting worthwhile, but secondary, values such as social responsibility, above profit making.

Finally, if we are to stay competitive we must monitor intensively and extensively because our US competitors do this. It is a sad fact of modern life that the lowest common denominator drives the bottom line. We also must continually find ways to be more efficient and productive if we are to compete with those in poorer countries that have few health and safety requirements and offer no employee benefits. Our high-tech solutions that measure it all are the only defense.

What's in it for me?

A lot! First, it's for your own good: it keeps the company in business, and without that, there is no job. The company business plan is defined by the need to maximize our competitive advantage. We are a profit-making organization, not a safe haven for the guilty, a spoils system for friends, or a charity for the lazy. Second, our system protects you from abuses by fellow workers and supervisors (yes, a few bad apples do get hired by mistake, but they don't last long). Video and audio recordings, drug testing, and access controls are there to protect you from being a crime victim and from false accusations. If a problem surfaces, we find it immediately, without requiring employees to spy on each other or us to suspect everyone. Surveillance honors that bedrock American principle of a fair day's work for a fair day's pay. You (and your work group) are compensated for how well and how much you produce, based on continuously revised scientific algorithms.

I haven't done anything wrong. Why do your practices make me feel like I have?

You may feel that way in the beginning, until you come to understand our company's culture. It's all about the learning curve and what the highbrows call "normalization." Our practices are based on the assumption that you are not guilty of anything and therefore are entitled to every opportunity to demonstrate that—hence our monitoring. Those who question our authority with respect to these personnel practices might inadvertently protect those who shouldn't be working here and hurt those who should, also alerting us that the questioner may be hiding something we need to know about.

What if I refuse to accept some of the company's surveillance?

That is certainly your right. In the rare instances when it turns out that we need to take some exceptionable search measures, you will simply be asked to sign a waiver granting us permission to do this. You don't *have* to sign but imagine what kind of a statement it makes if you don't. But it all comes down to the terms of our mutual contract. We value independence and personal choice. But basic fairness requires that you respect our choices as well. Corporations have rights too. If you don't like our policies, we are free not to hire you, and you are free not to work here. That is what makes America a great country—contracts based on *choice*, not coercion or some presocial sentiments like care or altruism that sound good but will quickly bankrupt a company. Our workers can vote with their feet. You actually have the upper hand here, and we know it! It is easier for you to quit than for us to fire you. However, complying with our policies shows that you are a "team player" and support other team players who participate without question. We are family. There is no I in team.

Why don't you just contact the job candidate's prior employer?

Good question. We wish we could, but we must do our own extensive testing and investigations because privacy laws and employer concerns over being sued have made it almost impossible to learn anything truthful about an applicant from a previous employer, other than to verify dates of employment and salary. A legal department requires bland assessments to protect the organization against defamation suits. Current legislation also prohibits some of the preemployment testing and questioning we previously did. For example, it is now illegal to use the polygraph as a hiring tool and to ask certain questions about health and marital status and some lifestyle elements (see, for example, copies of the Employee Polygraph Protection Act of 1988 and the Americans with Disabilities Act available in our library). These restrictions require us to find other legal ways to learn what we need to know to make the best decisions.

Is it true that employees are prohibited from riding motorcycles, hang gliding, and high-cholesterol diets?

Of course not. Recreation is important, and so is your freedom to choose. But just as we keep you informed about the company, the company needs to be informed about you. If you prefer such activities, you will pay higher insurance premiums. One reason why so many of our employees are fit and trim is that they receive annual bonuses for healthy living, as well as lowered premiums. However, we do draw the line at the use of illegal drugs because they are illegal, not because we want to tell you how to live your life away from the job.

Is it true that all employees must attend church services?

No! We do however ask that all employees attend nondenominational, team-building meetings once a month. Yes, attendance is taken. However a list is not kept of those wearing earplugs or using electronic devices during the inspirational messages, and *all* attendees are entitled to the refreshments and highly coveted gifts (such as T-shirts, caps, and tote bags with our logo) occasionally distributed at the end of a meeting.

Is there an employee's union?

That's such a twentieth-century question! With our company's success and philosophy of worker empowerment through information and sharing, you don't need one. We all have the same interests at heart. The age of the master-servant work relationship went out centuries ago! Of course workers need to be heard. We listen and even sponsor an employees' association that can elect its own leaders and use our corporate facilities with complete confidentiality (no monitoring!). We cooperate fully with the employee's association, especially in planning for holiday parties and in decisions about office decor and recreation equipment. We also support employee activity in nonpartisan charitable and political groups. You can earn comp time for volunteering in groups dedicated to creating a healthy environment so that companies like ours thrive. A list of approved groups is available. We realize that people hold different opinions on the issues of the day, but given our commitment to a peaceful, conflict-free work setting, the job is not the place to express them. To ensure such an environment we prohibit wearing attire, hats, or buttons reflecting political issues, and tattoos must be covered.

> **Aren't some of your policies pretty unusual and even "far out"?**
>
> Yes, that's what makes us a great corporation and why we are consistently rated at the very top of Fortune 500 companies on factors such as predictability, profitability, employee satisfaction, and cleanliness. Innovation is never easy and often requires adjustments and (the good news for you) incentives. We realize some of our policies have not yet become the industry standard, but that was said of the eight-hour day and laws against child labor as well. To help usher in the new normalcy, some of our programs are voluntary, and we offer rewards for participation, as with the chip implant and our zero-dependence policy. We build surveillance into routine activities. You won't even notice it after a while.

Contemporary Work Surveillance

Dominion-Swan, as an "omniscient organization," captures the essential features of the new surveillance in a major social setting where contracts play a key role. Information discovery is the little engine that said, "I know I can." Indeed, work environments increasingly create information floods, as technology blurs, weakens, or eliminates traditional boundaries and gives new meaning to the heretofore meaningless.

The explosion in the ability to collect, store, retrieve, combine, share, and analyze personal information is particularly strong in work settings, given competitive and productivity pressures and the less balanced labor-management playing fields of the United States.

The extent and form of monitoring of course vary greatly, depending on the state of the economy, cultural traditions, type of work, and worker.[3] I next consider some of those variations, particularly the social correlates of more intensive work monitoring, and then examine some links between the rhetoric and reality and factors that inhibit the full unleashing of the technology, as well as some unanticipated consequences that can accompany it.

The extreme forms of work monitoring are more prevalent in non-unionized settings that disproportionately employ unskilled workers, females, minorities, and immigrants in repetitive tasks that can be easily measured. Rather than the golden handcuffs of the Omniscient Organization, these workers are in iron handcuffs. Monitoring in the private sector is far less restrained than in the public sector, where the Bill of Rights and other federal legislation apply. A weak economy, pressures from competitors, and an abundance of workers seeking jobs supports more intensive surveillance, while the opposite conditions may result in diluted or ignored surveillance results.

A large proportion of employees in telecommunications, data processing, insurance, banking, and casinos are subject to electronic monitoring. In such settings information technology can be a central feature of the work product and of its control. The extensive and intensive monitoring is also found where the risks of failure can be catastrophic (e.g., nuclear power plants, airlines) and where the opportunity structures for misbehavior are plentiful and the need for legitimacy is high, as with those who work in government in contexts such as law enforcement and national security.

The new forms of monitoring, however, extend beyond employees who work directly with information technology, who lack power, or who face grave risks in their work. Drivers, waiters, and hotel maids (whose handheld computers remotely transmit information on their activities), as well as white-collar groups such as lawyers, stockbrokers, nurses, doctors, architects, and even professors increasingly face electronic monitoring.

Surveillance Unbound: Some Questions

The expanding of the supervisory gaze may have a variety of unintended and unanticipated consequences. While these are seen across settings, they are particularly clear in the work context. The rest of this chapter (along with chaps. 12 and 13), while not quite a rejoinder, could have been written by an independent consultant called in to evaluate the Omniscient Organization model.[4] The discussion below considers some techno-fallacy issues seen across surveillance contexts which are particularly well illustrated by controversies at work such as issues of monitoring by humans versus machines, equity, and an overabundance of data.

RHETORIC AND REALITY

Amid the chorus of entrepreneurs offering monitoring solutions and journalists delivering instant answers, it is easy to confuse the rhetoric with the reality of new technologies and to ignore unwanted consequences. While rhetoric can (and should) be analyzed on its own terms as a type of cultural data, it also requires empirical evidence.

One intriguing aspect of this topic is that in spite of the ethos of rational and scientific measurement as applied to workers and the industrial process, many of the new forms of monitoring have not been systematically evaluated. We cannot say with much certainty what the impacts are or, better, under what conditions different impacts are likely. The evidence supportive of strong and comprehensive technically based selection and monitoring practices seen in the United States is hardly overwhelming. In fact, there are good reasons to suspect that unrestrained monitoring can be counterproductive.

Drug testing nicely illustrates this. The reliability and validity of the tests, and the consequences of drug testing and use on employee performance have not been adequately studied, given how prevalent drug testing is. The research supporting the claims of advocates is underwhelming. Testing seems more driven by government and insurance requirements and public relations than by evidence that it is needed or cost effective (apart from areas such as emergency services, security, and transportation).

Given the vast expenditures on other forms of monitoring, it is striking that we have so little analysis of whether its claimed benefits are real. A study by the American Management Association, which asked whether its members collected statistical evidence showing that testing reduced absenteeism, accidents, disability claims, theft, and violence in their companies, found that only 10 percent reported such evidence (American Management Association 1996). The point here is that a possible negative impact on workers' physical and mental well-being may cancel out profits from supposed increased efficiency as a result of monitoring. We must ask: are there conditions under which monitoring is a cause of problems rather than a solution?

If monitoring were as effective as proponents claim, we would expect to see it widely adopted among industrial countries. Unlike mass production techniques, which quickly spread worldwide, some of the kinds of work monitoring recently appearing in the United States, such as drug testing, have not spread to the same degree (International Labor Office 1993a, 1993b; Wood 1996).

Some monitoring clearly has a fad-like, novel quality and reflects intuitive appeal or surface plausibility (one of the techno-fallacies identified in chap. 12). The symbolic goal here may be to communicate about corporate omniscience and monumentality. From this perspective, whether it truly works or not is irrelevant; the result is that employees and others may believe it works and feel humbled and in awe of the power of the organization. That of course can be risky if it is demonstrated that it doesn't work or has unwanted consequences.

As a result of varying work contexts, cultures, personalities, needs, and expectations, sweeping generalizations about impacts are suspect, and the patterning of variation needs documentation and explanation. Some workers favor a well-ordered, tightly run, standardized, hierarchical, transparent workplace with clearly defined, comprehensive expectations. A human supervisor's presence may make them nervous. The veiled, depersonalized authority of the machine may lessen feelings of inequality. Employees also may prefer receiving directions from a machine rather than a manager who has the potential to behave inappropriately or just haughtily. In an interesting reversal, the presence of the machine rather than a person may increase feelings of privacy (although the privacy implications of an enduring permanent record that can migrate remain). Additionally, some workers value compensation based on a highly detailed analysis of their individual or work-unit productivity, and pressure may serve as an incentive. They may believe that some sacrifices at work are required to keep the company competitive in a global economy (as the employers at DS hoped they would believe). The employer may be viewed as a concerned parent who has their best interests at heart. Such attitudes are consistent with the relatively low level of class-consciousness in the United States.

But other workers respond oppositely. They do not accept the creation of an expanding system of one-way mirrors into their work, private life, and even their bodies. They act back and respond in kind. As the many neutralization examples considered in chapter 6 indicate, in a free society humans are neither (morally nor practically) frail vessels to be automatically controlled by those with greater authority or power. Machines channel and record behavior, but humans are hardly indifferent or inert, unlike the raw materials of production. The machines use them, but they also know how to use the machines, as chapter 6 suggests.

Moreover, the technologies come with some ironic vulnerabilities. Every new form of control introduces new possibilities for failure, resistance, and deviation. Omniscient organizations invite the challenge of beating or retaliating against the system and may offer workers new ways of advancing their own interests. Unless done in a restrained fashion and with the cooperation of workers, the new surveillance can easily backfire and invite unwanted outcomes.

MACHINES VERSUS MANAGERS

Employers often introduce mechanical surveillance and engineered solutions without adequate analysis or preparation. Vendors present these mechanical solutions as quick and inexpensive—just purchase and plug in. "Have electricity, will control," they suggest, ignoring the delicately balanced and exquisitely complex nature of many human situations.[5]

In our culture, we sometimes grant computer-generated results, with their aura of scientific infallibility, an unwarranted legitimacy as fact. We rarely acknowledge that machines do fail (Perrow 1984; Neuman 1995; Vaughan 1996). Certainly machines can be more accurate and objective than an incompetent or biased supervisor. But what do they know about fairness, compassion, and mentoring?

The power of Chaplin's film *Hard Times* involves the automatic and repetitive quality of the technology in the face of the human. It is "dumb," and when things go out of hand, it may be too late to stop it.

Machines may fail to take account of atypical and extenuating circumstances because they have not been (and perhaps can't be) programmed to consider the richness of a dynamic reality. They are too literal, mechanistic, and acontextual, abstracting out only a limited number of factors. This is yet another form of the deskilling (Braverman 1974) associated with modern society, in which the machine replaces the skill of the worker (in this case the interpretive ability of the supervisor who, with discretion, can respond to events the computer was not programed to know). Consider, for example, an employee fired when he was caught taking an expensive tool home (the tool had an embedded chip that caused an alarm to go off when he exited). The employee had used (and returned) the tool many times previously on weekend jobs before the new monitoring system was in place and an aspect of the informal workplace culture had always tolerated this use. Or consider a telephone operator criticized because her average time spent on calls was a few seconds over the average—-a fact she explained by noting that she took additional time with the large number of calls received from the elderly and foreign born in her district.

Evaluations may favor what can be measured best by the technology instead of what may be most important (if more difficult to measure). In a form of goal displacement, the means may come to determine the end. Workers may seek to satisfy the measurement goal at the expense of what the goal is intended to measure. The enduring organizational conflict between quality and quantity tilts toward the latter.[6]

Relying on technology for control and automatic judgments to the exclusion of sensitive managers who can analyze problems, interpret data, and work at building trust and reciprocal relationships with workers is questionable policy. Traditionally, three major means of creating commitment and loyalty to organizations have been respected leaders, a shared history, and some sense of common destiny between managers and workers. But what happens if the supervisor's role is restricted to review of a printout highlighting deviations from general standards?

Productivity and loyalty are more likely to come out of the employee's commitment to others in the workplace than to be induced via technology (whether from remote electronic monitoring, embedding property and people with sensors, or manipulation via music, scents, subliminal messages, or diet). If managers have lost their authority, surveillance is unlikely to get it back and may even further erode it.

The more sudden and draconian the surveillance, particularly when introduced in a top-down fashion, the more likely it is to result in resistance. As the ethics chapter (chap. 13) argues, the process of introducing the surveillance may itself become an issue. Employees are likely to express indignation at the surprise discovery that e-mail is monitored or that a hidden video camera is in place, when no one has consulted or even warned them. When the surveillance itself violates basic expectations (as with cameras hidden in bathrooms or locker rooms or with an employee posing as a friend who has infiltrated the workplace during a unionization drive), anger will be intensified.

In settings with strong monitoring, workers may feel they are being treated like children (needing permission to go to the bathroom) and interpret the workplace to be saying, "We don't trust you. We expect you to behave irresponsibly, to take advantage, and to screw up unless we remove all temptation and prevent you from doing so or trick or force you to do otherwise."

To the extent that the technologies create feelings of powerlessness over the inability to have a say in the pace and conditions of work, to see the watchers, to know when one is being monitored, or to confront one's accuser, heightened and dysfunctional stress may be accompanied by feelings of dehumanization, invasion, estrangement, disrespect, demoralization, and anger.[7] Beyond the elements of gaming and self-interest, feelings of stress and alienation may accentuate the urge to rebel.

The quality and quantity of productivity may decline, and absenteeism, illness, errors, "time theft" (a term used by those selling monitoring devices to refer to loafing or socializing on the job), and material theft and sabotage may increase.

Chapter 6, table 6.2, lists various examples of beating the monitoring system in work settings. Consider typists who hold one key down to increase the number of keystrokes recorded and then delete the file later. Telephone agents may avoid calls that add to their average case time—by either disconnecting the call or giving out information that discourages the caller. In addition, monitoring may generate a market for means of getting around controls, as with various systems for creating false resumes and beating drug tests.

The coordinated and interdependent nature of production means that slowing down or obstructing one part of the system may spread to other parts, even if workers there are motivated to cooperate. The vulnerability of complex systems is the worker's silent ally and can serve as a brake, along with values, laws, and concern over negative publicity, limiting the full potential of monitoring. However, where the brakes are worn thin, and perceptions of inequity in application of surveillance are present, resistance is likely.

Chapter 1 noted distinctions between vertical and horizontal and nonreciprocal and reciprocal surveillance. Work settings are classically hierarchical and nonreciprocal, and as such, they raise fundamental questions about equity.[8] Are the techniques of surveillance available to workers as well as the company? Are all employees the subject of the tools? In casinos, at least with respect to direct observation, the answer is a resounding yes for patrons as well as employees.[9] As for the first question—whether the techniques are available to employees—some, such as miniature audio and video recorders, certainly are "available." Whether they are permitted is a different question. When workers can record managers, as well as the reverse, the situation is more balanced. But what kind of a work environment is it if the level of trust is so low, and suspiciousness or possible abuse so high, that people must be constantly on guard and recording all interaction?

The sweeping and categorical character of video and audio systems can be indiscriminate, catching all within their purview (whether work related or not and regardless of status in the organization). In principle, monitoring can extend up as well as down the organizational hierarchy. Card key systems required to enter a room or computer access codes make demands on all who encounter them, and drug testing can be mandatory for all, including the CEO. Systems for analyzing computer use can look at everyone. But do they?

If the advantages claimed for omniscient environments are real, then the same methods should be applied to managers and higher-level executives as to workers. In fact the case for monitoring the former as leaders and role models may be much stronger than that for monitoring those lower in the hierarchy—that is, if managers are performing inadequately or illegally, much greater damage can be done. We might even adopt a principle that the more central a position and the higher the costs from poor performance, the greater should be the degree of monitoring. The perennial question is who monitors those of highest status.

If management is often incapable of effectively watching itself (as white-collar crime—whether in banking, insurance, medicine, defense contracting, or environmental protection—suggests), then there is a strong case for independent groups (perhaps made up of employees, customers, and stockholders) to monitor managers and the overall organization.[10]

Imagine what could be uncovered if a full audio and visual record of all the job-related behavior of senior executive and managers were available. What if their files were subject to the same oversight as those of data entry clerks—for example, tobacco industry executives' discussions of health, smoking, and marketing, or banking and housing officials' discussions of derivatives?

Equity and efficiency would seem to require that controversial tactics used against less powerful members of an organization also be used against the most powerful—particularly if these methods are as effective as advocates claim. The credibility of those in management who advocate monitoring would probably increase to the extent that they are willing to apply the same rationales and technologies to themselves. Of course this suggestion is unrealistic. But the DS example at the beginning of the chapter illustrates stratification at work and the natural imbalances favoring those in higher-status positions with respect to the ability to see and not be seen and to know and to not be known.[11] The DS example also notes the enormous quantity of data management has.

DROWNING IN DATA: OLD AND NEW STANDARDS

Foucault (1977) writes of "indefinite discipline," where "never-ending judgments, examinations, and observation" emerge as a new mode of control. New areas become subject to measurement, and old areas are measured in greater detail. Precise formal standards are created against which individuals are judged. These may involve behavioral rules at work with or without a strong moral underpinning—for example, contrast the traditional "Don't steal" with "More than four trips to the bathroom require explanation to your supervisor." But many standards have nothing to do with behavior. They involve expectations about being a certain kind of person, only indirectly (if at all) related to the work tasks and the product, or even what happens at work—for example, dress code restrictions and rules about off-duty decorum.

Beyond using new standards for judging the individual, powerful discovery techniques may reveal more traditional infractions as well. Once technology can cross borders and merge previously distinct data, it can discover departures from expectations that in the past would have been unseen or ignored because they were not documented and managers could still look the other way and use their discretion without being called to task themselves.

The vast expansion of the supervisory gaze can mean an overabundance of data. Managers may find that they are drowning in the data, and even if they can separate the meaningful from the meaningless, they may face issues not anticipated by those who designed the surveillance system apart from a real setting.

In the context of this data flood, when a pattern of widespread rule violation is documented, it may not be possible to sanction all violators. Those who are sanctioned may feel it unfair and ask why they are singled out when everyone does it. Yet to not sanction anyone in the interest of being fair and avoiding claims of discrimination may send the message that the rules don't really matter—thus increasing violation. There are times when it is best not to know.

In another scenario, the abundance of information on violations may lead unscrupulous managers to misuse their discretion—singling out workers they wish to sanction for personal reasons, while they lack strong enough official grounds for doing so. Like a squirrel hoarding nuts, the manager may save up the data. Unless employers develop criteria for the relative importance of, and limits on, the retention and use of such data, they may apply it discriminatorily and long after the fact. When monitoring occurs secretly, workers may not know or recall the incident for which they are being sanctioned, raising due process concerns.

Vast quantities of minute data will probably reveal some infractions or potential failings by almost everyone (given a predictive profile and ideal standards against which the individual is compared, whether when hired or periodically on the job). If performance and personal conduct standards are continually raised and expanded to new areas on and off the job, fewer employees may be able to meet those standards, leading to a failure to feel appreciated and a decline in morale.

In turn, employers may find it more difficult to find and retain workers. Eventually the workforce (and social participation generally) may become more clearly divided between people thought to be good risks and others. Rigid preemployment screening and testing may create a larger and more permanent class of unemployables denied a second chance. In the past, when traditional records systems were less efficient, people could often start over. But now one's past may become an indelible mark. This would be an enormous waste of human resources. Yet to some extent this is happening, particularly for minority males (Patillo, Weiman and Western 2004; Pager 2003). If persons are denied chances for legitimate employment, we should not be surprised when they turn to illegitimate means or need to be publicly supported.

IF SOME IS GOOD, IS MORE NECESSARILY BETTER?

No!—as a techno-fallacy identified in chapter 12 suggests. Advocates of supposedly neutral data-generating technology seem to imply that all information is good. But the picture is more complex. The desirability of full rule conformity and complete openness regarding rule departures is a myth, and pursuing these goals too literally may have negative social consequences.

Intensive screening of new employees and the proliferation of inspections could lead to a narrow, even intolerant, timid, blindly conforming workforce lacking imagination and flexibility. Will creative persons be excluded or choose to avoid certain jobs because they don't fit conventional selection profiles? Will workers in general take fewer risks once on the job?

Organizations may be unable to function if held to full enforcement of their own rules (even if it could be effective). This leads to the notion of "bad" and "good" rule breaking and rule enforcement. For example, in the case of the good, one might see creative and innovative rule bending and stretching or the wise use of managerial discretion. Such rule bending may serve organizational and societal goals. Unrestricted transparency may undercut these positive but rarely acknowledged aspects.[12]

Increased transparency at work can interfere with the flexibility and discretion that are helpful in interpreting and applying rules in complex, ever-changing organizational contexts. The common refrains in some work settings along the lines of "You don't want to know" or "Look the other way" capture elements of this. Similarly, Merton's (1956) concept of "institutionalized evasion" serves as a way to paper over and avoid having to confront the uncomfortable dysfunctional aspects of rigidity and the problems that can accompany rules, which must of necessity often be written at a general level and thus become unable to offer direction for the extenuating circumstances that invariably populate human settings.

An enduring paradox is that group life is impossible without rules, and yet a too-rigid conformity to rules may undermine the group. Boundary conditions are necessary (or inevitable if interaction is to proceed), but so too is discretion. Pioneers, inventors, and innovators often use discretion creatively, pushing limits and extending gray areas, even venturing into forbidden zones to solve problems. Doing so can get them in trouble, but it can also make them heroes and lead to changes in the rules or new insights. The transparency that surveillance can bring to work environments, especially when accompanied by rigid rules regarding what it finds, makes innovation less likely. In short, the enhanced order and security of the omniscient organization may undermine its competitiveness relative to other more flexible organizations.

Work contexts are obviously quite varied, but their formal, contractual, and goal conflict aspects bring some uniformity in surveillance issues and in potentials for abuse. They contrast with the informal, caring, duty-minded, and shared goals that ideally exist in the context of family and children, the topic we turn to next.

Children: Slap That Baby's Bottom, Embed That ID Chip, and Let It Begin

Train up a child in the way he should go:
and when he is old, he will not depart from it.

PROVERBS 22:6 (KING JAMES VERSION)

As the many examples considered thus far illustrate, the seemingly omniscient, omnipresent, colonizing power of twenty-first-century new surveillance softly spreads ever outward and inward in society. The future gallops on in diffuse, almost invisible sensors embedded everywhere. Nowhere is this clearer than in the case of the hierarchal family with responsibility for the care of children. A focus on children and the home offers an ideal setting to see broader social forms and processes. The distinctive features of this context can enhance comparisons across tools, applications, life cycle stages, institutions, and geographic places as well as highlight some enduring tensions independent of these.

In contrast to the relatively more *impersonal, organizational, focused, formal,* and *contractual* surveillance of adults in *quasi-public* work settings in the previous chapter, attention shifts here to the relatively more *personal, diffuse, informal, dutiful,* and *caring* surveillance of *dependent* children in the *private* setting of the home. Here there is greater overlap in goals between parents and children. The emotional intensity of any conflict is likely to be stronger because of the closeness of the relationship.

Attention to childhood offers a unique transom into how we learn what it means to be watched and to watch, and how surveillance changes as roles and related rights and responsibilities shift over time. It also illustrates the unclear meaning of, and conflicts often found within and between, broad values and the hazy demarcation lines between different stages of childhood.

For our purposes, a unique feature of children is their dependence, which creates a presumption in favor of surveillance. Compared with other major institutional contexts, contracts and negotiation play a less significant role where children are concerned, and a sense of duty and shared goals of parents and children (or at least a greater overlap in goals) are initially present. Much parental behavior seems driven not by formal rules, but by a nonreflective, even automatic, sense of duty. As with other species this protection and nurturance of the young is probably instinctive.

A literature is slowly emerging on children and surveillance.[1] Most of it focuses on particular applications or needs. In contrast, this chapter treats the broader topic of surveillance of and by children. It is a composite drawn from interviews, observation, and documents encountered in the research. It begins with a satirical statement from PISHI (Parents Insist on Surveillance Help Inc.)—a fictitious social movement dedicated to protecting children through the use of technology. As with the other fictional narratives in the book, it reflects contemporary surveillophilliac cultural themes taken to an extreme. Yet as a composite based on actual incidents and products offered to parents, it should offer enough authenticity to provoke thought. It contains some moral and empirical truths that even the most anti-surveillance libertarian of parents would probably agree to.

The fictional narrative highlights the complexity and many of the conflicts associated with the topic. In an earlier, longer version of this chapter, the satire set the stage for a long descriptive empirical review of the many tools available to help parents meet the needs and wants PISHI identifies (Marx and Steeves 2010; and the deleted material on the University of Chicago Press web site for this book, at press.uchicago.edu/sites/marx/). Technologies examined span the years from preconception through the late teens and include prenatal testing, baby monitors and nanny cams, RFID-enabled clothing, GPS tracking devices, cell phones, home drug and semen tests, surveillance toys, and children as spies. These products inspired the PISHI statement and for reasons of space are not included here, although they are discussed and advertisements are shown in the deleted material on the Press' web page for the book.

The claims made by entrepreneurs selling surveillance to parents further illustrate aspects of the culture of surveillance. Responsible and loving parents, these entrepreneurs tell us, have an obligation to buy surveillance technologies to keep the child "safe" in a dangerous world. For the defenseless infant and child, danger lurks in the environment and the people around them. For older children with a tendency to lie and hide bad behavior, the danger may be found in themselves and in their peers. In health care and education settings, advocates argue that surveillance is needed to identify and "manage" children's undesirable genetic or behavioral deviations from the norm. A secondary emphasis is on parental convenience and the freedom technology can bring to busy, overtaxed and tasked parents as with remote baby monitors.

The PISHI section is followed by consideration of why these issues are so vexing, locates the distinctive character of contexts involving children, and considers some broader implications.

An Urgent Message to All Parents from PISHI
(Parents Insist on Surveillance Help Inc.)

Don't neglect, suspect! Be safe not sorry.

CHALLENGES AND OPPORTUNITIES

Children are expensive. According to some estimates a child born in 2015 will cost parents more than $325,000 before he or she finishes college. Is your investment protected? Are you looking out for your kids by looking at them in the modern way? Do you know what your kids are hiding from you? Do you know who their friends are? Do you know where they go? Do you know where the convicted criminals in your neighborhood live? And what do you really know about your nanny? You no longer need to guess or wonder what the answers are to such questions. The precise discovery tools of modern science—used by police, the military, and titans of industry—are now accessible to parents who care.

Given contemporary demands on parents, the many pulls away from the home and new dangers, watching children in the traditional, labor-intensive way is old fashioned, impractical, and irresponsible. The modern tools of scientific prediction and prevention make reliance on traditional surveillance unnecessary.

We can debate whether (or when) it is OK to read a child's diary kept in a drawer. But once that diary goes out on the Internet, the debate is over. It's a whole new ball game, with anonymous lurkers and communicators trying to make the team. Kids have always said and done silly things. But what if in doing these things, they leave a permanent electronic record? You can smell alcohol on a child's breath, but can you smell designer drugs? You unobtrusively can overhear their phone conversations, but can you see, let alone translate, their text messages?

The natural surveillance that works well for the very young fails with each passing day. As children grow older they are increasingly away from direct supervision and better able to take evasive action. Children should never be idle at home or in playgrounds, malls, or pool halls, or have uncensored, unobserved, and undocumented access to communications media. Unsupervised playtime is dangerous time. We don't let weeds volunteer in our garden but prefer things we plant. Idle hands are indeed the devil's tools. The young must be kept busy in circumscribed, directed, and documented activities with a purpose.

Children are our most precious asset, but they are also the potential enemy and victim. Even platinum left to the elements will dull if it isn't cared for. The world is not what it was. The waters are filled with sharks. The earth roils with vipers disguised as lowly worms.

WHO WE ARE

PISHI is a nonprofit, nonpartisan group of helicopter parents of all genders, races, religions, ethnicities, and regions who believe that technologically protected normal families are the basic building blocks of society. We are supported by socially responsible businesses that provide goods and services to help families help themselves. Generous grants from the SBC (Suspicion Breeds Confidence) Corporation and NHF (the Nothing to Hide Foundation) keep our prices on recommended products and services below market value.**

OUR GOALS

We are mission driven and child centered, dedicated to the development of persons who respect the rules and wisdom of the past even as they prepare to embrace the future. Our goal is to become "One Nation under Guard," in which security, like charity, begins in the home. Children must be trained in their communal responsibilities to be good economic citizens and to also watch and report on themselves as well as their peers.

We seek individuals who will fit in, not be cast out. Our four-part program provides you with expert-designed, predictive, and preventive control tools for infants, toddlers, preteens, and adolescents. Our products deliver healthy fun along with positive surveillance experiences in preparation for later life and are guaranteed to give your children what they will need to thrive in an advanced consumer society, filled with unprecedented risks.

Through our program children can acquire the requisite motivation and skills to watch themselves and others and to do their share for society as customers and (eventually) as employees. If our economy is to thrive, they must learn to be eager consumers of the bounty that is rightfully theirs.

Abundant childhood surveillance, communication, and consumption experiences—including playing and purchasing with our parentally controlled, award-winning CCK ("credit cards for kids") program, will produce ideal employees and entertained citizens who cheerfully welcome work monitoring and the new protections government must institute in a threatening global environment. They will be prepared to effectively monitor their progeny as well. Also on the bright side—if our government were to become less free (and let's face it: societies change and empires decline) the PISHI kids would be the best prepared for the new order.

In scientifically controlled environments, there is no longer a need to threaten or punish the child. Working together, we can organize the world so that our children (and those who would prey upon them) cannot do the wrong thing. As parents, beyond setting good examples, we must structure our children's environment so that they want to do the right things and are unable to do the wrong

Kids need to know that you are there because you care and that you are there even when you are not (the subtext—which there is no need to advertise—is "You can't get away with it"). Safety and security must become a seamless part of everyday childhood experience sweetened by invisibility. Look at the wonderful example of Disney World, where guards in Mickey Mouse and Donald Duck costumes roam the grounds making kids smile even as they are protecting them and with unseen audio and video tools reporting to the eye in the sky. Talk softly but carry a lot of gigabytes.

Some call it spying. Some call it overprotection. We at PISHI call it caring and responsibility. The horrors of delegating control to an overly intrusive, distant government of power-hungry, anonymous, lockstep bureaucrats are all too well known. We emphasize the opposite: local surveillance by the loving family. What starts in the family stays in the family.

THE PROBLEMS

Sadly, we all know the problems surrounding youth. We see them everywhere:

Substance abuse

Drugs
Smoking
Drinking
Glue

Sexuality

Birth control and its correlate, promiscuity
Sex without marriage
Concupiscence
Teen pregnancy
Abortion
Pornography
Predators online and in your neighborhood

Appearance

Tattoos
Body piercing

Unnatural hair colors and styles
Faces hidden by hoodies
Clothes that are too tight or loose or black
Morbid "jewelry"

School and academic issues

Bullying and harassment
The wrong kinds of friends
Gangs
Delinquency
Cheating on tests
Reading below grade level
Absence of civic knowledge and virtue
Vulgar, demeaning, ungrammatical, and incomprehensible language

Health

Obesity
Sexually transmitted disease
Violence
Suicide
Car accidents
Obsessive use of television, video games, and Internet for unhealthy purposes
Listening to loud sounds and vulgar lyrics that claim to be "music"
Moodiness
Snoring
High cholesterol and diabetes
Stress
Aggressive gum chewing
Junk food

Citizenship

Disrespecting authority figures
Lying
Spying on parents and infecting their computers
Corrupting younger siblings
Shoplifting
Gambling

Credit card abuse and poor consumer choices
ID theft
Lack of religious belief
Radical ideologies and im- and amoral relativism

Those facts speak for themselves! Aberrant has become the new normal. Yet megameltdown mode is not inevitable! We say NOT ON OUR WATCH. The problems can't be blamed on rampaging hormones (which, after all, are a historical constant). Rather they reflect an antiquated, misbegotten, and disproved psychology of permissiveness, experimentation, and faulty belief in the therapeutic effects of making mistakes. But there is no need to learn anything when mistakes are not made. The id in the kid needs a lid. For decades, so-called progressive psychologists have advised parents about the importance of letting go. Our message is the opposite—hold on, see through, and see it through.

OUR APPROACH

The tried and true expression "safe not sorry" valorizes our widely heralded emphasis: benign suspicion rather than negligent omission. Trouble rushes to those who send it an invitation. Stem the tide. Don't go with the flow. Dare to care! Listen to your children. Help them to reveal not conceal! Kids with nothing to hide get to ride. There are no secrets to safety! How many times have we heard parents lament, "If only I had known . . . ?" Well now you can.

One of our members, a mother who raised seven children, said, "Love them, but don't trust them." Remember how you hid things from your parents? Talk is cheap. Dissimulation is rampant. Trust can come only from the validation provided by scientific suspicion. We trust because we verify. We verify because we love. Until you test them, you can't be sure. Even then, all you can be sure of are yesterday's results, and things change.

With technology driving on autopilot, you can steer clear of fear. Parents must be prepared so their children can be clean in word and deed. One of our consultants, Tom "King" Leer, a famous mathematician who must know because he worked at Harvard, MIT, and Berkeley, summed all he had learned in two words, "Be prepared!"

THE PRICE IS RIGHT

Parents may enroll in only one of our programs or receive a special package deal when signing up for all four (recommended). If you accept the full package, we will include absolutely free a set of our award-winning games such as "I Spy," "Gulags and Guantanamos," "Can You Tap This?" "Ordinary People Renditions," "Find the Deviant," and "You Don't Have a Secret Anymore."

Beyond helping you to cover all the bases, the full package offers free access to our artificial intelligence virtual psychologist, which you can access from your home at your convenience and which some clients find more reliable than a human in terms of confidentiality and less embarrassing than revealing family problems when face to face with an outsider).

If you sign up—even with no purchases, as an awareness-raising public service we will give you a facsimile of the colorful preparedness patch created by the Girl Scouts of America in conjunction with the Department of Homeland Security.

It doesn't cost anything to become a member of PISHI and to learn about the many protective tools and play-learning toys that guard and educate children.*** But in return, we'd like to know a little about you for our files. We seek your feedback through online surveys. We hear you! We offer you and your children (known around our office as "the little pishers") a chance to participate and to make your voice heard. Make some democratic noise! Design the future! Get the attention of concerned merchants, educators, and policy makers, who, if they are to do their job well, need to know what you think. Stand up and be counted and join a global community of concerned parents. After filling out five surveys, you qualify for a free designer T-shirt with our logo, a plush toy, and an automatic upgrade to our top-of-the-kennel virtual pets.

The information you provide will help us to better serve you with life coaching, parenting advice, timely tips, updates, and information on the products you need and new must-haves. We will treat this information as if it were our own. It will stay within the trusted family of companies and nonprofits sharing our goals.

Finally, please note that because of our buying power we are able to offer highly competitive prices for the products we sell. But this is not about money. It is about love and the future of civilization. Your purchases show the love. Together we can make the world a better place—one child at a time!

NOTES

* © 2016 Parents Insist on Surveillance Help Inc. All rights reserved. We are a fully fictional, dysfunctional, off-island registered organization dependent only on the perspicacity of the author. Any overlap with existing agencies such as http://www .spyonyourkids.net; http://www.safekids.com; http://www.safeteens.com; http:// www.missingkids.com/cybertip; http://www.familysecurtymatters.org; http://www .firstcheckfamily.com; and http://www.OperationCheckpoint.com is purely coincidental. All our products are field tested on animals, prisoners, third-world persons, and computer simulators. Consistent with best practices for customers, please note that in visiting our web site you consent to our privacy policy. We are happy to take credit for anything good you find at the site, but since we are simply a conduit for information provided by others, we have no responsibility for the accuracy or legality of what we make available for you to draw upon. Please visit our Terms and Conditions section,

which establishes the use, disclaimers, and limitations of liability governing the use of our web site. You are welcome to use anything from our web site. We do not sell, rent, auction, or license ANY of our customer's personal information, but we reserve the right to give it away (or trade it) to help us better serve you. We encrypt that information using the latest secure sock-it-to-'em layer technology (SSL) and pretty bad privacy (PBP)

** To be an approved PISHI supplier a company must offer the right stuff and indicate support for our mission by donating a percentage of their proceeds. Since there is nothing worse than selling a problem without a solution, this mission includes facilitating rapid awareness of new problems, technologies, and services and assisting in the transfer of technology solutions to families, the government, and critical infrastructure marketplaces. Any corporate proceeds are used only for operating expenses. Each company undergoes thorough screening before they qualify to provide benefits to PISHI members. Continuous monitoring of customer service and product performance helps us maintain quality assurance and high standards. For additional details on many products and services offered exclusively to PISHI members, check out our kids-approved, privacy-certified, organic web site or the Discounts and Services Guide enclosed with your absolutely free membership kit. As part of community outreach, parents who sign our caretaker's pledge have access to the latest research and technology 60/60/24/7/30/365. We offer a toll free help line, "The Listener" (messages may be recorded for your protection and analyzed to better serve you). We also offer an online community for parents to share their experiences (www.parentswhocare/watchingiswinning.org).

*** We welcome partnerships with organizations, merchants, and media outlets that share our goals. If you are interested in becoming a Friend of PISHI (a big Pisher), a Strategic Partner, or in advertising in our newsletter ROC (aka the Rod of Correction) please contact us via the form on the web page. Point of view or opinions expressed above are those of PISHI, and do not necessarily represent the official position or policies of the US government or our sponsors (but they may not be far off).

[Material deleted here on the many tools to surveil children is at press .uchicago.edu/sites/marx/.]

Conflicts

The topic of surveillance and children involves several types and sources of disagreement. Parties may disagree about the relative importance of protecting children from others in their environment (including parents), protecting children from themselves and other children, and protecting society from the child. Is the emphasis on children as potential victims and vulnerable creatures in need of protection from evil outsiders (and insiders), or is it society that has to be protected from bad seeds and the incompetent and immature young? Is the home best seen as a sanctuary, a garrison, a prison, a clinic, a school, a market, an Exploratorium, Disneyland, or all of these? Is the home a refuge and a place where you have to be taken in, as Robert Frost suggests,[2] or is it a panoptic jail you can't leave (whether literally or symbolically)? Is the home a haven protecting the individual from the universal expectations of the public/communal sphere, or is it an extension of the broader society? How are tensions between competing goals and logics managed?

Any social setting of course is a mélange of conflicting cross-pressures and imperfectly integrated expectations. But the collisions seem particularly pronounced for children in the home. Awareness of opposing social logics offers a way to organize the varied beliefs and behavior observed. Much of the conflict and confusion surrounding children and surveillance come from the less-than-perfect meshing of factors and inherent value and goal conflicts, such as between protecting children and encouraging their development as autonomous persons, and between liberty and order.

The family is a special institution, and the home is a distinct place, involving a unique combination of social forces for the surveillance of children that set it apart from surveillance in other settings such as work, commerce, and citizenship and even such settings as schools, malls, workplaces, and public parks.

The largely unplanned conjunction of social factors noted in table 8.1 offers a key to the questions raised in this chapter. The distinctiveness results from the presence of informal and personal relationships, the diffuseness of an ethos of duty and caring, formal subordination, and vulnerability and dependence, all occurring within the private place of the home, wherein the child gradually gains ever greater independence. The family as a primary group and the evolving nature of parent-child interaction as the child grows are of particular importance.

Of Primary Importance

The family as a primary group involves informality and trust to a much greater extent than is the case in other organizations, with their formality and written rules. Trust (or at least its gradual extension as the child grows) is seen as fundamental to emerging self-control and healthy development. The use of formal means of assessment, as with drug testing of a child or recording all of their communication, can be unsettling, because it fundamentally undermines that trust apart from any questions of privacy (Rooney 2010). Such actions communicate a lack of confidence in the individual and undercut the foundation for personal and intimate relations. Lack of private spaces (whether physical, personal, or social) for children amid omnipresent parental oversight may also create an inhibiting dependence and fear.

A primary relation is partly defined by its diffuseness as contrasted with the narrower expectations associated with an organizational role. Family members are justified and indeed expected to attend to the most personal of issues, beyond what is appropriate and formally defined for an employer, government, teacher, or casual acquaintance. The breadth of the parental role can offer children a protective border and a safety net given the varied circumstances and surprises of growing up. Diffuse norms of attentiveness, care, and responsibility are pronounced in the case of children.

The shared physical space and the amount of time spent within the confines of the family mean closer observation and greater awareness of information that may be discreditable (whether to the child, the parent or both). In situations where a child's behavior conflicts with standards of the broader society, parents may withhold such information as a result of alternative standards, familial tolerance and understanding (or at least loyalty), self-protection and a desire not to lower the family's status, or denial.[3]

The ostensibly benign, broad prerogatives granted parents to protect and nurture their children justify intensive and extensive crossing of personal borders. Dependence on parents, the absence of formal rules, the vulnerability of children to their parents' threats, the degree of inequality, norms of family loyalty, and physical and legal borders separating the family and the home from external visibility can support parental abuse (whether involving doing too much or too little watching or exploitation). In short, the insulation of the home from observability provides rich opportunities for abuse and underscores the need for state oversight, child advocates, and perhaps even for a social movement urging children to watch their parents.[4] In that regard the cartoon (fig. 8.1) is illustrative of the double-edged potential found with any tool. In the image we also see how parents model surveillance behavior that children will copy (whether as kids or adults).

Kids Grow Up: A Process View

The last source of conflict in table 8.1 involves the dynamic nature of the parent-child relationship over time. Even if all the previously articulated conflictual factors were not present, the lack of clear points of transition as the child matures would generate conflict. This dynamic was discussed more broadly in chapter 5. The point is that the dynamic and transitional nature of children's development is a central factor in surveillance controversies, as the edges of transition are ragged and involve contradictory pulls.

FIGURE 8.1. The irony of the tool: sousveillance. (By permission of Steve Kelley and Creators Syndicate, Inc.)

TABLE 8.1. Factors characterizing parental surveillance of children

Variable	Value
Kind of institution	Family
Kind of relations	Primary
	Informal
	Personal
	Intimate
	Involuntary (no early exit)
Kind of place	Private
	Home
Subject resources for action	Dependent
	Vulnerable
	Less competent
Subject's position in hierarchy	Subordinate
Agents' rights and obligations (human and legal)	Special prerogatives and responsibilities and limits on parental authority and behavior
Relative fixity of interaction	Dynamic (explicit) goal changes from dependence to independence

The family is the ultimate, total institution. In the beginning parents have almost all the formal and informal power, but this situation changes form with age and can even be cyclical. It contrasts with prisons or workplaces, where external control remains more constant and where the individual is present for only part of the day. With appropriate socialization, the child's motivation and ability to comply develop, while in adult settings motivation and ability are more constant. For the developing child, surveillance and subsequent punishment may lead to change in the direction the parents intended. In contrast, for adults in the other settings, structural conflicts and their effects are relatively unchanging.

In the early stages of a child's life, formal (role relationship) family surveillance is nonreciprocal and nonnegotiable.[5] Parents define the goals and conditions and monopolize a rich mixture of traditional and new surveillance tools. The goals of parents and those of the young in need of nurturance and protection overlap. However, as the child moves from dependence to independence, the conflict potential and its breadth and intensity may accelerate.

Infants are poked, prodded, and observed by parents at will; almost nothing is out of bounds for responsible parental inquiry. Privacy and secrecy are meaningless for the very young. For the dependent infant or child, the *failure to cross* personal informational borders can be irresponsible, unethical, and even criminal. With maturity this situation is reversed, and the *crossing* of these borders can be wrong. Although this transition from openness to closeness may appear to be linear, it is often conflictual, and judgments of appropriateness must be contextual.[6]

At a year or two, naked toddlers are photographed joyfully frolicking together in wading pools. Parents inspect their bodies at will and dress and undress them in public. To the parent's consternation, the small child may freely disrobe in public. However, eventually the young child is likely to want the bathroom door closed, learns about modesty, and comes to value being clothed.[7]

The growing child comes to understand the physical and social borders that give meaning to the protection of personal information. Closed bathroom and bedroom doors, the clothed body, the privacy of desks and backpacks, and the urge to hide thoughts and feelings and communicate obliquely bring the individual greater control over personal information, whether as a result of changes in norms, physical borders, or new resources. With the development of language and motor skills children learn they can hide things and deceive parents.

From the absence or weakest of borders between the unborn child and the mother comes a gradual strengthening and defining of borders as the child emerges and ages. As an infant becomes a toddler and the toddler becomes a teen and then grows to almost adulthood, the varieties of protective surveillance (both regarding the environment and other people) decrease and change, and respect for the borders of the person increases as self-surveillance (and the related self-control) increase.

Childhood arenas expand beyond the clearly defined (and accessible and insulated) physical spaces of the home to the more distant spaces of day care centers, schools, malls, workplaces, cars, streets, and parks beyond direct parental observation. These changes bring a variety of new needs and challenges for parents and opportunities for children.

As children grow, the parents' goal of getting them to comply supplements protection. Surveillance seeks to discover and monitor new factors. Shared goals are joined by conflicts in goals. Children gain new rights and more informal power. The potential for negotiation and neutralization becomes more prominent. The young move from being subjects to also being agents of surveillance—within the family, as they watch younger siblings (and sometimes even their parents), and outside the family, as they observe their peers.

Responsible parents watch their children and the child's environment closely in each stage of development. But if socialization is successful, children increasingly watch themselves (and learn to watch others for signs of danger and to report misbehavior), and they are trusted beyond the range of direct parental observation, even as new grounds for distrust appear.

Parents gradually transition from imposing external, mechanical controls characteristic of situations where there is little or no trust (whether involving motivation or competence) to placing greater trust in the developing child's ability to control the self and avoid problems from the environment. The ratio of involuntary, external forms of control to internal self-control changes. Managing the speed and form of this transition is a central task of parenting and a frequent source of family conflict.

Children learn the joys of secrets and dissimulation as elements of game playing and may become comfortable with surveillance in such settings. Beyond games, they also learn that self-interest is often served by avoiding the parental and adult gaze. Shifts in surveillance occur as parents and teachers may come to see children as potential suspects, in addition to continuing to see them as in need of protection.

New technologies replace the direct observation and control that is possible with younger, less mobile children. As adolescence arrives, the greater opportunities for parentally disapproved behavior, the increased salience of personal borders, and new rights and resources make for less consensual surveillance and stronger reactions. The sharing of secrets with parents is likely to decline, and feelings of being intruded upon increase.

The dynamic nature of the maturation process illustrates the continuing relevance of context. A parent's curiosity about the communication and possessions of an eight-year-old looks very different when applied to a sixteen-year-old. In the case of the latter, parents may read a diary, letters, or computer files; overhear phone and other conversations; look through desks, drawers, and clothes (not to mention rubbing these for evidence of drug or sperm residue)—but all surreptitiously and ambivalently. They may also monitor credit cards, cell phones, and cars for location and even video evidence. Concerns involving drugs, liquor, companions, sex, driving, and academic performance may lead to new forms of monitoring and neutralization. As the child becomes an adult and leaves home, surveillance decreases significantly or becomes more discrete and, as noted in chapter 5, may be reversed with aged parents.

Concluding Thoughts and Lingering Questions

The examples in this chapter reflect the widespread changes associated with the new surveillance and emerging understandings of risk, responsibility, and technique across society. The concluding chapter (14) considers the broad social implications of these changes. Here I consider some unresolved issues with particular applicability to children.

Cultural expectations over what can and should be done for the young are tied to new forms of measurement and new tools for intervention. Consider, for example, public awareness of SIDS, ADD, teen drug use, pregnancy, and school violence. The mass media and advertising are central in shaping public knowledge and concern over these issues (Best 1999; Glassner 1999; Altheide 2006).

In some ways children in developed societies have never been safer across an array of measures. But public concern over a problem cannot be judged simply by comparative statistics. The manipulation of parental fears and anxieties in order to sell monitoring products considers risk only with respect to the extent of harm that could occur, rather than also considering the likelihood that it will occur. Those who set policy assess both (Slovic, Fischoff, and Lichenstein 1979; Slovic 1987). But for consumers, even if the risk is low, as it is with in-house child abductions or online stalking, the marketing of many products draws on the fear of what could happen.

If surveillance purveyors are successful in their relatively unregulated market, will children's lives be increasingly structured by an abundance of surveillance tools aimed at them and to be used by them as toys, and later as adults for real? Are we slowly and somnolently backing into a rather different world and creating a different type of child?

Will corporations be able to "mine" the family environment and commoditize social relationships in efforts to order and control the child's imagination and desires? Is the meaning and experience of childhood being redefined as this generation of children faces an unprecedented level of measurement and technical surveillance? What does the world look and feel like to the child subjected to the new scrutiny or the adolescent who can and may want to be in constant contact with mommy and daddy?

Will parental responsibility and even love increasingly be equated with the purchase of and provision of ever deeper and more inclusive forms of surveillance? Will external demands on already overextended parents lead to increasing reliance on machines to do parenting? Are physically removed parents who are still omnipresent and always on call really freer, or are they, like their children, more enclosed? Are there times when it may be best not to know?

Will we see ever more anxious parents produce children who might be safer but will become more apprehensive, dependent, and mindlessly conventional as adults? What will be the impact if the externally controlled fear of being caught (as long as the machinery works) overrides an internally controlled sense of right and wrong, or if finding one's own answer is replaced with relying on others for answers? Will awareness of the mechanical measuring and preserving of records of deviation encourage knee-jerk conformity, fear, and timidity in its subjects? Will constant monitoring work against children's developmental needs and make it harder for them to become resilient (Livingstone 2009)? Will it work against creating the kinds of trusting relationships that encourage children to comply with adult rules?[8]

Children need opportunities to interact with the world without being constantly monitored in order to develop a sense of autonomy (Livingstone 2009). Will the lack of respect for children's privacy as they grow inhibit identity formation and a growing sense of self-respect (Stern 2004), individuation (Tang 2006), and development of the facility for deeper, "connected thinking" (A. Davis 2001)?

Will more complex understandings of childhood as a time of innocence and savviness, protection and exploration, and nurture and autonomy be displaced by broader security discourses around the relationship of fear, risk, and resiliency and the simplicity of mechanical solutions? Will resources that might better be used in other ways, such as educating children and parents about a risk, go into products whose worth cannot be measured because the things they are to prevent happen so infrequently? Will the marketing messages deepen a view of children as both inconvenient and untrustworthy?

As the lines between home, play, and commerce become more permeable, will the home lose its role as a traditional refuge? As the child's information is converted to a commodity, will the home become one more source of market research data and point-of-sale transaction?[9]

Can parents find the autonomy to make decisions out of wisdom rather than fear in offering protection, safety, and security for children while also giving them space to develop, explore, stumble, and learn from mistakes? Must avoiding the costs of underprotection lead to the costs of over protection?[10]

Defenders of toy guns argue that their products are just make-believe and are harmless because they don't really work. Children can indulge their violent or protective fantasies without doing any immediate harm or confusing their game with reality. But that is not the case with many surveillance devices. They are attractive because they really may work. Children are no longer required even to pretend or to fantasize. In becoming accustomed to these, are the seeds of an amoral and suspicious adulthood being unwittingly cultivated? Will private bugging, wiretapping, video surveillance, and computer and location monitoring expand as a generation that has had these devices as childhood toys or as protection comes to see them as offensive and defensive necessities?[11] Will this generation be more likely to uncritically accept claims made by surveillance entrepreneurs? Survey data reveal that on the average those under forty who have had the most experience with new forms of surveillance are less critical of it. More than a few might even grow up to become like the somewhat-childlike Tom I. Voire, whose case is reported in the next chapter.

9

The Private within the Public:
Psychological Report on Tom I. Voire

It's not spying if you love someone.
BROADWAY DANNY ROSE

Unveiled women who show their hands and feet excite feelings of onlookers without
giving them the means to calm the excitement.
IRANIAN CLERIC

This chapter pursues aspects of the private within the public in looking at the
behavior of imaginary character Tom I. Voire through a clinical psychological
report. In the original, longer version of this chapter, Voire is the subject or
agent of more than one hundred forms of surveillance (the deleted material
is available at press.uchicago.edu/sites/marx/).[1] As the *subject* of surveillance,
he is a kind of everyman, facing the panoply of devices we all face. He also
performs in conventional organizational *agent* roles, as a soldier, lifeguard,
security guard, market researcher, and computer security specialist. The full
case study illustrates ambiguities and value conflicts in cross-gender surveillance and differences in male and female responses.[2]

But what is distinctive for the purpose of this chapter is his actions as a
male *free-range voyeur* whose discrete and indiscrete activities roam across
freely available public data. The male gaze shown in figure 9.1 is illustrative of
the many advertisements for personal devices that show men secretly watching women. Men on the average seem much more interested in the dazzling
power of surveillance technologies than are women. Advertisements directed
at women emphasize a more passive protection rather than pernicious spying.

In Tom's actions described in this chapter he is engaged in *impersonal,
non-role-relationship, nonreciprocal, low-visibility surveillance* in "public"
settings (or, better, settings where data are relatively unprotected).[3] His case
highlights tacit expectations about the "private" that remain within the "public" in the absence of role relationships and visible audit trails.[4] It also calls
attention to gender differences in responses to, and use of, surveillance. This
aspect is more fully developed in the longer article than in this abridged version.[5] Dubrofsky and Magnet (2015) offer a feminist perspective on the topic.

This chapter focuses on only one facet of Tom's visionary career—his en-

FIGURE 9.1. Just because it's legal does not mean it's right.

counters with one Eve Spectre—a woman he came to know, or perhaps better be aware of, as a result of his work in computer security at a women's hospital.

Contracts, care, and coercion define three of four fundamental surveillance contexts. As noted, these are illustrated by the workplace and consumption, the family and friends, and government. The fourth context, treated in this chapter, involves a type of information that spills over into the above but also occurs independently of them—"public" information. The compliance mechanisms for the first three are good-faith agreements, duty, and threat of force, respectively. In contrast, public information (by practical and often legal definition) is just *there* to be accessed or ignored.

Many of Tom's "encounters" with his subjects (whether here or in the full clinical report that space prevented including) involve neither coercion, contracts, nor care. There are some rules legitimating, mandating, or restricting access to (and use of) others' unprotected personal information, but the absence of clear rules is more common. There is a default toleration wrapped in common sense. Tom slips through the inevitable cracks in the conventional rules and exploits the absence of rules or conflicts between them. In probing those gaps in public settings he is not controlled by manners or a sense of propriety the way most persons are.

His composite story recounts how an individual who is off the wall (but who could make claims for not necessarily being out of the ballpark) might experience and use surveillance. It seeks to convey the subjectivity of the watcher and the watched—including the emotions associated with the discovery of covert surveillance and the seductions of secret knowledge. The story brings many of the tacit assumptions made about personal information to the surface and (in the next chapter) considers the kinds of harm that people may feel when these are violated.

The voice offering the report and commenting in the text and in the footnotes is that of the fictitious clinician A. Funt.

I. Clinical Report (Abridged Version)

This information is being released by the Sechel Clinic, 19 Bergasse St., Vienna, Va., upon receipt of a valid written authorization or as otherwise prescribed by law. The information contained in this document is CONFIDENTIAL and may also be LEGALLY protected. Further disclosure by the recipient without additional written authorization may be in violation of several federal regulations. If you are not entitled to read this document, stop reading at once. Repress any memory of it.

————————————————————————————————————

Pat. name: Thomas I. Voire AKA: Ret Marut; Alexandra Zuk; Zeke Hawkins; Joe Soy.

Pat. acct. # 21-18-19-13-1-18-20

Birth date: 6/6/66

Reporting physician: A. Funt

Presenting complaints: Subject seeks greater self-understanding and feedback on beliefs that he is a victim of a conspiracy to deny him his rights under the First, Fourth, and Fifth Amendments as these involve collecting and publishing information. Symptoms include possible sexual dysfunction, inability to distinguish media depictions from reality, voyeurism, paranoid and sociopathic tendencies and hyperheteronormality.

Date: 2/30/02

Insurance routing: Medical Insurance Bureau, Boston

WARNING: This medical report is CONFIDENTIAL and only to be seen by the more than 70 persons (or others in their agencies) who have a legitimate professional reason to see it. If the free and open communication between patient and professional is to be maintained, there must be a relationship of trust in an environment in which patient confidentiality is respected, and information is widely shared on behalf of our interlocking goals of quality treatment, efficiency, and profit maximization. Remember: there is no such thing as nonsensitive personal information. On the other hand, as professionals, we know that knowledge is good, and sharing it is a fundamental value of our occupational culture. We have nothing to hide.

———————————————————————————————————

CHILDHOOD

Whatever his deficiencies, lack of imagination was not among them. Unlike Peter Sellers in the film *Being There* or Jim Carrey in *The Truman Show*, he knew the difference between media fantasies and reality. He simply preferred the media. Thomas I. Voire might have grown up like any other typical American child (although he was born in Coventry) raised on comic books, film, and television, with an actress-mother and a science-fiction-writing father, were it not for the fact that he spent the first five years of his life in a full body cast. While other children played, he could only watch. But he didn't mind because seeing was so all encompassing compared to the constrictions of touching, hearing, or smelling. This experience made him a curious person in more than one way. But he did envy those who could play hide and seek, and he cherished his memories of playing peekaboo.

He devoured the mass media and became an astute and intense observer of other people—an eyewitness to the minutiae of the moment in which life is truly lived. He marveled at the taken-for-granted, cooperative actions and conventions of everyday social interaction. Yet common sense sometimes seemed like nonsense. What people said might or might not be true, and even apart from that, they might or might not believe it. He was naive, even childlike, in expecting honesty and consistency in such interactions and optimistic that he could find an inner logic to human behavior. He was nothing if not rigid and always sought clarity. He did not adequately grasp the social functions of ambiguity and of conflicting values, or of the salutary aspects of a mood apart.

As a frail youngest child, Tom was carefully observed by his parents. From an early age he was accustomed to being watched and to inspections and examinations of all kinds. His earliest memory is of a bright yellow transmitter with a bear decal that was always clipped on his pants. A warning alarm sounded if he strayed too far from his adult monitor. As he grew older the range expanded from twenty to a hundred feet before the alarm went off. His room had an electronic listening device and a video monitor that permitted his parents to supervise him during commercial breaks in the TV shows they watched and his computer use was monitored. As a teenager he gladly submitted to home drug testing, thankful that he had the kind of parents who cared about his well-being.

He loved comic books. Superman, with his x-ray vision, and Brenda Starr, who could become invisible by pressing her wrist, were his favorites. *The Saint*, a TV program with the same theme, was also a favorite, as was *Candid Camera*. In our therapy sessions he frequently referred to events from reality TV shows. Television served to legitimate his fascination with hidden observation. As he put it, "Everyone anonymously watches television all the time. The people on TV don't know we are watching them. So what's the big deal about discretely watching people on the street?

At the time he came to me (Dr. Funt) for therapy, Tom's job was in computer security at a women's hospital. He was tasked with probing patient records for security weaknesses and problems. He found many. Away from work with no fear of an audit trail, he exploited these for personal reasons.

He worked through a famous libertarian computer service in Northwestern Krokastan. Consistent with its ethos ("Information wants to be free and belongs to the people"), the service promised full anonymity (masking and then immediately destroying records of all searches or e-mails).

His goal: to scientifically find the perfect idealized fantasy woman to become involved with, without ever really being involved. To find his ideal partner Tom generated a software program that searched on 136 factors from the hospital's database. He used factors such as age, height, weight, hair color, education, ethnicity, and health to create a short list of ideal women. The list was then run against a variety of public and commercially available databases to further vet for objectionable and to select for favorable characteristics.

Using facial recognition tools, he created a template for his ideal woman. He then searched photos in the patient database (included as a security measure to avoid fraud) and found one that matched almost perfectly. It was a "good match," as Jane Austen would have hoped. Coincidentally the woman—Eve Spectre—also ranked high on the list from his first search.

EVE SPECTRE: EVERY MOVE YOU MAKE AND THEN SOME: "ENGAGED THROUGH SURVEILLANCE"

The full case study details Tom's difficulties with women. He simply did not understand them and was afraid of them. He had few friends of either gender and had always found technology more interesting, reliable, and controllable than people.

He used the following joke to characterize his personality: "I was walking down the street and saw a frog. The frog looked up and said, "If you kiss me I'll turn into a desirable princess and marry you." I picked it up and put it in my pocket. The frog then yelled, 'Hey kiss me and I will turn into a beautiful princess.'" Tom replied, "Been there, done that, and it's too risky. I am a computer guy who is leery of relationships, but it's cool to have a talking frog."

Nonetheless Tom was eager to learn all about Eve from a safe distance. Since he had her photo and knew where she lived and worked, identification was elementary. He was immediately curious about all aspects of her life (beyond what he already knew from her health records). From that moment on, he reports that his private life, or rather his life away from work (being a loner, he did not have a private life in the communal sense that term usually implies), was exciting as never before. He suddenly knew what the poets and balladeers of love were about and he felt a sublime inner peace.

To avoid problems he did not try to arrange even a contrived meeting with Eve. He followed (in both senses) the new laws on electronic stalking and knew how broadly they could be applied. Given his fear of the law, rejection, sexually transmitted disease, unwanted offspring, the pain of divorce, and his uncertainty about how men should behave in an age of acute sensitivity to sexual harassment, where telling an off-color joke, complimenting a woman on her appearance, offering a supportive touch, or even looking could get you in trouble, he preferred to be on the sidelines. It seemed rational to opt for a well-developed fantasy life where he was in full control.

Thus, it was never necessary for him to lie about having an affair, nor did he have to worry about rejection or disappointing a partner. He saw his commitment to physical celibacy as protective in yet another sense. He read that men in committed relationships who had children experienced a decline in their testosterone level, and he did not want that to happen. He vowed never to let social conventions like being in a real relationship undermine control of his body.

Combining his modest understanding of Buddhism (with its emphasis on desire as the source of human unhappiness) with a Harley Davidson advertisement, he organized his social [sic] life around the motto "The eagle rides alone."

His passive voyeurism received an enormous boost from recent developments in technology. New means of communication were appearing almost daily: cell phones, scanners, digital retouching machines, web video and soon "smart dust," "smart rooms," "smart roads," "smart clothes," mechanical telepathy and remote access tools (RAT) that permit rummaging around in another's computer and even turning on their webcam. For Tom, these were turbocharged machines speeding up and expanding opportunities for him to satisfy his needs.

Tom was happy as never before. The object of his fascination did not know that she had become the secret actress in a technologically enhanced fantasy. Eve never learned and so was in no way hurt by it (at least that is how Tom feels). The technology precluded the need for them to meet. Given his distinctive ways, she was much better off that way.

Tom is at pains to stress that his behavior is within the letter of the law. To ensure this, he even consulted an attorney and he audited a law class given by Droit Markenberg, a famous privacy advocate who had helped draft federal legislation regarding electronic privacy. He saw nothing wrong in his behavior and said it was parallel to the harmless computer hacking he had done. As with the hacking, he just wanted to unobtrusively take a look, taking or damaging nothing.

A full list of Tom's activities would be tiresome and serve no useful clinical purpose. Let me, however, offer a sample of what he calls his "research techniques" in creating "a safe imaginary friend."

After a few months of waiting he was able to rent an apartment directly across the street from Eve's. He set up a continuously recording video camera with a telephoto lens directed at her window. By never closing the blinds she unwittingly left herself unprotected. Another camera on his outside wall was aimed at her apartment's front door. He could have directly planted a hidden video lens in various rooms in her apartment. But to do that would require trespassing, or entering her apartment on a pretext such as by claiming to be a building inspector. The first was illegal and the second required lying, something he did not do. For several of her rooms, this wasn't even necessary, as the wireless video security cameras permitted access. These send an unprotected video signal back to a nearby computer or TV base station (and to anyone with a receiver up to one-quarter of a mile away). Tom spent hours gazing at her furniture. He appreciated her openness but worried that other less responsible observers would also take advantage of her gracious unencrypted sending of video signals. Since the cameras were only in some rooms, and even then there were blind spots, he closely followed developments in unmanned remote controlled photographic drone technology. However, the smallest commercially available drones were still too large for surreptitious entry, even if sending a fly-sized eavesdropping device through the screen was legal. Such miniaturized devices were in the planning stages and not yet available.

A parabolic microphone disguised as a satellite dish was also pointed at the window but only worked when the window was open. (He did not use a laser listening device that would have picked up sound vibrations through a closed window because that was illegal, nor would he entertain the idea of upskirt videotaping.) He attached a tracking device under her car's rear fender (he was careful to do this when the car was on a public street so as not to trespass). This continuously sent signals via global positioning satellite to his receiver, so he always knew where her car was, even when it was stolen.

He generated a "socio-metric" diagram locating her within a context of family and friends. He did genealogical research tracing her family history. He developed dossiers on her friends, initially identifying many of them from their license plate numbers when they parked in the visitors' space at her apartment. For a modest fee the Department of Motor Vehicles made additional information available to anyone. (The money the department made from this was used to finance a program putting video cameras at major intersections.) His network analysis was aided by the fact that he could legally purchase her cell phone records. These dribbled or flooded (depending on whom one believes) out, regardless of company policies against this.

He wanted Eve's vicarious company, but he also felt a manly need to protect her. Eve had someone to watch over her even if she didn't know it. Beyond satisfying his own needs, with this oversight Tom saw himself as a Good Samaritan, unselfishly providing a service in a dangerous and indifferent world. He believed that it was in her interest, as well as his, to have her under surveillance. For proof he referred to the time he called 911 when a gentlemen caller in her apartment became too aggressive. Another time when he knew she was at work and her apartment was vacant, the thermal-imaging device he also kept pointed at her apartment showed heat radiation from a living being. He called 911 from a pay phone and reported a possible burglary in progress. It turned out to be a neighbor's St. Bernard that she was temporarily caring for.

He next did a full search of a great many databases. Some of these he accessed directly (e.g., public record files), but for most he relied upon commercial services found online. He was not alone. He read in *People* magazine that more than 73.81 percent of Internet users had secretly Googled "a person of interest"—neither asking their permission nor informing them after the fact. New search services were regularly offered. For a search, all he had to do was supply the name and birth date, address, or social security number.

He could have accessed everything on her networked computers at work and home, (at home via satellite television). The password was insecure (birthday and initials), since she had nothing to hide. Even with better computer security, he could have deceived her into clicking on a malicious link to install RAT. But Tom resisted the invitation to spy here because to do so would probably have violated the 1986 Electronic Privacy Protection Act, not to mention the fact that it was unsporting and almost beneath his dignity, given the absence of any technical challenge. He even resisted the harmless act of watching her dog at a doggy day care center (the center offered real time images to pet owners via webcams).

From the video cameras (including one built into his sunglasses that he used to analyze her pupil dilation for possible drug use), his own still photography using a cigarette lighter camera, and images copied from her high school and college yearbooks (obtained from a company whose advertisement he saw on the web), he developed a photographic portfolio. He scanned his favorite pictures into his state-of-the-art computer. He digitally edited these so that he had only facial images of her. He then made modest changes to her appearance (changing her hair and eye color, making her ears flatter and a tad smaller, accentuating some parts of her form and reducing others).

Most persons seeing Eve and the new image would assume it was the same person (or perhaps her sister), even though the resemblance was not perfect. These minor editions meant that he could now claim that this was a work of art and not an exact photograph of a known person. This was also true of the images he created of her as a very young and much older woman described below. There simply was no analogue in "reality." If he was ever questioned, he could truthfully say, "I don't know her from a coat hanger."

Using a program that generated images of persons at various life stages he also created an age portfolio taking her from age fifteen up to seventy-five. He then did the same for himself. He digitally joined their images to create a photographic history of their "relationship" from the teenage years on up. In some cases (as with his high school prom picture), he used a "real" picture and simply placed her face over that of the girl he had taken to the prom. He added Thomas Edison's optimistic line "What the hand of man creates the head of man can control."

He put these images on his wall next to the homey touch he added with pictures of all her previous residences. He obtained the addresses from a data warehouse. He then obtained high-resolution satellite photos of these locations, reduced them, and created a collage.

Using a speech synthesizer he created simulated conversations between Eve and himself. The speech synthesizer made it possible for him to fairly accurately reproduce the sound and timing of her voice. Tom legally heard some of her phone conversations (until she obtained a more sophisticated cordless phone) through the UHF frequency of his old television set. Even if this had been discovered (which was highly unlikely), he could probably not have been found guilty for just having his television set on. If he wanted to, he could also have used a radio wave scanner purchased in 1984 before possession of this type was restricted. Or he could have purchased cellular interceptors, which were still available to those in law enforcement and for export.

He did not want to risk trespass and possibly other charges in attaching a transmitter directly to her telephone or hiding a transmitter elsewhere in her apartment, but he did obtain a voice sample from her answering machine. Through a trial and error process he determined the two-digit security access code for her answering machine and voice messaging system at work (although he could have also purchased a machine for doing this), and he thus kept current on her messages by remotely accessing her answering machine. He subjected her messages to voice stress analysis to detect lies. He also obtained some live speech data (always using a pay phone to avoid caller ID) by calling her at work and at home using a variety of subterfuges (wrong number, newspaper sales, charitable solicitations, public opinion polls). He took an average of her voice samples and generated the appropriate algorithms for voice simulation.

With those data he could program her to say anything and could actually create conversations in which they "interacted" and discussed everything. These were a far cry from the mournful nineteenth-century soliloquies of undying and unrequited love delivered in front of the mirror or scrawled in a diary or a never-to-be-mailed letter. Were someone to overhear the conversations, they'd be convinced that Eve was in the room with Tom (although hearing the same exact conversations over and over would have aroused suspicion and gotten boring). This might be seen as the ultimate in narcissism or as an ideal merging (as the guidebooks and poets counsel) of the selves of lovers. They certainly never had any fights, and it was clear who was in control. For a different perspective, he converted her sound waves into light patterns and was able to observe her in a unique fashion.

As noted, Tom was very up at this point and wanted to share the good news about being in love. After all, what was the point of being a voyeur if you couldn't advertise your triumphs? Unshared secrets were only half the fun, especially with the safety of cyberspace. He said his sociology class defined this as a chameleon insight.[6]

He did all the work needed to create a web site with a full account of his feelings for the woman and their imagined activities together, her past social and medical history, credit ratings, and consumption habits. He wrote about how angry he would become if she ever betrayed him (this was obviously academic since they had never met).

His entrepreneurial imagination ran wild. He thought of offering a service to help others like himself create such partners. His own personal web site would be proof of what could be done. For a modest fee, he would provide assistance. For an even larger fee, he would offer a complete package. He even thought that with his knowledge of databases he could serve as a sort of matchmaker in the ether. He would of course open the site by announcing, "Warning: This site does not condone or recommend participating in any illegal or questionable activities. This site is meant for entertainment purposes only." But for reasons that we are still exploring in therapy, he could not bring himself to activate the web site.

He was able to find other more, confined ways of communicating and sharing the joy. For example, he converted some of the images to postcards and he had others blown up to poster size to adorn his walls. Tom wasn't content with two-dimensional representations. He purchased five mannequin replicas of her. From Eve's photo, the fabricator was able to recreate her facial appearance. These he placed with appropriate dress around his apartment (on the sofa, sitting at the kitchen table, etc.). From working at a dress store, watching the fashion ads, and years of observation, Tom was very knowledgeable about women's clothes. He found it easy to reproduce Eve's type of wardrobe and even improve on it, using more expensive clothes and colors that better suited her complexion.

A final example of his bizarre fixation can be seen in the rag kept in a small jar prominently displayed on his mantle, right alongside his bowling trophy and his autographed pictures of Frances Ford Coppola and G. Gordon Liddy. In a criminalistics class, he had read of the high art form to which the East Germans had taken scent as a means of identification. Stasi offices were overflowing with neatly stacked sealed jars with little rags in them, each representing a suspected enemy of the people. Humans unknowingly constantly mark their territory. After suspects left an interrogation, police would wipe something they had touched or their chair with a cloth to get the smell and then label and bottle it. When graffiti or vandalism occurred, police would rub the site for scents and then use a specially trained dog to see if a match could be made. On balmy summer weekends, Eve often read on a bench in a nearby park. It was easy enough for him to rub the bench after she left in order to collect her scent (which he described as now belonging to him since she had left it in a public place).

Of course Tom didn't need this to identify her, since he already knew who she was (and where she was). But it gave him pleasure to think of Eve's presence always there on the mantle in the same room with him, much as those who keep the ashes of a loved one close at hand in an urn, or a lock of childhood hair in a necklace—even if the secret possession of her territorial markings didn't communicate the way the photographs, conversations and letters did. The distinctive smell was too weak for the human nose. Nor could he even test the ability of a dog to identify it, since his apartment prohibited animals. But as the secret colonizer of her scent, he knew her in a truly original way denied to others. The fact that a part of her was always there, for better or for worse and in good times and bad, filled him with awe about the universe. It was uplifting and wondrous to be reminded that there were many things under the sun that mere humans could not perceive. He had the same feelings in his moonstruck gazing at her DNA patterns described below.

YOUR TRASH AIN'T NOTHING BUT TRASH

Voire at first was very excited by the thought of the riches Eve's trash might provide. He knew that the US Supreme Court had concluded that it was OK to dumpster dive, so there was no risk there (although not in the city of Beverly Hills, where it was illegal even if contents had been shredded). True, he did learn a considerable amount about Eve's finances and her heating bills (her dwelling was overheated, according to EPA standards), to whom she made long distance calls (her mother, grandmother, a college roommate, and a famous psychic seen on national TV). He knew about her consumption habits from itemized credit card bills and barcode-generated receipts from grocery, liquor, drug, book, and video stores. In spite of his allergies, he occasionally sprayed her favorite perfume on the mannequins.

Eve's diet left much to be desired. It was high in polyunsaturated fats, and she did not consume the FDA-recommended minimum daily amounts of riboflavin, molybdenum, boron, or tin. Nor as far as he could tell did she take a calcium supplement. Her taste in videos included *Cooking with Moldy Cheeses*, and in books, *Walking Tours of the Sahara Desert* and the *Autobiography of Lawrence Welk*.

So compelled was he to know everything about her that he spent thousands of dollars having her DNA analyzed (the DNA sample came from cell tissue on her discarded depilatory wax). Ever the visual person, he enlarged the image showing her unique DNA sequences. It looked like some kind of 1950s modern art, what with the lines of varying width and length, to which he added colors of the rainbow. He did the same for himself and joined them in a large red heart shaped frame hung over his bed—a bit idiosyncratic but very personal and original. The DNA medical report was fascinating. He noted with pride that she would make a wonderful biological mother. Yet one thing was troubling. She had a genetic potential for an incurable disease. He thought for a long time about whether he should inform her of this. After posing this as a hypothetical on countless computer bulletin boards, he decided not to inform her. First, he couldn't think of an effective ruse to explain how he came to know about her DNA (although there is no law against this). After all, it's not like finding someone's wallet on the street or getting a letter for them addressed to the wrong address. But mainly his reason was that she could do nothing about it.

The DNA offered still other distant possibilities. Ever mindful of not wanting to intrude into Eve's life or in any way bother her, but very driven to want more of/from her, he became very interested in the idea of cloning. While he realized it was probably too late for him to clone her (unless a way could be found to vastly accelerate the growth process so he wouldn't have to wait twenty years), he thought how wonderful it might be for others (regardless of gender) if this could be done. It seemed like a win-win situation.

In spite of small gains, there was not much fantasy food in the garbage. He did not enjoy getting up at 4 a.m. to make his garbage runs. It was cold in the winter and smelly in the summer. He had to go through a number of trash bags to get to hers, and the bags sometimes broke. The world's insect overpopulation problem seemed to be centered in this row of trash. He had to compete with roving dogs and rats with rival interests in the garbage. Sometimes, homeless persons got to the trash first, and several times he saw a better-dressed person, whom he assumed to be a private detective, take a bag and leave an identical one in its place. He was amazed at what could grow on take-out Chinese food in only a few days. With so much rotting fruit, kitty litter, used tissue, and broken glass, the ratio of good stuff to garbage hardly made the search worthwhile.

He occasionally found some revealing personal passages in draft copies of letters to a girlfriend. But mostly the letters expressed concerns about a boring job, cellulite, shopping, a baseball team that always seemed to lose, and still waiting for Mr. Right. Among the pharmaceutical remnants there were no packages for birth control pills or aphrodisiacs but many for constipation, diarrhea, acne, and the removal of unwanted facial hair. In his words, "This stuff was a real turnoff."

At that point, a book he found at the laundromat by Professor Erving Goffman, *The Presentation of Self in Everyday Life*, led Voire to reassess his behavior. The book argued for the importance, and even sanctity, of backstage regions and personal borders. It claimed that these make it possible for us to cooperatively sustain appreciative illusions in our own eyes and in the eyes of others and are central to human dignity. It was then that he came to me for therapy.

Satirical stories are one thing and scholarly analysis another, even if both sometimes can be a joke. The next chapter moves from the lightness of fact filled fiction to the seriousness of analysis.

A Mood Apart: What's Wrong with Tom?

For any eye is an evil eye
That looks in onto a mood apart.
ROBERT FROST, "A Mood Apart"

In the full statement from which Tom is drawn (press.uchicago.edu/sites/ marx/) many of his experiences as a subject or agent of surveillance are broadly representative of the average person. As such, they require no special analysis beyond what would apply to others in the same settings.

My discussion here is restricted to what is unique about the case. Males as agents and females as subjects involve distinctive questions of sex and gender. Moreover, as noted, his behavior nestles within the separate context of open-field surveillance—meaning surveillance that occurs beyond that appropriately associated with a role, an organization, or a group. It introduces fascinating unsettled questions regarding what should be private even in "public" (whether defined as place or easy availability of information). By indirection, it also encourages thought on what should be public (or at least revealed to appropriate others such as employers, merchants, government officials, parents, and friends) within the private zone of the individual.

The deleted material from this chapter (press.uchicago.edu/sites/marx/) discusses aspects of gender, sex and surveillance, the male gaze and how the story of Tom might change if the genders and sexual orientation were different (if Tom became Tomasina). Given space limitations, this chapter only considers what is wrong with Tom's behavior. What he mostly violates are soft expectations about what is appropriate to impersonal, non-role-related, low-visibility, open-field contexts involving publicly accessible (unprotected) personal data. In the previous chapter Tom offers his justifications for peering at the private within the public.[1]

Outlaw or Pioneer, Victimizer or Victim?

How should Tom be viewed and by what standards? The multiplicity of social contexts and consequences makes this a challenging question. In the
full case study Tom represents much that is good about American society:
self-improvement, honesty, patriotism, respect for the law, and concern for
equality and justice (Willis and Silbey 2002). He is also mannerly, compas-
sionate, forgiving, loyal, and protective of those he cares about. He submerges
his own strongly felt needs in order not to inflict direct harm or embarrassment on others. He uses surveillance to act heroically, or at least in a socially
responsible fashion (e.g., alerting police when Eve has a disorderly visitor,
working as a lifeguard and store detective, and volunteering as a neighborhood watcher). Tom is also the beneficiary of positive surveillance—from his
parents, who successfully helped him become an adult, and the doctors who,
after extensive testing, evaluation, and monitoring, diagnosed and treated his
childhood illness. A vast array of unseen food, air quality, transportation,
product, and work safety inspectors also serve him. And in the full case study
he also suffers from many surveillance abuses (e.g., anonymous denouncers,
hidden cameras, telephone and computer taps).

He is caught in a miasma of cultural confusion not of his making. Given
conflicts in values and goals and the large interpretive, discretionary, and gray
areas surrounding many of these issues, taking a given line of expected behavior to an extreme or misreading the context, as Tom so often does, can
have unintended negative effects.

In logically following one set of values, such as freedom of inquiry and
expression, Tom runs afoul of others, such as the invasion of privacy. When
hired by his department store employer, he was trained to make eye contact
with customers and to be friendly. But then there were complaints that he
was too friendly. In simply looking directly at his female fellow employees,
he claims he is honoring them and that to not make eye contact can be seen
as arrogant, unfriendly, and disrespectful. Yet too much (or the wrong kind
of) eye contact can be seen as invasive, threatening, or hostile. As with some
medicines, there is an optimal point. Too much or too little (or the wrong
combinations) does harm. Properly socialized individuals of goodwill know
how to wend their way through these dilemmas.

Tom is poorly socialized and makes others uncomfortable. Yet he does
this with a clear conscience, aided by a confusing culture that offers him
abundant rationalizations and a vast unregulated and largely unregulatable
opportunity structure regarding the private in the public.

Tom is "way high on the 'creepy' meter" (Staples and Nagel 2002) and an unrighteous, duplicitous, and inconsistent sociopath who makes bad choices. His behavior—whether reflecting culture, gender, or genes—hardly absolves him of responsibility, but those factors can help us understand his actions.

From one standpoint, Tom is civil in not directly inflicting his actions on Eve Spectre. To follow from Goffman, is this then a case of *civil inattention*? Is it *uncivil attention*? Since his behavior does involve attention, a better term is lessened *civil attention*. He attends, but in such a way that she doesn't respond, because she is unaware. His attention is mediated by distancing technologies. In contrast, Goffman's use of the term *civil inattention* presumes that the other has *some* awareness of the person in their immediate presence who nonetheless feigns disinterest. When Goffman was writing in the 1970s, that meant physical presence, but with today's technologies, that need not be the case. She is the object (or subject, in terms used in the book) of his attention, but is this really to her or to her abstracted "persona"? A fuller rendering requires considering the agent's words and deeds, whether or not attention is directly to the subject and whether or not the subject is aware.

Is Tom then, like the society he reflects, just a giant Rorschach test in which observers offer their vantage point as the only truth? With respect to where the truth lies, can we do no better than the congressman who, in responding to testimony he did not agree with, politely said, "Well, I guess everyone is entitled to their own statistics?" I think we can do better.

Offensive Tom

Is Tom correct that actions such as his cause no damage? What are laws about personal information intended to protect or guard against? If neither Eve nor anyone else ever finds out about Tom and his data, is harm done? Can an individual be hurt by secret surveillance only intended for consumption by the collector? Yes! What you don't know can hurt you, and even if it doesn't, such behavior offends the broader society. Morality can hardly be said to take a holiday when infractions go undiscovered.

As Durkheim noted under modern conceptions of criminal law, offenses are viewed as an attack on the community at large, not just on the wronged party (whether he or she knows or cares about the violation). Further, with regard to privacy, Priscilla Regan (1995) and colleagues more recently (Roessler and Mokrosinska 2015) effectively analyze its social values apart from the individual. Much of the secret surveillance Tom engages in can be seen to debase our common civic culture through its violation of the taken-for-

granted world and the failure to appreciate the borders of the self. His behavior is consistent with Rochelle Gurstein's analysis (1996) of the decline of
nineteenth-century reticence.

The act of surveillance brings risks of broader revelation of data, even
with the best of intentions. Here a distinction needs to be drawn between the
momentary consumption of data by the surveillor's senses and the creation
of a reproducible record. Empirical artifacts reflecting the surveillance, such
as photos, video and audio recordings, and photocopies have a very different moral status than mere imagination. The risk of leakage or accidental
exposure with a permanent record takes the surveillance down several moral
notches relative to overhearing or watching without recording.

In Tom's case, for example, he could change his mind or undergo a psychological change that could lead him to want share his work. Even if he
remains steadfast, what if a cleaning service, a landlord, or fire or ambulance
personnel came upon it? What if his materials became public, whether because of his own carelessness,[2] a burglary, a police search, a news story, or
a trial? One of the cruelest ironies of all is that invaded persons may then
doubly suffer from the shock of discovery of the surveillance and from having
their information disseminated beyond their control.

Even given legal rights to easily available information, the would-be secret surveillor needs to consider certain questions: If the subject suspected
that she was under such surveillance, would she alter her behavior in any
way to block or deflect it? What is the psychological impact on persons who
learn that they have been spied upon? Does the agent want to be responsible?
Would the secret observer be embarrassed, humiliated, or ashamed at having
kamikaze surveillance behavior known? And finally, how would the secret
surveillor feel if his or her family members were subject to such treatment?

Kinds of Harm

In general we assume that those with whom we have only impersonal or no
relationships will not come to know (let alone accumulate) details that we
have not ourselves revealed. Under such conditions, it is unseemly for an individual to make inferences about another's health, happiness, beliefs, behavior, life chances, and so on, and to create representations in the way and to the
degree that Tom does. But what precisely are the undesirable consequences
from privacy invasions that the individual does not learn about and that result in no direct detrimental action?

Hidden observation threatens the trust that is so central to social organization. Deception does as well, and Tom can be faulted for behaving decep-

tively. While he prides himself on being open, he hides many of his data collection activities (cameras in dark glasses and a cigarette lighter, a parabolic mike disguised as a satellite dish, and the use of pseudonyms and pretenses in purchasing data about her). Tom is clever in arguing that he takes advantage of situations, not people, but his use of ruses and sophisticated technology to extract, record, and combine information means that he is hardly the passive agent he claims to be. He might rationalize his behavior out of a desire not to upset those he is interested in, but this is beside the point. Such behavior violates trust. We assume that under normal circumstances, both people and objects are as they appear to be. Expectations of trust are not restricted just to personal relationships, although they are strongest there.

While you can protect your physical property with borders of concrete and steel, the only protection that exists for your image, much of your personal information, and what people do with you in their imaginary world is their manners and sense of decency. The fact that appearance is in one sense a free good for the sighted, like air or the water of a rushing river, adds to the confusion in assessing Tom's behavior. However, if we regard a seemingly free good (such as the appearance others offer for us to look at) not only as one that can simply be taken in the world without physical resistance or technologies, but as one that the individual must be entitled to take (in anything beyond the most innocent regard), then the look or photograph are not free goods. They are surrounded by rules, levels of access, and a sense of propriety, and when these are violated, the social order is undermined.

Looking may be free in one sense, but it is not necessarily cheap. Mythology suggests that those who violate rules about looking suffer. Lot's wife was turned to salt after violating the command not to look back.[3] In Greek mythology, those looking at the female monster Medusa were turned to stone (except for the invisible Perseus, who was able to kill Medusa by using her reflection in his shield to aim his strike) (Gimbutas 1982). According to the seventeenth-century legend, when Lady Godiva made her naked ride, citizens were required to remain indoors. Peeping Tom, who looked out the window, was struck blind and dead (presumably in that order) (*New Encyclopedia* 1990). Note also the many cultures in which lower-status persons were to avert their eyes in the presence of higher-status persons and in which prohibitions were placed on looking at the ruler, as well as prohibitions today on photographing or being in the area of military installations.

People can harm others by violating the spirit, if not the letter, of laws protecting property, contracts, and legitimate access. Voyeurs take something to which they are not entitled. A trespass may occur in the ether and within the imagination, if not in physical space. Either what is taken has not been paid for, or access to it has not been granted.

A kind of rip-off occurs when Tom appropriates Eve's personal data with such intentionality that he colonizes her representations. One aspect of the rip-off involves the qualitative difference between the sum total and individual parts. While any single strand of information may seem inconsequential, multiple strands offer a fuller picture of the individual, revealing things that the person may not even know about him or herself. In acquiring multiple strands, Tom has crossed a threshold point in the aggregation of information. The creation of a "mosaic" in which, through a "value-added model," combining information (regardless of whether it is public or private or available to the unaided senses or requires extractive technologies) fundamentally alters its character. It may mean an end run around an individual's effort to protect information about the self.

In the totality of his behavior, Tom violates tacit assumptions that we make about how others will respond to our personal information. We assume that the kinds of information Tom gathers will not be much noted by others (absent a warrant to do so) and, if noted, will not be collected and aggregated, or long remembered.

The erotic looks that lovers may grant each other in public are not acceptable when offered by others. Tom is self-deluded in thinking that because he can with ease look lasciviously, or gather massive amounts of public data on an individual, he is entitled to do so.

Most people use such opportunities with discretion as a result of manners and/or a desire not to be thought poorly of or to invite unwanted reciprocal attention or sanctioning. We learn to avert our eyes even as we could look. This is often the case with a dead body or when someone does something embarrassing—what Goffman (1963) refers to as disattending. Children are taught that it is bad manners to stare. It can also be dangerous. We offer respect for the other by not watching too attentively or by not recording and, in so doing, we also affirm something about the kind of people we are.

It is not that women or men do not want to be looked at and noticed, but that they have a proprietary interest in controlling who looks at them and in what ways. A part of personhood is defined by the autonomy, ownership, and control individuals have over their data and image, whether in face-to-face interaction or beyond, and adhering to a visual honor system works in public as part of this system. One can marvel that men and women are so relatively (if not equally) inhibited in their looking.

Unknown (as against suspected or identified) secret watching has an additional element of unfairness. It permits the agent to evade the natural moderating effects of reciprocity and countercontrol that are possible when the subject is aware.

When individuals have reason to suspect they are under such surveillance, they may take steps to prevent it (e.g., closing blinds, using a shredder, not using a cordless phone, debugging rooms, unlisting a phone number, encrypting computer and phone communications including answering machines, and when there is interaction, perhaps even obtaining a restraining order or getting a guard dog). Most people do none of the above because they assume there are no Toms seeking to be a vicarious part of their life. This leads to the issue of the harm that can come from discovery.

Pain and poignancy are both consistent and striking in the voices of those who speak out about their discovery of voyeuristic behavior and related forms of inappropriate personal border crossing. Four recurrent themes beyond the possibility of strategic disadvantage are feelings of betrayal, paranoia, embarrassment, and shame, and overarching these is fear.

BETRAYAL

Secret watching and recording often involve the breaking of trust within relationships or in places presumed to be protected, in which individuals feel free to reveal themselves. The trust subjects routinely assume offers temptation and an opportunity structure for violations. This trust varies from those who share close relationships—lovers, family members, and friends—to those one knows as a result of contractual relationships, such as a landlord, to those organizations with which we interact and in which we place a generalized trust.

The closer the relationship and the more protected the place, the greater the sense of betrayal. For example, the discovery of a person on a street corner peering into an open window, however discomforting, is unlikely to be as harshly judged as when a hidden camera is discovered in a hotel room, locker room, tanning salon, or bathroom. The person in a restaurant at an adjacent table listening to a conversation does not arouse the same feelings as a telephone technician selling unlisted phone numbers or listening to or recording intimate conversations.[4] The law tries to conceptualize this in terms of whether, in a given situation, there is a reasonable expectation of privacy.

UNCERTAINTY AND PARANOIA

Beyond the momentary shock of learning that personal borders have been crossed, one's view of the world can change in a more enduring way. The victim experiences a loss of innocence associated with the violation of trust and new uncertainties. Once one discovers an invasion, it is natural to wonder if it will happen again. The victim may also feel less confidence or faith in the world, questioning whether persons, places, and material objects are what they appear to be and whether they can be trusted. People are justified in posing such questions, as a sampling of commercially available places for hiding a camera includes a bottle, ceiling speaker, clock, emergency light, exit sign, jacket, lamp, mirror, mug, pager, phone, picture, plant, smoke alarm, computer speaker, book, tie, watch, sunglasses, and cigarette pack.

The urban angst Erving Goffman (1971) describes in writing about "normal appearances" beautifully applies. The individual may respond with an immobilizing paranoia, vast energy put into defensive measures (showering in clothes or in the dark, frequent room sweeps for bugs, changes of phone number, use of mail drops, formal contractualizing of personal relationships, as with nondisclosure statements), and a constriction in activities.

Once secret surveillance has been discovered, the victim also worries about dissemination. Who else has the results or could have? Do others see me in a new way as a result of their knowledge? Am I being treated differently as a result? With a permanent record of personal information that can be easily circulated to others, the victim may relive the memory of the recorded event(s) and imagine it being seen or heard over and over, whether by new persons or the initial recorder. Such repercussions seem particularly characteristic of smaller communities, where knowledge and gossip spread widely and where anonymity is less likely. The web is of course the ultimate example of the impossibility of fully calling back information.

EMBARRASSMENT

A sense of unease accompanies being involuntarily naked (whether literally or metaphorically with respect to personal information). Even if an individual is not strategically disadvantaged or revealed in a negative light, his or her modesty and reticence have been transgressed. This is the nakedness of Eve and Adam once they become conscious that their behavior has been monitored. We feel uncomfortable revealing aspects of ourselves to strangers, and even to doctors, absent reasons for doing so. The secret filming of nudity or sexual activities is an example. Even in a non-Victorian age of self-advertising and revelation, most persons would be outraged and embarrassed at the unauthorized collection and exposure to others of such personal information.

There can also be concerns even with authorized exposure. A scene in Steven Soderbergh's film *Sex, Lies, and Videotape* (1989), in which the character acknowledges talking about her sex life on camera for a male friend, illustrates this. Her straight-laced sister is shocked when she learns of this and says, "How could you do that? He has probably already beamed it on satellite to some dirty old man in South America." Her horror involves the possibility of having intimate details revealed to some anonymous faraway man who would not know her name and whom she would never meet.[5]

SHAME

A related element is the sense of shame and humiliation if what the surveillance reveals is discrediting, or at odds with the image the individual publicly projects. A hidden camera in a bedroom or bathroom might reveal a wig, prosthetic device, birthmark, scar, or surgery, as well as things that may be hidden, such as an extramarital affair or homosexuality.[6] Inappropriately accessing a database may reveal equivalent information regarding criminal records, bankruptcies, bad credit, or mental and physical illness that the individual wishes to withhold. The subject may feel disgraced and stigmatized as a result of the unauthorized knowledge access, independent of any strategic disadvantage.

Judging Tom

Chapter 13 explores judgment issues in more detail. Here I wish to merely hint at the kinds of factors that should inform evaluation. The context and comportment themes are of course central. In order to judge, one must analyze the kind of setting (e.g., a park vs. a home), the goals of the surveillance, the role relationships, the established rules and expectations, and the kinds of data collected (e.g., personal or impersonal, visual or audio). Analysis requires differentiating between thoughts and overt behavior, real and simulated information, awareness and lack of awareness of the subject or object (overt or covert data collection), the presence or absence of consent to collection of information, and the degree of equality or reciprocity. Some other factors include whether the information is available to the unaided senses or requires a technology to extract, and, if the latter, what the characteristics of the technology are.

Motive, while hardly fully exculpatory, is also a factor in judging.[7] A desire to intentionally do harm is distinct from actions that unintentionally cause harm. However, actual behavior (and the structure of the situation) may be more important and easier to empirically determine and analyze. Thus, information overtly collected with the subject's knowledge and consent without a technology, in an impersonal and/or public setting, clearly has a different moral status from that secretly collected without awareness or consent, using a technology in a private setting involving a personal relationship.

As another variation, an actual record may have a different moral status from a composite or simulated record. The former can draw on a morality of authenticity and perhaps a higher truth value, at least with respect to an actual case. On the other hand, the latter may be justified precisely because it isn't "real," as that term is usually understood. Moreover, those records that protect the anonymity of subjects are different from those in which subjects can be clearly identified.

Additional factors of major significance are how the information is used and who consumes it. Private information used for private purposes has a very different status from that which is broadcast. Assuming that the surveillance does not break the law and that the goal is private consumption, a factor in moral assessment may be how good the secret surveillor is at keeping the results secret (the security question). As noted, there is the risk of revelation, even with the best of intentions, although this is less likely when there is no documentary record. Chapter 13 offers a list of questions that can be asked to help assess any personal data collection activity.

Learning from Tom

In describing Tom, I emphasized the bizarre and the atypical to surface and highlight the issues. In the fuller Tom case study the harm he causes and suffers are in general not life threatening, and his naïveté and some of the occurrences are humorous. But that is not to suggest that these issues are unworthy of serious attention. In contrast to the other major narrative contexts which involve role playing based on care, contracts, or coercion, Tom is in a sense beyond or outside an organization or group. He ranges across personal information settings and rummages through life remnants largely unbounded by the rules and interaction order that structure much behavior. In such open fields, order, such as it is, must rely on supports other than law, rewards, or penalties.

The variety, conflicting expectations, and difficulty of enforcement in Tom-like situations would severely challenge the law's blunt and general quality—even if there weren't commonly a lag between development of a new tool and means of regulating it. Law can't control everything we may find offensive, nor can it redress all hurtful behavior. As a wise jurist said several hundred years ago, "The eyes cannot by the law of England be found guilty of trespass."[8]

Even granted that some of Voire's behavior, while legal when it occurred, might become illegal (e.g., secret videotaping or remotely listening to another's answering machine messages), the law can only go so far. It is hard to prove that those using legal software for remote computer access or a parabolic microphone have criminal intent. Mostly what Voire is guilty of is bad manners and insensitivity. And his bad behavior helps us see the extent to which we need awareness and standards to guide easy-to-use invasive technologies under conditions of anonymity. Public discussion and education are central for this.

Nevertheless, decent behavior must flow primarily from custom and manners rather than from the threat of coercion or the agreement of contracts so central to the other narratives in this unit.[9] Tom's actions must be seen against the soft control of manners and the vast space for unseemly and inappropriate behavior available to anonymous agents acting secretly.

However extreme, Tom's behavior and responses are at one end of a continuum. He illuminates (as both subject and agent) potential uses of the new technologies and the lack of adequate formal or mannerly protections against violation. Whatever his distinctive psychology, he reflects elements of our culture and conflicts within it.

The issues around information technology do not just involve large organizations and their treatment of individuals, or organizational rivals, but also the behavior of individuals toward each other.

Tom does not come from the far reaches of American society. He has been formed and affected by surveillance experiences in mainline institutions—the military, education, work, and therapy. His ideas are not drawn from the sanity-defying fringe media but from mainstream sources such as reality TV and the popular press.

Given the ambiguity, elasticity, and frequently conflictual nature of values and norms, how is it that we have the degree of social order that we have? Given the vast social space for this, why aren't there many more Toms? Or perhaps there are and we prefer not to know.

Tom's case shows how easy it is to rationalize highly questionable behavior and how muddled expectations regarding all of this can be. A bit of Tom's curiosity nestles in all of us, regardless of gender, although in our culture more in men than in women. To varying degrees, we also share something with the subjects (or perhaps they are objects when treated in a depersonalized way) of Tom's covert activity.

In offering Tom as satirical fiction, I do not wish to detract from the mundane and omnipresent reality of the topic, or from its seriousness. Tom may be an outlier and even an outlaw, but it is premature to conclude that he does not offer a window into the future. The same can be said about the Honorable Rocky Bottoms, the subject of the next fictional account. Rocky's career has unfolded in both coercive and contractual contexts and in new forms that blend government and the private sector. Whether Tom and Rocky and their ideas and tools are indeed the turbulent wave of the future or only a brackish backwater remains to be seen.

Government and More: A Speech by the Hon. Rocky Bottoms to the Society for the Advancement of Professional Surveillance

I am here to fight for truth, justice and the American way.

SUPERMAN, 1978

As long as the genuine security problem exists, there will be persons whose imagination will be set boiling with excited apprehension.

EDWARD SHILS, 1956

This "true fiction" speech by Mr. Richard ("Rocky") Bottoms to the annual Las Vegas convention of the Society for the Advancement of Professional Surveillance is a composite of remarks, many of them direct quotes gathered in this research.

The talk reflects the optimistic, techno-surveillance worldviews of many of those broadly within the surveillance and security community. The speech argues for maximum use of the new technologies of security and surveillance and for prevention, categorical suspicion, nonconsensual data collection, the soft and hard engineering of behavior, and the increased blurring of borders between public and private security and more generally government and civil society.

Regardless of the varied settings in which Bottoms works, his actions involve surveillance that is *impersonal, nonreciprocal, and organizational* and involves *internal* and *external* constituencies. When Bottoms acts as an agent of government, a key structural aspect of his position is the legal power to coerce. His claim that his work is also about care mixes the ingenuous and the disingenuous. When his surveillance actions are in the private sector involving employers and consumers, the central mechanisms are contracts and persuasion.

Dossier on R. Bottoms

Mr. Richard Bottoms was born in Repressa, California. His home was adjacent to Folsom State Prison, where his parents were employed. Growing up in the protective orbit of the prison, under the guidance of stern parents and a strict religion, he came, at an earlier age than most, to appreciate the virtues of order and the need for strong controls.

A relative in the toy business had provided him with an endless supply of heroic police and military toys—from action figures to junior detective spy tools. His certainty about the righteousness of his cause and his attraction to the use of power to do good are traced to a Prussian ancestor who fled Europe under a death sentence for the clear air and golden streets of America after the failed revolutions of 1848. His acute awareness of the exceptionalism and special mission of the United States traces to historical circumstances involving the Reformation and Calvinist traditions, which powered his belief in individualism and free markets with religious zeal.

He gained his first law enforcement experience in an Explorer Boy Scout Troop sponsored by his local police department. For his Eagle Scout project he organized an undercover sting operation against merchants selling cigarettes and liquor to underage students. Scouts went to the stores and were often successful in purchasing contraband. However, the project was eventually called off after several scouts consumed the evidence.

He studied at the prestigious Briareus University under the renowned philosopher and futurist Professor Doctor Ralph Hythloday. In his studies he was strongly influenced by Plato's *Republic* and Thomas More's *Utopia*. He has several advanced degrees and was trained as both a sigint and signet (signals intelligence and networking) engineer with a strong dose of humint (human intelligence—with an emphasis on psychology and market research). From an initial interest in uses of the electromagnetic spectrum to remotely collect, as well as to send, signals to the body, he became interested in the potentials of exponential technology. He worked on Skynet, a self-aware system of interconnected computers.

Mr. Bottoms's career is a case study in continuous crisscrossing between the dark and the light side. He began as a military police officer, where he realized the benefits of cooperation and exchanges involving the military and law enforcement and developed software permitting easy data exchanges between operating systems and organizations. As part of his military service, he spent time as a sheep-dipped knuckle dragger and had his legends and indeed, in some circles is a legend!

After military service and several years as director of intelligence for a large urban police department, he went to work for a secret government agency. Because of his communication skills, he was seconded to Hollywood for two years, working to ensure that defense and security concerns were appropriately communicated to, and through, the mass media. He knows that symbols matter and repetition sells. He next served as a liaison officer charged with increasing cooperative relations through harmonization of security practices, information sharing, and joint training with European security services and public and private security providers.

He then spent several years as the Director of Marketing and Security for a national department store chain. Over the next decade, with several leaves of absence to work directly on government projects, he was employed by SeeSecCor, the large international private security company. Among his innovations there, he introduced a common vision; standardized control methods across the manufacturing, marketing, and security units; and oversaw implementation of RFID projects that put chips in all employees and in company property.

He was a strong advocate of predictive models of human behavior based on data mining and big data sets. His award-winning program SnagEm, written for the US Marshall's Fugitive Task Force, is now widely used in the commercial sector. As he often says, "A search after all is a search, whatever the goal." He currently heads the international private security firm WIT (Whatever It Takes) known for its flexible organizational and ethical approaches. He serves on the American Board for Certification in Homeland Security and is a member of the American College of Intel–Don't Tell Examiner's Institute. He is alone among his peers in having both the martial arts black belt in Wan Hun Low and the coveted communication arts green belt (seventh chord!) in Verbal Judo. He is a frequent commentator on television and the author of the best-selling book *Crossing Informational Borders for Security and Profit*, for which he received the coveted Mikey award.

NATIONAL AND CORPORATE SECURITY
Unauthorized Disclosure Subject to Criminal Sanction
ORCON (OC) Originator Controls Dissemination and Extraction
PROP (PR) Caution—Proprietary Information Involved
PRE-SEN (PS) Pretty Sensitive
SECURITY CLASSIFICATION (YEO)
[Note: the bracketed numbers in the speech refer to statements analyzed in chap. 12.]

THE WONDERS OF MODERN SURVEILLANCE:
A CALL TO ACTION

By R. Bottoms

Never before has society faced the dangers it does today. Will our profession rise to the challenge? Will we be in the driver's seat on the information superhighway leading the charge into the future? Or will we be roadkill in a deep pile of hurt waiting to be scavenged by those who get there first? Sir Frances Bacon really put the meat on the table when he said, "He that will not apply new remedies must expect new evils" [28].

There is too much talk these days and not enough action. I want RESULTS, not theories. I like my waffles for breakfast, not in my strategic plans. As police leader

Ollie (OC) Capsicum, in referring to President Truman's decision about the atomic bomb, asked, "If the technology is available, why not use it?" The answer is self-evident. We have the answers. Let's apply them! I say, let's turn the technology loose, and then we'll see the benefits flow [2].

When it comes to security and surveillance tools, the legal power of the state and the inventions and know-how of the private sector point the way. While the challenges we face are great, both the Big Guy and the technology are on our side. In this period of unique opportunity and crisis, it is time to unleash the full potential of surveillance technology and let the chips (pun intended) fall where they may. Where there is the slightest whiff of suspicion, or if costs of failure are great, it would be irresponsible not to use all the ammunition in our arsenal. Do I sound paranoid? OK—that's because I am the one with the facts and know what we have to worry about. If the public only knew what we know (but of course can't tell them), our job would be a whole lot easier.

The genius of the human species is invention, and this is taken to its highest form in Western Civilization, especially in the United States. Human betterment is directly tied to the inexorable march of information technology. The Christians might have made some mistakes over the centuries, but they got it right when they saw that history moves in a linear, progressive fashion. As surely as day follows night, the new must replace the old [1]. You can't stop progress, and no right-minded person would want to. The technology is here to stay. The question is, are we?

We are only now beginning to realize the potential of information technology. We need to vastly expand our R&D budgets and develop more powerful machines [38]. Above all we must turn to technology and do away with the human interface—that is, "get the humans out of the loop" [8]. We've got machines now to do the work, and they do it better. With drones, nanotechnology, and satellites, the sky is no longer the limit. Nor with robo-flys are window screens a barrier. John Lenin got it right when he sang "Imagine"—a song about vision.

We must anticipate virtual dangerous futures in order to prevent them. That requires continuous data collection as well as continuous probing of the security of our own methods. We need to view the world in systemic terms and use the tools of simulation. We must apply the insights of the life sciences, which tell us that all livings things are systems of information exchange. Meaning lies in fusion—in converting and combining streams of data into integrated information systems.

Most of the social issues we hear so much about are technical problems to be mastered, not social questions to be analyzed—or worse, to be negotiated. When untoward incidents occur, the cause must be seen as a technical systems failure [34]. Some say we must ask "why" regarding the motivation of rule breakers. But this only gives them a megaphone for self-serving, justifying rhetoric and encourages them to ask for even more.

Too often we hear from the "fruits and nuts" crowd (the civil-liberties/anarchist, dodgy, Luddite perps and potential perps who hang around universities and so-called public interest groups), that the term "technical fix" is somehow negative. But what can be better than a technical fix when you consider the alternative? These means offer cost-free solutions [10].

The electric eye never sleeps. Indeed, it never even blinks. Always on the job, it doesn't screw up, talk back, cut corners, miss work, lie, join unions, file lawsuits or engage in corruption, cover-ups or sexual harassment. It exceeds humans in the depth, scale, and speed of its work.

Technology just offers us the facts, which speak loudly and clearly for themselves [4]. Seeing is believing. We can help people believe by creating and telling them what they see before they see it. As a student of perception and marketing, I know the truth in the statement "If I had not believed it, I would never have seen it." All we do is report the neutral facts that enable security agents, employers, or parents to reach appropriate conclusions.

Our engineering experts base their no-nonsense actions on science, the unsullied simple purity of numbers, and the diamond-hard facts of EC (empirical correctness). If we can't trust them, who can we trust? Surely not the squishy sentimentality and sullied claims of contemporary political correctness and social nonscience [3, 26]. If we must have sociology, let it be with people who think like Ronald Regan (America's most famous undergraduate sociology major).

Technical solutions are reliable and secure. Real file cabinets defile, and paper records are easily lost, destroyed, or compromised. Personal information is best protected when the computer rather than a possibly prurient, dishonest, or curious clerk collects, reviews, and analyzes cases. Personal information is best discovered by sensors and computers. Research from a prestigious national science group has found increased validity and subject comfort when those being interviewed can respond to questions on a computer screen rather than directly to an interviewer.

Furthermore, with respect to managing complaints, our studies on effective client communication find that "the computer says" is a very persuasive rhetorical device, as is the claim, "I'm sorry that is not in the computer." Technology makes it real.

Another advantage of technical solutions is that they are egalitarian. In the United States, relative to those unfree Europeans (who can't even buy weapons or many state-of-the-art surveillance tools for personal use), the technology is available to all. We are not talking multimillion dollar aircraft or computer programs that require a degree from MIT to run, but laptops, video cameras, home drug and pregnancy testing, and electronic location-monitoring devices that are within everyone's reach and become cheaper, faster and easier to use almost daily. Even satellite imagery relying on a billion dollar infrastructure and traditionally restricted to just a few governments is now available for nothing, or almost nothing, on the web.

When programmed not to consider certain personal characteristics, technology offers the ultimate nondiscriminatory tool. In short, security cameras catch the rich as well as the poor if they try to steal from a loading dock or sleep behind the mall or even under a bridge. The camera doesn't care about your gender, color, or accent. Computer-based decision making relying on quantitative indicators and artificial intelligence has done more for fairness and justice than all your lawsuits and so-called protest movements put together [6]. The sword of surveillance comes into the world because of justice delayed and justice denied, and it cuts!

We have to categorize in ways that meet our goals and maintain the image of our systems as fair and rationalized. The kinds of discrimination or, if it sounds better, distinctions we make are not based on the old irrational, imperial, ethnocentric, and sexist beliefs.

But we don't profile—that can get you a whole lot of bad press and besides it's illegal. Rather, we rely on rational criteria clearly understandable to the average person. Our actions are based on facts and fairness. But I will tell you, we do look a little more closely at people with last names suggesting ancestral ties to contentious areas. We do that to protect them from false accusations and hate crimes and to gain their help in identifying foreign agents. We need to be guided by scientific correlations and common sense—not by the passions of the prejudiced.

We sell freedom from fear by offering prevention.—a point well made in one of my favorite films, *Minority Report*. INVENTION FOR PREVENTION is the name of my game. As the community of surveillance professionals, then, our job is to help clients predict the future in order to control it. It does no good to close the barn door after the horse has bolted.

It is perfidious mendacity of the worst kind to claim, as some of our critics do, that we create problems to which we then sell solutions. No! That is ass backwards. We are bell ringers and problem solvers. Sadly, many of our potential clients are woefully ignorant of the risks they face. We have a moral and professional obligation to help them understand these risks and bring the good news that there are solutions. Above all, we must explain the contemporary idea of prevention and that being modern means we can almost eliminate risk, or at least price it fairly. I stress "almost" because completely eliminating the risk would be bad for business. Thus, we have a delicate communications and strategic challenge. We need to inform potential clients of the dangers so the need for our services is recognized while remaining upbeat.

Quantitative data and simulation [26] allow us to detect early warning signals before problems occur. Remember, even the worst offenders started off with clean records. Personal information is too valuable a commodity to waste, now that so much, about so many, can be so inexpensively obtained by so few and we face problems of such magnitude [24]. Think of the great things that could happen if we really were able to fully use all the available personal data that surveillance technology can provide. It is now cheaper to store all data than to cull it. A record, like a diamond, should be forever. We must purge our systems of troublemakers and subversives, not data, and that is why I strongly oppose policies that mandate the destruction of data after a short period. Because you never know.

In economics there is even a scientific theory that proves that good information lowers costs. One of our members, Ron "Pudge" Grais, hit the bulls-eye when he said, "information is the new gold. You can not know too much about the data subject and you dare not know too little" [39]. In short, the future is both knowable and shapable if only we invest the resources and have the courage to act. We need real-time documentary records that can be continuously combined, analyzed, and reviewed.

What has changed to upset the apple cart? Why are these technologically based goals and tools needed now? Look no further than to borders, both geographic and organizational, that are either too rigid or outdated, or that are broken, giving a free ride to invisible enemies. Traditionally our country's dynamism depended on isolation from the decadent Old World and the avoidance of foreign entanglements. The oceans were our natural borders. Tread on us and our military would wage war over there, while at home police dealt with internal threats. Neither our military nor our intelligence agencies could act at home, and our many national and local police agencies were restricted in gathering intelligence, even that which private-sector agencies could gather. While these restrictions added to inefficiency, we could manage. My friends, that is no longer the case.

In the twenty-first century those old separations are dysfunctional. Now, since we export our ideals and more, the borders of America have expanded to include the planet earth (and as our vital program of space research shows, beyond).

What is more, we can no longer as easily separate the enemy within from the enemy without. Potential enemies could be anyone and anywhere. Joseph McCarthy long ago realized that we are at risk from the febrile enthusiasm of conventicles who are shielded by liberties designed for others. We have barnacles on our borders and viruses within our systems. Mobility and decentralized structures make them hard to identify.

What we must do, then, is purge our systems of harmful elements, whether social or biological. The old borders need to be redrawn and reengineered. Those in remote locations beyond our physical borders can do terrible damage to our infrastructures. In a radical break with the past, our new infrastructures can be used against us (like those poor people who are allergic to their own sweat). Our airwaves are polluted. Our financial flows are corroded by dirty money. The bottom line here is survival of our way of life, economic growth, conservation of resources, and health.

Germs and ideas cross borders with equal impunity, and some ideas are pathological in the worst organic sense. In the dangerous world of today, crime, political violence, and germs merge as never before. Terrorists, for example, engage in narcotics trafficking and counterfeiting to finance chemical and biological weapons, and apolitical criminals sell muscle to the highest bidder.

Criminals and terrorists increasingly are part of shifting organizations and global networks. Like the child with a coloring book, Intel needs to fill in the blanks. But the picture in our coloring books is far more complicated. Rather than being two dimensional, linear, and fixed, these new dots may look almost random, although they are not. Making matters worse, the dots are hidden, fluid, and changeable. They appear and disappear, mutate and migrate via transparent, evaporating bridges. The enemy is an ambulatory masked rhizoid whose root-like filaments parasitically attach to our personal and social bodies and use our fluids in the hope of destroying us. Like those children's toys called transformers, they morph.

People and goods move as never before. And we can be right there with them using the body and its various offerings to track who has been where, when, and with whom else. We must offer a giant "No!" to anonymous mobility and a big "Yes!" to transparent and controlled mobility for those with the right stuff. We need to identify and exclude, or otherwise immobilize, those with the wrong stuff, in order to preclude. To do that we need to scan, pan, and ban. The modern way uses virtual patrols via robots, cameras, sensors, and databases, not inefficient meat and meet police patrols of physical spaces.

No, my friends, borders aren't what they used to be. With an avant-garde, borderless business plan reflecting the above changes, the distinction between in- and outsourcing evaporates. There is no more inside and outside, and if we aren't careful there will be no more *ourside*.

We must respond to changes in international borders that are beyond our control by reconfiguring other borders that we can control. For example, restrictions on sharing public- and private-sector information need to be lessened. Limitations on the domestic activities of military and intelligence agencies need to be rethought. Information must be shared within national borders, and we need more information from other countries. Local police must become more like the military in their ethos, tactics, and organizations, and the military must cultivate the good community relations assets of our better police departments. For some purposes and in some locations, cities (or at least special areas within them) need to be thought of as hardened battlefronts under siege rather than continuing to be soft targets for crime and terrorism.

We are all in this together now, and we need to think in terms of a world community of good people who can equate the law with the right. The law ain't perfect, but it's all we got. We don't need the divisive idea of civil-society and competing security groups. What we need instead is one big Government that is synonymous with community and society [20]. We need undivided loyalty. The government is the people, and it has to look out for its people. The restrictions on information gathering, sharing, and cooperative actions faced by our security forces within government just make it harder to get the job done.

Consistent with this, we need more exchange between our private and government databases. As recent events suggest, we separate this information at our peril. The underutilization of merged and mined (and minded) databases is a national disgrace. As long as they pay for it, the government should be allowed to access private-sector databases. It is simply wasteful to have duplicate systems of data collection. Cooperative public-private data collection efforts must draw on the authority of government to compel disclosure and the efficiency of the private sector to collect, protect and distribute information, generating taxable revenue in the process.

The restrictions on the private sector's ability to access most government databases must also be eliminated. We pay with our tax dollars for the creation of government data, and like asphalt highways, they should be more available for public use, repackaging, and resale, especially by those of us in security work serving the public good.

In short, our commercial and security databases must be mutually reinforcing. For example, crime data must inform insurance rates and business location decisions, and credit card data must inform national security—whether this involves the excessive indebtedness of government employees who could be corrupted or the anomalous credit patterns of visitors and citizens.

And I have another point to make about borders as the borders between organizations with different goals have become more blurred and less distinct under the sway of technology. Here, I refer to the healthy convergence and overlap in recent years between the military, law enforcement, corrections, management, and marketing. Vast untapped fields of electronic and biological detritus that humans leave are waiting for our harvesting, whether for security or commercial purposes. Finding the enemy, looking for criminal suspects, identifying persons with contagious diseases, creating safe environments through target hardening and suspect weakening, and monitoring those under some form of judicial supervision are really no different from looking for customers and clients, determining eligibility, checking creditworthiness, making predictions about persons and risks, and monitoring workers. Commercial fulfillment centers or Homeland Security fusion centers—it's all the same. Just get the right algorithms based on the red flags and choke point data, and you have your person—whether crook or customer.

Overall, then, we must have more synergy and institutional cooperation. Consider a nice South Carolina example involving law and medicine. Low-income pregnant women who came to a clinic were automatically tested for drug use. Imagine their surprise when those who tested positive were arrested. With one easy collection, something that would otherwise get flushed away serves an important law enforcement, health, and child protection goal.

Another promising biosocial example can be seen using the great advances in neuroscience to proactively control those prone to violence. Rather than having to rely on an imperfect judicial system this is based on a scientific risk assessment profile drawing on genetics, biochemical, and social environmental factors. Consider the scenario offered by Adrian Raine (2013), a prominent psychologist and creator of a brain imaging center. In this account, after age eighteen all males would need to have a brain scan and a DNA test in search of the malfunctioning violent brain. These results would be combined with an array of other data (medical, school, neighborhood) to create an "all-encompassing data set" and score for the subject. Those with a high LOMBROSO (Legal Offensive on Murder: Brain Research Operation for the Screening of Offenders) score would be held in "indefinite detention". There would be periodic reassessments, and if scores came down, they would be returned to the larger community but would remain under "continuous auditory and visual scrutiny." Zones of community "containment" could be created for potential trouble makers who would know via electronic warnings to stay away from zones of "exclusion." Indeed broader application of such a scheme would help clean up urban spaces and make for clearer boundaries.

Many misguided and uninformed persons will dismiss such ideas as unrealistic —whether those opposed to the march of progress, privacy fetishist fundamentalists or those with ulterior motives. They fail to understand that information wants to be free and like molecules to bond and share and that, unlike many forms of property, information increases in value when it is used. The sharing of data is fundamental to an open society, citizenship, and personal relations.

However, I want to add a caveat here. In the case of the press, we have the opposite problem: *too much* sharing of information and the *lack of restrictions*. Our job is made much more difficult by all those investigative reporters and information leakers of doubtful loyalty who publicize our mistakes and failures. What we need here, then, are new and stronger information walls guarded by those with the tools to discover and retribute. That is common sense, not censorship. Security requirements to protect sources and techniques, along with classification and privacy restrictions, mean that our successes often cannot be known. Our guys do lots of great work that just can't be talked about in public. But trust us. Look how far we have come.

Of course, in everything we do, we must obey the law. But the law, like the Big Guy, is on our side. And whether you are now working in the commercial sector, law enforcement, or national security, I know that law and ethics are fundamental factors for your work. But the striking thing about most of the new surveillance technologies is that they are generally legal for everyone, and especially for the government and those organizations it delegates authority to [22]. When they aren't legal, we just need to come up with better names or reinterpret or change the law, as President Bush did through executive orders. Later he worked with Congress to pass appropriate legislation extending the data collection abilities of NSA and other agencies—whether via warrantless wiretaps, indefinite detention, or library records—further reducing any questions about legality. When we can't change the law, we may need to find a better organizational setting ("jurisdiction shopping"). Thus in 2003 Congress gave us only a temporary setback when it refused to fund the Terrorist Information Awareness program, because we were able to resurface it as a classified NSA program. And when some of our special operations military units in Afghanistan were too constrained by military policies, we were able to have them work with the CIA under its broader combat authority.

For a nice example of the kind of innovation our profession is justly famous for and that gracefully avoids the messes of politics, consider the tactic we adopted as soon as the cell phone appeared. The laws about accessing basic cell data are confused and vary by state, federal district, and cell company. Rather than bother with warrants, permits, lobbying, or the excessive fees charged by cell phone service providers, we simply cloned the phones of interest. Thus, even when they were turned off, we could monitor prior usage with respect to factors such as location, time, and number connected to. We have other tools that simulate cell phone towers and can intercept messages. Of course, such tools have to be used with discretion, and it would be wrong to actually listen in on conversations without cause. But since the goals—whether for security or marketing—so often involve patterns rather than content, that is not a problem.

When tactics are appropriately restricted to government, private-sector contractors need to be sure delegated authority and appropriate exemptions cover them. Even when we are prohibited from using a tactic, the pie is big enough for everyone. In football, defensive linemen get the same pay as offensive linemen. One good example: When wiretapping was fully criminalized for the private sector in 1968, it was an easy move for us from selling our offensive skills, such as bugging, to selling our defensive skills, such as antibugging and data protection.

Some contemporary interpretations of the Constitution have stressed the power of the executive, particularly in times of crisis, to do whatever is necessary. And the president is elected by the people! President Nixon said, "When the president does it, that means that it is not illegal." Dick would certainly have agreed with another of my heroes, Dashiell Hammett, who said, "Never break a law that violates your integrity." The willow which bends to the tempest endures while the rigid oak will snap. Do you want to stand on ceremony while the platform collapses?

President Nixon may have made a few mistakes (what great leader doesn't?), but he understood that "guarding the guards" was eternally problematic. Given that administrative problem, you can't always rely on conventional agencies or the loopholed law to keep your own house in order. He didn't' create his off-the-books plumbers' unit to get rich or help his friends, but to control the illegal leaks that were damaging national security. Perhaps his high police agents went too far in plumbing depths, but their first mistake was the incompetence that resulted in their getting caught. I even wonder if they weren't set up to embarrass the president. But that's a topic for another speech.

Fortunately the new technologies generally give us the latitude to act offensively, as well as defensively. In contrast to Europe, this country's free-market economic system and civil rights and liberties mean that we can go very far in using technology to gather personal information, and if necessary, to stand our ground in guarding our information and other property. The protections in our Bill of Rights evens the score and are intended to restrain government, not the private sector or citizens. These new technologies are not only legal to use in the sense that they are not prohibited, but they are legal in the sense that we have an affirmative obligation to use them. For those in government, given the equal protection clause of the Fourteenth Amendment, it would be unconstitutional not to use them.

And speaking of civil liberties, what about the civil liberties of the entrepreneurs whose rights to information are denied? I wouldn't be quite so critical of the civil-liberties lobbies if they were at least consistent. After all, the First Amendment gives me the right to freedom of information and expression. I have a right to know, collect, and use data. The Constitution says that I have the right to own property, and the personal information we collect and add value to is our property [16]!

The US Constitution is crystal clear about the importance of an informed citizenry for democracy. Our basic rights to free speech, assembly, and association are inconceivable without the right of the right people to know and communicate, factors given an enormous boost by surveillance technology. The first civil liberty is SECURITY. Without collective rights, individual rights mean nothing. Without order based on engineered solutions, there is chaos, anarchy, and unnecessary illness.

Question: "What would Machiavelli call a lie to preserve real truth and save the empire?" Answer: " Smart." Some may call what we do spying. But wars are won by spying. Let those who live in a perfect society behave like angels; the rest of us better be on guard. As our vice president Gigi Lesser, author of a book on helping women find out the truth about cheating spouses, told Oprah Winfrey, "Sure we sometimes do the wrong thing, but for the greater good." Our means can mean their ends.

It would be self-destructive for us not to use every means necessary out of some vague concern over privacy (a term not even mentioned in the Bill of Rights and its European antecedents or valued in the wonderful worlds promised by our best utopian thinkers), or because of concern over hypothetical problems that have never happened [42].

As a wise judge once said, "The Constitution is not a suicide pact." When everyone is standing in the mud, you can't afford to be the one looking to the stars. Our competitors and enemies both at home and abroad are using the technologies [25].

There is a lot to be said for principles up to a certain point, and we need to work closely with PR and our Maxi-True Ministries on message massage, but principles don't do you any good when you lose. What does it profit a person to gain a soul if there is no world left in which to enjoy it?

Beyond being legal and justifiable in the higher ethical planes of self-defense and property, the data we need are mostly free! We have so much going for us that it's rare that we need to risk a bad fudge in a gray area. As Narciso Gonif, spokesperson for the large personal data warehouse No-Choice Point, said, "Never underestimate the willingness of the American public to tell you about itself. That data belongs to us! . . . It isn't out there because we stole it from them. Someone gave it away, and now it's out there for us to use" [15]. In other words, if I'm in the data stream, don't tell me I can't swim or siphon off the water I need.

The information is public, not locked in a box behind closed doors and walls. What people kindly offer is just waiting to be processed by our sensory receptors. We can no more be stopped from gleaning that information than we can be stopped from breathing the air. A free good is a free good, after all. Some things are just givens waiting to become takens. If they transmit it, we can receive it. If they don't block it, we are invited to take it.

Those who choose to walk or drive on public streets, enter a shopping mall, use a credit card, or work at a particular place have made a choice to reveal personal information because of the obvious benefits they gain. By not protecting the information, they show that they don't expect it to be restricted. I don't have much sympathy for those anticommunity persons who try to protect their information. We all know what people do who have things to hide. Traditionally some law-abiding persons made themselves suspect in official eyes and in the eyes of their fellow citizens by not co-operating out of some misunderstanding of what the real threats to civil liberties are. Fortunately with modern ways we have less need to be concerned with them, because we can so easily search everyone without their cooperation or even letting them know.

The triumphant rock of visible verisimilitude ensures justice and is the foundation of society. Do you know the origin of the ritual of shaking hands? It was meant to show the other person that you were not carrying a weapon. Only those who have something to hide [18], or who are callously indifferent to pressing problems of productivity, national security, health, drug abuse, and crime will fail to understand the case I am making [17]. As Harry Caul, the hero in the film *The Conversation*, which honors our profession, said, "I have no secrets. My life is an open book." In our society of strangers, that book better never be closed.

I welcome the collection of personal data as the bridegroom welcomes the bride. It is only fair that I should pay less on my insurance because I eat healthily, exercise, have good DNA, and don't smoke. Anyone is invited to know what kind of cat food I buy and what magazines I read. The cell phone company needs to know where I am for service and billing purposes and for emergency help.

I'll tell you a little secret—I like to look at myself on store video monitors, they make me feel safer, and in reducing shoplifting, they lower prices. I also like using the latest wireless video tools so I can always know where my children and my wife are and observe my dog at his doggy day care center. They understand that given the security issues in my line of work, it can't be reciprocal.

I know from my government work that the eagle only dumps once a month and these are tough economic times. It is hard to keep up with the consumption and lifestyle challenges we face in the modern world, as the mass media offer us ever-improved visions of how we should live based on the latest developments and trends. But if a frequent-shopper card guarantees better prices at the super market—hey, I'm on board. The same for all the very personal ads I receive. I know I matter to someone when I get all that targeted mail.

Moreover, even if information isn't public and you have done nothing wrong, in these dangerous times we all have a moral responsibility to cooperate with the necessary initial screenings. In particular, those who do wrong have no right to avoid even more intense scrutiny. In electing to be in settings where surveillance is required (as well as to break the rules), they have made a choice. Such freedom of choice is the American way. This value was well put by member Pebble Blech, a personnel director who said, "We don't force *anyone* to undergo drug testing, only those who want to work here."

As our past president, phone company executive Sammy "Slick" Ringer said during the controversy over caller ID, "When you decide to make that phone call, you have agreed to release 'your' (actually the phone company's) telephone number" [15]. In turn, in choosing to have a telephone, you are inviting people to bring you courtesy calls about when the aluminum siding and carpet cleaning people will be in your neighborhood or about important political events and charitable causes. You like the convenience of your smart phone, so don't complain that the pings it sends out lets us know where you are even when the phone is turned off.

Likewise, if you use my corporate resources to make a toll-free call, look at company web pages, or stroll in the air-conditioned zone sanitaire of our malls, it's only fair that I get something in return, like your phone number, address, or image, and unobtrusively record your behavior as a consumer and for liability protection. If you don't like that, fine. Use the regular long-distance number, write letters, and shop at expensive mom-and-pop stores. In the case of the web pages, for example, we don't charge you for all the information we provide there, or for the suggestions we subsequently offer based on our understanding of your behavior and preferences. It's a simple matter of exchange.

And there's more. If you don't want your neighbors to share in your intimate moments, then close the shades or live in a rural area. We can't return to that golden age of manners and respect for other's information found in earlier centuries and rural places [35]. If you really want privacy, then give up your electronics, don't say anything, or use the earlier American invention of smoke signals.

Unlike the surveillance in a police state, our surveillance activity increasingly responds to consumer demand, whether for our material products or for the feeling of safety they provide. Yes, security is a product, too, and we need to think about it as a marketable commodity. We have to educate the public about that, just as they are educated about dental hygiene for themselves and their pets. Even in situations where we might expect surveillance technology to be rejected, it may be welcomed. In prison settings, both guards and prisoners support use of video cameras and feel protected by them. The documentary record permits us to discover the truth, rather than settling for conclusions shaped by the more powerful party, or those who sympathize with the underdog. Consider, too, the well-established principle of inspection as a vehicle for mutual deterrence in international treaties.

More broadly, we can hardly keep up with the public's demands. Surveillance is nothing more than "listening to the people"—the true merger of democracy and capitalism. It's what sets our government and economy apart from the despotic regimes of history and less developed countries. The public interest is whatever we the public is interested in—from reality TV shows to increased security, to the ease of using credit cards and the web, to checking up on each other. Do you really know who your neighbors, friends, and workers are?

My message to the surveillance profession? Find a need and fill it [40]. If we don't, someone else will. For example, as the possibilities for real-time monitoring of all consumer behavior, preferences, location, and communication have become clearer, consumers are demanding the personalized services made possible by modern segmented marketing over the inefficient mass marketing and service delivery of the past. Furthermore, be aware of how the means can play a vital role as well in helping us determine the end [11].

That is one reason why I love this business and why it is such a win-win situation. We get to work both sides of the street. Clients—whether government, corporations, or individuals—want data on others and to protect their data. They need surveillance and countersurveillance.

Why does our approach work so well? I'm no psychologist, but as an employer, a parent, and a former law enforcement and intelligence officer, I know people are most likely to conform when they are afraid of getting caught. The greater the likelihood of being discovered (or the more uncertainty about that, given the expense of catching everyone all the time), the better the result [10]. As intelligence expert Camie Cyparis, who did such great work for our company and the nation in tailing and nailing environmental extremists, said, "If they hear us, they will fear us and think that we are everywhere (which we just might be!)." Security and justice bloom when one plants seeds of doubt in a garden of paranoids. And we need to help those who are wavering become paranoid.

A leading New York State anticorruption prosecutor, Maurice Nadjari, got it right (even if he was fired for doing his job too well): "If we cannot have absolutely honest public officials, then let's have frightened public officials" [13]. I would extend that to employees, tenants, customers, children, spouses. You name it.

Some say that surveillance technology is overpowering, but I say that it is *empowering* because it induces self-control via rational appeals and setting examples. Many of those in this room know about Bentham's Panopticon. Well I'd like to create one inside people's heads so they can always be watching themselves. My kids call me strict, but my God they have a superego because they know that I watch them to aide them in self-control. Surveillance helps people help themselves. Monitoring also lets subordinates know what is expected, protects them from false accusations, and can clear them of suspicion.

When one of our searches fails to get the goods, that doesn't mean the suspect didn't do it (or do something else). It just means they didn't get caught this time. Lack of evidence may simply show how clever they are, especially when they have reasons and resources to deceive. Even when you get your man, never stop looking for the guy behind the guy.

Things are not always what they seem. My man Machiavelli knew all about *dietrologia*. When the evidence strongly contradicts opposition to what, based on your intuition, you know is probably true, be especially on the lookout for conspiracy. Sometimes the evidence is so overwhelmingly negative that it can only mean a conspiracy (and not a very good one because it is just too perfect). Even when the evidence supports your intuition you better keep looking because things change. What is true today might not be tomorrow.

As surveillance specialists we are committed to objective intelligence—that means we provide our intelligence analysts with the objectives and they come up with data that supports them—or we get new agents who understand what is expected of them.

One of our contract employees, the former head of the East German Security Service (Stasi) got it right when he said, "Everyone is a security risk." His agency needed to keep records on more than one-third of the population, so he ought to know (but even that wasn't enough to stop the collapse of his government). Better to collect first and filter later. You can always throw the nonguilty back, kind of like catch-and-release fishing. With a big net you never know what you will catch.

Be open to creative connections with enemies; every crook is a potential policeman. Find those 'flapjacks' and flip 'em. I know it can get gray out there and the Chinese expression "clean water kills the fish" won't sit well with the public, but those of us in the trenches know it rings true. For obvious reasons I can't go into detail about the contributions that the so-called "man without a face" (actually should be the "men"—as there have been many from Markus Wolf to Keyser Söze) made to public order and security. Whether for national security or crime fighting, you have to be flexible and cast a wide net. Let's be honest. Thus, whether dealing with politics, employment, or family and friends, we must learn from a paraphrased and praised Thomas Paine that "those who expect to reap the blessings of freedom must always undergo the fatigue of restraints on liberty." As the next figure from one of my former employers shows "Freedom isn't free" (see fig. 11.1).

You can't make an omelet without breaking some eggs. Casualties and collateral damage come with war. Just ask Harry Lyme [19]. Hey! No pain, no gain. Yes, we make

Freedom isn't free . . .

Do your part, Practice Good SECURITY!

FIGURE 11.1. But how is the price set and who sets it? (Courtesy of the U.S. Army Center of Military History.)

mistakes, but given the documentary record which keeps us accountable, even our mistakes are a blessing, since we can work to avoid them next time. Some of those closet anarchists, who don't understand that we can have no liberty without order and who are indifferent to our many societal problems, worry about their so-called freedom. They conjure up fears of a Big Brother type of society. I don't know about you, but I loved my big brother because he looked out for me. But apart from that personal note, the United States is the longest-running democracy in history. Hell, 1984 came and went a long time ago. I can't judge George Orwell as literature (I am already suspicious because he wrote under an alias—as my man Mark Z, whose company has done so much to help us, said, "Having two identities is an example of a lack of integrity"), but Eric Blair (Orwell's real name) is a failure as a prophet. Technology didn't enslave us. It freed us. Any way you slice it, his argument is baloney. Even Orwell, who did so much to scare people, knew with Kipling that the veneer of polite civilization rests on the hidden and when necessary, not so, heavy hand.

Technology is the driving force in creating social expectations. The Supreme Court has found that as technology advances, "reasonable expectations of privacy" must recede [5]. The head of a large computer company said, "You have no privacy— get over it."

Furthermore there is no concern about privacy when data are merely collected by a computer and not used. As with unspent ammunition, it is use, not the collection or possession, which should be regulated. There can be no harm when the technology, rather than a person, collects and sees the data. Whether in the case of computers or guns, information and bullets are nothing more than inert potentials. It would be as irresponsible for those of us in security to go around with unloaded weapons as with computers that are not uploaded.

Certainly privacy is a value to be considered. But Americans like bargains and also to be noticed—just look at the successful business model of the social media. History tells us that this mania for privacy is a very new idea and one that on balance has had negative consequences [29]. Our country is not a mushroom farm. In contrast, the more authentically American ideals of openness and visibility are central to our democratic notions of accountability. Privacy as we define it has been unknown in most societies and throughout most of history. While they have their problems, the Chinese and Russians with their righteous emphasis on the family, the community, and the state, until recently, did not even have a word for individual privacy. If that isn't enough, what is the origin of the word privy and what do you associate with it?

Contrary to the hysterical claims of those who are against progress, there is nothing really new here other than opportunity [29]. We are continuing well-established practices, but more efficiently and cheaply. A computerized database is only a faster file cabinet. Work monitoring is just another supervisory tool. E-mail is just a postcard. A video camera focused on a street is no different from a police officer on the beat. Caller ID harks back to the original system when all calls went through an operator. Using a scanner to listen to telephonic radio transmissions is no different from reading lips or overhearing a conversation on the subway. Using one of my minidrones, a satellite, or a soldier in a balloon with a telescope to collect visual data is no different from looking directly at someone you find of interest.

Maybe I should qualify that. There is something new. While the goals of surveillance have not changed, the new means are less coercive and draconian than the old means, and they are very cost effective. The modern way is soft, unobtrusive and often invisible. No need to force people to do anything when you can create the desire within them to do what they should. Discipline is so DURE and nineteenth century. Sure, I read *Guns and Ammo* magazine and I am packin' whenever it is necessary, but

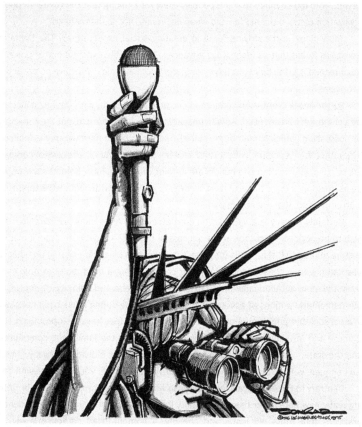

FIGURE 11.2. But who is watching her? (By Paul Conrad. Used with permission of the Conrad Estate. This item is reproduced by permission of The Huntington Library, San Marino, California.)

I know that I get more out of my horse with an oat bag than a whip, and at the summer place, I get more flies with honey than with vinegar. Rather than punishing or coercing, we get people to do what we want—I mean, what *they* want—through training and rewards. Behavior thus reflects the inner person manifesting democratic freedom of choice and self-restraint, whether in consumption or law-abiding behavior. If some inhibited disparager calls that seduction, that's AOK with me. We are a modern society that acknowledges the importance of sexuality. We need to learn from everyone, especially women, who know you don't need a cattle prod to be in control.

As Teddy Roosevelt, one of my heroes, would have said if he were around today, "Talk softly and carry a little machine." The next figure nicely illustrates that—the Statue of Liberty welcoming all to her shores, talking softly but caring a big microphone and binoculars [fig. 11.2]. There is no need for the coercive crudeness and bad publicity of the big stick when we have the quiet, gentle engineered jiu jitsu of modern technology [27]. To paraphrase one of my distant relatives and a great American, Barry Goldwater, "Technology in the defense of liberty is no vice. Limiting technology in the pursuit of justice is no virtue."

A Common International Culture of
Surveillance and the Blurring of Borders

The next chapter assesses the content of this speech and the other narratives in this unit. But first a brief note on how Bottoms's career illustrates contemporary themes in security and control. His story reflects the emergent, complex breaking, reconfiguring, and hybridization of a variety of borders. He fuses work forms and settings that traditionally were distinct and even opposite. Bottoms is a poster boy for the postmodern—offering an anamorphosis of social control and security (Palidda 1992). His career has involved jobs in several levels of government—local police and the military, national and international security agencies, and private security. As he moves from setting to setting, he encounters an increasing overlap in worldviews, technologies, personnel, and (whether parallel or cooperative) surveillance endeavors.[1] This overlap can be seen within and between countries and across forms and subjects and with the delegation of tasks. Here we see the morally ambiguous area of what Bob Hoogenboom (2010) calls *grey policing*. Authorities may creatively delegate investigative tasks to private individuals, groups, and other countries not bound by the laws and policies that restrict state agents.

Bottoms is the paradigmatic security professional, whose experience reflects major strands of the new surveillance. His career moves reflect the significant harmonization, migration and blurring between, and even merging of, public- and private-sector ideas, tools, practices, personnel, roles, and forms of organization within a global network. The shadowy, standardized revolving doors keep moving, even as it is not always clear what rooms they offer access to or from. Bottoms travels in the circuits of the global political economy of surveillance and helps sustain it (Wood 2012).

We can speak of economic or political man and also of *security man* (or *control person*). Rocky represents a blending of security and control sectors into a new multifaceted, professional field reflecting a nodal governance network in perpetual motion (Shearing 2005; Schuilenburg 2016). He is the *homo securitas* of nightmares or dreams, depending on who is somnolent.

In Bottoms we see overlap and convergence in the structure and functioning of diverse institutions, such as the military, criminal justice, schools, medicine, manufacturing, and commerce, which are all technology based and concerned with controlling people and information, whatever the more specific goal. These developments may result from their common culture, shared perceptions of threats, and similar interests and opportunities, entrepreneurial export, fads and fashion, and processes of globalization.

Consistent with Bourdieu's (1984) broad conception of a field and as elaborated in Bigo's pursuit of global security (2006), we see the merging of security and commercial sectors into national and transnational fields of security and control.[2] These are constantly changing and expanding under the sway of technology, but also acting back upon it.

There is increased congruence and convergence in belief and behavior among agents (indeed not infrequently the same ones) with experience in public and private organizations, in the military and in police and at home and abroad.

Bottoms and his colleagues move easily between government (whether the military or police) and the commercial sector and between local, national, and international settings. They engage in war making and peacekeeping or institution building, as well as in intelligence and in operations, and in risk, threat, and opportunity assessments—whether for security, sales, insurance, banking, or employee human resource management. Indeed from an emerging-control perspective, it is all just one big technical security, prevention, and sorting problem (or aggrandizing opportunity), and the tools, personnel, and legitimating rationales are increasingly interchangeable. Apart from the circulation of personnel there is also the introduction of military and police models and tools into other institutions such as schools, malls, and factories. There is also the incorporation of business models into police and the military.

The traditional distinction between "us" and "them" and inside and outside a society change with globalization and new technologies. These changes in government and the private sector and "public" and "private" information are captured in a variety of overlapping terms such as *globalization* and *deterritorialization*, the breaking, blurring, merging, and morphing of traditional borders, and the appearance of new barriers (whether spatial, geographic, juridical, organizational, functional, or of the senses).

The story illustrates contemporary themes snaking through world society. In response to fear, threats, risks, disasters, pandemics, and critical incidents, surveillance agents use means based on profiling, pattern recognition, transactional data, data mining, embedded sensors and ambient intelligence, intercepts, satellites, passwords, spyware, biometrics, authentication, audit trails, and target hardening. They emphasize prevention, proactivity, and preparedness.

Bottoms expresses these themes in his preference for signals intelligence over human intelligence and means that are automated, integrated, remote, unseen, involuntary and soft, and that involve real-time data flows. He pays attention to systems and networks as well as individuals. He folds surveillance into routine activities and seeks an immediate link between data collection and action.

Some of the above are contradictory. Depending on the level of analysis and sector, we see change, variation, and competition, unifying and polarizing forces, and different emphases (e.g., between groups such as the FBI and CIA or domestic, foreign, and international security agencies). These are all parts of the Hindu tale of the somewhat coherent elephant whose varied parts can be hazily seen through pixilated shadows and fog. A twenty-first-century version of the tale requires a morphing elephant.

The narrative stories of this section of the book can stand alone as tales of our age (with only a little exaggeration). Much in them makes sense. In the case of Bottoms, for example, some of what he says is eminently supportable, some is legitimately debatable, and some is clearly over the edge. Yet in neither style nor substance is he a crude yahoo whose extreme views would be more easily identifiable. Rather, he is a smooth talking, worldly, public relations-wise operator, educated at the best schools. As with the other narratives, truth and falsehood are mixed. Kris Kristofferson's line in "He's A Pilgrim" applies to Rocky: "He's a walking contradiction, partly truth and partly fiction." Because of that, some readers may even miss the satire and uncritically accept the perspectives offered (just as Rocky missed the meaning of fig. 11.2). Yet there is much that is fallacious in the four narratives' rhetoric, whether logically, empirically, or ethically, that requires decoding. The next chapter identifies a series of common *techno-fallacies* redolent of the narratives and of the modern period.

PART 4

Ethics and Policy

Let us begin by committing ourselves to the truth. To see it like it is and tell it like it is, to find truth, to speak the truth and to live the truth.

RICHARD NIXON, 1968, Republican convention acceptance speech

In parts 1 and 2 the emphasis was on neutral analysis in describing and categorizing concepts, data, and some theories. The categorization, description, and explanation in those earlier chapters are distinct in important ways from the normative (if also related to it). In contrast, part 3 was unabashedly normative in reflecting surveillance advocacy perspectives (if of the speaker, not the chronicler). The views there often relied on blind faith or self-interest masquerading as morality and science.

Clearly a degree of skepticism is needed with respect to all perspectives (including the oft-noted paradox of doubting an imperative about questioning). Yet no matter how rigorous, systematic, and empirical our standards of scholarship and writing are, we bring our values and passions into the work. They enter into the topic and methods we choose for study, the elements we emphasize, and the interpretations we make. And as C. Wright Mills argued, objectivity need not mean antiseptic detachment. The appendix expands on the role of value in this inquiry.

My concerns go beyond knowledge for its own sake, however central that is. Values are reflected when considering the conditions needed to sustain a free and open society, the dignity of the individual, and the distortions that may enter the power, knowledge, and practice trilogy. The desire to encourage public policy informed by logic and evidence is also a value position. In short, exemplary social inquiry encompasses a grand tradition that seeks to bring together, rather than isolate, the empirical and the normative or value questions.

With respect to the value questions, we ought not to be forced into rigid adherence to any single principle with the passion of the prophets, however emotionally gratifying that often is. Rather, as Selznick (2002) suggests, we need to weigh consequences and be guided by a principle of responsibility to both the dignity of the individual and the well-being of the community in a sea of often contradictory principles and imperfect evidence.

Chapter 12 analyzes the worldview of strong surveillance advocates by identifying forty-four "techno-fallacies of the information age." Chapter 13 deals with the ethics of surveillance by suggesting a series of questions that embody broader values or principles necessary for judging. The concluding chapter notes trends supportive of and undermining the surveillance essay views noted earlier in the book. It also identifies value conflicts, considers broad implications the topic raises, articulates unresolved and emerging issues, and offers suggestions for better understanding the role of surveillance in society.

Techno-Fallacies of the Information Age

There is no doubt that we must conduct more detailed research into the connection
between the practices of security professionals and the systems of justifications of their
activities, as we ponder on how procedures of truth claims are formulated.

D. BIGO 2006A

This chapter is concerned with public policy, but not with specific laws, regulations, or guidelines. Rather it seeks to identify the broad justifications and
often veiled assumptions underlying surveillance policies and practices. For
reasons of space this chapter is shortened; the deleted material is available
online at press.uchicago.edu/sites/marx/.

Among the nations of the world, the United States most clearly reflects
the optimistic, techno-surveillance worldview found within a broader technocratic and commercial celebratory ethos. And the satires all reflect a strong
version of this view, as it is presented to the public by those broadly within
"the surveillance community."[1] But the ideational environment which nour-
ishes these technologies needs to be better understood through examining its
empirical and value assumptions.

Sometimes these rationales and assumptions form a relatively coherent
and self-conscious ideology, or at least a perspective, as with governments,
political parties, and interest groups such as the American Manufacturing
Association, the International Association of Chiefs of Police, and the National Association of Security Companies. More often, however, the beliefs
can be found in dangling ad hoc snippets drawn on to justify an interest
group's claims and actions.

The arguments in the narratives illustrating the basic surveillance contexts are paraphrases or direct quotes from specialists seeking to justify their
behavior and convince wider audiences. Their views do not represent a to-
talizing, monolithic, closed ideological system. Rather they are loosely constructed self-serving worldviews.

These conceptions of the world and forms of consciousness involve problem definitions, explanations, justifications, and directions for action. And

they share with more comprehensive, coherent, and logically consistent ideologies a limited number of basic assumptions about the social world, certainty about its truths, an intermingling of values and facts, and a related action program.

The kinds of views characterizing the four narratives illustrating basic surveillance contexts show elements of belief systems that Karl Mannheim (1955) identified as both ideology and utopia. For example, the "Bottoms doctrine" articulated in the last chapter certainly is intended to serve the interests (however varied) of the more powerful and is therefore one variant of a traditional ideology. Yet the Bottoms narrative also offers a utopian perspective— that is, the love affair with futuristic technology that promises to be transformative and fundamentally alter the meaning of the human and the social.

For Mannheim the beliefs of emotionally hooked activists are tied to their social location and interests and hence relative, partial, potentially disingenuous, and distorted. In contrast, Mannheim suggests that the free-floating intellectual, divorced from traditional interest-group social pressures, could get closer to the truth than the autonomic believer. Listening to all views and straining them through the lens of scholarly inquiry would offer a more accurate view beyond the fog of self-serving ideological stances. The analysis of surveillance worldviews is in that tradition, if more humbly and with awareness of the paradoxical nature of claiming that the outsider really could be fully outside.[2]

The analyst of ideology has traditionally had two tasks (Seliger 1976; J. Thompson 1990). The first is to report the central ideas of a worldview (weltanschauung), and the second is to analyze them. This chapter offers a logical, empirical, and ethical critique of the worldviews portrayed in the four satires and in culture more broadly.

The emphasis here is on showing how some aspects of this worldview are empirically wrong, logically inconsistent, and morally questionable, but the analysis does not cover all possible fallacies.[3] Nor is this a total rejection. As pedagogical devices (and as in some realities) the worldviews in the narratives intermingle compelling values and social analysis with the dubious and even the outrageous. Some statements within the surveillance rhetoric are eminently supportable and ring true.

Nor do I claim that the worldviews discussed here necessarily stand apart from other ideological systems, which also contain inconsistencies, self-serving claims disguised as high principle, deceptive facades, misleading statements, empirical errors, and both unsupported and irrefutable claims. The dominant surveillance discourse is not necessarily richer in these than the belief systems of opponents (a task for systematic empirical research to determine). However, consistent with Gramsci's (Gramsci 2000) observations, it is *dominant* and serves to legitimate current practices. Those with different views do not have equivalent resources to create and propagate their perspective. Because of that imbalance, there is a case for analyzing the dominant views in more detail.[4]

Techno-Fallacies

Many [technical means of discovery] are excellent when kept in their places, but when pushed forward as infallible methods, they become forms of quackery.
                    DASHEILL HAMMETT

Society is in its animal, emotional state that is the equivalent of the dark ages. We are in this transition period where all that is hidden in darkness will come out through statistical evidence.
          HEDGE FUND EXECUTIVE, on human analytics

In listening to surveillance rhetoric over several decades I often heard things that, given my knowledge and values, sounded wrong, much as a musician hears off-key notes. The off-key notes involve elements of substance as well as styles of mind and ways of reasoning.[5] Below I identify forty-four "information age techno-fallacies." Sometimes these fallacies are frontal and direct; more often they are tacit—buried within seemingly commonsense, unremarkable assertions. It is important to approach the commonplace in a critical fashion—whether we initially agree or disagree with the ideas.

This approach to analyzing the rhetoric of technology advocacy and consequences follows in the broad tradition of Mumford (1934), Ellul (1964), Weinberg 1966, Winner (1988), Postman (1992), Tenner (1997), Scott (1998), Marcuse (2002), and Rosner (2004) and of the more focused work on topics such as computers, the environment, energy, and crime (e.g., Wiener 1967; Weizenbaum 1976; Morozov 2011; Mander 1992; Hilgartner, Bell, and O'Connor 1982; Marx 1995a; Grabosky 1996). While I could have identified fallacies (as well as truths) unique to particular information-extracting tools (e.g., Corbett and Marx 1991 on electronic monitoring of offenders) and contexts (e.g., schools), the emphasis is on ideas that apply across the surveillance field.

Beliefs may be fallacious in different ways. Some are empirically false or illogical. With appropriate evidence and argument, persons of goodwill holding diverse political perspectives and values may be able to see how they are fallacious, or in need of qualification.

Fallacies may also involve normative statements about what matters and is desirable. These reflect disagreements about values and value priorities. To label a normative belief a fallacy more clearly reflects the point of view of the labeler and goes beyond Mannheim's methodological neutrality. However, normative positions are often informed by empirical assumptions (e.g., favoring a hidden rather than overt watching because it is believed to be more effective). In sniffing out fallacies, one must identify and evaluate the intermingling of fact and value and the quality of the facts (Rule 1978; W. Bell 1997). At a very general level, people often agree on values (though they often dissent over prioritizing and implementing these). Disagreements also commonly occur over what evaluation measure(s) and specific tools for judgment are most appropriate and over how evidence is to be interpreted—both with respect to what it says empirically and to its meaning for a given value.

Below I identify forty-four surveillance-talk assumptions I find questionable, or worse. These are organized into five categories:

A. Fallacies of technological determinism and neutrality
B. Fallacies of scientific and technical perfection
C. Fallacies involving subjects of surveillance
D. Fallacies involving questionable legitimations
E. Fallacies of logical or empirical analysis[6]

Information Age Techno-Fallacies

A. FALLACIES OF TECHNOLOGICAL DETERMINISM AND NEUTRALITY

1. The Fallacy of Autonomous Technology and Emanative Development and Use
2. The Fallacy of Neutrality
3. The Fallacy of Quantification
4. The Fallacy That the Facts Speak for Themselves
5. The Fallacy That Technical Developments Must Necessarily Mean Less Privacy

B. FALLACIES OF SCIENTIFIC AND TECHNICAL PERFECTION

6. The Fallacy of the 100 Percent Fail-Safe System
7. The Fallacy of the Sure Shot
8. The Fallacy of Delegating Decision-Making Authority to the Machine
9. The Fallacy That Technical Solutions Are to Be Preferred

10. The Fallacy of the Free Lunch or Painless Dentistry
11. The Fallacy That the Means Should Determine the Ends
12. The Fallacy That Technology Will Always Remain the Solution Rather Than Become the Problem

C. FALLACIES INVOLVING SUBJECTS OF SURVEILLANCE

13. The Fallacy That Individuals Are Best Controlled through Fear
14. The Fallacy of a Passive, Nonreactive Environment
15. The Fallacy of Implied Consent and Free Choice
16. The Fallacy That Personal Information Is Just Another Kind of Property to Be Bought and Sold[7]
17. The Fallacy That If Critics Question the Means, They Must Necessarily Be Indifferent or Opposed to the Ends
18. The Fallacy That Only the Guilty Have to Fear the Development of Intrusive Technology (or If You Have Done Nothing Wrong, You Have Nothing to Hide)

D. FALLACIES OF QUESTIONABLE LEGITIMATION

19. The Fallacy of Applying a War Mentality to Domestic Surveillance
20. The Fallacy of Failing to Value Civil Society
21. The Fallacy of Explicit Agendas
22. The Legalistic Fallacy That Just Because You Have a Legal Right to Do Something, It Is the Right Thing to Do
23. The Fallacy of Relativism or the Least Bad Alternative
24. The Fallacy of Single-Value Primacy
25. The Fallacy of Lowest-Common-Denominator Morality
26. The Fallacy That the Experts (or Their Creations) Always Know What Is Best
27. The Fallacy of the Velvet Glove
28. The Fallacy That If It Is New, It Is Better
29. The Fallacy of Equivalence or Failing to Note What Is New
30. The Fallacy That Because Privacy Rights Are Historically Recent and Extend to Only a Fraction of the World's Population, They Can't Be Very Important
31. The Fallacy of the Legitimation via Transference

E. FALLACIES OF LOGICAL OR EMPIRICAL ANALYSIS

32. The Fallacy of Acontextuality
33. The Fallacy of Assumed Representativeness

34. The Fallacy of Reductionism
35. The Fallacy of a Bygone Golden Age of Privacy
36. The Fallacy That Correlation Must Equal Causality
37. The Fallacy of the Short Run
38. The Fallacy That Greater Expenditures and More Powerful and Faster Technology Will Continually Yield Benefits in a Linear Fashion
39. The Fallacy That If Some Information Is Good, More Is Better (see fig. 12.1)
40. The Fallacy of Meeting Rather Than Creating Consumer Needs (Demand vs. Supply)
41. The Fallacy of the Double Standard
42. The Fallacy That Because It Is Possible to Successfully Skate on Thin Ice, It Is Wise to Do So
43. The Fallacy of Rearranging the Decks Chairs on the Titanic instead of Looking for Icebergs
44. The Fallacy of Confusing Data with Knowledge and Technique with Wisdom

Discussion of these is available at press.uchicago.edu/sites/marx.

One Person's Fallacies Can Be Another's Truths

A necessary condition of wisdom is identifying and evaluating the web of tacit assumptions that are so intertwined with beliefs and action. The techno-

FIGURE 12.1. Techno-fallacy 39: If some information is good, more is better. (© Chris Slane, used with permission.)

fallacies differ in seriousness and are not universally shared, or held with equal intensity, by diverse surveillance advocates. Moreover, the list is illustrative and not exhaustive The major point of this chapter is not to argue in depth against statements I view as techno-fallacies (see the fuller version of this chapter [online at press.uchicago.edu/sites/marx/] for more detail). Rather it is to argue for the importance of critically examining how we think and what we say about any new (or old) surveillance practice.

The techno-fallacies are especially prominent among technophiles favoring maximum security and minimum risk. They too seldom appreciate the virtues of civil society, the advantages of traditional informational borders, the necessity of trade-offs, and the limits on human rationality and control, let alone on human perfectibility.

Contrary to the fears Rocky Bottoms expresses in his opening speech, I do not identify these techno-fallacies with a goal of prohibiting new technologies of surveillance. Rather, I do so in a spirit of sensitizing conservatism, asking us to pause in the face of any proposed change and raise questions.

The views of all claimants must be examined, not only surveillance advocates. Technophobes with extreme libertarianism and/or prejudicial skepticism too often fail to appreciate the advantages of technology, the virtues of community, and the dangers of anarchy, thus holding their own fallacies, or sharing some with their opponents—for example, too cleanly separating the human and the machine or giving one value priority over all the others.[8] By adding "never" or otherwise reversing many of the techno-fallacies, we have some mirror image fallacies of the technophobic (e.g., the fallacy that technical solutions are never to be preferred).

A speech given by privacy advocates could contain some additional fallacies: the fallacy that with new technologies the end is near and the apocalypse approaching; that if you can envision bad things happening, they surely will; that the people always know what's best (the populist fallacy); that privacy is an unlimited good (or if some privacy is good, more must be better); that privacy is primal (i.e., that it ought to take precedence over other values); that privacy is only an individual value rather than a social one; that privacy can only be taken from someone, rather than be violatd by being imposed upon the individual; that because something worked (or failed) in the past, it will in the future; that technology is always the problem and never the solution (the Luddite fallacy); and, related to this, that technology can only be used to cross informational borders rather than to protect them.

Of course, Karl Mannheim notwithstanding, the academic analyst who tries to stand above the fray and between supporters and opponents also has perspectives. The analyst sees and speaks from a particular social location with values and interests. Those on the front lines of surveillance technology promotion or resistance—don't necessarily share the analyst's perspectives.[9] Yet another fallacy list is needed to surface the tacit and debatable assumptions of the academic.

Such a list might start with these:

The fallacy of risk-free Monday morning quarterbacking

The fallacy of the overly broad academic generalization

The fallacy of dressing common sense (or non-sense) in multisyllabic jargon replete with esoteric references

The fallacy of using Ockham's razor to nit-pickingly slice the world into too many categories

The fallacy of unduly timid waffling (the Nero-Libra "I like to watch" fallacy) in the face of complexity and always imperfect data or the opposing fallacy of never wavering ("Trust me I am an expert and it is crystal clear what must be done")

The fallacy of sacrificing scientific neutrality along with scholarly credibility by taking advocacy positions in the name of science that far exceed the evidence

The fallacy of failing to clearly enough differentiate value statements from scientific statements

And the related fallacy of failing to specify how the empirical within the value might be assessed

The apocalyptic fallacy of believing that the sky is falling and the fallacy that thinking makes it so—if you can imagine bad things happening, they are likely to happen

The fallacy of hegemonic power ("Them that got is them that get," according to Ray Charles), in which technology is simply always only another tool by which the more powerful further their control over the less powerful, and the related idea that surveillance is always nonreciprocal and asymmetrical, only flowing downward

The related fallacy of surveillance as only a rational strategy of domination, rather than as a tool applicable for a variety of goals such as efficiency, caring, entertainment, and truth claims, and something inherent in the human condition—even endemic to living things involving the protection of system borders (whether individual or social)

In order to further constructive dialogue besides understanding any claimant's assumptions and possible fallacies, we also need to know what rules the claimant plays by. The worldview of those who start with advocacy rather than analysis is by definition self-serving. The rhetorical devices expected there differ from those of the academic analyst, who must start with questions, not answers, and question all claimants. The scholar of course serves his or her interests in the pursuit of truth. But especially because scholars are making truth claims, they must also strive for consistency and a strong tilt toward logic and evidence.

An academic analyst should offer data, methods, concepts, and theories in an open, civil, self-interrogating, and critical environment. These should be accompanied by healthy doses of qualification, caution, and humility (given dynamic situations, measurement challenges, and the paradoxes of the sociology of knowledge) in the face of complex, interdependent problems.

Yet for complex issues of social and technical policy, limits must be acknowledged, but they must not immobilize. One can rarely wait until all the data are in and there is scientific consensus. Even then, the nonscientific aspects of values and goals remain.

With the above cautions, the analyst may nonetheless wish to give advice, particularly for topics of social import. In doing so, she or he must try to keep statements of fact distinct from statements of value, while acknowledging the tensions and interconnections between them. The key is awareness and tentativeness (or at least continual openness to examining assumptions and alternatives).

The presence of values, however, is nothing to run from. Indeed, the failure to acknowledge values and to cloak them in the camouflage of pseudoscientific neutrality, necessity, certainty, and precision is at the heart of many problems. The next chapter continues the consideration of values by offering a framework for judging surveillance practices.

An Ethics for the New (and Old) Surveillance

If it doesn't look right, that's ethics.

I'm in computer science. I took this class [on surveillance] because eventually I want to do the right thing.

This chapter stresses the difficulty of applying a single set of ethical standards to the rich variations in surveillance behavior and settings. The deleted material from this chapter is available online at press.uchicago.edu/sites/marx/. As noted, to a significant degree, evaluations are contingent upon the context and the behavior within it.

The chapters in the first three sections of the book (chap. 1–11) sought social science objectivity. Those are my team's rules. Yet at the end of a project dealing with social issues, the scholar who reports only the findings but fails to evaluate them runs the risk of moral abdication. The righteous witness of course faces other risks.

Underlying this inquiry and interlaced with the empirical questions are moral concerns. Is a given practice good or bad, desirable or undesirable? How should the new surveillance forms be viewed—as efficient, equal opportunity, scientific tools of productivity and protection in the face of ever greater crises, or as crepuscular, sugar-coated tools of domination? A related question: how should neutralization efforts be viewed—as courageous and inspiring expressions of the human spirit in the face of the soulless domination of the machine in the service of the more powerful, or as sneaky and disheartening expressions of self-interest on the part of those who are inadequately socialized and disrespectful of the community's rules?

These questions are at the core of surveillance as a contemporary issue. However, posing questions in such a general way is not helpful. The only honest answers are, "yes and no," "sometimes," and "it depends." The empirical and normative task for etiquette, policy, and law is to suggest what the evaluation of surveillance does, and should, depend on.

What's Wrong with This Picture?

Public opinion polls consistently show that a very large percentage of Americans and indeed persons everywhere are concerned about surveillance issues (Zureik, Stalker, and Smith [2010] provide international data; and, for the United States, Westin [2003], Pew Research Center [2014], Acquisti, Brandimarte, and Lowenstein [2015]). But the elements of this concern are rather muddled, muddied, and inconsistent. Many persons feel a sense of discomfort in the face of indiscriminate drug testing, hidden video cameras, electronic work monitoring, airport screens, drones, and the collection and marketing of their personal information—even as they favor security, responsible behavior, efficiency, economic growth, and credit-card-aided consumption. Given the newness of the technologies, opinion here is less well defined and coherent than it is for many more settled issues.

Persons often have trouble articulating what seems wrong with a surveillance practice beyond saying that it doesn't seem quite right—often with a vague reference to the invasion of privacy. What's the fuss all about? What is it about the new technology that is troubling, and why is it difficult to take a consistent position? By what standards should we conclude that a given practice is right or wrong or at least desirable or undesirable? How should surveillance activities be judged? Where is contention most likely to be found, and what does it involve?

Popular expressions such as "It doesn't look right," "It just seems wrong," and "You don't treat people that way" speak to ethics embedded in folk culture. Data gathering and protection efforts imply ethical assumptions that are often unstated. In what follows I suggest an ethical framework for thinking about the surveillance of individuals whether involving the new or traditional means (e.g., such as informing and eavesdropping). At a very general level there are shared expectations in American culture, and perhaps to a degree more generally in Western and industrial capitalist cultures, whose violation underlies the discomfort, or at least ambivalence, experienced in the face of many personal border crossings.

This chapter suggests some basic questions for identifying factors that would lead the average person to view a surveillance practice as wrong or at least questionable—whether in general or in a specific case (or, conversely, as acceptable). The chapter ends with a consideration of the values these questions imply.

The questions for judgment in this chapter build on efforts to inductively define *surveillance* and related terms such as *privacy* and *publicity*. In such efforts the analyst starts with an array of behaviors seen as right or wrong and builds up to some more general categories. William Prosser (1960) is the godfather of this approach to privacy issues. To illustrate a range of generic surveillance problems, I draw from my interviews and participation in various policy inquiries, court cases, and mass media accounts and from examples in works such as those by Alderman and Kennedy (1995), Smith (1997), Privacy Rights Clearinghouse (2011), and Electronic Privacy Information Center (2011).

Have We Got Questions

This chapter's ethical analysis emphasizes the watchers rather than the watched, the potential harms that can result from the watching, the potential harm to the individual rather than the group or organization, and the short rather than the long run. However, many of the ideas can be applied more broadly.

The perspective I offer applies to conventional domestic settings in a democratic society for those with full adult citizenship rights. In situations of extreme crisis such as war and pandemic or when dealing with very different countries or cultures, the incompetent and dependent, or those denied juridical rights such as prisoners, a somewhat different discussion is needed, and the lines in some ways will be drawn differently. Such cases of course call for extreme vigilance, but they also present a danger of exploiting the fear and of normalizing states of exception.[1]

The ethics and/or wisdom of a practice can be assessed at each stage of the surveillance occasion noted in chapter 5 and with respect to its larger milieu. With the exception of section 6 that deals with harm, the evaluation questions presented (see below) are structured so that answering yes is likely to support a broader value and related principle. Given the book's emphasis on variation and complexity, no simple additive score is possible. Much depends. Yet, other factors being equal, the more these questions can be answered in a way that affirms the underlying principle (or a condition that supports it), the more ethical and wise the use of a tactic is likely to be. This is often, but not always, in the form of a yes answer.

Questions are organized according to the following categories: initial conditions, means, goals, connections between means and goals, data collection and analysis, consequences for subjects and others, rights and resources for subjects, consequences for agents and third parties, and data protection and fate.[2]

Questions for the Ethics of Surveillance

1. INITIAL CONDITIONS: POLICIES, PROCEDURES, AND CAPABILITIES

Formal procedure and public input in the decision to adopt: Does the decision to apply a potentially sensitive technique result from an established review procedure in which affected parties (whether within or beyond the organization) are consulted?[3]

Role reversal: Would those responsible for the surveillance (both the decision to apply it and its actual application) agree to be its subjects if roles were reversed? How would the agents who are now in the role of subjects view efforts to neutralize surveillance?

Restoration: Does the proposed technique radically break with traditional protections for personal information? Can, and should, these traditional protections be reestablished through other means (whether legal, informal expectations or technical)?

Unwanted precedents: Is the tactic likely to create precedents that will lead to its application in undesirable ways?

Symbolic meaning: Do the tool and the way it is applied communicate a view of citizens who are due respect and who have rights appropriate for a democratic society?

Reversibility: If experience suggests that the policy is undesirable, how easily can the means be given up in the face of large capital expenditures and vested interests backing the status quo?

Written policies: Does an agency have policies to guide use of the tactic, and are these periodically reviewed?

Agency competence and resources: Does the organization have the resources, skills and motivation to appropriately and effectively apply, interpret, and use the tactic?

2. MEANS

Validity: Are there publicly offered grounds for concluding that the tactic in general is valid and to periodically check it?[4] Are there means to verify specific results?

Human review: Is there human review of machine-generated results—both basic data and (if present) automated recommendations for action?

Alternative means: Is this the best available means? How does it compare to other tools with respect to ease of application, validity, costs, risks, and measuring outcomes? Is there a tilt toward counting (in both senses) what can most easily and inexpensively be measured, rather than toward what is more directly linked to the goal but may be more difficult to assess?

3. GOALS

Clarity in goals: Are the goals clearly stated, justified, and prioritized?

Appropriate versus inappropriate goals: Are the goals of the data collection legitimate and consistent with the information expectations of the setting?

Unitary usage: Are data used for the defined purpose and consistent with the subject's understanding (and, where appropriate, agreement) by agents entitled to it?

4. CONNECTIONS BETWEEN MEANS AND GOALS

The goodness of fit between the means and the goal: Is there a clear link between the information sought and the goal to be achieved?

Inaction as action: Where the only available tool is costly, risky, and/or weakly related to the goal because what is of interest is difficult to detect or statistically very unlikely to occur, has consideration been given to taking no action or to redefining the goal? The potential for resilience is a factor to be considered here (chap. 13, note 9).

Proportionality: Do means and ends stand in appropriate balance?

Timeliness: Is a tactic that is initially justified still needed or has a goal been met or a problem reduced such that it is unnecessary and even unwise to continue to use it?

5. DATA COLLECTION AND ANALYSIS

Criteria for subject selection: Are universalistic standards applied? Where there are no grounds for treating persons differently, are all subject to surveillance, or do all have an equal chance of being surveilled, even if few are actually chosen.[5]

Minimization: Are the data gathered with minimum intrusiveness and invasiveness, with only the amount and kind of personal information necessary for the goal collected and analyzed? Are personal data from different contexts kept separate rather than aggregated and, where appropriate, is identity buffered through various anonymizing techniques?

Border crossings: Does the technique cross a sensitive and intimate personal boundary (whether bodily, relational, spatial, or symbolic) with notice and/or permission if consent is given, is it genuine?

Violation of assumptions: Is application of the technique consistent with the assumptions that subjects make about the conditions under which their personal information will be collected?

6. HARMFUL CONSEQUENCES FOR SUBJECTS

Harm and disadvantage: Does surveillance at any of the stages noted cause unwarranted physical, psychological, or social harm or disadvantage to the subject, the agent, or third parties? Figure 13.1 offers an example for a canine agent.

"I'm starting to really like the smell of cocaine."

FIGURE 13.1. Surveillance can be addictive. (Matthew Diffee/The New Yorker Collection/The Cartoon Bank.)

Lack of fairness: Is surveillance used to gain unfair strategic advantage in discovering information that a subject is entitled to withhold?

Manipulation: Is surveillance used to gain manipulative advantage in persuading or influencing a subject?

Unfair treatment: Is surveillance used to restrict social participation or otherwise unfairly treat persons based on information that is invalid, irrelevant, acontextual, or discriminatory?[6]

Reputational harm: Does surveillance damage a subject's reputation as a result of unwarranted publication or release of personal information?[7] State laws that protect against privacy invasion, false light, and defamation attempt to remedy this.

Trust violations: Does the surveillance betray confidences and violate trust because of procedural violations and exaggerated claims (i.e., efforts to create the myth of surveillance) even if the information is neutral or positive for the subject?

Intrusions into solitude: Does the surveillance whether in collection or use involve unwanted intrusions into solitude, as individuals lose the ability to control the access others have to them?[8]

Subject: Does surveillance only profit the agent but not the subject whose data are being marketed?

7. RIGHTS AND RESOURCES OF SUBJECTS

Right of inspection: Are subjects aware of the findings and how they were created?

Right to challenge and express a grievance: Are there procedures for challenging the results and for entering alternative data or interpretations into the record?

Redress and sanctions: If an individual or group has been wronged, are there means of discovery and redress and, if appropriate, for the correction or destruction of the records? Are there means for minimizing or preventing problems that require redress and sanctions? Are there audits and sanctions to encourage fair and responsible surveillance? Is there a strategy and resources for *resilience*?[9]

Equal access to surveillance tools: In settings of reciprocal surveillance are the means widely available, or are they disproportionately available (or restricted) to the more privileged, powerful, or technologically sophisticated?

Equal access to neutralization tools: In settings where neutralization is legitimate (whether because the rules permit it or because unwarranted agent behavior may be seen to justify it), are the means widely available or limited to the most privileged, powerful, or technologically sophisticated?

8. CONSEQUENCES FOR AGENTS AND THIRD PARTIES

Harm to agents: Can undesirable impacts on the values and personality of the surveillance agent be avoided?

Spillover to uninvolved third parties: Can the data gathering be restricted to appropriate subjects?

9. DATA PROTECTION AND FATE

Periodic review: Is the system regularly reviewed for effectiveness, efficiency, fairness, and operation according to policies? Are there audit trails and inspections?

Data fate: Are there rules regarding the retention or destruction of the data, and are these honored?

The nine types of ethical question are discussed at press.uchicago.edu/sites/marx.

Questions about Questions

> She was a sociologist, and I don't like sociologists. They try to reason things out too much.
> BROWARD COUNTY PROSECUTOR[10]

As suggested, the more the principles implied in these questions are honored, the more ethical the situation is likely to be, other factors being equal—which of course they rarely are, given, among many other concerns, the importance of prioritizing and weighing values. The questions thus require several kinds of evaluation.

First, do the procedures and policies cover the basic areas? Once we have this answer, we can move to questions about substance: Are they good policies? Are the policies followed in practice? Are there regular and surprise audits and inspections? Is the subject likely to be aware when a policy fails?

Inquiring whether the policies are followed can be looked at across all, or a sample, of cases as well as in any given case. For example, the validity and consequences of a specific type of drug testing as a class can be considered. But questions can also be asked about the application of a particular form such as a urine drug test to a given individual or at a specific location. The point is that a means that meets general standards for validity can still be incompetently or erroneously applied. Distinctions are also needed between rejecting, limiting, or revising a tactic—say, the polygraph—because of questions about its efficacy or contextual appropriateness as against rejecting a particular flawed application of a tactic.

When failings are identified, are they idiosyncratic and seemingly random or systemic (as was the case when Congress limited use of the polygraph)? Is it the apple or the barrel? How often do individual problems have to appear before agents conclude that the problem is in the system rather than an unfortunate, but tolerable, occurrence? If it is the former, can it be mediated in the given case?

Context and Comportment

> Systematic reasoning informed by practical wisdom and artful judgment that guides us away from missteps, suggests heuristics and rules-of-thumb, and clarifies what is at stake in these dilemmas may point the way to better if not certain judgments.
> HELEN NISSENBAUM, *Privacy in Context*

The analysis thus far has hopefully demonstrated a central point of the book: *surveillance is neither good nor bad but context and comportment make it so* (at least most of the time). The variation in tactics and contexts presented here illustrates the importance of making distinctions and identifying assumptions—whether for purposes of social science or judgment.[11] As the examples and argument throughout the book suggest, a situational approach to analysis and ethics is needed. This broader approach stresses the need to look at the setting, to go beyond (but make room for) important variables such as the tool in question or the type of data, and to consider structural conditions such as reciprocity and whether state or nonstate actors are involved, or whether an overarching first principle such as privacy or publicity is at stake.[12] These factors need to be seen within a specified context, rather than in isolation from it.

The irony and much of the sense that something is off in the stories of the Omniscient Organization, PISHI, Tom Voire, and Rocky Bottoms are related to a mismatch between surveillance behavior and what seems right for the milieu in question (work vs. home, personal vs. impersonal relations, the state vs. civil society). A key factor in this mismatch is the interplay of various personal and institutional borders, as seen in the fit of technologies, rules, expectations, setting, and behavior. The surveillance occasion (chap. 5) viewed as a dynamic process over time needs to be broken into its sequential strips and interrogated by the questions in our list, above.

In seeking to understand and evaluate the privacy-related problems raised by new information technologies, Helen Nissenbaum (2010) creatively develops ideas of contextual integrity. She calls for detailed analysis of how a change—say, for example, the increasing ease of communicating information or aggregating it in combined databases—affects the goals sought and traditional expectations regarding factors such as who the information is about, what kind of information it is, and what the principles for its transmission are.

As the many examples considered thus far suggest, building up from the facts on the ground to reach conclusions is central to understanding and judging surveillance. The emphasis on context with its direct acknowledgment of the variation in settings of personal information is a key to a more comprehensive understanding. A perspective such as Nissenbaum's is necessary for analyzing the roots of the many concerns over the new technologies. My approach is even more general in seeking ways to judge all surveillance—whether traditional or new and whether or not it comes to be defined as problematic.[13] Privacy is only one of the major issues raised by surveillance and, as noted, can be analyzed independently of it.

In treating established information norms as the standard against which any new means should be compared, Nissenbaum does not necessarily favor the status quo. She notes that sometimes new information-gathering means will better meet the dominant goal(s) of a given context such as health care or voting than did traditional means. My initial concern, however, goes beyond comparing new and old to suggesting ways to judge the desirability of traditional means, apart from any change brought by emerging means, and to identifying the correlates of disagreements (or structural roots, as they say).

In studying undercover police practices in 1988 I stressed the importance of rules and of less formal expectations in *specific contexts* as against the intrinsic elements of a tool or universal principle in reaching conclusions. This also holds for other forms of surveillance. As noted, a given means can be used for different goals (contrast a location-monitoring device carried by a skier in case of avalanche with the surreptitious application of such a device to a rival's car.) A given goal, such as the prevention of drug use, can be sought and evaluated with respect to a variety of means from mandatory to voluntary testing of various kinds, informers, stings, dog searches, education, supply restriction and methadone (or Antabuse for alcohol), and various treatments.[14]

Simply having a technique that is morally acceptable is obviously not a sufficient condition for its use any more than a good goal is justification for using a morally challenged or unduly risky or costly means. But even with appropriate means and ends, ethical concerns can also arise at other stages noted in chapter 5, such as collection, analysis, data protection, and data fate.[15]

The ethical status of a technique can vary from cases in which the means, goals, conditions of use, and consequences are wrong or even abhorrent, to those in which they are all acceptable or even desirable, to varying combinations. A more precise and richer analysis is possible when judgments are related to the distinctions the book suggests.

To be sure, some means of personal information collection strike most observers as wrong or at least troubling, apart from how and why they are done, and whether or not they appear to be valid and effective. Torture and biological weapons are obvious cases. Harming or threatening innocent friends or relatives of a subject is another. Similarly, most persons recoil at (and the courts tend to prohibit) information collection involving coercive bodily intrusions such as pumping the stomach of a suspect believed to have swallowed evidence or removing a bullet from the body for ballistics matching.

Other surveillance means such as lying, deception, and manipulation (as in undercover work), while not automatically beyond consideration, are hardly initially preferred. As Sissela Bok (1978) argues with respect to lies, they should be used only under limited circumstances and when a convincing case for them has been made. Such means always present a moral dilemma. No matter how compelling the justification for use in a specific setting, in our culture neither lying and trickery nor physical force and coercion are morally preferred techniques.

Yet, viewed against the astounding number of surveillance events occurring daily, publicly acknowledged use of tactics that are abhorrent or of last resort are uncommon.[16] The law, concern with public relations and reciprocity, the values of the agent, and the move toward soft means of data gathering can block or temper the harsher applications. While some data collection means are inherently undesirable and even prohibited, categorical prohibition of a means is rarely an issue. Most contemporary disputes over domestic practices do not involve the means as such; rather, they are more likely to be found in a disjuncture between the context and the means and/or the goal, or to involve lack of reciprocity or concern over faulty or absent rules or the failure to follow appropriate standards for collection, analysis, and data protection and use.

Values

> You're right from your side,
> I'm right from mine.
> BOB DYLAN, "One Too Many Mornings"

Context and the specifics of a situation apart, the questions presented in this chapter imply some broader principles or values that can be sources of conflict. The unifying function of values is aided by their level of abstraction and vagueness of meaning. But given the lack of clarity in definition, there is much room for disagreement. What does the value mean? When values conflict, how should they be prioritized? When does a value apply?

Even when the meaning of values is not disputed, conflicts between values are often present—for example, liberty and order or publicity and privacy; rights and obligations of the individual over the community; universalism and particularism; individual rights and efficiency, effectiveness, and rationalization; free markets and regulation; freedom of religion and gender equality; and freedom of expression and honesty. Conflicts are often between the good and the good, rather than between good and evil.

When values conflict, rather than rejecting them outright, people often disagree over how they should be weighed. Since 9/11 supporters and opponents of the Patriot Act and enhanced surveillance argue endlessly about the relative importance of security and privacy.

When the meaning or prioritization of a value is not in dispute, people may disagree over when it applies. Disagreements about transitions between the borders of social positions are an example. Consider parents and teenage children—with parents justifying surveillance because they see adolescents as irresponsible, or at least in need of guidance, while the latter argue that they have become responsible (whether of legal age or not).

A related disagreement is about what value should apply to an object. There is little debate about the reasons for protecting information contained within the first-class letter, or about the accessibility of information offered by a postcard. But when a new means of communication, such as e-mail, appears, should it be treated like a first class letter or like a postcard?

Complexity? Yes. Abstention? No. Complicated? Often

On the best of all possible planets for the philosopher, an ethical theory needs to be grounded in a formal normative argument that offers justifications for its principles, indicates their logical implications, and leads to clear conclusions. Such an argument would anticipate and respond to likely objections and would be consistent across types of justification (e.g., it would not mix arguments based on categorical first principles with those based on empirical consequences, as is done here).

Like a kaleidoscope with a unifying light source, an integrated ethical theory should illuminate and link the varied shapes and shades of surveillance.[17] It would be nice if the world had been created such that a simple deductive Rosetta stone for judging surveillance was possible.[18] But given the world in which we live, such an effort would need to be so general and banal as to be of modest interest or use ("do good, avoid harm") and so for now we are left with practical reasoning rather than an ethical theory.

The alternative offered here—an inductive approach that asks about the ethics of heterogeneous settings and behavior—also has limitations. A comprehensive consideration of the myriad factors that can go wrong or right with surveillance may overwhelm the observer. Casting such a wide yet thinly meshed net brings the risk of being unwieldy and unrealistic, let alone unread—even by those with time to reflect and the will to read more than an executive summary.[19]

This can easily lead to quick solutions that ignore complexity and the potential fallacies of quantification—falling back on automatic bureaucratic decision making based on ethics by the numbers (e.g., simply counting up the "yes" and "no" answers to the questions above and declaring that the majority wins). Equally troubling is to ignore moral conflicts and the dangers that come of failing to acknowledge the "Dirty Harry problem" and seeing that hard choices must sometimes be made between the bad and the horrible.[20]

I have sought an intermediate position—casting a net broad enough to capture the major variations and filtering these through some basic values. This chapter's emphasis on surveillance agents reflects concern over the abuses associated with the tilted nature of private-sector, organizational, and authority playing fields and unequal access to surveillance resources. At the same time, I try to avoid the demonology and glorification involved in viewing data gatherers as invariably up to no good and surveillance subjects as helpless victims whose rights are always trampled.

We all play multiple roles and rotate between being agents and subjects. Organizations and those in positions of authority are prone to emphasize their rights to gather and use personal information over their duties or the rights of subjects. In turn, subjects generally show greater interest in protecting their own information than in the informational rights of others and are relatively unaware, or uninterested, in the information of organizations.

Under appropriate conditions agents have a right and even an obligation to surveil, but they also have a duty to do it responsibly and accountably. Reciprocally, those subject to legitimate surveillance have obligations as well (e.g., not to distort the findings or threaten agents), even as they also have rights not to be subjected to some forms of surveillance.

The multidimensional nature of personal information, the extensive contextual and situational variation related to this, the value conflicts, and the dynamic nature of contested social situations prevent reaching any simple conclusions about how crossing informational borders will (empirically) and should (morally) be evaluated. Such complexity serves well when it introduces humility and qualification, but not when it immobilizes. Real analysts see the contingent as a challenge to offer contingent statements rather than throwing up their arms in despair. The point is that in spite of all the factors (whether contextual or inherent in values) that work against broad generalizations about the ethics of surveillance, some moral threads that swirl within and between the questions can be noted.

Some values are desirable as ends in themselves—for example, honesty, and fairness. But values may also be a means to some other ends—for example, democracy as a support for legitimacy, privacy as a support for intimacy or challenges by political organizations, and transparency as a support for accountability. Asking why (and when) a value is important as an end itself as against as a means to other valued ends and offering standards for prioritizing values are central to the ethics of surveillance. In democratic societies operating under the rule of law, a cluster of value justifications underlie the questions in our list. The most overarching and important are the Kantian idea of respect for the dignity of the person and respect for the social and procedural conditions that foster a civil society.

At the beginning of the book I noted that its central questions involved empirical description, conceptual elaboration, cultural analysis, and finally, ethics and policy. This chapter, which treated the last two, concludes the effort. The final chapter briefly returns to these themes and also explores some broader questions, such as Where is our society headed with respect to dystopian and utopian claims? How should we think about the verdant trends, countertrends, ironies, conflicting goals, and emerging questions the topic brings? What are the major unresolved and emerging issues in the social study and regulation of surveillance? I conclude with some directives to guide future researchers.

Windows into Hearts and Souls: Clear, Tinted, or Opaque Today?

The king hath note of all that they intend,
By interception which they dream not of.

WILLIAM SHAKESPEARE, *The Life of Henry V*

Consistent with Talmudic wisdom, which asks, "Why spoil a good question with an answer?" a project which in one sense began when I was in graduate school can't really be concluded, but it can be stopped. The more I look at the forms, processes, and borders of personal information, the more I find to ponder and learn. I enjoy musing about these issues, and new data to feed the muse continually appear. William James quipped that knowing what to ignore was a central part of wisdom. The same might be said for knowing when to stop searching.

A major goal of this book was to generate a conceptual framework to order, describe, explain, and evaluate the questions and data raised by new surveillance technologies. I have sought to identify a skeletal structure assessing the most varied surveillance tools and activities. When one's goals are conceptual, a moment arrives when the latest development or newest entry fits comfortably within the existing categories. I have reached that point. Whatever the latest iteration for collecting, analyzing, and using personal information, the basic questions and concepts presented endure.

I will not offer a summary of the many concepts. I will, however, restate some of the central themes and arguments. The concepts in a sense will speak for themselves if researchers and policy makers can successfully apply them. In other words, the value of the organizing ideas lies in their usefulness, and that is largely untested, although I have sought to demonstrate their worth by way of illustration—a method far from the systematic potential of current social scientific methods. I hope the concepts can be further developed, made more operational, and applied to hypothesis testing and public policy discussions.[1]

Of Queens and Bards

What would Queen Elizabeth I or Shakespeare say if they were to look down on the contemporary surveillance scene in democratic societies? Are the windows today into "men's hearts and secret thoughts" (the quote that opened the book's introduction) clear, tinted, or opaque, and, whatever the answer, is this good or bad?[2] To paraphrase what Shakespeare said of Henry V, do kings and other power wielders today have note of all we intend, by interception which we dream not of? Certainly they know a lot more about their subjects than did kings and queens in the sixteenth century, but there is also much more to know (or potentially knowable). Individuals today are not at a loss for dreaming (even if of the nightmare variety) of what means might be used to intercept their private thoughts, and kings are more limited in their power in democratic societies. Conversely, what do people know today of kings, or of each other, given the more egalitarian distribution of the means of knowing and the greater openness associated with democracy? Related questions apply to what neighbors in the medieval village were likely to know of each other, as against what urban neighbors now know of each other (or are capable of learning of others) in today's global environment and to the borders between public and private, state and civil society, employers and employees, merchants and customers, and the individual and the group.

The Beat Goes On as well as a Counterbeat

Dial F for Frankenstein.

ARTHUR C. CLARKE

Toward the end of the last century, as the new surveillance became headline news, Huxley, Orwell, and Foucault provided the foundation for much of the emerging work in surveillance studies, including that of modern surveillance essayists. With respect to the means of data collection, storage, analysis, and communication at the center of the new surveillance, there has been a continual decline in cost and size, and an increase in sophistication, power, scale, speed, memory, integration of distinct forms and data sets, remote accessibility, and ease of use.[3] The list below elaborates on these developments.

Trends Supportive of a Broadly Defined Panoptic Perspective

Thou art about my path, and about my bed; and spiest all my ways.
PSALM 139:7

1. *Increasingly information-based society*: a larger role for empirical data, information, and knowledge as against tradition, superior physical force, and direct coercion in social organization and interaction

2. *Increase in elite access to data*: disproportionate determination and control of knowledge by, and available of knowledge to, those in higher-status positions, sustaining and increasing their power and other resources while increasing the exclusion and marginality of the less privileged, who know ever less about elites

3. *Technical progress*: decline in cost, increased efficiency, and ease of application at various stages of a surveillance occasion (e.g., collection, analysis, and communication)

4. *New visibility and meaning for data*: appearance of tools for making the unseen or meaningless meaningful

5. *Border busting*: breaking through borders of time, space, covertures, and varied formats that protected information

6. *Border blurring*: decrease in the distinctness of lines between public and private places, making personal information more available

7. *Data integration*: merging of previously compartmentalized data

8. *Lessened anonymity*: decline in the ability to be unnoticed and unidentified or, if identified, to be known about

9. *Expanded categorical surveillance*: generalized suspicion of all

10. *Data collection built in*: Embedded, automated, and increasingly remote surveillance that is integrated with and involuntarily becomes part of the activity itself

11. *Softer data collection*: collection that is less overtly coercive or visible and relies instead on persuasion and benefits for subject compliance

12. *Expansions*: growth in the breadth, depth, temporality, quality, quantity, and invasiveness of personal data collection, covering (and recovering) ever more areas of life

13. *Restrictions of opportunity*: lessening of choice through the standardization and homogenization of behavioral engineering

14. *Increased ignorance and uncertainty*: lesser subject knowledge about the collection and use of surveillance data and, when there is awareness of its potential, whether or not one is a subject

15. *Increased granularity*: systematization and ever finer differentiation of categories for classifying people

16. *Increasing subjection to mandates*: expansion of laws, policies, and procedures requiring that agents seek and subjects provide information

17. *The arrival of cheerful, reward-seeking subjects*: glad, gleeful, and unreflective acquiescence in providing personal data, whether for rewards, convenience, or protection

These developments fan the flames of the "nowhere to run," tighten-the-noose, death of privacy under the velvet-sheathed, modern Leviathan State of the Dystopic imagination. Yet countertrends exist as well. These generally receive less attention from critical scholars and the media. The *Hux-Orw-Fouc* view must be tempered by noting the opposing developments—both short- and long-term.[4] The list below summarizes a number of these developments.

Counter Trends Not Supportive of a Broadly Defined Panoptic Perspective

Surely the darkness will hide me and the light become night around me
PSALM 139:11

1. Improved means for *protection of the jewels*: the development and spread of technologies for protecting individual information
2. New *alternatives to core identity and expanding choice*: the development of anonymous and pseudonymous forms of identification
3. Increasingly *destigmatized and diversified identities*: greater acceptance of some previously discreditable identities and introduction of new opportunities to choose and shift identities
4. Increasingly *individualized surveillance*: greater focus on intense scrutiny of particular subjects as against (or after) general surveillance
5. Increased *spillover*: data increasingly gathered (often nonintentionally) on those beyond the subject of interest
6. Increased *sharing of tools*: broader availability of many tools for data collection and analysis cooperatively used by distinct organizations
7. Increased *decentralization and networking*: information collection, analysis, and communication by agents not requiring a center
8. Improved means for *resisting*: improving neutralization tactics
9. *New normative protections and cultural expectations*: principles, laws, rules, policies, ethics codes, and manners that guard personal information and establish standards
10. *Informed subjects with choices*: increased awareness among subjects about whether or not information must be provided, and how much information must be provided
11. Surfacing of *Achilles' heels*: increased agent and public awareness of ironic vulnerabilities and failures
12. *Reduction of objectionable methods*: less intrusive and invasive means of data collection
13. *Contraction*: some retrenchment and desistance in use of surveillance means after initial appearance

There have been many failures of surveillance systems. Minas Samatas (2014) details the impressive failure of a $300 million state-of-the-art C41 (command, control, coordination, communication, and integration) system for the Greek 2000 Olympics. The 9/11 Commission documents some of these (National Commission 2004) and later, even with unprecedented levels of surveillance, the Boston Marathon, Mumbai, Paris, and San Bernardino. Many more known to insiders will probably never become public. In spite of the world's largest and most expensive and sophisticated manhunt by orders of magnitude, it still took ten years to locate Osama Bin Laden, and human intelligence was integral. Note also the failure of massive international searches to locate Edward Snowden and the missing Malaysian Airline flight 370.

Every complex system has ironic vulnerabilities and Kafkaesque absurdities. Albert Camus and Woody Allen, not to mention Sisyphus, are always waiting in the wings for an entry on stage right. The Keystone Kops need to be joined by what Jean-Paul Brodeur and Stephane Leman-Langlois (2006) call "big bungler" the other side of big brother. They as well need to make room for some obdurate ironies involving the potential insecurity of security.

That technologies may bite back in unexpected and unwanted ways is a common theme in our culture (Seiber 1981; Tenner 1997; Vamosi 2011). Efforts to solve old problems may bring new ones. One strand of this insecurity was well illustrated by the case of WikiLeaks and of NSA insider revelations.

While the means may be highly focused and individualized, yet because of spillover, far more data may be gathered than are needed or can be used, and data may be gathered that the agents would prefer not to know and on subjects they have no right to know about—for example, DNA on family members revealed from a sample of an appropriate subject, or miscellaneous people caught by the sweep of an audio or video recording that also catches the subject.

In conflict settings, an initial advantage may be lost as adversaries come to use the tools or learn to defeat them. Early successes may have resulted from encountering the easiest cases. Heterogeneity among subjects will probably mean that a technique that works for some may have the opposite effect for others—for example, video surveillance can deter some subjects while offering a platform for those who seek notoriety and sanctioning, whether as exhibitionists, attention seekers, activists, or would-be martyrs.

With the twentieth-century expansion of civil liberties and civil rights has come a significant expansion of laws, policies, and manners that limit and regulate the collection of personal information and its subsequent treatment, including requirements to keep, seal, or destroy after a period of time. Bennett and Raab (2006) document this international trend. *The Privacy Journal* regularly publishes compilations of these laws and regulatory efforts (Smith 2013), and privacy law itself is a growing specialization.[5] Moreover, rather than a one-size-fits-all approach, informed-consent policies often bring the choice to opt in or out of data collection efforts or to pay for a greater level of privacy or be rewarded for accepting a lesser level (fast-track options for air travelers, G-mail or Facebook accounts).[6]

Alternatives to full identification, (e.g., to the core identity discussed in chap. 4) are more available. The absolute number and relative importance of noncore forms of identity offering varying degrees of anonymity has significantly expanded. A variety of pseudonymous certification mechanisms intended to mask or mediate between the individual's name and location yet still convey needed information are available. Moreover, the distance-mediated, remote interactions of cyberspace (e.g., searches, phone communication, toll road scanners, and many consumer transactions) require authentication which can be met through alternative forms of identification, including those that are fully pseudonymous.

Identities with varying degrees of anonymity will probably become an increasingly common and accepted form of presenting the self for particular purposes, whether as a unique individual or as a member of a particular category. A cartoon showing a talking bird who speaks, but only anonymously, illustrates this.[7]

Contrary to the "nowhere to hide" image, in some cases it may be easier to automatically destroy electronic records than paper records. For example, libraries delete a user's record once a book is returned, and greater anonymity comes with automated searches, as they eliminate the traditional need to ask a reference librarian or clerk for face-to-face help. The greater anonymity in communication is a central factor in the rapid expansion of pornography from movie theaters to VHS/DVD to the Internet.

Seen through a broader lens, social and cultural changes toward greater openness and tolerance can mean people have less need to protect some kinds of information previously considered stigmatizing—for example, that involving divorce, homosexuality, birth out of wedlock, race, religion, adoption, and some illnesses. Greater acceptance and new legal protections take the wind out of the sails of certain prior forms of discrimination, not to mention blackmailers, and they also can eliminate the need for control via surveillance.[8] Indeed, with new pride, those with formerly disparaged identities are less fearful of powerful means of discovery and may publicly assert what previously had been hidden.[9] Along these same lines, newer, blurred identities—as with race and ethnicity or gender and sexuality—make it more difficult for traditional categorizations.[10] Furthermore, with new kinds of communication come lessened expectations for controlling certain forms of information—as with postings on social media or YouTube that can be widely seen.

While traditional records may be more permanent, forms of identity and appearance need not be, raising questions about the currency of archived data. Individuals in some ways are freer both morally and tactically to make or re-make themselves than ever before (Marx 1991). When online, some inherited or historically fixed identities such as social status, religion, ethnicity or region can be more easily altered, changed, or simply made invisible (as with accent). The proliferation of television "makeover" shows and self-altering products also reflect this potential, as does the use of photo-editing tools. Such opportunities, along with the increase in non-face-to-face interaction, reflect the possibility of having multiple personas in cyberspace and a more protean self whose nature may vary depending on the audience and will of the person.

Within limits, the self can be seen as a chameleon commodity and as an object to be worked on and fitted to the situation. Identities, then, are becoming relatively less unitary, homogeneous, fixed, and enduring, as the modernist idea of being able to choose who one is continues to expand, and as globalization further blurs aspects of identity previously restricted and determined by geography.

Even seemingly permanent physical attributes such as gender, height, body shape, or facial appearance can to some degree be altered, whether by hormones, surgery, or beauty parlors. The ultimate change is the emerging technology of total face transplants. The latter raises interesting questions about facial recognition systems. These opportunities complicate simple assumptions about Big Brother's fixed knowledge of the person.

In addition to these less fixed and less unitary identities we are developing, we have access to an increased range of tools for protecting individual information and for neutralizing surveillance. New encryption tools, for example, offer a degree of confidentiality, accountability, and data protection in communication never before seen. Home security systems and software to provide computer security and protect privacy are also increasingly available. In short, the expansion of surveillance creates markets that entrepreneurs are glad to fill. New tools and ways of blocking, distorting, deceiving, or destroying the surveillance means (whether legitimately or illegitimately) are commonplace and appearing at a rapid pace.

Beyond the aforementioned defensive measures that individuals employ to protect their personal information, there has been a massive democratization, as consumers and activists have begun to benefit from the same surveillance tools initially enjoyed by elite users but at lower cost and with enhanced power and ease of use. The offensive use of surveillance tools has spread far beyond the military, police, and large organizations and may now be directed at them and also used by individuals in the interpersonal relations of daily life. Data collection, aggregation, analysis, and communication once restricted to the major governments, corporations, and the most privileged can be used by less powerful nations, smaller organizations, and individuals.

This democratization allows greater reciprocity in watching (whether openly or covertly), as it moves from a one-way mirror to two-way transparent glass.[11] Consider the rapid diffusion of cell phones with video cameras, home video security systems, and computers, with real-time video capacity among many other forms.

In Bentham's *Panopticon*, an unseen guard watched many prisoners. Likewise, the surveillance essays emphasize the monopolization of information and communication by a small number of interconnected, low-visibility elites, not unlike the workings of the early telephone systems, where all calls had to be initiated and connected through a central operator. Television and radio channels had a central location to reach the public.

Today however, as has often been noted in hailing the virtues of the computer, we depend less on centralized networks and engage in much peer-to-peer surveillance and communication.[12] Center hubs and main offices, while hardly irrelevant, can frequently be bypassed as once-isolated individuals directly engage in remote interaction without an over-the-shoulder looker. This may enhance the civil-society pluralism favored by democratic theorists since Tocqueville, who are uncomfortable with ever larger governments and corporations and with recent blurring of the lines between them.

Decentralized information collection, analysis, and sharing mark a significant departure from the early fears of the 1960s of one big centralized database on a large square block in Washington DC (Burnham 1983). The ability of protesters to use surveillance tools such as cell phones to document the behavior of social control agents and to use social media to communicate among themselves and with the outside world is illustrative.

The Internet offers the enterprising searcher astounding tools for learning about others. And the net makes anyone with access a potential publisher, independent of the traditional centralized sources and censors. That blurs the borders between the professional journalist and the chorus of reporting citizens. The potential for surveillance results to be presented as news and/or entertainment might also moderate some elite excesses because of fear of being on and being the news. Finally, even when high-status individuals control the tools, they may be under legal obligation to share the fruits of their surveillance with subjects (e.g., those arrested or rejected for credit). In short, the information provided by the omnivorous device does not always favor the elites.

FIGURE 14.1. But does that excuse not taking a position? (Mischa Richter/The New Yorker Collection/ The Cartoon Bank.)

Figure 14.1 captures the frequent lack of agreement among scholars with respect to the empirical, but disagreement also extends to the values that inform how we assess the facts even when they are clearer.

Value and other Conflicts

Now Adam's prize was open eyes,
His sentence was to see.
TOM RUSH

Lyndon Johnson, in his first job interview, to be a teacher in 1928, was asked where he stood on the then-contentious issue of Darwin and evolution, he paused before saying he thought he could teach it either way. So it is with the great surveillance debates. That indecision regarding the most contentious issue of his day applies to ours. Certainly we need systematic ordering, careful measurement, and the testing of hypotheses to understand where surveillance in society is going.[13] But even the best concepts and empirical data will be unlikely to do much to resolve disagreements over values, holding apart the emergent, interweaving dynamic nature of a fluid topic.

Thus, whether scholars determine that the trend is toward or away from a maximally developed surveillance society (and within specific contexts), there would be disagreements about whether this was desirable or undesirable, particularly within specific settings. With conflicts over values and policies (e.g., whether to put resources into prevention or into ameliorating known problems or to focus on rewards or punishments), disagreements rest largely on beliefs and existential dilemmas, not on the presence or absence of data. This makes it difficult for the well-tempered intellect to take broad and consistent positions.

I saw this in studying undercover police, as I identified a number of ironies, trade-offs, risks, and operational paradoxes (Marx 1988a, 200–205). Many of these apply more broadly to surveillance-related issues. While not full Greek tragedies in which a virtue is also a flaw, the multiple goals and complications of the empirical world often result in unwanted consequences, only partial victories, and trade-offs in which there is no consensus about how they should be approached. In this situation, interested parties must remain aware, weigh (if not necessarily balance) what is at stake, tolerate second- and third-best outcomes, and try to identify and then mitigate unwanted collateral consequences.

The empirical record itself often does not clearly and strongly point in one direction. Even with eyes wide open, goodwill, competent agents, and best practices, the surveillance actions taken (or not taken) may have multiple consequences for legitimate values and interests—serving some while undermining others. No amount of research, training, new tools, policy analysis, or public relations can alter that. We can't have it all; repasts always cost someone something, somewhere, sometime. The bountiful optimism of the Renaissance, the Enlightenment, and utilitarianism meet their match in the natural and social complexity, fluidity, contradictions, and limitations of the world. We are rarely prescient or adequately prepared for the full consequences of innovation and social change.

A number of contradictions or conflicts can be noted. First, we seek privacy and often in the form of anonymity, but we also know that secrecy can hide dastardly deeds and that visibility can bring accountability.[14] On the other hand, too much visibility may inhibit experimentation, creativity, and risk taking. And while we value disclosure in the name of fairness and just deserts, we also believe in redemption. New beginnings after individuals have been sanctioned, or after they have otherwise overcome limitations or disadvantages, are fundamental to the American reverie.

Second, in our democratic, media-saturated, impression management societies, the reality is that many of us want to both see and be seen, even as we also want to look the other way and be left alone. We want to know, and we also want to be shielded from knowing. The accelerating contemporary desire to be noticed is reflected in the self-help and self-presentational industries à la popular talk and reality shows, YouTube, social media, blogs, celebrity tell-all books, and public relations. But note also the high degree of expressed concern over privacy invasions (if not always behavior consistent with this) revealed by public opinion polls.

Third, we value freedom of expression and a free press but do not wish to see individuals defamed, harassed, or unduly humiliated (whether by the actions of others or their own). We also desire as ideals honesty in communication and also civility and diplomacy. In interpersonal relations (in contrast to the abrasive talk shows) we may work hard to avoid embarrassing others by not seeking certain information or by holding back on what we know. We value the right to know, but also the right to control personal information. The absence of surveillance may bring freedom from censorship but also open the door to the worst demagogues, liars, and self-deluded snoops, such as the Tom Voire's of the world. Yet undue surveillance chills nonconforming communication and is the companion of repression.

Fourth, individuals expect organizations to treat them in a fair, accurate, and efficient manner and to judge them as unique, not as undifferentiated members of a general category, while at the same time they hesitate to reveal personal information and desire to have their privacy and confidentiality protected.[15] Meeting the first set of goals necessarily requires giving up personal data, and up to some point, the more one gives up, the more accurate and distinctly reflective it will be of the unique person. Yet the more data one reveals, the greater the risk of manipulation, misuse, and privacy violation. At the same time, knowing more can bring new questions and less certainty to surveillance agents. Depending on their role and social location, individuals and groups differ in the relative importance they give to privacy as compared to accuracy.[16]

The individual's expectation to be assayed in his or her full uniqueness may conflict with an organization's preference for responding to persons as part of broad common aggregates—something seen as more rational, effective, and even efficient. The idea of due process and fairness to be determined in each individual case can radically conflict with an organization's utilitarian goals and bottom line.

In the criminal justice context, for example, civil liberties sometimes conflict with the goal of effective enforcement.[17] The case for *categorical surveillance* (without cause) versus *particularized surveillance* (only with cause) and for prevention versus after-the-violation responses can be well argued either way.[18]

Fifth, culture sends contradictory messages. On the one hand, individuals are expected to submit to surveillance as members of a community that supports the common good and fairness (e.g., the required census or social security number that apply to all) or that allows one to participate in certain behaviors such as traveling, buying on credit, or obtaining an entitlement. Yet, fairness apart, when such surveillance goes beyond minimal verification and is done in a coercive manner, it may conflict with the expectation that before personal information borders are crossed, there need to be some grounds for suspicion. The Fourth Amendment elevates this principle to high law, but the idea infuses the culture more broadly. When there are few clear clues to what is sought and the searching is invasive, charges of discrimination will be avoided if all are searched or have an equal chance of being randomly surveilled. If the search is relatively modest, yet bears fruit, it also clears the way for more invasive searches that would be supported by the Fourth Amendment's requirement of probable cause.

If agents have to wait to do surveillance until they have cause in situations where there is evidence of preparatory actions or where violations are of low visibility or hidden outright, many violators get a free ride. This limitation protects the innocent against unnecessary searches. Yet it can also mean failing to prevent terrible events—for example, in the case of 9/11, where well-intentioned policies from another era as well as many informal factors blocked the FBI and CIA from exchanging information about the perpetrators.[19]

As has been said, if your tools work and if you search them all, you will probably get the guilty, not to mention the innocent. Profiling as a surveillance tool permeates society far beyond ethnicity, religion, or national origin. In contemporary society, with its emphasis on prevention, the push is toward broader and deeper searching absent cause. The dilemma can be identified but not solved, because observers differ in judging the trade-offs between equality, fairness, grounds for suspicion, invasiveness, prevention, effectiveness, and the likelihood and seriousness of risks.

The above discussion involves conflicts between abstract values. But more concrete conflicts may also appear in applying the tools. The intrinsic properties of a device may work against the agent's desire for secrecy. While much contemporary surveillance is defined by its ability to root out the unseen and unknown, it also paradoxically may reveal itself through electrical and chemical and other forms of data. That which silently gathers the emanations of others, if not exactly a mirror image, nonetheless emanates itself, offering discovery possibilities and means of neutralization to technically competent adversaries. As noted, the watchers may also be watched by the means they apply to others.

Social control systems contain ironic vulnerabilities (Marx 1981, 1988a, 2012, 2015b; Sewell and Barker 2006; Hoogenboom 2010). In the case of secure borders, what is included is also in a sense excluded, and these can be

linked in a bizarre dance. The need for exchanges with the environment creates the possibility for illegitimate, as well as legitimate, entrance and egress.
To securely enclose can mean no escape. To protect the jewels in a safe gathers them all together for predation.

This ironic potential is seen in films such as *Enemy of the State* and *The
Panic Room*. The former offers hope as the hero (Gene Hackman) attacks
obliquely and is able to convert the system's strength's into weaknesses. But
the latter suggests how the contradictions of surveillance can be a trap, not a
trade-off. In the film, the guards/guarded become the imprisoned. The room
that was to protect a mother and her daughter and prevent fear and panic
instead becomes the "panic room" surrounded by burglars (Kammere 2004).
If an agency publicizes a surveillance system that has as one goal making
citizens feel more secure, it may in addition have the opposite effect because
it sends the message that dangers are so great as to warrant the need for such
a system. Or this same publicity may alert committed malefactors to the presence of surveillance, triggering evasive, blocking, or displacement means—a
kind of unfair (at least to the law-abiding public) warning (note the presence of some security cameras designed to be conspicuous, with vibrant blue
lights, as against others that are hidden). Thus, advertising the means versus
keeping them secret highlights the potential conflict of goals between deterrence and apprehension so apparent with undercover work.[20]

The existence of practices with a good potential for abuse traditionally
leads to demands for regulation. A bureaucratic and legalistic response may
lessen problems, but ironically, it can also lead to expanded use of potentially
troubling means. In contrast, without a formal mandate legitimating and acknowledging the tactic, agents may hesitate to use it because of uncertainty
about where to draw the lines.

And so, having presented these thoughts on the inconsistent evidence,
competing values, and conflicts inherent in the surveillance process, I next
turn to an effort to make some broader sense out of them. While I can't adequately resolve the contradictions, I can suggest some ways to approach them.

The Moral (or Immoral?) Ambivalence of the Elves[21]

> There are two problems with the new surveillance technologies. One is that they don't
> work. The other is that they do.
> ANONYMOUS SOCIAL STUDIES SCHOLAR CIRCA 2000

Much of the debate in this field reflects a misguided *either/or* fallacy—
whether emerging from self-interest, ideology, the narrows of culture, dis-

ciplinary socialization and specialization, or selective perception. Engineers tend to be drawn to binary thinking as a result of training, and politicians and single-issue advocates fall into the same trap as a result of rhetorical needs. In contrast, many academics get splinters from fence sitting as a result of their culture or personality predispositions.

When patterns are not unidirectional, the challenge is to see if seemingly opposing ideas can be empirically linked and woven together, even if they abstractly remain logical opposites despite the empirical linking. Such efforts might involve identifying a time sequence that makes room for opposing patterns (e.g., the initial absorbent sponge of general surveillance gives way to the focused laser of a probing tool to a specific case).

Some disagreements may be more apparent than genuine when we consider the different definitions and meanings assigned to the same word or practice (consider *privacy, liberty, choice,* or *search*). Yet conflicting claims may result from looking at different parts of the social order. Thus, in the case of organizational trends, there is evidence of ever more specialized surveillant roles, but also of generalization and dispersal across roles (e.g., introducing various reporting hotlines such as "see something, say something" or training all retail employees to look for shoplifters). Or consider a concurrent increase and decrease in inequality (e.g., communications and behavior monitoring by government and large private organizations as against the wide availability of cell phone cameras and covert recording devices that can be turned against the more powerful).

But duality can also be seen in looking at one social setting, as with the simultaneous presence of contracts, coercion, and care in workplaces (although not to the same degree). Even the same goal, such as control, may show dominating and liberating aspects. Indeed dualism and more are a central theme of the book. The point here is to be open to its presence and not to prematurely fall into taking sides and offering intellectually indefensible claims.

The Four Questions

When we turn from wrestling with the conflicts and contradictions of the present to the historical questions with which this chapter began, a different approach is required. To get beyond the rhetoric, four important questions regarding broad historical patterns in the treatment of personal information need to be considered:

1. What is the ratio of what a technology is capable of to how extensively it is applied? (*surveillance slack ratio*)

2. What is the ratio of what is known about a person to the absolute amount of personal information potentially available ?[22] (*personal information penetration ratio*)

3. What is the ratio of what individuals wish to keep to themselves to how able they are to do this, given the technology, laws, and policies?[23] (*achieved privacy ratio*)

4. What is the ratio of what superordinates know about subordinates to what subordinates know about superordinates? (*reciprocity-equity ratio*)

These questions are central to a consideration of privacy concerns and limits on others' access to personal information.[24] Taken together they offer a more nuanced way of thinking about the social implications of the new surveillance.

Surveillance slack, the size of the gap between what a technology is capable of doing and the extent of its application, varies over time.[25] The slack was low in the Middle Ages, when technology was relatively weak but there were few restraints on applying it.[26] Conversely, consider situations of high surveillance slack, perhaps where technology is very powerful but there are significant restraints on applying it, for example, content wiretapping in the United States. Both of these pictures contrast with situations in contemporary authoritarian societies, in which the technology is strong and the restraints on its applications are few.

The personal information penetration ratio (what could be known given the means of discovery relative to what is actually known) was probably much smaller in the nineteenth century and in the medieval period than today. The weakness of the technology then was matched by the fact that there was much less to know about the individual's behavior (given a less differentiated society and greater homogeneity in ways of living apart from greater power of the technology), even if those in authority were less restrained in using their power to discover it.[27]

However, new tools (including formal record keeping) and changes in societal scale, density, mobility, differentiation, specialization, writing, and communication vastly increase the quantity of information.[28] Having large amounts of information available as a kind of raw material fits well into a society where most things are marketable. It also raises questions about where the outer limits on treating the personal as a commodity are, or ought to be. While people had less personal information to protect in the past, they also perhaps had less reason to protect what was there, at least within the small village. When personal information becomes something to be bought and sold, its value (and a desire to control it) may increase for both subjects and agents. Thus, if we compare preindustrial, industrializing, and contemporary societies in absolute terms, the amount of personal information that is potentially knowable would seem to have increased markedly but with varying degrees of surveillance penetration of that information.

Important here is the scale and relative ability (including speed, ease, and cost) of linking personal data to the core identity and location of particular individuals (chap. 4) and of linkages across databases.

Moving to the achieved privacy ratio (no. 3 above), apart from the *amount* and linkages, there is also the *content* of information individuals seek to and/ or are able to protect. This of course ties to tools and rules and to what surveillance agents desire to know, or not to know, about people and organizations. Do people overall today have, or want, to hide or communicate more than in the past, and how is this need or desire conditioned by the nature of the information? How well are the preferences realized in practice? To what extent do agents honor the legitimate preferences of their subjects?[29] How does what individuals hide from agents vary under different historical circumstances and how do the agents hidden from vary? What is the fit between the preferences of subjects and agents?

Our understanding of what people are willing to reveal, or have a choice about revealing, will increase to the extent that we compare particular kinds of information across historical periods. One window into change is to observe the contrast between today and the Victorian period, with its rich literary vocabulary for the examination of personal issues. That task keeps segments of the book and film industries in business and would reveal very different attitudes toward personal information among Victorians than we see today.

With respect to question 4, regarding trends in the extent of reciprocal knowledge,[30] we can identify three broad possibilities of particular interest using as an example access to, or denial of information to, government and citizens relative to each other.[31]

1. The ratio of what government knows about citizens to what citizens know about government increases (government knows more and more about citizens, who know less and less about government).
2. The ratio of what is reciprocally known by government and citizens stays about the same even as it varies only within moderate limits.
3. The ratio of what government knows about citizens to what citizens know about government declines (governments knows less and less about citizens, who know more and more about government).

The same alternatives fit any two-party relations, such as consumers and merchants or doctors and patients.

The first option characterizes a totalitarian society. The third option might seem preferable but would be organizationally impossible and severely dysfunctional. From the standpoint of classic democratic theory the ideal state is somewhere in the middle. However, this leaves blank the question of what the degree and kind of reciprocity between contending (or at least distinct) groups should be. The ratio of what groups should be able to know about each other obviously will vary depending on current events such as major crises and threats, the kind of information, and the context and roles played.

Orwell or Fitzgerald?

> Ring the bells that still can sing
> Forget your perfect offering
> There is a crack in everything
> That's how the light gets in.
> LEONARD COHEN, "Anthem," 1992

Much disagreement in the surveillance debate is about what the varied empirical contours mean in some overall sense for the individual and society. At the extremes are the utopians with their cotton candy promises and the dystopians with their gloomy disaster predictions.[32] Neither perspective describes social change well—in the past or, I suspect, for the near future.

To construct an adequate answer to the "Where is society headed?" and "Is it good or bad?" questions, we need to consider the various components of control over personal information, various forms of privacy and types of data on people, and the tools used to uncover, record, and protect personal information, and we need to do so across contexts and at the various points of the surveillance occasion.

In the fullest analysis, even if we were to look just to implications for privacy, we would need to look at informational, physical, aesthetic, proprietary, and decisional forms of privacy (chap. 1, pp. 27–29) as well as the various subtypes of data on persons (chap. 4).[33] And we must also consider the types of tools used to uncover, record and protect personal information and the role played (chap. 2, pp. 55–58). As well, consideration needs to be given to the various contexts treated in the three-C narratives of coercion, contracts, care, and the residual free-range surveillance type apart from an organization or appropriate role. The various points of the surveillance occasion (chap. 5) also require consideration. This, unfortunately, would yield a vast number of places to look, and an analysis so broad as to be unworkable, as well as the conclusion that until more comprehensive analysis is done, it is tricky to argue that individuals now have lesser or greater control over personal information.

By way of illustration and suggestive of the challenges to facile conclusions, elsewhere (Marx 2002) we can see the complexity of assessing efforts to intercept and protect just one form—telecommunications—that began in mid-nineteenth century.

Almost as soon as the telegraph appeared, so did wiretapping and the sending of messages in code. New means may initially spread in the absence of any restrictions, but as problems appear, so do counterefforts and regulation (e.g., the Privacy Protection Act of 1986) often including a degree of self-regulation. Among some recent examples, cordless and cell phone communication and e-mail could be legally intercepted until the passage of the Privacy Protection Act in 1986. The sending of junk fax and automated phone dialing was prohibited not long after. Or consider the relatively short time between the commercial availability of DNA testing for insurance and employment and the passage of the Genetic Information Nondiscrimination Act of 2008. The speed of recent legislation is noteworthy, considering that it took almost a century to significantly restrict wiretapping.

My review illustrated the difficulty in reaching an overall conclusion about whether the protection of personal communications (as a proxy illustrative of the wide range of surveillance fields) has expanded or contracted.[34] Reaching strong conclusions requires measures of absolute and relative data for multiple forms and settings of communication, with particular attention to time lags, displacement, and the appearance of functional alternatives.

Looking just at the period *before* regulation and neutralization appear might give the impression that the sunset of liberty is upon us as predicted. On the other hand, looking just at the passage of so many new data protection laws (absent consideration of their content or implementation) can give the impression that things are getting better all the time. The evidence suggests neither the fast track to dystopia nor the slow crawl to utopia. In goal- and conflict-rich, constantly evolving dialectical environments of human frailty, there are frequent slips twixt desired goals and outcomes, and major impediments to sudden radical change, regardless of its direction, just as there are lags in identifying and responding to new problems.

In short, within democratic societies over the past half century there has been something of a rough moving equilibrium (but, to be sure, with jagged lines up and down) between the availability and protection of personal information. The fluid patterns and changing forms of personal data collection and protection and the diverse interpretations that can be applied to them ought to slow (although not put an end to) broad generalizations about where society is headed and whether this is for good or bad, absent clear definitions of the forms and time periods.

The muddy waters of the empirical record in the face of the imprecision of language have implications for George Orwell's (1968) famous call for clarity in expression. In *1984* he satirically illustrated this need with the word *doublethink*. F. Scott Fitzgerald (1936) developed a related idea some years before Orwell. In contrast, Fitzgerald's idea was not meant as satire, but as appreciation and admonition: "The test of a first- rate intelligence is the ability to hold two opposed ideas in the mind at the same time, and still retain the ability to function"—a view many Jungian and cognitive developmental psychologists would endorse.

The value of clarity and honesty in expression, as Orwell advocated, is hardly debatable, but when complex topics are involved, it is well, with mathematician and logician Alfred Whitehead, not to rush to find clarity and consistency at a cost of "overlooking the subtleties of truth." We need to acknowledge and understand the breadth and heterogeneity of the fields, the ambiguities in meaning, and the conditions that permit social forces and values to move in opposite directions, whether literally or within the perceptions of the observer. There is need for a concept that captures these tensions.

The Perhapsicon

> She [Laura] oscillated uncomfortably between being somewhat scared and somewhat skeptical, never quite the one or quite the other; an agnostic on this as on so much else, a little envious of the true believers for their easy certitude.
>
> JONATHAN RABAN, *Surveillance*

So, again, where do we stand? We have the trends and countertrends observed but rarely quantitatively documented across cultures, contexts, and historical periods. And we have the ironies, unintended and uncontrollable consequences, and multiple value conflicts that make the topic so interesting and challenging. Mushrooms do well in the dark, and so does injustice. And all this appears to work against sweeping empirical or moral conclusions (other than this one). Perhaps then a nuanced *perhapsicon* model better captures our situation than either a *panopticon* or a *utopicon* model. To the Right Honourable Jeremy Bentham and M. le Professeur Foucault and their traveling fellows, such a model says, "Perhaps, sometimes, perhaps even often, *but* sometimes never, and in addition, make room for counter evidence, conflicting values and outcomes and new factors."[35] Foucault himself of course was not above honoring conflicting ideas.

Those who look optimistically at information technology as the solution and those who view it as the problem too often talk past each other. For persons within the orbit of the Omniscient Organization, PISHI and Rocky Bottoms, the message is to be aware of complexity and value conflicts and the need for empirical reality checks. Liberty and democracy (which, after all, can be good for business) are fragile and not self-sustaining. The message for the independent scholar is to avoid premature commitment to the camp of either the optimists or the pessimists. Usually, the best answer is "It depends."[36] The moral mandates for study that conclude this chapter offer some further directives.

Modern democratic society is a farrago in a cauldron of conundrums accompanied by myths shielding harsher realities. The challenge is to acknowledge this without creating an immoral relativism and an immobilizing cynicism. Surveillance rules and transparency are needed for accountability but without straitjackets that eliminate organizational discretion, flexibility, and innovation or that stifle personal questioning, honest communication, and experimentation. Surveillance as part of presumably rational, external, engineered behavior control needs to avoid creating persons who do the right thing only because they think they can't get away with doing the wrong thing. Are the assumptions in the security mantra "Trust but verify" necessarily incompatible?

Contradictory and ironic elements are a sign of reality's overflowing the either/or categories favored by our culture and brains. Why, for example, during the Cold War were computers and related means seen as technologies of freedom (de Sola Pool 1983) in authoritarian countries, while in the West they invoked fears of Big Brother? This calls for empirical inquiry and for theories that can take account of the complexity. Understanding and acting wisely require seeing multiple sides and awareness of dialectical processes (e.g., between democracy and bureaucracy or expertise) and levels of analysis. Unlike beauty, truth isn't quite in the eye of the beholder, but it is powerfully conditioned by where, when, and what one looks with, for, and at. Double vision is bad for the viewer, but good for wisdom.

Next we turn attention to some questions that are unsettled partly because the technologies are so new and there hasn't been time to find good or adequate answers, whether empirical or ethical.

The Questions Just Keep on Coming

Let me note some enduring big "So what?" and "Where is society headed?" questions that the new surveillance raises.

The meaning of the human: What are the implications for traditional understanding of human dignity, uniqueness, free will, responsibility, choice, and control when persons are reduced to abstracted bits of information and when their behavior is predicted based on simulation models that claim to foresee aggregate behavior? What happens when people are ever more defined in categorical and profiled terms rather than by relationships? Is there a point at which the scientification and parceling out of the soul destroys something sacred? What happens to interior life if thoughts and feelings can be determined apart from what people choose to disclose? Should masks be prohibited? Should people be prohibited (whether for reasons of convenience or by rules) from being able to compartmentalize their multiple selves, and even in the absence of formal mandates, will we back into such a condition because of perceived advantages of technologies such as Facebook and the identification and location powers of other means? Are the lines between the human and the nonhuman becoming more blurred as information gathering and controls become a part of the body? At what point does something uniquely tied to a person—for example, DNA, gait, or "personal" microbes, which are in a sense "freely" offered to anyone close enough to capture them—cease to belong to that person? In the face of such capabilities, do we need a more fluid conception of the person and his or her rights to control the "personal" when it transcends the body?

The meaning of a search: Searches based on the unaided senses that physically cross protective barriers such as walls, desk drawers, briefcases, or bodies are already well understood. But what of technologies that read what persons or places radiate with no need to enter and remove what is within? How does search by an "impersonal" machine or animal differ in its consequences and desirability from that by a human? Is due process honored when an individual is singled out not because of wrongful behavior, but because of how close he or she fits an aggregate statistical model believed to be associated with wrongful behavior? At what point does momentary surveillance in a public place (as with a police officer noting the license plate of a parked car) evolve into the kind of search prohibited by the Fourth Amendment without a warrant? Consider the detailed geographic location records for vehicles that are now so easy to generate. Are the new abilities to read what persons involuntarily give off consistent with the Fifth Amendment?

The limits of pragmatism: The new surveillance tools raise new questions about the role of technique in human society. Dazzled by the potentials, the inspired may easily assume that if the technology can do something, it should be done. Yet the technology is part of a broader social environment, and the human is something more than a subject with problems and potentials controllable by interventions, no matter how high minded the goals or intellectually exciting the puzzle to be "solved." Yet just what this is and ought to be is to a degree negotiable under ever changing conditions.

Competing social and psychological needs: How does (and should) the hu-

man need for community, attention, and response from others enhanced by
social media and new forms of visibility and communication affect other human needs for personal space, solitude, down time, back stages, and apartness from others?

The appeal of omniscience: What happens to the sacred, the magical, and
the mythological, let alone the civil and diplomatic, under conditions of full
knowledge? Do facades and ignorance serve social and psychological functions?[37] What if the eyes of God are not always upon us? How can society deal
with the inevitable gap between formal rules and the need to get important
jobs done? Just because something can be known, should it be? Why did Sa-
tan tell David to take a census of Israel, incurring God's wrath with a plague
upon the land (1 Chronicles 21)? What of the Cyclops, whose eye to see the
future led him see his own death? Is there wisdom or stupidity in the New
England folk belief that warns, "Look not at a knot-hole less you be vexed"
(any supporting evidence here from Adam, Narcissus, Lot's spouse, and Lady
Godiva?). How can we reconcile the importance of openness and visibility in
democratic government with the expectations of privacy and confidentiality
of personal information? What would a society be like with perfect visibility
regarding government, organizations, and persons? What would society be
like without the ability to deceive?[38]

The collapse of time and space: What are the consequences of remote and
instantaneous communication of sound and images? What changes when the
time between events, their communication, and the ability to act is immediate
(e.g., crowd sourcing)? What happens when the insulation from observability
offered by geographic distance is obliterated by telecommunications? What
are the consequences of communicating privately with far-flung others without the knowledge of those in your immediate environment (creating both
new individuation and new community)? Alternatively is distance-mediated
communication more conducive to hostile expressions (e.g., cyberbullying
and vigilantism, doxing, anonymous slandering) and fraud than face-to-face
communication?

Trust and doubt: Will confidence and trust (whether in other individuals,
organizations, or institutions) and sociability and community increase as a
result of new surveillance vetting, enhanced knowledge, record keeping and
analysis, and engineered behavior, or will they decline?

Are we entering a new age of suspicion? Will people increasingly wonder
if there is more there than meets the eye? Will fear, timidity, demoralization,
and even immobilization reign as we are ever more aware of risks (e.g., terrorism, crime, global warming, poor air and water quality, disease, the safety
of food, manufactured goods, and buildings, the mental health of airline pi-

lots? Are the mundane objects of everyday life what they appear to be? Might a backpack contain explosives? [39] Might a cuddly teddy bear or a smoke detector contain a video camera? Might a letter contain anthrax? Does this bottled water contain *E. coli* bacteria? Might a hidden voice stress analyzer be used during a job interview? Will individuals in the crowd at a protest rally be identified by their face and/or cell phone? Will drones and robots become the tools of voyeurs? Might a friend or a neighbor "see something and say something" about us? Might a former friend post a private or unflattering image or message on the Internet, a blog, or social media? Can our personal communications remain private? What kinds of decisions are made about us and by whom using algorithms and reconfigured data of which we know not?

Because deception, covert means, and even lying are known to be in the government's arsenal, will confidence in authority further decline—perhaps aided by less reliance on the immediate senses, lack of understanding of how data are produced and applied, and awareness of the simulations and distortions made possible with digital editing? Should the claims of leaders be believed about the seriousness of the threats, their competence and the promises of technology to protect us, and their ability to resist the temptations for abuse new rules and tools offer? Are the confidence, comfort, and sense of ease associated with familiar places, objects, and persons eroding?[40] What are the practical, psychological and social implications of living in a society of uncertainty, fear, doubt, cynicism, and paranoia? Per Rocky Bottoms's suggestion, today is the paranoid the one with the facts? Will the line between paranoia and reality cease to be meaningful? As agents and as subjects will we become ever more suspicious of everything and everyone (chap. 10, p. 237)?

While the paranoid, the suspicious, and the duplicitous may be more likely to live to play another day, the psychic cost and the cost to community can be great. Maria Los (2004), who fought for Polish freedom in the 1950s, notes how knowledge that informers are rampant leads to a suspicion of others but also has a personal cost, because the person knows that others are looking at her as a possible informer. In Burma, where George Orwell served as a young imperial policeman involved with intelligence gathering, informers were called *pasein yo*—"the handle of the axe." In this wonderful symbolism, the tool used to bring down the tree is made from the wood of the tree itself (Larkin 2004). Czeslaw Milosz's *The Captive Mind* and Arthur Koestler's *Darkness at Noon* followed *1984* in depicting the obliteration of community under conditions of distrust.

Machine error: If, as H. L. Mencken believed, people do the right thing because of an inner voice that warns them that someone (or something) may be watching, what happens to social order based on technology when the machine fails?[41] What does machine-mandated conformity imply about moral judgments?

National distinctions: Is there a move toward a uniform world surveillance society driven by a common ethos, problems, and technology developed in Western societies? Or is the commonality based on convergence and amalgamation drawing on the cultural and historical distinctiveness of different societies? Or, instead, will we see a world of uncommonality, where local differences in narratives and uses remain strong, even as common technologies are adopted? What happens to traditional national and local borders when intangible information can flow freely across them? What of new electronic borders and enclosures?

Privacy, private property and community: To what extent are notions of privacy and individualism inherently tied to ideas of private property? Does an emphasis on strong protections for personal information necessarily come at the expense of a more inclusive community and mean a more secretive, atomized society?

Social stratification: What are the implications for equality and inequality? Will information as a resource displace traditional patterns of inequality in class, status, power, and identity or be assimilated into them? Will the gap between rich and poor within and between nations continue to accelerate? What would society be like if knowledge were freely and equally available to all?

Remembering and forgetting: What would a society be like that never forgets? Is there a danger of creating new forms of scarlet letter and permanent stigmatization reminiscent of medieval branding? Will the contours and size of deviant and suspect populations markedly increase, even to a point of straining processing systems, as nets become wider and their meshes thinner? Should there be a right (or at least a normative tilt) not only to be let alone, but also to be forgotten?[42] And what about an expectation to at least being momentarily acknowledged, if not long remembered?

Some Metamethod Moral Mandates

I hope you do not assume yourselves infallibilitie of judgement when the most learned of the apostles confesseth that he knew but in parte and saw but darkly through a glass.
SIR RICHARD SALTONSTALL

Brother Saltonstall, whose words are inscribed on the Watertown, Massachusetts, statue I biked past for several decades, does proud the sociologist of knowledge and the psychologist of perception. All looking occurs of course in parts and with varying degrees of illumination. Whether peering through the looking glass, or looking at those who use it, modern social science is more likely to encounter haze than darkness. Still, one can sometimes see with clarity and consensus to the extent that she or he follows several imperatives for advancing knowledge which have guided this book. They are discussed next. The imperatives are for anyone concerned with understanding personal information practices (whether as scholars, practitioners, or informed and affected citizens).

Disaggregate and then aggregate! Break the world down into manageable analytic and empirically measurable bites. Disentangling the multiple and often crosscutting dimensions of surveillance contexts, structures, processes, occasions, and strips brings greater precision and makes measurement possible. Yet what is broken up analytically must also be put back together in ideal types and typologies.

Adopt a loose (but not too loose) systems approach: While we must identify variables, avoid the simplistic determinism and reductionism that come from overemphasis on a given causal factor. But do not cop out by concluding that therefore all causes are equal in their importance. Be attentive to feedback and to reciprocal influences, including those between soft and coercive forms of control. Study the subjects and the agents of surveillance in interaction, rather than as isolated elements. Appreciate their creativity and choices, but also the limits of the situations they find themselves in. Attend to how exogenous influences are affected by and affect those that are endogenous as well as how technical and social factors may influence each other.

Attend to beginnings (or at least prior circumstances): Everything was preceded by something, and new ways of meeting human needs must be compared with old (functionally alternative) ways.

Recognize that some things change and others stay the same: Start by locating the broad constants and constraints found in any surveillance context and within these the major areas where variation in form and process can be identified. Whether approaching the material as a researcher, practitioner, or concerned citizen, look at both structures (material, organizational, legal) as relatively enduring entities, at the fluid and even unpredictable dynamics of face-to-face interaction, and at related broader system changes over time.

Be aware of the difference between changes in degree and in kind: Appreciate that some new surveillance developments are in fact qualitative, revolutionary, deep lying, and fundamental, while others are quantitative, minor, and superficial. But all operate within certain enduring natural and social conditions.

Study surveillance practices as interaction processes over varying time periods: The dynamic, "no final victory" quality of many surveillance-conflict settings tells us that studying the topic requires attention to changes in the game and moves of the players. Make the effort to understand atrophy, entropy, neutralization, escalation, evolution, devolution, contraction, displacement, and border changes. Appreciate the independence and creativity of actors in the face of sweeping structural influences. Doing this requires a historical perspective (whether short or long term) and an awareness of the possibilities of cycles. Surveillance, like love, is a process, not an outcome or inert tool.

Duck when the boomerang comes around, and be sure you want to play the game: Doing this requires being prepared and alert to unintended consequences, systemic impacts, and long-run consequences, and also asking whether unwanted outcomes can be mitigated or are worth the cost. Remember that inaction is sometimes the better part of wisdom. Leaders need to know both when and when not to act.

Don't automatically associate correlation with causality: Samuel Johnson (1734) warned against mistaking "subsequence for consequence." It is necessary to critically reflect on surveillance results and what they appear to arise from. A correlation may be invalid because of weak measures or incompetent application of strong measures. Even when valid, inferences from a correlation or a match may be spurious, as Dr. Johnson suggested. The facts may mumble, but they do not speak clearly absent adequate controls for confounding factors, awareness of what was measured, and how results are interpreted. What the facts are claimed to mean, of course, is often related to the interests and social location of the observer.

Be cautious in moving from aggregates to individuals: Realize that probabilistic statements made with great accuracy at aggregate levels need not apply to inferences about any given case—one reason why profiling is contentious when it encounters ideas of justice and individualized treatment.

Be attentive to kinds of causation and levels of analysis: Causes exist at many levels. In popular understanding, the reasons people give for their behavior are often seen to be sufficient as explanations.[43] But what individuals say generally does not exist within a context or institution that the individuals have chosen, or are necessarily aware of. A focus on the broader, prior factors in a surveillance setting—its nature, history, culture, law, attributes of the technology, and types of data (whether as raw material or as transformed and presented)—calls attention to different levels and questions within which individual beliefs and motives are found and thus causation more broadly understood. Realize that the same causal factor(s) can have different outcomes and that equivalent outcomes can have different causes. How we account for and judge surveillance should depend on the role played and the characteristics of the tool, data, goals, and values present.

Neither a pessimist nor an optimist be, in the absence of good data! Don't let fears and hopes confound either the analysis of the empirical record or the importance of having a dream.[44] Keep distinct statements about the world as it now is from predictions or descriptions of what *might* happen. When making broad statements about dystopic or utopic trends regarding history, society, and liberty, be clear about the implied evidence, causal mechanisms, and values.

Where's the beef! Have an argument! Make some noise! Let the reader know where you stand, even if at times it is only to indicate why it is hard to take an unequivocal position for or against. Offer the reader logical and empirical criteria with which to evaluate arguments and results. Doing so necessitates clear definitions and, when appropriate, specification of independent and dependent variables.

Don't forget the "So what?" test: In the case of academic work make clear why the academic work should matter to broader audiences, beyond a self-referential group of scholars in increasingly fragmented settings, speaking languages only the natives can understand.

Talk to strangers: Listen and learn from those beyond your academic and political comfort zone. Integrate knowledge from the many strands of surveillance inquiry. The advancement of knowledge is not well served by specialized scholars speaking in code only to their tribe.

Carry a big tool kit: Laws, organizational polices, and technologies are crucial to protecting the borders of personal information. But so too are manners and education.

Differentiate facts from values: Do this while remaining mindful of their interweaving and the importance of values and passion in social inquiry. The assumptions of ethics and law need to encounter the findings of social science. Distinguish judgments based on ideal standards from those comparing known societies and actual behavior. This requires asking not only how one society or institution compares to others but also how close or far is it from the ideal.

Remember that no matter how sound the method or clear the findings, a leap to values, ethics, and political choices always remains in what we come to count as facts and the ends to which surveillance is put. But inform value positions by examining their empirical assumptions and the frequent presence of trade-offs bearing ironies. Be aware of how the abstract and conflicting nature of values often means that well-meaning persons will disagree. However, in spreading humility and appreciation of the complexities, do not become an academic eunuch, or a legitimator of the status quo—absent empirical, logical, and moral analysis.

Ask about the appropriateness of both means and ends: Desirable ends do not justify doubtful means, and good means can be misused. Good goals and purity of motives are not sufficient justification. Consider the acceptability of means and ends independently as well as in their relationship to each other. Recognize that a given tool can serve a variety of goals and that a given goal can be met by a variety of tools.

Be clear about what team you are on and the game you are playing: When making claims about the world, be clear about whether you are doing this as a scholar in pursuit of knowledge or as a citizen or organization member in pursuit of a policy goal. The former are subject to cross-observer evaluation by the canons of scholarship, while the latter are assessed by their political instrumentality. Still, one would hope that scholars are not immune to some of the passion of the latter, or that activists are immune to the truth standards of the former.

It is OK to study it just because it is there: As with the mountain climber's proverbial answer to the question "why?" Erving Goffman (1983) wrote that social life should be studied because it is there and is ours (meaning the social scientist's). But he also offered something for those who wished to be more than wry observers on playing fields that are often unfair, where what is taken as knowledge tends to follow the contours of power: "If one must have warrant addressed to social needs, let it be for unsponsored analyses of the social arrangements enjoyed by those with institutional authority—priests, psychiatrists, school teachers, police, generals, government leaders, parents, males, whites, nationals, media operators, and all the other well-placed persons who are in a position to give official imprint to versions of reality."[45]

Eyes and Windows

The intriguing English proverb "Eyes are the windows into the soul" reflects the biblical claim (Matthew 6:22–23) that probative looking into another's eyes reveals who the other person is. Yet this is imprecise. Whose eyes? What kind of window—open or closed and when and for whom and under what conditions? Whose soul? Is the eye evil? Does the eye bring insight and/or incite? Do the eyes belong to the subject looked at or to the agent looking? Or is the *same* eye both the tool of discovery and the data? That is the case with self-surveillance when the subject (also here the agent) looks in a mirror or a pond (or uses some other technology) to see what lies within him- or herself. *Different* eyes are involved when an agent looks at another individual (whether into the eyes or at other aspects and emanations). Is what is of interest what the eye itself reveals directly (color) or what is presumed to be hidden behind the eye (an ophthalmologist seeing blood vessels as an indication of health or a detective viewing eye movements for signs of deception or a physiological psychologist seeing signs of character).[46] Or is the eye merely symbolic of looking at the person whatever the means rather than literally involving an eye and an eye? Where does the ability of the subject to deceive fit (e.g., in the classic scene in the film *Minority Report* where Tom Cruise has the eye of Mr. Yakamoto implanted in order to foil the hi-tech system presumed to identify people by their eyes).

The stirring words of Queen Elizabeth I, who wanted "no windows into men's souls," speaks to the highest ideals of our civilization. The jagged (if overall positive) trajectory of liberty since her time has meant many more opaque windows for official eyes and looking away even when it was technically possible to look through. Hers is a mandate calling for protection *from* wrongful government actions and more broadly from those with the power to see through or break the windows. Much contemporary concern over surveillance appropriately draws attention to the destructive *power over side*, rather than to the *empower side* of the Renaissance's call for scientific knowledge and the Enlightenment's hope for a rational ordering of society according to what is technically possible.

The "thou shalt not" expectation is both secular and sacred, although even to mention the latter puts the scholar at risk of being thought of as not a real scientist. Protecting the information borders of the person is of course secular in furthering the individual's strategic interests (e.g., life style, consumption, work, self-presentations), but it is also sacred in acknowledging the dignity due to persons. That dignity was expressed in the ideals of the Magna Carta and the French and American Revolutions and is legitimated by the idea of God-given rights. Surveillance abuse goes far beyond material disadvantage and can be seen as an assault on the soul—the very essence of the self beyond the tangible. There is need for an intangible *courtoise* in the development and use of technology. This old French term goes beyond courtesy or politeness. As the Italian scholar Emilio Mordini (http://www.rtexpert.com/#!technologie-courtoise/clzgj) suggests, it involves tools that are respectful, proportional, and, when appropriate, even gentle and sympathetic in taking the measure of the person.

In a world where surveillance is both a threat and a response to threats, the condemnation of wrongfully crossing the borders that sustain civil society and the dignity of the person need to be seen alongside the commendation of rightfully crossing borders. For the latter the sacred imperative to regard the other—"thou shalt"—is positive and calls for an ethics of care with actions that are desired, not prohibited. Eric Stoddart (2012) and David Lyon (2014) call attention to this meaning of surveillance as protection, concern, and acknowledgment of the other's soul or personhood beyond any legal rights, conventional cost-benefit analysis, or technical potential. Underlying this concern is awareness of a transcendent loving and protecting eye in the sky (whether literal or mythical) and the belief that the dignity of the person is sustained when borders are associated with the sanctity of personhood. The ethics of eyes, windows, and souls thus resides in acts both of omission and of commission.

A Remarkable Piece of Apparatus?

> Had I been present at the Creation, I would have given some useful hints for a better ordering of the universe.
> KING ALFONSO THE LEARNED, thirteenth century

But he wasn't, and so we are left with a complex, complicated, interdependent, and dynamic world awash in unknowns, uncertainties, and empirical and moral contradictions. The book has emphasized the contingency. A given surveillance strip or occasion, the life history and consequences of a tool, or a full-fledged program all depend on context, comportment, and setting. Behavior is fluid and emerges out of the patterned and chance intersection and interaction of many factors. The lines between the possibility of a given tool, its actual design, and subsequent social uses and consequences are wavy at best. Outcomes have a degree of indeterminacy, and while the characteristics of the tool, problem/goal, and the intentions of those with authority matter, so too does the behavior of surveillance subjects—either in their personal response to a given surveillance activity or in their collective political action. This yields variation to be explained, the need to weigh expected consequences and to develop rules responsive to situational differences. Success or failure need to be viewed at various levels and ever mindful of the moving targets and uncertainties that contravene the best laid plans.

In what could be the motto of many social scientists' natural-born doubts about reform, the Italian social theorist Antonio Gramsci calls for "pessimism of the intellect, optimism of the soul." Keith Guzik (2016) and Christian Fuchs (2008) note how too rigid a focus on determinism can lead to hopelessness and failure to see that political will and an aware public can make a difference with respect to more humane and democratic uses of technology.

The ideal ought to be a *positive information society* based on fairness, dignity, care, openness, trust, security, autonomy/participation, and communality, rather than a *negative surveillance society* based on unfairness, commodification, coercion, secrecy, suspicion, insecurity, domination/repression, and atomization.

If it is correct that *surveillance is neither good nor bad but context and comportment make it so*, then a central task for analysts is to understand variation within and between contexts, while a central task for citizens is eternal vigilance. Cherished values are ever precarious, and freedom is indeed a constant struggle. Threats may come from within and beyond, from above and below, from government and the private sector, from organizations or individuals, and from *action* based on the hubris of the unexamined assumption as well as from *inaction* based on the ambivalence of the overly reflective. As a result, we must begin with doubts, as Sir Francis Bacon advised. This calls for a humble skepticism regarding claims about the unalloyed virtues or vices of a tool or a goal, but at the same time we must embrace a tentative willingness to doubt one's doubts, as Sir (and later Saint) Thomas More advised. We must attend to the empirical details of complex and dynamic systems on playing fields that are frequently unleveled, where knowledge is often imperfect or obfuscated, where values conflict, where trade-offs are rampant, and where consequences vary depending on the time period and level of analysis.

A thread running through all systems with an ethos of total control—whether totalitarianism in a state, a prison, or a demanding cult—is for the authority to deny individuals the right to control information about themselves while maintaining full control over information about the authority itself. It has been said that a civilization's nature can be seen in how it treats its prisoners. It might also be seen in how it treats personal information, communication, and group formation independent of the state. As de Tocqueville, informed by Aristotle, noted, a democratic society requires that individuals be free to come together in associations apart from the domination of the state or other all-powerful organizations.[47]

The growing field of surveillance studies (Ball, Haggerty, and Lyon 2012) serves as a reminder that while they—whether the state, commercial interests, new public-private hybrids, or free-range voyeurs—are watching us, we are watching them. The mist and ambiguity so often enveloping the topic call out for sustained inquiry, dialogue, and negotiation. And as baseball player Yogi Berra said, "You can see a lot by looking" and by asking. Making surveillance (and any technology) more visible and understandable hardly guarantees a just and accountable democratic society, but it is surely a necessary condition for one.

As Justice William O. Douglas observed, such a society is hardly self-executing, and liberty is fragile.[48] We are in something of a twilight zone now with respect to basic rights, what it means to be human, and how we think about society. As darkness does not come all at once, neither does the light. Ambivalence about technology is a hallmark of our age as we navigate between hope and dread. The fragile irony of needing protection both by authority and from it abides, particularly in periods of rapid change and heightened perception of threat.

The question is not only whether the discovery machines are growing ever more powerful, but also whether accountability and control mechanisms are keeping up with them and are honored (Norris et al 2016). Where inequality is legitimated and accountability mechanisms are in place, can citizens trust them? Restrictions on liberty will justifiably vary depending on events, context, agent competence and trust-worthiness, and time period. Secrecy in review (e.g., closed hearings and briefings, in camera proceedings) may be necessary at times.[49] The initial absence of adequate means of review was a major problem in the hurried initial passage of the Patriot Act in 2001. However, as Sissela Bok (1978) argues, secrecy (or any other social practice with a high cost of abuse) should not be the default position; rather, a case for such practices must be made, and they should be periodically reviewed.

If the agents of such practices are not required to make their case, we face the possibility of becoming an even more stratified society based on unequal access to information, with the result that individuals involuntarily live in glass houses while the external walls of large organizations are one-way mirrors. In short, there almost always seems to be a gap between the capabilities of the new surveillance technologies and cultural, legal, and technical responses.

The danger is not so much a catastrophic event resulting in a sudden fall into a cold and dark dungeon, but rather a Teflon slide into a climate-controlled, well-lit, but opaque society where meaningful individual and political choices are engineered away.[50] Perhaps such a society would be more orderly and efficient, but surely it would be less free and creative, with a decided tilt toward the community and organization over the individual.

Can we grant that in complex and dynamic settings, knowledge is imperfect and rules are often unclear or in conflict; that means and ends are imperfectly integrated; that obtaining one goal may mean sacrificing another; that societies are awash in moral dilemmas and trade-offs; that desirable as well as dastardly deeds can occur under cover of darkness; that sunlight can illuminate as well as blind; that those in positions of authority sometimes do the wrong thing in order to do the right thing; and that while Dr. Faustus may sometimes be granted a place at (or under) the table, he must be invited reluctantly and only with oversight?

FIGURE 14.2. Ye who enter here, don't abandon all hope, but be careful! (Arnie Levin/The New Yorker Collection/The Cartoon Bank.)

In teaching I often used the cartoon in figure 14.2. Students were asked to identify two meanings of the cartoon. The cartoonist certainly intended the first, in which the technology is simply an alternative to the traditional warning about a dog. I don't know if the second deeper meaning was intended, about the societal dangers the technology can portage, but it is a wonderful visual summary of a central concern of this book.

In a semiopaque world that muddles through with its conflicting pressures, it is premature, and perhaps even sacrilegious, to conclude with a Cyclopian eye to the future that information technology will destroy us. Yet the epigraph that began this book, from Kafka's 1919 cautionary short story "In the Penal Colony," remains instructive.[51] The story is about a new technology described as "a remarkable piece of apparatus"—a highly acclaimed, state-of-the art machine invented by a corrections officer for punishing inmates. The story ends when the machine malfunctions and kills its operator—an enthusiastic advocate of the benefits and infallibility of the machine.

Appendix

A Note on Values: Neither Technophobe nor Technophile

The world is filled with technophiles, often nesting in engineering, computer science, business, and government environments, who too often uncritically and optimistically welcome the new surveillance as a counterweight to the challenges and risks of the twenty-first century. As with Rocky Bottoms, they claim expertise in both identifying problems and delivering solutions. Society is at grave risk if it fails to appreciate the magnitude of changed conditions and new dangers and fails to make full use of the new technologies they claim. When the technophiles acknowledge problems with a new tool, they then call for improved or breakthrough technology to resolve it.

The world is also filled with technophobes, often isolated in social science and humanities environments, who too often talk only to each other. Sometimes they raise their concerns about technology explicitly, but more often their concerns appear as underlying themes or subtexts—for example, that we should be skeptical and suspicious about contemporary surveillance, and that the social analyst has a responsibility to sound the alarm. The extensive and intensive recording of "every move you make, every breath you take" is seen as a major element in the destruction of the human in an increasingly engineered, antiseptic, fail-safe, risk-adverse society. In the technophobes' worldview technology furthers inequality and domination and eliminates meaningful choices. Critics further argue that publicists for surveillance often deny the real motives and ignore unintended consequences.

As a citizen concerned with calling public attention to the unequal playing fields of social control technology, whether involving undercover police and informing, computer matching and profiling, drug testing, electronic location and work monitoring, or new communications, I have walked among the strident. Yet as a social scientist partial to the interpretive approach and the need for empirical grounding, and with an awareness of the richness, complexity, and fluidity of social reality and an interest in maintaining credibility by being an honest broker, I have often been uneasy about the tensions between activism and scholarship, at least in democratic societies. Strong political feelings and emotions can distort scholarship. As Montaigne says of his work, much of what this book offers "is by way of discourse" rather than "by way of advice." Yet the quest for absolute objectivity and nonjudgmental fiddling can make one a moral eunuch in the face of a deaf world on the brink.

For me, Berkeley and the 1960s inspired allegiance to both social responsibility and scholarship, but without much guidance as to how they might be reconciled. For five decades I have been concerned with this tension, occasionally displeasing activists on the right and the left, as well as positivists and humanists and quantoids and qualtoids, in an effort to give each their due without being wholly captive to anyone.[1] I have urged social responsibility among the scientists and respect for the canons of scholarship among the applicators and activists.

Scratch a social scientist and you will often find a closet moralist. For many social researchers coming of professional age in the 1960s and 1970s, the scientific aspect of social science was not enough. Inspired by writers such as C. Wright Mills (1959), we wanted to do research that mattered, not only in terms of its elegance, sophistication, innovation, clarity, and cumulative influence, but in terms of its contribution to ameliorating the social problems we saw. We were interested in understanding how what are experienced as "private" troubles could be implicated in broader public issues.

Yet in playing an independent (and often "critical") role, the scholar is nonetheless *engaged* in reflecting back a world that he or she believes the informed citizen needs to see. Here the scholar simultaneously seeks both engagement and objectivity. This, then, is a third way between the technophobes and the technophiles and the firefighters and the fiddlers. Quan-Hasse (2016) in summarizing central technology and society ideas offers a very readable example.

However, passionately desired ends are often best pursued through dispassionately applied means. We must exercise minds as well as passions—and maybe even exorcize the latter a bit. The empirical scholar has the best chance of making a contribution by listening to all claimants, subjecting their claims (especially the ones we like best) to logical and empirical analysis, disentangling questions of fact from questions of evaluation and interpretation, and, where appropriate, seeking the integration of diverse perspectives. The scholar needs to identify and help overcome gaps in knowledge, identify tacit empirical and moral assumptions, and suggest criteria by which competing claims can be assessed. The scholar must go beyond the fundamentalist who says, "It's true because I say it's true"; the relativist who says, "It all depends on your point of view"; and the single-factor reductionists of whatever flavor who explain everything by reference to one variable or who advocate public policies in which only one value is considered.

My topic selection is driven more by an interest in understanding actual and potential problems the techniques can raise than in providing solutions to the problems they are intended to solve. That is not because the problems are unimportant, but because given the social contexts in which these techniques are found, strong, established interests actively encourage their adoption.[2] By comparison, the forces concerned with misuse and unintended consequences pale in comparison, as do those concerned with the public interest as broadly defined.

If the book occasionally tilts toward the critical, that is because the cheerleading has a way of taking care of itself, while the bad news is too often unreported. Our liberal economic system offers ample room for the successful pursuit of self-interest and media attention on the part of the technology's purveyors. The positive aspects of surveillance such as protection, guidance, documentation, and entertainment speak loudly for themselves. The less visible negative aspects, such as domination, repression, intimidation, and wrongful exclusion speak more softly, if at all.

There is an important role for academic analysts to play in calling attention to unexamined societal beliefs and processes that often invisibly tilt toward favoring more powerful groups and traditional approaches. However, the point is not to uncritically represent the muted voices of the less powerful and to ignore other voices. Nor is it to resist change. Rather the task for scholars is to start with questions instead of answers, to surface tacit and manifest assumptions, and to expose them to the flames of the empirical world, logic, and morality. Ultimately their goal is to serve a broadly defined public interest—while remaining ever aware of the difficulties in defining that interest.

Critical kibitzers benefiting from domestic abundance and security also need to appreciate the challenging tasks of the sometimes-fallible persons who are actually in the ring.[3] Such practitioners usually must act with imperfect tools in a messy world, one in which second best can still be pretty good. Kipling, whatever his failings as an apologist for the sins of empire, put it well in his poem "Tommy" about the importance of not "makin' mock o' uniforms that guard you while you sleep." Those Tommies, however, were at least identified by their British uniforms.

This book is guided by critical *social science*. Such social science encourages attention to social stratification as well as to documenting and understanding the frequent gaps between our values and our practices. As the book argues, new technologies and the information they generate are in many ways not socially neutral and can sustain or enhance unfairness and undesirable forms of inequality. Unchecked they may strengthen existing (and perhaps create new) undesirable forms. In addition, the most influential ideas and means of communication in any time period and place tend to disproportionately reflect the imprint and interests of dominant groups.

For these reasons, the often tacit assumptions and legitimating claims surrounding a new technology must be carefully examined in light of the interests served, the normative and empirical claims made, and the questions not asked. The search for socially constructive uses not envisioned by the developers and initial adopters should be encouraged. For example, what technologies might be developed and/or applied to meet the needs of socially disadvantaged groups that lack lobbyists, publicists, and research and development departments?

This book, however, is also guided by a conservative spirit, which asks us to pause in the face of any proposed change and consider likely short- and long-range consequences. Tradition is sustained not only by power and sometimes by ignorance, but to a degree by common sense, based on historical experience. The parts of a society are significantly interdependent, and unreflectively and too rapidly tampering with one part may have unexpected and undesirable consequences. We need not agree with eighteenth-century Irish politician and theorist Edmund Burke—who reportedly said, "Don't talk to me of reform, things are bad enough already"—to know that the status quo is rarely perfect, but at least it is known. Given the politically charged nature of the topic, many accounts either welcome the technologies as solutions or fear them as problems. Of course they can be both or neither, depending on the observer and the situation. Here I emphasize their potentials. This book is neither pro- nor antitechnology (at least to the best of my knowledge)[4]—although it is pro to being thoughtful and broadly analytic about technology so that we go with it or against it with our eyes open and relatively well informed.

As an academic analyst I come as neither a torchbearer for the Luddites nor as a beacon for the entrepreneurs. We are as ill served by indiscriminately bashing technology as we are by unqualifiedly advocating techno-fixes. The orderly utopia promised by the peddlers of new technologies is hardly imminent, although neither is the doomsday foreseen by critics. The sky is not now falling, even if that offers only modest grounds for rejoicing. There are, after all, holes in the ozone layer.

Notes

Preface

1. Perhaps surprisingly, that holds even for age. Work by Hoofnagle et al. (2010) finds that large proportions of young adults do care about privacy. Boyd's 2014 ethnographic work reports on youth and the internet and Young and Quan-Haase (2013) on privacy protections youth use on Facebook.

2. Our subjects, particularly in far-removed settings, rather naturally also suspect social scientists asking questions—but so too do police and intelligence agencies when they are the subjects. Social researchers are also the subjects of surveillance, whether in their self-studies or in those by authorities (Keen 1999; Price 2004).

Introduction

1. Attributed to her by her adviser Sir Francis Bacon (2011). Bacon was an advocate of science and the unfettered pursuit of truth but was also very secretive and appreciative of the links between knowledge and power. He is a forerunner of both modern science and modern surveillance.

2. In complex social matters there are of course no free meals, and irony almost always has a seat at the table. Her actions also were accompanied by more sophisticated and expansive state surveillance, which kept her in office and gave her the power to carry out her reforms. Bacon, her key adviser, was an advocate of freedom of thought and of the advancement of knowledge but also was a player in darker fields. Sir Francis Walsingham, the queen's ambassador to France and later her private secretary, played a central role in the development of modern, more systematized, external and internal spying. Budiansky (2005) offers a popular account.

3. Walton (2001); Subcommittee on Africa (2006); Klein (2008). In a more democratic context using fingerprints and iris scans, India is developing a national registry of persons (Polgreen 2011). Each of India's 1.2 billion people will be given a unique twelve-digit number. Using inexpensive handheld devices tied to the mobile telephone network, the system would serve to verify the identity of any Indian anywhere in the country within eight seconds. Unlike the Chinese program, it contains only minimal identity information.

4. Marx (1988a, 221).

5. Given a meaning of society as involving shared standards and a freely chosen sense of

responsibility to others, the term "surveillance society"—implying engineered and mechanistic external control, is a contradiction in terms, although for dramatic effect I ignored this when I first used the term (Marx 1985).

6. An important initial effort to remedy this is Ball, Haggerty, and Lyon (2012).

7. In looking at structures, tools, goals, culture and process and interaction I draw from Talcott Parsons's (1970) AGIL framework and Kenneth Burke (1959) filtered through Goffman in considering act, scene, agent, agency, and purpose.

8. Another possible title, *Just Looking*, was taken (Updike 1989). *Observing Surveillants and the Surveilled* would have worked as well.

9. Two chapters that deal with popular music, advertisements, cartoons, art, graffiti, and T-shirts were cut and are available online at press.uchicago.edu/sites/marx/.

Introduction to Part 1

1. Depending on one's will, goal, and resources, inclusive general concepts can be broken into ever finer distinctions. There is a sense in which a classifier's work is never done, given the variety of the empirical, change, and new discoveries. Cessation must be heuristic after parsimoniously categorizing the similarities and differences of interest to a given researcher. The scholar hoping to capture it all through continual differentiation is engaged in a Sisyphean task. This can involve endless gradation, not unlike the proverbial couple on the sofa who, moving one-half the distance between them each time will never touch.

2. Intellectual poachers shouldn't be unduly bound by the disciplinary borders specialists erect around their fields. The inquiring mind concerned with a broad topic can never come close to being up on it all. Trying too hard to master too many fields in the hope of avoiding criticism by the real experts can mean never letting go (of either your product or your imagination). Better to trust your instincts and go with your riffs, straining the richness of so many fields of inquiry through the particularities and idiosyncrasies of your scene in the hope of some integration or at least having a good time. Academic colonizers need to rely on the kindness of colleagues in other fields willing to share their knowledge.

3. Goffman (1981) writes, "I believe that the provision of a single conceptual distinction, if it orders, and illuminates, and reflects delight in the contours of our data, can warrant our claim to be students of society. And surely, if we can't uncover processes, mechanisms, structures and variables that cause others to see what they hadn't seen or connect what they hadn't put together, then we have failed critically. So what we need, I feel, is a modest but persistent analyticity: frameworks of the lower range." Further, "better perhaps, different coats to clothe the children well than a single splendid tent in which they all shiver." However difficult, the search for the warm tent ought not to be abandoned, but simply given a lower priority.

Chapter One

1. Illustrative of the surveillance essay is work such as that by Stanley Cohen (1985), Giddens (1990), Poster (1990), Gandy (1993), Lyon (1994), Bogard (1996), Brin (1998), and Staples (2000). In general, it draws on newsworthy accounts and secondary empirical data and, in offering broad theoretical accounts, tends to sweep across contexts, countries, and technologies. Journalists take even more license (Mike Davis 1990; S. Garfinkel 2000; Parenti 2003).

2. Horowitz (2009) notes how dogs' reliance on their strong sense of smell gives them a very different experience of the world than does our strong reliance on the visual. Dogs can "smell

time" and therefore have an immediate window into the past and the future. Because odors become less strong with time, a weaker odor indicates time past, and the future may be smelled in what the breeze brings (with the preservation of the past and prediction of the future offered by the computer we may however be closing the gap a bit). Dogs are less able to identify the location of a sound than are humans, needing only to know its general direction; at that point their more acute sense of smell and sight take over.

3. Taste is the most underutilized of the senses for surveillance. However, consider the tasters who sampled the food and drink of kings and queens for poison, wine connoisseurs, and baking contest judges.

4. The interplay of the senses and culture, even how many there are, goes beyond biology (e.g., Howes 1991; Classen 1993; Ackerman 1990; Jay 1993). Imagination and visualization in simulation, cyberspace interactions, and the changing meaning of place and time seem likely to lead to new conceptions of the senses and knowing.

5. Why is there no English verb *to surveill*? The closest English equivalent is *to survey*. This less-than-clarion term has two meanings: (1) to take a general or comprehensive view or appraisal and (2) to view in detail, especially to inspect, examine. The supervision and vigilance aspect is much less apparent than with the other languages.

6. *U.S. News and World Report*, October 15, 1973, 59.

7. The noun *surveillance* and the verb *to surveil* are the same figures of speech as *privacy* and *to privatize*. The latter, however, have their opposites in *publicity* and *to publicize*. But where are the equivalent opposites for *surveillance* as a noun and a verb?

In English there is no easy term for the action which is the opposite of surveillance (although there are antonyms). The verb form *to surveil* suggests actively surveying by an agent, just as the verb form *to privatize* suggests actively protecting (although the more common usage involves property rights, as with privatization). While *publicize* is the opposite of *privatize*, the best-worst term we have for a potential surveillance agent who doesn't act is that he or she demonstrates anti- or nonsurveillance or perhaps unobservance. The agent chooses not to act or to know (as with the proverbial three monkeys).

8. However sometimes the inattention is feigned, as with the so-called *brush pass*, in which two people who appear to be simply brushing past each other are handing off spy material in the best tradecraft tradition.

9. Contrast this with various other patterns, such as those of nonconfidentiality, where both can or must reveal, or where the surveillance subject also is expected not to reveal. The presence or absence of reciprocity and prohibitions or prescriptions on discovering and reporting are important variables in structuring and judging surveillance settings.

10. This suggests another typology of not only who the rules apply to, but of whether the interests of the parties to the secret are shared or conflicting. Consider the secrecy sustaining elements of those having affairs, involved in conspiracies, and the reluctant symbiosis of players in the game of blackmail,—as against situations where the parties have nonoverlapping interests in revelation and concealment.

11. For this view we can blame Georg Simmel: "The secret is . . . the sociological expression of moral madness" ([1908] 1950, p. 331). While Simmel is the classical theorist I would most like to meet if had I to write about that for an SAT essay test, he missed it here. Marx and Muschert (2008) and Coll (2012) argue for Simmel's continuing relevance a century later, particularly with respect to secrecy and information control, new forms of sociation and information as a new medium of exchange.

12. For the word *private* the opposite is *public* but what is it for *secret* (*nonsecret*) and what does the lack of an equivalent term imply?

13. The physical border perspective has limits too, thus taking or giving a urine or breath sample or a photo involves using things that have already left the body and are different and beyond the literal physical protective border of it. Garbage placed on the street in a protective container is physically (although not impossibly) bordered as well, and in some jurisdictions is also legally bordered.

14. Defining cases such as Griswold v. Connecticut, 381 U.S. 479 (1965), and Roe v. Wade, 410 U.S. 11 (1973), involve decisional privacy with respect to personal and intimate matters such as family planning, birth control, same-sex marriages, or physician-assisted suicide. Proprietary privacy—use of a person's information without consent for commercial and other purposes— also involves control and liberty questions and the extension of market principles to symbolic material that is often immaterial (at least physically).

15. In Marx (1997, 2001, and 2005b) some blurred forms considered are space, distance, darkness, time, and social and cultural orders.

16. The largest category is probably residual, in which there are no rules (although there may be softer expectations). What is the ratio of rules that prohibit revelation, as with public nudity or nursing, to those that mandate revelation, as with the obligation of sellers of a car or home to come clean, and what are the ratios for prohibiting or requiring asking for information?

17. These distinctions can get hazy and be sequentially linked. Consider implants which enter the person but can then send data back from the person under external or internal triggering as with an RFID chip or bombarding a person with stimuli and then "reading" the response, as with one of the MRI brain techniques.

18. Vance Packard was prescient here in writing about both taking information from and imposing it upon the individual, although the dates (1964 and 1957) of his publications reverse this logical sequence. As chapter 3 argues, goals do not seem to have changed, even as the tools have (e.g., Duhigg 2012; Turow 2014; Calo 2014).

19. *Subjects* and *agents* here refer to the roles played and are intended to be nonevaluative terms. This contrasts with some contemporary treatments in which the targets (or recipients) of surveillance are viewed as either objects/victims with an implication of denying their humanity or as subjects subjected to unwanted treatment. Our use is more visceral and inclusive than the Foucauldian use, in which the subject is an abstract object of knowledge created by the specialist. It also differs from the use of *subject* in psychological experiments. Further distinctions are noted in chapter 2 when we consider whether the agent and subject are human or nonhuman. Subjects (objects?) may be things associated with humans such as sentient environments, artifacts, or biological remnants.

20. The experiences of the CIA in Iran and the East German Stasi illustrate the shift of agent and subject roles that followed the changes in those countries in 1979 and 1991. The hunters became the hunted, and subjects became agents.

21. In a Nevada brothel's practice of using a live intercom to monitor interaction between prostitutes and customers we see both protection and control. As an employee of the organization doing the surveillance, the sex worker is in the role of agent and a beneficiary of the goal of security. Yet she is also the subject of surveillance, since it serves as a check on her honesty in reporting the agreed-upon price (Meade 2001).

22. Getting on the list appears easier than getting off. The New Jersey State Control Commission rejected a request from a man who sought to have his name removed (*New York Times*,

January 18, 2007). In Alberta, Canada, in 2010, gamblers could be fined up to $250 for violating their self-exclusion agreements.

23. The Gospels are spot on here in advising that we keep enough oil in our lamps, because we don't know when God's judgment will arrive: "Therefore keep watch, because you do not know the day or the hour" (Matthew 25:1–13).

24. Mail Goggles, a nonreciprocal, private-audience self-surveillance and control experimental feature of Google's Gmail program, seeks to help with drunken e-mailing. The user needs to perform some simple math problems within sixty seconds before an e-mail can be sent between 10 p.m. and 4 a.m. on weekends.

25. The mutuality may lie in parallel actions, as with demonstrators and police filming each other, or with a trusted third party, as with independent agencies charged with monitoring treaties.

26. In work reported in Mann, Nolan, and Wellman (2003), for example, the one-sidedness quickly becomes apparent when, with no appreciation for the humor or irony in the situation, Steve Mann is told to leave a store he is videotaping in.

Chapter Two

1. One reading of recent Western literary history suggests the centrality of paranoia to the emergence of modernism (J. Farrell 2006).

2. For a sampling of work in which such ideas are developed see Shils (1956), Silver (1967), Fogelson (1977), Foucault (1977), Nisbet (1980), and S. Cohen (1985).

3. Among useful explorations of this dossier, actuarial, risk-adverse, predictive society are Laudon (1986b), Beck (1992), Feeley and Simon (1992), Gandy (1993), Lyon (2001), Haggerty and Ericson (2006), Harcourt (2007).

4. On Civil War balloons see Hayden (2000).

5. Nor is a commonly used form of classification based on the type of technology, such as electronic location or communication monitoring, very helpful (e.g., US Congress Office of Technology Assessment 1985), nor for most social analysis is a system based on what is technically monitored (e.g., Petersen 2001). For our purposes a list based on function is more useful, as seen in Nogala (1995) and Nelson (2010).

6. With the presence of a human interpreting and acting on results another level is added. That richness is also seen in microphones that collect and relay the barks of guard dogs (filtered by computer programs believed to identify stress or aggression in the animal) to a human agent. This is reminiscent of the carrier pigeons used in World War I whose harnesses carried miniaturized roll-film cameras with pneumatic timing mechanisms and took pictures over enemy territory.

7. The absence of a corresponding sense for detecting cell phone, power line, and nuclear radiation is probably a factor in the lack of public understanding and fear associated with these. This contrasts with proprioception and nociception information.

Chapter Three

1. Or it may merely embarrass or shame. Note Target's data mining that identified pregnant women based on unrelated purchases and then sent targeted ads for the expectant. Hill (2012) reports on the surprise this caused in one family.

2. This list is hardly exhaustive and simply reflects one way to pose the question. Additional

goals that may cut across these or fit within them include kinds of control or influence, categorization, determination of accountability, and inclusion or exclusion involving access to the person and the person's access (whether to resources, identities, or physical and social egress and exit).

The surveillance of (or, better, through) social media might be another goal, but this tends to cut through other goals such as discovery, strategic advantage, curiosity, and self-knowledge and sociability. The net and social media are tools or locations for other activities rather than goals as such. As tools they lend themselves well to the agent anonymously surveilling others (Trottier 2012; Brown 2014; Marx 2013; Fuchs and Trottier 2015; Lane 2016; Schneider 2016).

3. I marvel at the security assumptions about the consistency in behavior that led to my being interviewed more than three decades later about a student being considered for an important government position.

4. This can be further complicated by separating persons who really believe what they are saying from those who know they are lying, and, in the case of the former, identifying whether their belief is correct. For the inquiring agency the central point is accuracy.

5. In the case of prevention, there is the more elusive question of what might happen, as presumably revealed by big data analysis, even if what might happen is not yet planned and the incipient planner is unaware of causal mechanisms fatefully pushing toward some action.

6. However, in the case of video cams worn by police in some jurisdictions policy may require the permission of those recorded.

7. Sometimes the answer is surprising. A cartoon that appeared after Edward Snowden revealed the extent of NSA eavesdropping shows a little boy talking to President Obama: " My Dad says you're spying on us." The president responds, "He is not your dad."

8. This may indirectly even be seen to serve security needs, particularly internally.

9. Note the empirically erroneous response of Secretary of State Henry Stimpson, who closed down a US cryptography unit in 1929, claiming, "Gentlemen do not read each other's mail." During World War II his viewed changed (Kahn 2004). After the revelations that the United States' NSA listened to her cell phone, German chancellor Angela Merkel also said, "Spying between friends, that's just not done." Yet given the halls of mirrors and smoke and competing agencies and rogue nooks or agents, one must ask to what extent higher authorities are really in charge and whether they know what lower-level operators are doing. That is particularly the case when those with legal training are responsible for judgments involving technology they may not understand. Note Chancellor Merkel's embarrassment several months later when it was revealed that her own intelligence service was complicit in spying on the European Commission and the French president.

10. In a related context I have suggested that the efforts to achieve the goal of control can be broken into removal, devaluation, or insulation of the target, incapacitation or exclusion of the offender, and identification of the offence, offender, or target (Marx 2015c).

11. This contrasts with the threat of publicity as the means of influence for blackmailers and as a negotiating resource. Nor is publicity necessarily desired in national security cases, particularly where tactics of challenged legality are present or operational details would be revealed.

12. For example, the Acorn antipoverty organization workers captured on tape giving tax advice to a "pimp" and a "prostitute" in a video later revealed as a contrivance of a conservative group (Montopoli 2009).

13. There may be unintended symbolism as well. Thus, for some persons, wearing a monitoring anklet can be a status symbol of being a badass.

14. Yet in cases where self-knowledge is wound up with knowledge of others, the ethical and policy issues are hazier. Information controversies around family adoption and some medical situations work against unduly sweeping generalizations.

15. This is the distinction between knowing that there is a secret and knowing in addition what it is. There is a kind of glee and insider quality to knowing which is strongest when others know you know and they don't know. When the very existence of the secret itself is unknown the satisfaction is probably less pronounced.

Chapter Four

1. The following exchange between Howard Hughes and actress Ava Gardner (presumably based on real events) nicely illustrates the different evaluation of reading versus the fuller data available from listening. Hughes bugged Gardner's telephone conversations. In the film *Aviator*, when she discovers this, she angrily says to him, "You listened to my phone calls?" He responds, "No! No! No! Honey I'd never do that.... I just read the transcripts, that's all."

2. In some cases the failure of an agent to offer, ask, or collect can be problematic. Note Emily Post's advice: "Women frequently ask whether they should call an unzipped fly to the wearer's attention, unless you are a total stranger do" (1992, 242).

3. I contrast types of information, not evaluators beyond the subjectivity of the person. An approach useful for other purposes focuses on what individuals mean by *privacy* and *publicity* and the actions taken with respect to these, a topic Chris Nippert-Eng (2010) unpacks in her rich ethnographic study.

4. Does the fact that something is public lessen the extent to which it is personal? This depends on the dimension of the personal. There is a correlation between the personal and the private, or a tilt of the person toward the private, except when it is for notoriety, attention, celebrity, or to make a political point. Among those legally deemed to be public figures, there is less formal protection for backstage and backmask information. When they are wealthy they can protect their information more easily—whether hiring body doubles, using personal assistants and image spinners, or avoiding public transportation.

5. One meaning of *impersonal* is "anonymous," as it involves "safety in numbers" through accessible categorical information not pegged to an individual whose identity or residence is known. This information flooding is seen in the expression "the faceless crowd" (although video and facial recognition systems may make that anachronistic).

6. A related issue is what can be done to works of art or film by owners who are not its creators or subjects.

7. It is curious that one has to pay for an unlisted number, while businesses pay to have their phone numbers listed. With respect to listed numbers, one can argue that the phone company should pay individual consumers for being able to market their numbers in directories or deliver them as part of a caller ID service. While we now talk of *privacy by design*, the appearance of caller ID in its original form in the 1980s is one of the first examples *eliminating privacy by design*.

8. In a literal sense, this is a structure or form issue rather than a content issue. There is ambiguity in talking about "kinds of information," since this may include content, form, or both. Sartre (1993) captures the security aspect of realizing one is not alone: "What I apprehend immediately when I hear the branches cracking behind me is not that there is someone there; it is that I am vulnerable; that I have a body which can be hurt; that I occupy a place and I cannot

in any case escape from this space in which I am without defense, in short, I am seen." This fear requires awareness, as does the challenging of the danger, elements that are lacking when the surveillance is transparent or unseen.

9. The privacy tort remedy of intrusion attempts to deal with the subjective and emotional aspects of harm from incursions into solitude when personal borders and space are wrongly crossed (Alderman and Kennedy 1995).

10. Pamuk 2007.

11. Erving Goffman, in stressing the situationally specific nature of identity, would probably reject the idea of a core identity. However, my discussion begins with the objective facts of birth, not the individual's perception or social offerings regarding this.

12. A Chinese law, for example, requires that all Internet cafés videorecord users.

13. An account for Internet access or a cell phone will probably require a geographic address. The cell phone involves various temporal, geographic, and social information—registration and billing information, call origination point and time, and locations during a mobile call.

The ability to access an Internet account from anywhere involves a similar potential disjuncture of registration and use. A central variable for accountability purposes (always resting in an uneasy relationship with anonymity) is the kind of certified personal information needed to use a communications device. Biometrics offer some advantages for agents but may come with other costs and are not as fail-safe as some advocates claim.

14. Nor will either the caller or the called necessarily know whom in fact they are sending to or receiving a message from. A phone number or an address need not be unique. There may be multiple users of the same address or phone number. A major inference error here is to assume that the person in whose name a means of communication (phone, computer, typewriter) or a vehicle is registered is in fact the one using it as captured by surveillance. Absent other verification (biometric, photographic, or an encryption signature), that may not be the case. As well, erroneous inferences may be drawn when addresses and devices are deceptively and fraudulently used.

A related inference problem involves multiple latent fingerprints on the same surface. There is however a technique for disentangling the prints of those who have touched explosives or drugs from those that have not (Ifa et al. 2008).

15. Developments linking postal addresses, census block data, and GPS coordinates mean that the actual location of every address and land and cell phone can now in principle be known to within a limited number of meters.

16. Whether this ability to know where is accompanied by the presumption that it is also acceptable to have interactive access to the person is an evolving issue of manners, law, and policy faced by any new means. Beyond the contemporary case of spam, consider early twentieth-century debates about whether it was appropriate to be telephoned by those one had not been formally introduced to (Marvin 1990; Fischer 1992).

17. An issue of *Surveillance and Society* edited by Bennett and Regan (2003) offers an informative set of articles on mobilities.

18. The identity authentication issue is also present with traditional letter writing (and it is often related to content validity). While signature, writing style, and stationery offer clues to identity, the absence of face-to-face interaction in real time may abet dissimulation as well as honesty. The greater ease of validating the identity of a phone caller (at least one whose voice has previously been heard) than a letter writer offers another example of how the material properties of a means can condition behavior.

19. In Marx (2015b) I reflect further on the intersections of cultural and physical ("natural" before human intervention) borders as these relate to the flow of information. I discuss seven components of information accessibility: awareness, collection, understanding, a record, sharing, private property, and usage. I suggest hypotheses that predict normative responses to revealing and concealing personal information and expand on issues raised in Marx 2015a and 2011b that could not be included here.

Mireille Hildebrandt (2015) offers a related approach to the question of what information is as this connects to its materiality. She notes that it is a relational and relative concept that depends on technological expression and cultural framing and that involves primary, secondary, or tertiary retention. Three distinct properties of information are identified: accessibility, propertizability, and appropriateness.

20. Lipreading is a fascinating tool: the reader has data access whenever someone can be *seen* talking, while having the advantage of a hidden tool leaving no remnants (not unlike gambling card counters). Evidence from a lip-reader cannot be used for prosecution without a warrant. But it can certainly embarrass as with the 1968 Democratic convention, when Mayor Richard Daley was caught only by a videotape speaking uncivilly to Senator Abraham Ribicoff, who was criticizing police violence directed at demonstrators outside the convention hall.

21. Nonsurveillance forms of conversion include technologies that convert material from web sites and e-mail to Braille and audio, as well as various means of converting speech to written form and visual images to signals that the blind can interpret and in a sense see. These forms share with the surveillance forms the sociology of knowledge and philosophical questions of truth, knowledge, meaning, and understanding.

22. Claims about the past are at least subject to an empirical standard, however musty the memories and degraded the material artifacts. Past failings may also be more excusable than those predicted for the future (e.g., "She has learned her lesson"; "He has grown up"; "That mistake was paid for"). In contrast, future claims are always speculative.

23. Here it is not only that the content offered by the subject is erroneous, but also that the person is revealed to be dishonest.

24. The logic here is that the unwarranted taking of information in actually reflecting the person would be seen as worse than an abstract category applied by others for which the individual can say à la Pamuk and his passport, "That's not me."

However, one could as well argue the opposite. The latter in being artificial and in less realistically, or at least less self-evidently, claiming to represent the person, is worse than the seeming more real natural information. A relevant factor, of course, is whether the characterization supports or undermines the individual's interests or persona.

This is an aspect of backstage behavior. The individual's sense of a unique self is partly found in the less-than-perfect fit between cultural expectations and the situation (regarding both attitudes and behavior). Goffman's (1961b) concept of role distance and the idea of distinctive identity lying partly in the cracks of the roles played fit here.

The quote from Pamuk on p. 100 contrasts with the epigraph from Traven that opens this chapter. For Traven, the issue is not one of fit, but that who he is is his own business, not that of petty officialdom.

25. Of course, appropriate skepticism is needed precisely because this tilt toward such data creates rich opportunities for deception. The Chinese expression "A picture is worth a thousand words" must be tempered with attentiveness to whether and when "seeing is believing" or "believing is seeing" or when they should be disconnected. The same holds for seeking evidence

for the assumption that a machine that converts disembodied raw data to quantified meaning is necessarily more objective and reliable than the interpretive work of humans—granted that they may discriminate and cover their mistakes and rule violations.

26. Beyond lack of accountability, there also can be a lessened likelihood of bystander intervention as anonymity increases (Latane and Darley 1968).

Chapter Five

1. Myra Marx Ferree (2004) examines the reciprocal of men softly controlling women, in a context of social movements through ridicule, stigma, and silencing.

2. Discussed at greater length in Marx (1992) and Leo (1992, 2009).

3. In 1958 Huxley (2004) revisited his novel in light of developments since its publication in 1932.

4. As Ayse Ceyhan (2012) suggests, surveillance through biopower, where the emphasis is on the human body and its movements, brings new ways of managing individuals. This approach is embedded in domestic life, rather than through territorialized biopower of the sovereign and the market of the nineteenth century,

5. The *categorical suspicion* tactic of rounding up all the usual suspects (and then some) is still rare in the United States for historical, legal, and logistical reasons but clearly increasing in new forms.

In considering whether the tactic "works" varied outcomes need to be considered. A review of 20 instances found that the overwhelming majority of DNA dragnets did not lead to success. In seven of the cases traditional investigation methods did (Electronic Privacy Information Center 2005; see also Walker 2006; Chapin 2004; and Grand 2001).

6. The engineering of softness and the minimization of the onerous are of course central themes in unrelated aspects of modern life now laced with surveillance potentials. The modern toilet, for example, can offer controlled access and medical sensors that automatically send results to appropriate authorities—not to mention heated seats, music, automatic flushing, and air deodorizing. The talking toilet can greet the customer and also respond to voice commands (*Wikipedia* 2011). Braverman (2010) offers a clean and incisive treatment of automated public toilets and notes their control and exclusionary roles. Among the innovations are doors that open after fifteen minutes and (if a body is sensed to still be there) relay a message to control agents and the use of blue lighting so that unwelcome drug users cannot see their veins.

7. Here science may come to the defense of folk prejudices which hold that the "other" smells differently. Will the passive reading and tracking of involuntarily transmitted personal data become as widespread as the use of air-sniffing radiation detection devices aimed at places?

8. But should the remote reading of brain waves become possible and workable, science fiction would once again become science and another technological weakness that protected liberty would disappear. Ray Bradbury's heroes in *Fahrenheit 451* who resisted a book-burning, totalitarian regime by memorizing destroyed books would need to find alternative means. Larkin (2004) reports how a contact in Burma asked her to memorize, not write down, the address of a person she sought to interview. Memorization serves a way to *avoid* and *block* surveillance per the *categories in chapter 6.

9. However, with the advent of bomb-injected undergarments, that may be only a temporary inhibition. This threat has given rise to jokes and cartoons about flying naked as the next control technique.

10. Prior to the 1968 Olympics female competitors were required to walk nude in front of a panel of doctors to verify their sex (Vilain 2012).

11. Harper (2008) reviews one role played by some contemporary psychologists with respect to security interrogations. Conflicting views on the appropriate role of anthropologists can be found in Price (2008) and Lucas (2010) and the debates regarding social scientists embedded within military units (http://fabiusmaximus.wordpress.com/anthropology-war/) and, for an earlier period, Project Camelot (I. L. Horowitz 1967). Some related issues appear with respect to social science and marketing research.

12. Here we borrow from the tools of forensic analysis of e-mails used so creatively to establish lying in the Enron case. Given the potential for subject untruthfulness and the biasing effects of direct interviewer questions, passive means are almost always preferable.

13. We want to emphasize that all of our techniques are research based and validated. For example since the famous study by A. L. Chaiken et al. in 1976 we have known that self-disclosure is more likely in warm, comfortable rooms with soft lighting. We have learned a great deal more since then.

14. Consider, for example, life insurance customers using "Fitbit" wearable computer monitors that automatically upload health data (glucose, gym visits, etc.) to the company in return for a better rate or driving data reported to car insurers for a discount (Siegel 2015).

15. The increased commercial offerings of "detective" services for checking up on the fidelity of romantic partners that play on, or seek to induce, suspicions are noteworthy here. Beyond the trust issues there are "reality" issues. Is it the case, as one service provider said of the attractive wired females he rents out for testing unsuspecting males, "I just set the table. They decide to eat"?

16. The well-known example here is the QWERTY typewriter keyboard.

17. Controls over wiretapping contrast with those over computers. It took almost seventy-five years between the widespread use of the telegraph and telephone and the appearance of the Katz decision and 1968 congressional legislation for wiretapping to be outlawed. In the case of computers this took less than two decades with the appearance of the Electronic Communications Privacy Act of 1986 (ECPA Pub. L. 99-508, Oct. 21, 1986, 100 Stat. 1848, 18 U.S.C. § 2510–2522). This broadened government limitations on tapping phones to include transmissions of electronic data by computers and data stored in computers. This was an amendment to Title III (the Wiretap Statute) of the Omnibus Crime Control and Safe Streets Act of 1968. Communication-technology-law-lag issues are relatively understudied given their significance and pervasiveness.

18. In solidarity and in an appeal to federal employees, President and Nancy Reagan, Vice President Bush, and seventy-eight high-level officials volunteered to undergo drug testing. An official was "sure it would be noted" if someone refused to provide a sample. For those taking the test, results would be kept confidential "out of respect for their privacy." If drug use was suspected, officials would be given counseling (de Lama 1986).

19. Note the curious case of aspiring politicians who feel compelled to offer the results of their drug tests and affidavits attesting to their marital fidelity after their opponents have publicly done this.

20. There are gradations here, and a variety of responses can be observed, from outright bans, to mandatory uses and conditions for use, to the absence of legislation or court cases, to standards for evidence in courts.

In the case of audio or video collecting tools there is most often a restriction on certain uses rather than an outright ban. In the case of parabolic mikes, for example, the ban is on listening to other's conversations, rather than on outright possession, although there is a ban on some receivers that pick up police and military communications.

21. Such databases serve as both methods of inclusion-exclusion and as a compliance mechanism. According to the agency, "We tell them that we would not want to see them ruin their excellent credit standing and damage their future creditworthiness. . . . A tenant knows that his or her own actions will determine what information will go on his or her permanent record" (http://www.thelpa.com/), accessed June 12, 2012.

22. Or at least the need to be able to read the data if they contain identity information. Consider the case of a thoroughly modern friend who had an identity chip embedded in her cat. The pet was lost and to my friend's consternation the local animal shelter did not have the technology for reading the chip.

23. For example, electronic monitoring for those judicially required to remain at home, which began only with locational data, quickly moved to remote audio and video transmissions and telemetric alcohol and drug testing. The latter then moved from remote breathalyzers in response to a telephone call from an agent to devices such as SCRAM (secure continuous remote alcohol monitor). This "offender or patient bracelet" remotely reports every hour on molecules of ethanol coming off the ankle, because "five percent of everything you drink comes out your body."

24. As noted in chapter 4, there is a reaction against this reflected in the increased use of unique identifiers specific to a given use that cannot be easily linked across uses. Note also the minimization seen in the request for zip code rather than telephone number in some retail sales settings. For market research purposes that can be sufficient, given what can be inferred from the area of residence.

25. Many of the provisions were extended until 2019. NSA will no longer be able to directly obtain mass metadata. The Patriot Act was replaced by the USA Freedom Act (Uniting and Strengthening America by Fulfilling Rights and Ensuring Effective Discipline over Monitoring Act of 2015). While not "comprehensive reform," an ACLU official said, "the passage of the USA Freedom Act is a milestone. This is the most important surveillance reform bill since 1978" (*Privacy Journal*, June 2015, 7).

26. Of course given the covert nature of this, it is hard to know how much of the iceberg is beneath the surface. See, for example, cases such as that of Los Angeles private detective Anthony Pellicano (Hall and Abdollah 2008).

27. Yet as Samatras (2004) observes, some skepticism about whether files were fully destroyed or simply moved may be appropriate. In the United States, consistent with privatization, prohibited functions may be delegated to the private sector where, actions may be more difficult to discover and less subject to regulation. Given the ease of electronic copying, storage, and communication, hiding information may be easier now than with bulky paper files, although audit trails and other security measures may work against this. Tackwood (1973) offers a case of the apparent circumventing of legal requirements to destroy paper files in Los Angeles. There may be other reasons for not destroying files, as when they are needed for reconciliation programs, as in Germany and South Africa.

28. Yet following what Samatas (2014) terms the "super-panopticon scandal" involving the 2004 Greek Olympics some of these hard-won civil liberties eroded in the face of a draconian antiterrorist law prescribing mass surveillance, spying, and grassing and efforts to have surveillance viewed as the new normal.

29. This short time frame contrasts with the very broad view seen across centuries and countries—as with Toynbee's (1950) and Sorokin's (1956) analysis of shifts between societies with

greater or lesser emphasis on rationality and liberty and differing views of the appropriateness of crossing personal borders.

30. These issues are a staple of social problems research see, for example, Gusfield (1984), Best (1999), Spector and Kitsuse (2001), and Glassner (1999).

31. Research on background factors is found across many areas. A selection of other illustrative work includes, on the military, Dandeker (1990); on welfare, Gilliom (2001); on drug testing, Tunnell (2004); on video, Norris and Armstrong (1999); on computer monitoring, Regan (1995); on the polygraph, Cole (2001); on fingerprinting, Alder (2007); and on registries for automobiles and cell phones, Guzik (2016).

32. These phases connect to the distinctions and questions in the chapter on policy and ethics. Policy responses need to be more closely connected to the phase where a problem occurs.

33. When the focus is on a particular person or object this may involve *registration* (which answers the "which one" question, *inspection* to be sure that standards of functionality (a person's competence or an object's safety) are met, and subsequently *regulation* in use. Guzik (2016) notes how the content of these were altered as the national Mexican government sought to exert greater control through RFID chips on cars.

34. However, that is less true in general for the end stage involving the fate of the data, particularly if the data are circulated in digital form.

35. Goffman discusses strips and occasions (1974) in referring to face-to-face interaction. However, as used here, they refer to bundles of discrete activity from the point of view of the observer, and most do not involve face-to-face interaction of agents and subjects.

36. Decisions about *who* is responsible for doing the surveillance and the design of the technology could be treated as the initial strips as well. However, attention here is on the next stage directly associated with doing the surveillance.

37. This is said mindful of the fact that it is always possible to make ever greater differentiations within the categories identified and to push the causal chain back farther. However I think this conceptualization captures the major natural breaks in activity once a problem in need of personal information has been defined and an agent designated.

Chapter Six

1. This contrasts with the original meaning of *neutralization* within sociology (Sykes and Matza 1957), which involved attitudes thought to permit rule breaking, not the behavior itself. In the case of resistance to surveillance, however, the frame of reference is less clear for defining legitimacy. Some cases of neutralization are moral (and legal) violations, just as some cases of surveillance are.

2. Here I won't consider the efforts of subjects to stop information from being shared or publicized once it has been gathered. Stopping collection may be physically and legally very hard—for example, capturing visual images or sound in a public setting. An area for inquiry that brings in censorship questions is how those whose images or words have been captured seek to pressure those with the data (a very different issue from insidious and harder to identify self-censorship for authors, teachers, and, in every day communication, Marx 2001a). Subjects may try to protect their data by invoking confidentiality protections, making threats, seeking injunctions, or bringing civil suits. Such actions run the risk of further calling attention to the data. The "Streisand effect" entered popular culture in 2003 when publicity about legal action the singer brought to block aerial images of her mansion (taken to document coastal erosion) from being seen on the Internet led hundreds of thousands of viewers to then see it (*Wikipedia* 2012).

3. Of course the possibility of resistance does not mean it will be successful, and some may even be tolerated as a way of denying other realities. The spread of technological control and personal data collection to so many areas of life also means that some resistance is futile or fool-hardy (unless one embarks on a fool's errand out of principle rather than expediency).

4. The ethos of empirical inquiry must also be directed toward laws and policies prohibiting, limiting, or mandating surveillance. Just because rules can be identified on paper, it does not follow that they are uniformly implemented and respected. The variation here (along with that legitimately present in the form of discretion) should be a central topic of study. The National Research Council's reports on the polygraph (2001) and on other forensic tools (2008) indicate the kind of independent and public research needed for the other major tools.

5. Thus when the TSA instituted more stringent security procedures in 2002, air travel de-creased by 6 percent. According to one estimate there were an additional 130 automobile deaths every three months from traffic fatalities because ground was substituted for air transit (Blalock, Kadiyali, and Simon 2007).

6. For example, we can note that self-testing, substitution of clean urine, flushing one's system, adding a distorting substance such as bleach to a sample, or accounting for a positive finding by reference to a medication taken are all *drug test* neutralization means. We can also consider these examples of the *generic forms* that will be discussed, involving discovery, switch-ing, distorting, and explanatory moves.

7. The United States, France, and Italy may stand out in that regard relative to England, Canada, and Germany.

8. Scott is talking about these as used by "relatively powerless groups." Yet the new surveil-lance cuts across traditional form of stratification and may even reverse some patterns, as with the electronic traces disproportionately left by the more privileged, who may also have better tools to resist.

9. What are the connections between strategic and nonstrategic individual responses? Are they alternatives or complementary and, when linked, what sequences are likely?

10. Consider the awareness raising and lobbying of new organizations such as the Electronic Privacy Information Center and Electronic Frontier Foundation, the Center for Democracy and Technology, Computer Professionals for Social Responsibility, the Privacy Rights Clearing House, the Privacy Foundation (University of Denver), Privacy International, and Statewatch .org and traditional organizations such as the American Civil Liberties Union (in particular, its project on Technology and Liberty), Consumers Union, Adbusters, and Consumers against Supermarket Privacy Invasion. Bennett (2008) identifies a number of groups with an interest in protecting privacy.

There are also groups with specific concerns, such as the National Rifle Association regard-ing gun sales and ownership, the National Abortion Rights Action League regarding reporting requirements for abortions by minors, and universities concerned over reporting and monitor-ing requirements for foreign students. There are also, of course, many industry groups active in lobbying and in offering communications about the topic, such as the US Chamber of Com-merce, which has concerns over work monitoring, and the Direct Marketing Association, with an interest in third-party commercial uses of computer data.

11. Thus, in Japan after the launching of a controversial national identification number some cities cooperated with the national government, some, such as Yokohama, gave citizens a choice of whether to allow their data to be entered into the system, and some refused to cooperate (Wood, Lyon, and Abe 2007). In the U.S. United States following passage of the Real ID Act of 2005, which imposed federal standards for driver's licenses, a number of states indicated they

would not cooperate, and the Supreme Court has overturned surveillance legislation at all levels of government. Note also the interesting case of states offering driver's licenses to undocumented persons. Guzik (2016) documents equivalent local state resistance in Mexico to national programs aimed at increasing the central government's control over automobiles.

12. YouTube offers an abundance of materials on Big Brother and related themes. The ACLU's Pizza Palace surveillance clip is a classic (http://www.aclu.org/pizza/).

13. There are parallels to Charles Tilly's (1995) work on *repertoires of contention* by protest groups (e.g., demonstrations, strikes, boycotts), although the emphasis is on individual rather than organized and collective responses as a means of exerting influence.

14. In considering just biometric surveillance Ball (2005) notes resistance strategies to interrupt the flow of information from the body and to alter the timing and codings of the body.

15. As if it were a game of hide and seek, as teenagers in Hollywood we took pride in believing that we were always able to identify the "juvies" (juvenile police officers) by their stock four-door, blackwall-tired, brown or gray Fords and Plymouths as they slowly drove around. When out of the car, black shoes and white socks were also presumed to be indicative.

16. Reppetto's (1976) classic statement regarding crime displacement applies more broadly.

17. A company claiming to offer "the definitive list of companies that drug test" is at http://www.testclear.com/dtcompanies/searchcompany2.cfm.

18. With some machines now all copies are digitally scanned and stored on a hard disk or network.

19. As with landlines, even when turned off, cell phones can be made "hot on the hook"—converted to ambient microphones transmitting room audio. Under court order roving bugs can be applied by either remote activation or by hardware added to the phone. Some handsets are fully turned off only when the battery is removed.

20. Mickey Cohen in writing about his life in organized crime reports, "Important messages never came by phone. Anything to do with a hit, a gambling operation, to go somewhere or to see somebody, was by courier. See, we worried about wiretaps thirty years ago [1945]. . . . Even money was only transacted person to person. If anybody had money coming or going, you put a man on a plane." (Cohen and Nugent 1975).

In the contemporary international context, the use of couriers and simple walkie-talkies have their own limitations, but as the Black Hawk incident in Somalia in 1993 indicated, vulnerability to high-tech satellite listening devices is not among them.

21. Such presumptions can be wrong. Consider the film *The Conversation* (1974), in which criminals mistakenly felt safe talking in a rowboat in the middle of a lake, or the Philadelphia organized crime figures who were arrested as a result of electronic surveillance of meetings they held in the offices of their doctor and lawyer. They wrongly assumed that the doctor-patient and lawyer-client privilege precluded such places from police surveillance (Decourcy 1994).

22. They might also wish to invest in disposable undergarments, given the availability of sperm detection test kits for home use, "the easiest and most cost effective way to put an end to the nightmare of suspicion and doubt caused by the infidelity of a cheating spouse." Guilty until proven innocent?

23. Ken Tunnell (2004) has written a richly informed book on the interdependent and interactive drug-testing and detox industries.

24. There are of course risks. According to one account (http://en.wikipedia.org/wiki/Whizzinator), "In 2006, a Pittsburgh-area woman and her friend were charged with disorderly conduct and criminal mischief after they asked a convenience store clerk to microwave one of the devices so the woman could pass a drug test. The clerk, thinking it was a real penis, called

police. The couple were required to reimburse the chain for the cost of a new microwave: OSHA regulations do not allow microwaves to be used once bodily fluids have been in them. The solemnity of the United States Congress was brought to bare (so to speak) on the issue in hearings (US House of Representatives, Subcommittee on Commerce, Trade and Consumer Protection 2005).

25. Home meters for gas and water are other examples.

26. The New York City police department's use of lasers against demonstrators can be seen in http://www.youtube.com/watch?v=dVaCGHn8LnY. However, in that case the device did not work well enough to prevent images of it from being taken, and as demonstrators are heard singing, "This little light of mine, I'm gonna let it shine" (R. Davis 2011).

A *New Yorker* cartoon ("No cameras beyond this point") showing a police barricade expresses this goal. In another example of light being used to both illuminate and to shield, police can purchase the MII Flashcam tactical flashlight with its hidden video recorder and night vision technology.

27. The operator knew the phone number of both the caller and the called, although not necessarily who was using the phone. The smaller the area, the more likely it was for the operator to be familiar with the voice.

28. This of course is at a cost of being unable to receive incoming signals as well.

29. A major policy decision involves how much discretion the electronically monitored have. With various smart badge systems or cell phones individuals may simply leave the badge on their desk or keep the cell phone off. In the first case the individual will miss instant notification of messages and the system will know where the badge is, but not necessarily where the person is. In the second (depending on the system) location may not be known and the person is insulated from the message. But in being unavailable the individual also sends a message and may be suspect. As we note later, there may be strong pressure to participate—nonparticipants are seen as lacking in manners or having something to hide.

30. Of course, ironically, the effort to hide identity may bring notice that something is up. Rather than directly hiding identity, there may instead be efforts to alter the perception of the person it is hidden from, as with blindfolds, darkness, and smoke or shocks that focus attention elsewhere.

31. A nice example of this is the Guy Fawkes masks seen in recent antiglobalization protests and a symbol of the online hacktivist group Anonymous and the Occupy movement. The masked Ku Klux Klan drew on the same means.

32. In some quarters this is still viewed as top secret. Note the April 1999 news stories regarding efforts of the CIA to prevent FOIA revelations from 1917 of documents regarding this.

33. A related form is getting rid of objects that can be identified with a subject (e.g., throwaway cellphones) or destroying items such as clothes worn at the scene of a crime.

34. Wearing a bandana or a mask that looks like a mask is a form of blocking, not masking as the term is used here. When agents do learn that masking is present, we see another contingent process, as neutralization efforts seek to discover what was prior to the mask.

35. Such endeavors, of course, are not without risks of various kinds. Note the case of Mexican crime boss Amado Fuentes, who died during plastic surgery and liposuction undertaken to change his appearance (Dillion 1997).

36. Schemes varying in their complexity expanded (as did efforts to defeat them) as governments and other organizations came to be interested in the identity of travelers, merchants, and those claiming benefits in the late medieval period. Groebner, Kyburz, and Peck (2007) offer an

informative account of identification means in early modern Europe with strong parallels to several of the means discussed in this chapter.

37. This example of applied philosophy was developed at NYU by Helen Nissenbaum, a philosopher, and Daniel Howe, a digital artist and media researcher.

38. See for example, EPIC v. FAA 2015; Froomkin and Colangelo 2015.

39. When given a choice, opting out of providing data or of having one's data shared beyond the initial use, we see another kind of behavioral refusal, but on legitimate terms. In contrast, the kinds of refusal this chapter considers are seen as illegitimate refusal by agents. Contrasting people who employ these two types with those who simply cooperate suggests another source of variation to be explored.

Olympic sprinters Kostas Kenteris and Katerina Thanou, who resigned on the eve of the 2004 Olympics, appear to offer a case of avoidance and saying no to both the rules against doping and the rules about taking a drug test. They were found guilty (although later exonerated) of a conspiracy with their coach to fake a motorcycle accident in order to avoid the drug test (Press Association 2011). That contrasts with simply denying the use of prohibited substances, as with the perjury trial of baseball player Barry Bonds years after the suspected use.

40. Depending on the specifics, neutralization logics and rationales will differ. The refusal to obey a rule (such as "Don't smuggle drugs") is probably different from the refusal to cooperate with a drug test.

41. "Trouble over Privacy in Japan," *Economist*, August 8, 2002.

42. In 2001, 45 percent of respondents in a study for the industry trade group the Council for Marketing and Opinion Research said they had refused to participate in a survey in the last year, up from 31 percent in 1992 and 15 percent in 1982 (Jarvis 2002). According to a 2003 Pew Research Center survey, about seven out of ten telephone calls answered do not result in completed interviews. For later data see the 2007 report by the Council for Marketing and Opinion Research on professional image. Their euphemism for resistance is "respondent cooperation"— the title of a conference held by the group in 2008.

43. A related form involves strategic deception with the *cry wolf* strategy, wherein subjects intentionally trigger an alarm several times and quickly depart. By the third or fourth time agents assume it is a false alarm again and subjects have an informal license to trespass.

44. This offers another way to approach variation. Where the surveillance goal is to discover compliance there is a fourfold typology derived from bringing together responses to the rule (obey/disobey) and cooperation with the surveillance procedure (cooperate/neutralize).

45. Note two marines who refused to give DNA samples because they did not trust the government to use them only for identification purposes in case of death (Essoyan 1995).

46. Such an explanation was good enough for tennis player Andre Agassi (2009) to avoid sanctioning after he failed a drug test. In a letter of explanation to the governing board he blamed it on an assistant named Slim: "I drank accidently from one of Slim's spiked sodas, unwittingly ingesting his drugs. I ask for your understanding and leniency"—which he received. The explanation turned out to be a classic deceptive move. He had in fact knowingly taken meth in another form.

47. They are also ideally suited to thwart such systems when they are turned inward. This is one reason why "who guards the guards" is always problematic.

48. But even means such as satellites which seem out of sight (in both senses) to the ordinary person are available for short-term hire at modest cost.

49. This suggests a qualification to Simmel's observation that adversaries come to resemble

each other in their use of tactics. For those motivated by high democratic principles the means used may be as important as the ends. This also involves the distinction between a given tactical means and a broader strategic effort to alter or stop use of a tactic.

50. This includes the Whizzinator, which the Congress learned about in a hearing (US House of Representatives 2005).

51. The disclaimers may bring a reassuring smile to the most hardened cynic: "just for fun," "for educational purposes," for "personal use only," or for "self-defense," and not for "any other use that can be construed as unlawful."

52. In the surveillance context the limitations of such responses are considered by Martin (1998) and Monahan (2006).

53. Many variables condition this, and it goes to the heart of efforts to explain surveillance practices. This could serve as a dependent variable with some ideal types in various social contexts. Of particular note are situations of minimum surveillance slack and maximum neutralization slack, as in the most repressive settings, versus situations of lots of surveillance slack and little neutralization slack. This can be related to the historical cycles of repression and liberalization. Availability can be considered as legitimated or merely tolerated. It can also refer to whether are not tools are available to access the information, apart from whether this is acceptable to do. That availability can be through open or black markets.

54. Gilliom (2001), McCahill (2002), and Tunnell (2004) offer examples of the supportive agent.

Introduction to Part 3

1. In using the term *culture of surveillance* Staples (2014) emphasizes legitimating ideas and related behavior rather than the elements of popular culture.

2. While it is the actor who constructs all self-presentations, as Goffman (1956b) suggests, only some are inauthentic in projecting an image the actor knows to be false. The same distinction can be applied to stories told about the social world.

3. This contrasts with the practical "legal fictions" of the law in which the court—for jurisdictional purposes and to avoid outmoded procedural rules—acts as if certain factual conditions were present which need not be.

4. Of course, this is not a problem for those who view social science as mostly fiction anyway, whether because of the complex, ever-changing nature of its topics, the illusiveness of subjectivity, relatively weak methods, or the biases of its practitioners.

5. Note the enduring power of Lon Fuller's (1949) article on the speluncean explorers for generations of law students.

Chapter Seven

1. This expands on a satire published in 1990 purporting to be from the year 1995 (Marx 1990). Several decades later the fundamental issues remain, even as some of the details change. As written today, for example, the company plan includes mandatory smartphones and tablets, requirements to use social media but also to provide the company with any social media IDs and passwords.

2. At that extreme see the practices of an employer described in the *Wall Street Journal* on December 1, 1994, whose nonunionized employees are particularly vulnerable as a result of lack of skills, immigrant status, and gender.

3. Among early sources on work and technology I learned from Howard (1985), Shaiken (1985), Zuboff (1988), and the latest Carr (2014) and Gray (2015). Ball (2010) offers an overview; Sewell (2012) locates technological surveillance within the broader context of employment and pretechnological forms. He identifies variation by combining direct and indirect and subjective-embodied and objective-disembodied dimensions.

4. After the article on the Omniscient Organization appeared in the *Harvard Business Review* (Marx 1990), I was told by several colleagues that I would receive many consulting invitations to analyze company practices. I did get some requests—but only from persons wanting to know what company it was based on and where the technologies could be purchased.

5. The efforts to engineer behavior the same way one engineers manufacturing is at the core of modernization. Such control shares many issues with raw material but also differs in profound moral ways and is a more difficult task. In the criminal justice context, see Byrne and Marx (2011) and Marx (2015c).

6. Wachtel (1985) offers a nice example of this for police work.

7. Smith et al. (1992) find that electronically monitored workers on the average experience greater stress and dissatisfaction than those not so monitored. There is variation within each group as well. But in comparing monitored with nonmonitored workers in the communications industry what is striking in the Smith et al. study is the high level of stress reported by both groups of workers (thus, eight out of ten of the former reported high tension on the job, but so too did almost seven out of ten of the latter). Aiello and Shao (1993) report that workers subject to individual monitoring report greater stress than those subject to team monitoring. After a study of monitored telephone workers revealed that 67 percent experienced high or very high pressure, Bell Canada restricted monitoring to training purposes only (DiTecco et al. 1992).

8. An illustrative case: two Nissan employees fired after they referred to their boss as *numbnuts* in personal e-mails, which they assumed were protected. They learned to their detriment that the Bill of Rights as currently interpreted tends to stop at the company door. They were not permitted to encrypt their messages. They would have seen a different outcome had they been able and chosen to encrypt there message to each other. Companies vary in the extent to which they permit employees to engage in private communication and, when they do, whether it can be protected from computer system managers.

9. The film *Casino* nicely captures this. Ace (Robert De Niro), looking out over the operation says, "In Vegas, everybody's gotta watch everyone else. . . . The dealers are watching the players. . . . The box men are watching the dealers. . . . The floor men are watching the box men. . . . The pit bosses are watching the floor men. . . . The shift men are watching the floor men. . . . The shift bosses are watching the pit bosses. . . . The casino manager is watching the shift bosses. . . . I'm watching the casino manager. And the eye-in-the-sky [the domed ceiling camera] is watching us all." As he is talking, the camera pans to each actor.

He might have added that cameras also watch patrons as they enter—identifying high rollers for red-carpet treatment and those on lists of people banned from entering. There are as well an abundance of paparazzi at work.

10. Beyond access to classified, secret, and private files, this can involve "private" entrances, elevators, doors, bathrooms, and dining areas, not to mention the deference that informally accompanies higher status. Physical segregation, beyond its symbolic meaning, can also ease the discomfort when interaction is equitable, as when a manager and employee simultaneously approach a vending machine.

11. In other respects there may be greater visibility, beyond the glare of media attention—

government leaders must file disclosure statements, stock companies need to follow reporting requirements—but at the same time secrecy protections may go beyond what is organizationally functional, or at least legitimate, to cover bad behavior.

12. Here *transparency* is used to mean full disclosure of all that goes on, rather than the more conventional organizational-public meaning of how decisions were made.

Chapter Eight

This chapter had its origins in an earlier happy collaboration with Val Steeves (Marx and Steeves 2010) that contains many visual images of tools, and I am grateful for the chance to draw from it here.

1. See, for example, Jorgensen (2002), C. Katz (2006), Wagnsson, Hellman, and Holmberg (2010), Nelson (2010), Steeves (2012), and an issue of *Surveillance and Society* (2010, vol. 7, no. 3/4), edited by Val Steeves and Owain Jones.

2. In "The Death of the Hired Man" Frost (1915) writes, "Home is the place that when you have to go there, they have to take you in." In the twenty-first century, it might read, "Home (or at least the parental gaze) is the place you can't leave."

3. Anita Allen (2003) offers a moving account of the conflicts a protective and caring family (spouses, children, siblings, close relations) faces with respect to the desire to help, the privacy of a wayward member, and the role of the legal system, with its potentially helpful as well as punitive potential.

4. Such a movement can be imagined in the case of KISHI (Kids Insist on Surveillance Help Inc.), an organization founded by kids for kids at Foucault Regional High School in French Lick, Indiana. Its fictitious press release: "Calling all kids! Now is the time to take charge of our lives! We live in dangerous times. But we can make a difference. We want to love our parents, and given the right environment, they will do the right thing. But no one can go it alone. Parents need lots of help. The home can be a dangerous place for kids. Consider that 80 percent of child abuse occurs in the home, and that a healthy (actually *very* unhealthy) percentage of parents who live in energy-inefficient homes don't recycle; serve food too rich in sugar, salt, and cholesterol; smoke, drink, and use illegal narcotics; have sexually transmitted diseases and family-destroying affairs; gamble; and are profligate with funds needed for toys and college. Unlike kids in earlier times, we know all about adults from watching television and using the Internet."

On children as informers Marx (1986, 1988b) and the section that was cut: "Playing for the Future: Simulations, Spy Toys, Children as Informers, On-line Playgrounds," at press.uchicago .edu/sites/marx/.

5. Well, not quite. Even infants and those a bit older surveil their environment and are especially attentive to where their mothers are and often cry when the parent is out of site. As children grow older, this is reversed, as they seek to avoid the parental gaze. Peekaboo is a game rich with meaning for these questions and the transition to being beyond the parent's view.

6. For example, surveillance that denies a six-year-old girl with a love of tutus the chance of wearing them can hurt her development. On the other hand, failing to provide any limits on the clothing choices of a thirteen-year-old can be harmful in a different way.

7. The process is slow and uneven. While babysitting, I accompanied a three-year-old grandson to the bathroom as he requested. Then he said he wanted some privacy. But when the door was closed and I left the room, he began to cry and asked for the door to be opened.

8. For example, Kerr and Stattin (2000) found that monitoring children did not encourage prosocial behavior; instead, children were more likely to behave in prosocial ways when they were able to voluntarily disclose information to adults with whom they shared a bond of trust.

9. Merchants may seek to legitimize this commodification by positioning the child as agent (Shade and Decheif 2005). Kids are no longer minors with special needs; instead, they are savvy computer users and consumers who—at the young age of thirteen—can consent to the collection and use of their information (see Children's Online Protection Privacy Act 1998). This type of presumed contractual protection has been criticized, especially in the context of children's privacy (Hertzel 2000; Grimes and Shade 2005; Steeves 2009).

10. The former is *surveillance smothering*, and the latter, *surveillance slack* (Marx 2002 and chap. 14, 303–304). The question of what holds back parents from exercising their full surveillance needs to be joined with that of the failure to surveil. Are these best seen as the ends of a continuum of surveillance implementation reflecting linear impacts of shared causes or as distinct factors requiring separate explanations?

11. At a minimum there could be warning labels on such listening devices indicating that their use in certain ways is illegal. The toys might also come with guidelines for appropriate use and instructional materials to help parents discuss with children the moral issues around surreptitious listening and recording.

Chapter Nine

1. A still earlier version (2002) is at http://web.mit.edu/gtmarx/www/voirerevised.html. I considered revising this a decade after it appeared to bring it up to date. The spread of social media forms offers rich possibilities for the curious, not to mention other forms such as drones. But I decided to freeze the case. It can never be brought up to date. However, revision of the case (and the other narratives in this section) every decade or so would offer a way seeing change and continuity.

2. Men on the average respond differently to the case than do women, not experiencing the same shock and indignation.

3. The data of course can be "personal" in any of the several ways discussed in chapter 4, but my emphasis in this chapter is on the nature of the relationship, not the kind of data.

4. On this topic see Nissenbaum (1998), Marx (2001; 2015a). Here in some of his behavior Tom is engaged in uncivil attention, even under the guise of civil disattention. The opposite issue involves what should be public (whether broadly or to selected others) within what is otherwise private, as in not being easily available to others.

5. To take only a few of many examples from the longer article where surveillance and gender intertwined to Tom's detriment—at his security guard job he was accused of contributing to a hostile work environment for women because he wore a T-shirt with a provocative image of a woman; had a revealing pin-up on the inside door of his work locker; and sometimes used the women's restroom. Some women complained that they didn't like the way he looked at them. He felt it was unfair that he could not monitor the cameras in the women's dressing room, although female guards could monitor those in the men's dressing rooms.

As a result of the above he was put on notice. That angered him, and he was eventually fired after a hidden camera caught him urinating in the coffee pot in the executive suite. Under unclear circumstances he was then arrested for soliciting a decoy police prostitute; after the arrest, a citizens' group, as a deterrence measure, paid for a picture of him to appear in the local newspaper before his trial.

But in each case he felt he was doing the right thing. The locker was like his private property and he had rights with respect to what he posted inside it. He acknowledged wearing a salacious T-shirt but said that was to help him fit in with other customers while he looked for shoplifters. Yes, he did, in an emergency, use the women's restroom, but that was because he had a stomach condition (documented by a doctor's note) that required sudden visits and, besides, he said the nice chaise lounges and stalls with doors were much more inviting than in the men's rooms. He didn't understand the accusation of looking at women, he said he looked to honor them and not to look, or to look away, was to deny their very being and to disrespect them.

He acknowledged it was wrong to urinate in the coffee pot, but said that paled into insignificance when considering the use of secret cameras. Granted, he made a mistake this time, but what about all the times he didn't urinate into the coffee pot, let alone all the other good things he did at work—don't they outweigh one tiny mistake?

6. I (A.F., Tom's therapist) believe he refers to Simmelian insight here.

Chapter Ten

1. Among his central points were that he broke no law, he intended no harm and no harm came to her, Eve never learned of his actions, in not protecting her information she invited others to share it, and the law gives him the right to look and certainly to have his own private thoughts and forms of artistic expression intended only for himself.

2. Debra Gwartney (2012) offers a poignant, searing account of the terrible fear caused by a voyeur who thought that as long as he remained unseen and unknown no harm was done. As in the film *One Hour Photo*, he was accidently discovered when he turned in film for processing. In the film the protagonist states, "I just took pictures." In an effort to balance the liberty of the individual vs. harm to others, the law treats the act of secretly collecting (or intercepting) private personal data much less seriously (if at all) than publicizing or selling it. There are kinds and degrees of invisibility here. On the one hand the subject is invisible to the agent because he or she is not seen as fully human, the agent in being hidden is invisible to the subject (absent accidental revelation) as in the above case. Gwartney notes yet another kind of invisibility—most of the victims given the chance to know and to act, preferred to look the other way.

3. "Escape for thy life; look not behind thee, neither stay thou in all the plain; escape to the mountain, lest thou be consumed." Genesis 19:17.

4. In the earlier days of analog phones, an engineering student who supported himself by working nights at a phone company reported that his colleagues kept a list of "hot" lines to listen in on while ostensibly monitoring transmission quality.

5. But not to worry, the participating sister responds, "That won't happen because he promised me confidentiality." With her more relaxed style she probably would not be deeply upset if he broke his word. Yet as long as he keeps his word (or his promise is kept, which isn't quite the same thing), her privacy cannot be said to be invaded because she willingly talked in front of the camera, just as those in pornographic films are usually assumed to agree to perform, although in return for compensation. The issues of consent and the promise of confidentiality separate the film example from settings where one or both are absent.

6. As always, there are exceptions. Consider the case of the intelligence agency that secretly filmed some compromising positions of an individual it was hoping to compromise. When confronted with what the agency assumed was an embarrassing sexual image, the subject was unwilling to cooperate but was pleased with the picture and asked if he could have a copy.

7. This is not to imply that the feelings of the subject are unimportant, but in criminal cases intention is a defining element. A number of state stalking and harassment laws require direct communication between the defendant and the victim. As of 2015 it was not a crime to publicize nude photos of a person, even knowing that the individual did not consent (e.g., the posting of "revenge porn"). The Federal Video Voyeurism Prevention Act of 2004 criminalizes intention-

ally capturing images of a private area of a person when they have a reasonable expectation of privacy, but only if this happens on federal property. Citron (2014) makes clear the need for legal reform as technologies have changed.

8. *See* Entick v. Carrington, 19 Howell's State Trials, 1029 (1765).

9. Some initial thoughts on manners as applied to new forms of communication are in Marx (1994).

Chapter Eleven

1. At least five kinds of interweaving (initially noted for undercover work, Marx 1987) can be seen: joint public and private investigations, public agents hiring or delegating authority to private police (privatization), private interests hiring public police (incorporation), new organizational forms in which the distinction between public and private is blurred, and the circulation of personnel between the public and private sectors.

2. A variety of literatures have conceived these changes well, although the conceptual has generally raced ahead of systematic empirical documentation. Consider, for example, work on security and technology from an international relations and comparative perspective such as Fijnaut and Marx (1995), Katzenstein (1996), McDonald (1996), Deflem (2002), Sheptycki 2003), Bonditti (2004), Scott and Jackson (2004), Dillon (2003), Bigo (2005), Zureik and Salter (2005), Abrahamsen and Williams (2006), and Andreas and Nadelmann (2006).

Chapter Twelve

1. Within the broader culture, if not necessarily within the cheering squads of the surveillance professions, there is deep ambivalence and a counter to this view (Dr. Frankenstein stories). The advocacy in chapters 7–10 contrasts with the antisurveillance themes commonly found in the work of artists, cartoonists, novelists, filmmakers, and university-based social scientists (this is discussed in the material hosted at press.uchicago.edu/sites/marx/.) Their work also contrasts with the prosurveillance perspective more commonly found in radio talk shows, advertisements, industry-sponsored think tanks, and public relations efforts.

2. Of course intellectuals have social locations, interests, and blind and obfuscated spots as well. Believing in empiricism, logic, and the higher aspects of Western civilization reflects value commitments. But there are some central differences as well, such as adhering to an open, self-interrogating critical standard beyond specific contexts and awareness of the paradoxical nature of the sociology of knowledge.

3. The number of fallacies is already too long (and to honor no. 39, more need not be better). Some additional ones: confusing the simulacra with the phenomenon; that saying I'm sorry makes it OK; that crooks and suspects have no rights; that contemporary wars can be won with finality; that if a democratically elected leader does it, it is not illegal; confusing what is possible with what is or is probable; that good motives excuse bad outcomes; imputing competent, technique-based intentionality to outcomes we like in the face of fortuity while imputing ill will, incompetence, and conspiracy to outcomes we don't like; the rush to talk about inherent tradeoffs before analysis of whether these are genuine and what is being traded.

4. The elasticity and vagueness of symbols and concepts is also illustrated. Thus Bottoms supports his case by reference to John Lennon (although in an interesting slip he refers to him as John Lenin). Freedom, liberty and choice are also resources in the verbal arsenals of those Rocky criticizes.

5. See, for example, Lee and Lee (1939), Lowenthal (1949), Shils (1956), and Hofstader (1965) regarding the simplistic, manipulative, nonrefutable, demagogic, sloppy, heated, energized, dark, conspiratorial, paranoid, apocalyptic, Manichean, true-believer rhetoric and propaganda that seem to find particularly fertile ground in certain geographic and social sectors of the United States.

6. Examples and a fuller discussion are available online at press.uchicago.edu/sites/marx/.

7. This commodification or monetization of private and personal data is part of a broader issue of the moral limits of markets. What should be salable? Given their social meaning and implications in an unequal world, there must be limits in spite of the advantages of free markets and the sanctity of individual choice (Walzer 1983; Satz 2010; Sandel 2012).

8. The distinction between the human and the machine worked for much of human history. But with the increasing interdependence seen with cyborgs, advanced robots, and people hooked up to machines, the lines are less clear now.

9. Being criticized by those with opposed viewpoints can be one indicator of speaking unpleasant truths. Such critics often fail to appreciate the substantive and strategic contribution that objective analysis can bring and to reflect on the basis of their own strongly held views. Our National Research Council (2007) report on privacy was attacked by several activists because "it had too many academics on board" and "there was too much waffling."

Chapter Thirteen

1. Note Governor George Wallace's call in the 1960s to "let the police run this country for a year or two" to stop the disorder (Kazin 1998). On states of exception more broadly see Agamben (2005).

2. Given space limitations, here I list only the questions; a fuller discussion of them is available online at press.uchicago.edu/sites/marx/.

3. An Important initial policy tool here is the *privacy impact* (or, more broadly, surveillance) assessment statement (Wright and de Hert 2012). Such inquires consider a project's feasibility, goals, and a range of possible consequences based on prior evidence, research, and best estimates—with input from an array of those deemed to be "stakeholders."

4. It is not simply that research is needed (even if it alone will rarely be enough to alter an entrenched policy or lead to a new policy, at least in the short run). Rather, the research must be well done. Consider electronic monitoring, a well-researched surveillance area and one in which supportive answers to the questions in this chapter are lacking (and an area which also brightly illustrates a number of the techno-fallacies from chap. 12). Renzema and Mayo-Wilson (2005) reviewed 119 studies in asking, "can electronic monitoring reduce crime for moderate to high risk offenders?" They report that only three of those studies met the standards for adequate methodology they set. The less-than-strong evidence for effectiveness led them to conclude: "After 20 years, it is clear that EM has been almost desperately applied without adequate vision, planning, program integration, staff training and concurrent research." They are pessimistic and ask if this is not another form of what Latessa, Cullen, and Gendreau (2002) call "correctional quackery." Lilly and Nellis (2013) reach a similar conclusion.

5. The consistency principle here, which asks whether the tactic is applied to everyone, is different from asking, What if everyone applied it?

6. For example, Oscar Gandy (1993) has noted how market research on consumption behavior can work to the disadvantage of the least privileged.

7. There may be a procedural violation in the initial collection or in the wrongful release

of the information. These two kinds of harm are further compounded when the information is wrong. The embarrassment to the falsely accused, labeled, or identified is a rarely considered form. A mild form is in the momentary (and widely experienced) inconvenience caused by a search that leads to an invalid conclusion, such as having an alarm go off by mistake as one walks through a detection device in a store or library or the rejection of a valid credit card. In contrast, less sympathy is likely for revelations regarding those shown to be guilty and/or worthy of being embarrassed or worse, even if the means of discovering or releasing the information is wrong.

8. Derber (2000) treats the rarely studied issue of demand on another's attention as a stratification issue. This overlaps norms regarding information seeking, protection, and revelation.

9. Resilience is something of an alternative or a supplement to prevention and anticipation. Starting with the assumption that stuff happens in a complex and complicated world, the issue becomes how a society best can respond to, and limit, harm when uncertainty is so often rampant about the likelihood of, and damage from, risks, not to mention the effectiveness of preventive measures (Wildavsky 1988). A large project offering a wealth of data completed in 2014 for the European Union applies the concept to surveillance societies. It finds that the open nature of democratic societies makes them more vulnerable to attacks on infrastructures and people but also can make them more resilient. The handbook *Surveillance, Democracy and Resilience* suggests options for enhancing resilience (IRISS 2014) see also Wright and Kneisel 2014.

10. Rimer 1990. The prosecutor lost his 2 Live Crew obscenity case and was commenting on mistakes made in jury selection.

11. Conceptual differentiation is a central aim of the book, even as there are cognitive and pragmatic, if not natural science, limitations on how many angels can find room at the inn or on the pin. Natural science limits, however, may apply in locating the angels.

12. However, as Winner (1988) notes, there are conditions under which some technologies clearly have political and social (and by indirection) ethical implications. For example, the decision to use nuclear power will of necessity imply centralization and high levels of security. Enormous capital expenditures in the creation of a system will exert pressures to continue it in the face of evidence that it does not work as well as other means or has other unwanted consequences.

13. This of course makes room for contrasts, as in chapter 2 between traditional and the new surveillance and between practices that the analyst as outside observer using the framework the book develops would see as problematic but that are not seen that way by the public, as well as the reverse. This is the classic issue of whose point of view is being expressed—the person in the situation or the removed outside observer.

14. Disagreements about surveillance may occur because actors are referring to different components of the surveillance occasion and talking past each other. Untangling these may bring greater clarity to the discussion.

15. These may overlap, as when a system of retinal eye pattern identification instantly results in access or its denial. But they are always analytically and (usually) temporally distinct.

16. Infrequency is hardly a justification, but it is a factor in considering what is likely to receive policy attention.

17. Thus it would need to take account of the behavior of individuals, organizations, states, and the international order, as these involve crossing borders to impose upon and to take from subjects; the rights and obligations of various parties; the ethical meanings of doing good and avoiding harm; and various levels of analysis, such as kinds of institutions and roles, the crosscultural, and the short and long run.

18. Kevin Macnish (2014) offers a good beginning for nonconsensual surveillance based on nine principles tied to the just-war tradition. See also the 2014 commentaries on the article by Hosein, Stoddard, Palm, and Marx.

19. There is tension between getting it all down and the realization that if a conceptual space involves more than three variables, most persons won't bother to absorb an argument. Furthermore, the failure to go the Kantian imperial, deontological route and offer overarching first principles puts one at the risk of being captured by those with the best access to communication and the most passion. To argue on a case-by-case basis also risks being accused of ad hoc, inconsistent, and partial responses. As the case of Tom Voire suggests, clever advocates, whether lawyers or not, can usually find a way to justify behavior that seems outrageous to others.

20. Klockars (1980) wisely discusses this. "Failure lies in not acknowledging and analyzing a moral dilemma in which there is gain and loss no matter what path is chosen. Note also happier choices between the good and the good, and the good and the better.

Chapter Fourteen

1. Given the historical, theoretical, and observational approach of most surveillance studies scholars, there has been little direct hypothesis testing.

2.. See the quotation on p. 1 in the introduction.

3. The doubling of processing speeds every eighteen months and disk memory capacity every year (National Academy of Sciences 2006) are illustrative.

4. Relative to the many articles proclaiming, but not welcoming, the arrival of a surveillance society there is only a modest literature critical of, or expanding on such articles. Among articles I find useful are Yar (2003), Haggerty and Ericson (2006), Wood, Lyon, and Abe (2007), Dupont (2008), and Elmer (2012). This section draws material from Marx (2005a) and Marx and Muschert (2007).

5. This list expanded from only eight pages and 160 state and federal laws protecting personal information or on surveillance when first published in 1975 to more than eighty pages and about 1,500 statutes in the 2013 edition. Among the most significant federal legislation: the Fair Credit Reporting Act, the Privacy Act of 1974, the Video Privacy Protection Act, the Gramm-Leach-Bliley Act of 1999, the Children's Online Privacy Protection Act, the Heath Insurance Portability and Accountability Act, and the Genetic Information Nondiscrimination Act of 2008.

Of course more than legal authority and workable laws is needed. Those charged with oversight and enforcing the law, particularly for intelligence and national security issues, must not only be wary of being deceived by professional deceivers on a mission, but they must have the will and resources to act independently. The State Department's former top legal adviser observes, "This is an area where Congress notoriously doesn't want to know too much" (Mazzetti 2015).

6. Whether law and policies go far enough or are effective and how they compare across institutions and cultures are important research questions. Paying for an enhanced level of privacy and security brings other issues, such as fairness and inequality when all can't easily afford to pay.

7. Mort Gerberg, "Yes, he does speak but only on condition of anonymity," cartoon, *New Yorker* (July 10, 2000), http://www.cartoonbank.com/assets/1/44031_m.gif.

8. Consider teen sexuality: some parents in Scandinavia, rather than testing for telltale signs of sexual activity (as advocated in PISHI) instead accept their children's sexuality and even encourage sex within the security of the family home.

9. Of course new forms that the actor has an interest in hiding or at least controlling also ap-

pear. Diagnostic tests involving DNA or predictive profiles for those at risk (no matter of what) can create new forms of stigma and interests in concealing or revealing.

10. For example, consider the millions of Americans who, as products of a mixed marriage, consider themselves both Christian and Jewish, white and black, or Asian and Hispanic. Note also recent questions of transgender and male or female categorization.

11. The strong case that science fiction writer David Brin (1998) makes for the benefits of increasing mutual visibility must be appreciated. However, we also need to note the desirable or at least defensible aspects of secrecy and privacy and to consider the settings and criteria that would justify overriding reciprocity. A suspicious society where all watch and record all is hardly desirable, even if better than a society where technology is a one-way street monopolized by the more powerful.

12. The creation of redundant structures was a defensive means to keep the system going in the event of a nuclear attack, but it had the ironic consequence of making it harder for the center to control and creates infinite possibilities for abuse.

13. Once concepts are defined and variables identified, the next step is the generation of hypotheses and the specification of conditions under which they apply. The field has lagged here. For example, the comprehensive volume edited by Ball, Haggerty, and Lyon (2012) is filled with terrific ideas, but few in the form of hypotheses that can actually be tested—that leaves the field to those with the best networks and biggest megaphones. Marx and Muschert (2007) offer a sampling of tested (or testable) hypotheses for democratic societies. Psychologists working in carefully defined areas such as work performance (e.g., Stone-Romero, Stone, and Hyatt 2003) or conformity have gone much further. A sociological exception is Horne et al. 2015. In studying Smart Meters they offer hypotheses and some documentation suggesting that demands for privacy protection norms are most likely when a tactic can harm subjects (with Smart Meters this could happen through revealing protected details of home life, selling information to third parties, or limiting individuals' control over their use of home electricity). When goals are shared and subjects have meaningful choices, the demand for norms to control technical changes is less likely. Some related issues are raised about the appearance of norms for both subjects and agents with respect to seeking, offering, and withholding information (Marx 2011b).

14. The New Testament (John 3:20–21) observes that "everyone who does evil hates the light, and will not come into the light for fear that his deeds will be exposed. But whoever lives by the truth comes into the light." The vagaries of truth apart, it can be a bit more complicated. Consider controversies involving store changing rooms or public bathrooms with respect to physical barriers to visibility. The presumed increased security may come with lessened privacy (e.g., removing doors from bathrooms and stalls within them).

15. This is even truer of primary relations than of those found in the formal organization. A further qualification is also needed here with respect to whether a fuller picture and more unique identification (or characterization) of the individual permits more or less advantageous treatment. Thus, the stigmatized fearing wrongful discrimination or, in a judicial context, the guilty person may not desire unique identification. There is also the issue of the dignity that may extend to being acknowledged by name rather than by a number discussed in chapter 4.

16. Rule (2007) has long argued that we would be better off collecting less personal data, even at a cost of less efficiency.

17. From another perspective civil liberties when associated with belief in the legitimacy of government may of course help law enforcement.

18. *Particularized surveillance* could be labeled *categorical particularized surveillance*, but that is awkward. The terms *indiscriminate* and *discriminate surveillance* work better. The discriminate can be categorical in looking at all who fit into the suspicious category.

19. Less delicately, this lack of intelligence sharing between agencies is reflected in the film *The Departed* when a Massachusetts police sergeant in a special investigations unit says, "My theory on Feds is that they're like mushrooms, feed 'em shit and keep 'em in the dark."

20. Yet there are also times when a visible police presence may smoke out a violator who would otherwise be undiscovered. Consider traffic enforcement in HOV lanes. With tinted windows and children's car seats in the back, it can be difficult for police to identify violators. However, a marked police car driving in an adjacent lane will often lead a violator to self-identify by getting out of the lane. In contrast, unmarked police cars are more effective at apprehending speeders.

21. This is from J. R. R. Tolkien, who advises, "Go not to the elves for counsel, for they will say both yes and no." As elves with magical powers they are free to indulge their indecision and yet avoid the worst of the places in hell that are reserved for the indecisive—a privilege not available for academics, even with tenure.

22. Related measures could include comparing what individuals know about themselves or are capable of knowing versus what outsiders and experts know or can know about them. Other measures can be created based on the size of the audience of knowers and comparisons made between different types of audience. Marx (2011b) asks about the rules for the different parties regarding what must or must not be asked or told, as against their being discretion about this.

23. This assumes that the preferences for withholding information are themselves legitimate—a culturally relative and changeable topic that is clearest at the extremes.

24. As argued in chapter 1, equivalent questions can also be asked about the ability of individuals and groups to *publicize* information within or across settings and time periods, and to the interrelations of the rules regarding both subjects and agents with respect to seeking, offering, and withholding information (Marx 2011b).

25. The concept of *neutralization slack*, considered in chapter 6, can also be used here. The slack measures may be too relativistic for many observers. A lesser evil is still evil, and a greater good is not the best. For those in the biblical tradition of the prophets, or believing in the inevitable cascading of slippery slopes, the only standard is the absolute ideal. To make judgments based on empirical data is irrelevant when the principle is the standard. The empirical analyst concerned with these issues as a citizen may also wonder if the kind of scholarly analysis suggested here creates undue complacency in the face of potential dangers.

26. But as Locke (2011) shows in a fascinating history, there were certainly restraints on citizens observing others. The Magna Carta (however short lived and narrowly focused on rights for the privileged) illustrates the uneven temporal and other contours of restraint.

27. A most interesting category is the box where no tools exist to pry out information. In that case rules will be unlikely. But if a broad set of standards to permit, limit, or prohibit the crossing of personal information borders exists, then this box would be empty. This ties to ideas about the functionality of rules appearing when there is a "need" for them (Marx 2015b). Yet these also exist in a bath of broader symbols and values. There is some relevance in the contrast between the United States and Europe, with the former more likely to judge based on the technology per se and the latter on more transcendent principles such as the right to personhood in the Council of Europe proclamations.

28. The growth of vocabulary also makes possible more expansive thought.

29. Of course preferences for withholding or offering personal information must themselves be legitimate, something that is culturally relative, changeable, and clearest at the extremes.

30. A related question involves whom information is known to.

31. This frame fits any two-party relations, such as workers and managers or parents and children. In considering information rights and responsibilities for the relevant parties, it looks at the structure of relations and changes over time.

32. Some of these ungrounded claims are aptly described by a fifth-century BC statement, "Since the Temple was destroyed, prophecy has been taken from prophets and given to fools and children." Babylonian Talmud, Tractate Baba Bathra, 12b (http://www.come-and hear.com/bababathra/bababathra_12.html#PARTb), accessed February 26, 2012.

33. Whether *privacy* is the best term to apply to current personal data and new surveillance issues is subject to debate. In an informative exchange in *Surveillance and Society*, Collin Bennett (2011) acknowledges the limitations of the concept but makes a strong case for using *privacy* as a catchall term for a variety of relevant information issues beyond itself (Boyd 2011; Gilliom 2001; Regan 1995; Stalder 2011).

34. One area where there clearly has been an expansion of protection is with respect to the privacy of traditional mail. However, to the extent that communication becomes ever more electronically based, the latter's constancy is less significant in considering the overall picture.

35. Certainly there are many unreconstructed Foucauldians, particularly in the humanities, with little interest in contemporary empirical results or conceptual elaboration. Lots of blooming flowers keep it interesting, and, as they say, "Chacun à son goût." However, the meal would be improved with greater attention to empirical research and equivalent prior ideas developed by Max Weber, Karl Manheim, and Erving Goffman.

36. This recalls a story about a young rural couple who are very excited about taking the train for the first time. They arrive at the station and ask the wizened conductor, "Will the train be on time?" He takes out a schedule, studies it for a long time and says, "That depends." They then ask, "What does it depend on?" He then looks at another schedule, looks up and down the track, pauses in deep thought and finally replies, "Well, that depends too." Any conclusions about more or less or better or worse depend too. It is the scholar's task to indicate what they depend upon.

37. "You don't want to know," a phrase encountered in my earlier research on police, nicely captures one aspect of this.

38. A film by Ricky Gervais (*The Invention of Lying*) offers one approach to the topic.

39. Goffman (1974) unpacks the rarely surfaced normalcy assumptions we make about the prosaics of everyday life. Neyland (2008) and Harper (2008) and offer updates for the surveilled society.

40. Noble (2005) applies Giddens's (1990) concept of *ontological security* to the discomfort experienced by strangers who feel distrusted and do not trust their immediate surroundings. Bauman (1999) suggests that this existential insecurity with its uncertainty and fear go beyond the events of the evening news and characterize modern society more broadly.

41. And what happens when the people know they are not being watched? Note a 1930s comic line, "Do you work here?" "Only if the boss is watching."

42. In contrast to the US, Europe has a comprehensive approach to privacy that involves rules about the collection, use, and storage of personal data by both the private and public sectors. This is based on the European Union's 1995 Data Privacy Directive and the European Court

of Justice. A decision in 2014 gave citizens the right to request that search engines delink results that are inaccurate, irrelevant, or excessive (European Commission 2014).

43. Apart from whether such accounts are true or false or believed by those who offer them, we show respect for those we study by closely listening to their accounts even when they are unsupportable.

44. There is a path, however twisting, changing, and bramble and illusion filled, somewhere between Tennyson's early nineteenth-century optimism, as seen in his poem "Locksley Hall" (Tennyson 1989: "For I dipt into the future, far as human eyes could see, saw the world, and all the wonders that would be"), and Einstein's twentieth-century worry that technological progress can become like an axe in the hand of a pathological criminal (Folsing 1998).

45. This statement is in opposition to the dominant trend at the time to study lower-status and outsider groups such as the poor, minorities, prisoners, and the ill. Here Goffman echoes themes expressed by Mills (1959) and Becker (1963).

46. An example of the latter is seen in research in Sweden suggesting that what the subject eye offers (in the form of iris patterns) is correlated with personality characteristics (Daily Mail 2007). Those with densely packed crypts (threads which radiate from the pupil) were more warmhearted, tender, and trusting, while those with a pattern of contraction furrows were more neurotic, impulsive, and likely to give way to cravings. Iris prints may come to be used not only for identification purposes (access and security), as is the case today, but as a tool for character assessment.

47. In book V of his *Politics* Aristotle (2013), the grandfather of all statements about undemocratic societies, notes that the Persians were the "great master" in the administration of such governments (something that countries here only since 1776 might take note of in negotiating nuclear agreements). His thoughts are at the base of all civil-society advocacy and, although not mentioning material technology, also inform most writing on dystopias. Tyrannical regimes must engage in *prevention* through the creation of atomistic populations, the blocking of private communication, the elimination of borders to visibility, and the sowing of suspicion and discord among their subjects.

The sustainable tyrant "must not allow common meals, clubs, education, and the like; he must be upon his guard against anything which is likely to inspire either courage or confidence among his subjects; he must prohibit literary assemblies or other meetings for discussion, and he must take every means to prevent people from knowing one another (for acquaintance begets mutual confidence). Further, he must compel all persons staying in the city to appear in public and live at his gates; then he will know what they are doing: if they are always kept under, they will learn to be humble. In short, he should practice these and the like Persian and barbaric arts, which all have the same object. A tyrant should also endeavor to know what each of his subjects says or does, and should employ spies, like the 'female detectives' at Syracuse, and the eavesdroppers whom Hiero was in the habit of sending to any place of resort or meeting; for the fear of informers prevents people from speaking their minds, and if they do, they are more easily found out. Another art of the tyrant is to sow quarrels among the citizens; friends should be embroiled with friends, the people with the notables, and the rich with one another."

48. Douglas wrote, "The United States Constitution with its Bill of Rights guarantees to us all the rights to personal and spiritual self-fulfillment. But the guarantee is not self-executing. As nightfall does not come all at once, neither does oppression. In both instances, there is a twilight when everything remains seemingly unchanged. And it is in such twilight that we all must be most aware of change in the air—however slight—lest we become unwitting victims of the darkness" (W. Douglas 1987).

49. Rosen (2004), Landau (2011), Chesterman (2010), Rotenberg, Horwitz, and Scott (2015), Schneir (2015), and Pasquale (2015) are illustrative of books with specific policy and behavioral recommendations.

50. This recalls the story of the acquiescing frog that stayed for dinner after being put into a pot of cold water on a low flame—that gradually came to a boil. But absent a frame of reference, even velocity may not spur awareness. Consider the case of the individual falling out of a two-hundred-story building who, at floor 100, when asked by a spectator "How is it going?" responds "So far so good."

51. Note also the chilling Philip Glass opera based on the story.

Nathaniel Hawthorne (1980) offers a similar morale in his short story "The Birthmark"—first published in 1843. An alchemist seeks to "correct what Nature left imperfect in her fairest work" by ridding his wife of a small blemish. He is certain that "unless all my science have deceived me, it cannot fail." The operation succeeded in removing the blemish, but the patient expired.

A more modern version of the story reflects the victim's (our?) complicity in these "days of miracle and wonder."—In the not-too-distant future three persons are about to be guillotined for unspecified thought crimes revealed by a new noninvasive technology that routinely, inexpensively, and democratically scans everyone for the broadest array of imperfections and future misdeeds. The first person is placed on the block, the rope is cut, but the blade does not fall. This very religious individual, looks up and says, "It's a sign from God," and is released. The second person, a constitutional lawyer, is led to the block and again the blade does not drop. On grounds of equal protection of the law this person is also freed. The third person, an ever-optimistic, American can-do, go-to guy with degrees in engineering and business, looks up at the problematic blade and says, "Hey, wait a minute, I think I can fix that." Such a response was not permitted Mary Queen of Scots when the executioner's axe missed her neck the first time (Fraser 1993).

Appendix

1. Reflections on these tensions have been an enduring interest (Marx 1972, 1984, 1995a, 1997, and 2002). Related tensions and the search for balance between individual rights and the common good under changing social and technical conditions have been central to the work of another 1960s-Berkeley-trained sociologist, Amitai Etzioni (2015).

2. Though here it is well to note that the idea of a "problem" presupposes a definition. Managers and workers, insurance companies and potential customers, and those within and beyond gated communities will often define this differently. For those subject to contested surveillance, the problem may be defined as the surveillance technology rather than the problem it is said to be directed against. Yet there are also areas of common good and overlapping definitions.

3. Teddy Roosevelt's enduring words (see http://www.theodore-roosevelt) should be ever in the awareness of those with the responsibility and leisure to pontificate: "It is not the critic who counts, nor the man who points how the strong man stumbled or where the doer of deeds could have done them better. The credit belongs to the man who is actually in the arena; whose face is marred by dust and sweat and blood; who strives valiantly . . . who knows the great enthusiasms, the great devotions, and spends himself in a worthy cause; who, at best, knows the triumph of high achievement; and who, at the worst, if he fails, at least fails while daring greatly, so that his place shall never be with those cold and timid souls who know neither victory nor defeat."

4. That qualifier is an acknowledgment of the limitations on fully knowing our intentions. It contrasts with the prevarication reflected in Richard Nixon's prefacing his answers to questions about Watergate by saying, "To the best of my knowledge and belief."

References

Books and Journal Articles

Abrahamsen, R., and M. Williams. "Privatisation, Globalisation, and the Politics of Protection in South Africa." In *Policing the Globe: Criminalization and Crime Control in International Relations*, edited by J. Huysmans. New York: Oxford University Press, 2006.

Ackerman, Diane. *A Natural History of the Senses*. New York: Random House, 1990.

Acquisti, Alessandro, Laura Brandimarte, and George Lowenstein. "Privacy and Human Behavior in the Age of Information." *Science* 30 (January 2015).

Agamben, Giorgio. *State of Exception*. Chicago: University of Chicago Press, 2005.

Agassi, Andre. *Open: An Autobiography*. New York: Knopf, 2009.

Aiello, John R., and Yang Shao. "Electronic Performance Monitoring and Stress: The Role of Feedback and Goal Setting." In *Human-Computer Interaction: Applications and Case Studies*, edited by Gavriel Salvendy and Michael J. Smith, 1011–1016. Amsterdam: Elsevier Science Publishers, 1993.

Albrecht, Kathy, and Liz McIntyre. *The Spychips Threat: Why Christians Should Resist RFID and Electronic Surveillance*. Nashville:Thomas Nelson, 2006.

Alder, Ken. *The Lie Detectors: The History of an American Obsession*. New York: Simon and Schuster, 2007.

Alderman, Ellen, and Caroline Kennedy. *The Right to Privacy*. New York: Knopf, 1995.

Alexander, Jeffrey C., Gary T. Marx, and Christine L. Williams. *Self, Social Structure, and Beliefs: Explorations in Sociology*. Berkeley: University of California Press, 2004.

Allen, Anita L. *Why Privacy Isn't Everything: Feminist Reflections on Personal Accountability*. New York: Rowman and Littlefield, 2003.

———. *Privacy Law and Society*. Minneapolis: West Publishing, 2007.

Altheide, David. *Creating Fear: News and the Construction of Crisis*. Hawthorne, NY: Aldine de Gruyter, 2002.

———. *Terrorism and the Politics of Fear*. Lanham, MD: AltaMira Press, 2006.

Aly, Gotz, and Karl Heinz Roth. *The Nazi Census Identification and Control in the Third Reich*. Philadelphia: Temple University Press.

Andreas, Peter, and Ethan Nadelmann. *Policing the Globe: Criminalization and Crime Control in International Relations*. Oxford: Oxford University Press. 2006.

Andrejevic, Mark. *iSpy: Surveillance and Power in the Interactive Era.* Lawrence: University of Kansas Press, 2007.

Aristotle. *Politics: A Treatise on Government.* Translated by Williams Ellis. London: J. M. Dent and Sons, 2013.

Ash, Timothy. *The File: A Personal History.* New York: Random House, 1997.

Bacon, Francis. *The Works of Francis Bacon.* Edited by James Spedding. Cambridge: Cambridge University Press, 2011.

Ball, Kirstie. "Organization, Surveillance and the Body: Toward a Politics of Resistance." *Organization* 12, no. 1 (2005): 89–108.

———. "Workplace Surveillance: An Overview." *Labor Studies* 51, no. 1 (2010).

Ball, Kirstie, Kevin Haggerty, and David Lyon, eds. *Routledge Handbook of Surveillance Studies.* London: Routledge, 2012.

Ball, Kirstie, and L. Snider. *The Surveillance-Industrial Complex.* Oxon, UK: Routledge, 2013.

Ball, Kirstie, and Frank Webster, eds. *The Intensification of Surveillance: Crime, Terrorism and Warfare in the Information Era.* London: Pluto Press, 2003.

Baluja, Shumeet. *The Silicon Jungle: A Novel of Deception, Power, and Internet Intrigue.* Princeton, NJ: Princeton University Press, 2011.

Balzacq, Thierry. "The Three Faces of Securitization: Political Agency, Audience and Context." *European Journal of International Relations* 11, no. 2 (2005): 171–201.

Bart, Peter. *Infamous Players: A Tale of Movies, the Mob (and Sex).* New York: Weinstein Books, 2011.

Barth, Alan. *The Loyalty of Free Men.* New York: Viking Press, 1951.

Baudrillard, Jean. *Simulacra and Simulation.* Ann Arbor: University of Michigan Press, 1994.

Bauman, Zygmunt. *Liquid Modernity.* London: Polity Press, 2000.

———. "Modernity and Ambivalence." In *Global Culture,* edited by M. Featherstone. London: Sage, 1990.

Beck, Ulrich. *Risk Society: Towards a New Modernity.* New Delhi: Sage Publications, 1992.

Becker, Howard. *The Outsiders.* New York: Free Press, 1963.

Beckett, Katherine, and Stever Herbert. *Banished: The New Social Control in Urban America.* New York: Oxford University Press, 2009.

Bell, David. "Surveillance Is Sexy." *Surveillance and Society* 6, no. 3 (2009): 203–212.

Bell, Wendell. *Foundations of Futures Studies: History, Purposes, and Knowledge.* Vol. 1. New Brunswick, NJ: Transaction Publishers, 1997.

Beniger, James R. *The Control Revolution: Technological and Economic Origins of the Information Society.* Cambridge, MA: Harvard University Press, 1986.

Bennett, Colin J. *Implementing Privacy Codes of Practice: A Report to the Canadian Standards Association.* Rexdale, Canada: CSA, 1995.

———. *The Privacy Advocates: Resisting the Spread of Surveillance.* Cambridge, MA: MIT Press, 2008.

———. "In Defense of Privacy: The Concept and the Regime." *Surveillance and Society* 8, no. 4 (2011): 485–496.

Bennett, C. J., and K. D. Haggerty. *Security Games: Surveillance and Control at Mega-events.* Oxon: Routledge, 2011.

Bennett, Colin J., and Charles D. Raab. *The Governance of Privacy: Policy Instruments in Global Perspective.* Burlington, VT: Ashgate Publishing, 2006.

Bennett, Colin J., and Priscilla M. Regan. "Editorial: Surveillance and Mobilities." *Surveillance and Society* 1, no. 4 (2003): 449–455.

Bentham, Jeremy. *The Works of Jeremy Bentham*. Edited by John Bowring. Vol. 4. 11 vols. Edinburgh: William Tait, 1838–1843.

———. *The Panopticon Writings*. Edited by Miran Bozovic. London: Verso, 1995.

Berger, John. *Ways of Seeing*. London: Penguin Books, 1972.

Berry, Wendell. *Farming: A Hand Book*. New York: Harcourt Brace, 1971.

Best, Joel. *Random Violence: How We Talk about New Crimes and New Victims*. Berkeley: University of California Press, 1999.

Bigo, Diedre. "La Mondialisation de l'(in)securitie? Reflections sur le champ des professionals de la gestion des inquietudes et analytique de la transnationalisation des processus d'(in) securisation." *Cultures & Conflicts* no. 58 (2005): 53–100.

———. "Globalized (In)Security: The Field and the Ban-Opticon." In *Translation, Biopolitics, Colonial Differences*, edited by Naoki Sakai and John Solomon, 109–156. Hong Kong: Hong Kong University Press, 2006a.

———, ed. *Illiberal Practices of Liberal Regimes: The (In)Security Games*. Paris: l'Harmattan, 2006b.

Bigo, Diedre, and A. Tsoukala, eds. *Terror, Insecurity and Liberty: Illiberal Practices of Liberal Regimes*. London: Routledge, 2008.

Bijker, Wiebe E., Thomas P. Hughes, and Trevor Pinch, eds. *The Social Construction of Technological Systems: New Directions in the Sociology and History of Technology*. London: MIT Press, 1987.

Black, Edwin. *IBM and the Holocaust*. Crown Books, 2004.

Blalock, Garrick, Vrinda Kadiyali, and Daniel Simon. "The Impact of Post 9/11 Airport Security Measures on the Demand for Air Travel." *Journal of Law and Economics* (November 2007).

Blomberg, Tom. "Criminal Justice Reform and Social Control: Are We Becoming a Minimum Security Society?" In *Transcarceration: Essays in the Sociology of Social Control*, edited by J. Lowman, R. J. Menzies, and T. S. Palys. Surrey: Gower, 1987.

Bloom, Amy. *Normal: Transsexual CEOS, Crossdressing Cops, and Hermaphrodites with Attitude*. New York: Random House, 2003.

Blumer, Herbert. "Collective Behavior." In *New Outline of the Principles of Sociology*, edited by A. M. Lee, 166–222. New York: Barnes and Noble, 1957.

Boersma, Kees, Rosamunde Van Brakel, Chiara Fonio, and Pieter Wagenaar. *Histories of State Surveillance in Europe and Beyond*. London: Routledge. 2014.

Bogard, William. *The Simulation of Surveillance: Hyper Control in Telematic Societies*. Cambridge: Cambridge University Press, 1996.

Bok, Sissela. *Lying: Moral Choice in Private and Public Life*. New York: Pantheon Books, 1978.

Bonditti, Phillipe. "From Territorial Space to Networks: A Foucaldian Approach to the Implementation of Biometry." *Alternatives* 29 (2004): 465–482.

Bourdieu, Pierre. *Distinction*. Translated by Richard Nice. Cambridge, MA: Harvard University Press, 1984.

Boyd, Danah. *It's Complicated: The Social Lives of Networked Teens*. New Haven, CT: Yale University Press, 2014.

Boykoff, Jules. *The Suppression of Dissent: How the State and Mass Media Squelch US American Social Movements*. New York: Routledge, 2006.

Boyne, Roy. "Post-panopticism." *Economy and Society*, 2000.

Braverman, Harry. *Labor and Monopoly Capital*. New York: Monthly Review, 1974.

Braverman, Irus. "Governing with Clean Hands: Automated Public Toilets and Sanitary Surveillance." *Surveillance and Society* 8, no. 1 (2010): 1–27.

Breckenridge, Keith. "The Elusive Panopticon: The HANNIS Projectee and the Politics of Standards in South Africa." In *Playing the ID Card*, edited by Colin Bennett and David Lyon. London: Routledge, 2008.

Brin, David. *The Transparent Society: Will Technology Force Us to Choose between Privacy and Freedom?* Cambridge, MA: Perseus Book Group, 1998.

Brodeur, Jean-Paul, and Stephane Leman-Langlois. "Surveillance Fiction or Higher Policing?" In *The New Politics of Surveillance and Visibility*, edited by Kevin D. Haggerty and Richard V. Ericson. Toronto: University of Toronto Press, 2006.

Brown, Ian. "Social Media Surveillance." In *The International Encyclopedia of Communication and Society*. New York: John Wiley, 2014.

Brown, Simone. "'Everybody's Got a Little Light under the Sun': Black Luminosity and the Visual Culture of Surveillance." *Cultural Studies* 26, no. 4 (2012): 542–564.

———. *Dark Matters: On the Surveillance of Blackness*. Durham, NC: Duke University Press, 2015.

Budiansky, Stephen. *Her Majesty's Spymaster: Elizabeth I, Sir Francis Walsingham, and the Birth of Modern Espionage*. New York: Penguin, 2006.

Burawoy, Michael. *Manufacturing Consent: Changes in the Labor Process under Monopoly Capitalism*. Chicago: University of Chicago Press, 1979.

Burke, Kenneth. *A Grammar of Motives*. Berkeley: University of California Press, 1969.

Burnham, David. *The Rise of the Computer State*. New York: Random House, 1983.

Byrne, James, and Gary T. Marx. "Technological Innovations in Crime Prevention and Policing: A Review of the Research on Implementation and Impact." *Cahiers Politiestudies* 20, no. 3 (2011): 17–40.

Byrne, James, and Donald Rebovich. *The New Technology of Crime, Law and Social Control*. Monsey, NY: Criminal Justice Press. 2007.

Calo, R. "Digital Market Manipulation." *George Washington Law Review* 82 (2014).

Caplan, Jane, and John C. Torpey. *Documenting Individual Identity*. Princeton, NJ: Princeton University Press, 2001.

Carr, Nicholas. *Automation and Us*. New York: Norton, 2014.

Cate, Fred H. *Safeguarding Privacy in the Fight against Terrorism*. Washington, DC: Department of Defense, 2004.

Ceyhan, Ayse. "Surveillance and Biopower." In *Routledge Handbook of Surveillance Studies*, edited by Kirstie Ball, Kevin Haggerty, and David Lyon. London: Routledge, 2012.

Chaiken, A. L., V. J. Derlega, and S. J. Miller. "Effects of Room Environment on Self-disclosure in a Counseling Analogue." *Journal of Counseling Psychology* 23 (1976).

Chapin, Aaron B. "Arresting DNA: Privacy Expectations of Free Citizens versus Post-convicted Persons and the Unconstitutionality of DNA Dragnets." *Minnesota Law Review* 89 (2004): 1842.

Chesterman, Simon. *One Nation under Surveillance: A New Social Contract to Defend Freedom without Sacrificing Liberty*. New York: Oxford University Press, 2010.

Citron, Danielle. *Hate Crimes in Cyberspace*. Cambridge, MA: Harvard University Press, 2014.

Clarke, Roger. "Information Technology and Dataveillance." *Communications of the ACM* 31, no. 5 (1988): 498–512.

———. "The Digital Persona and Its Application to Data Surveillance." *Information Society* 10, no. 2 (1994): 77–92.

Classen, Constance. *Worlds of Sense: Exploring the Senses in History and across Cultures*. London: Routledge Publishing, 1993.

Clavell, G., and P. Ouziel. "Spain's *document nacional de identidad*: An e-ID for the Twenty-First Century with a Controversial Past." In *Histories of State Surveillance in Europe and Beyond*, edited by K. Boersma, R.Van Brakel, C. Fonio, and P. Wagenaar. New York: Routledge, 2014.

Cohen, Julie E. *Configuring the Networked Self: Law, Code, and the Play of Everyday Practice.* New Haven, CT: Yale University Press, 2012.

Cohen, Mickey, and John P. Nugent. *Mickey Cohen, in My Own Words: The Underworld Autobiography of Michael Mickey Cohen, as Told to John Peer Nugent.* Englewood Cliffs, NJ: Prentice Hall, 1975.

Cohen, Stanley. *Visions of Social Control.* Cambridge: Polity Press, 1985.

Cole, Simon A. *Suspect Identities: A History of Fingerprinting and Criminal Identification.* Cambridge, MA: Harvard University Press, 2001.

Cole, Simon A., and Henry N. Pontell. "'Don't Be Low Hanging Fruit': Identity Theft as Moral Panic." In *Surveillance and Security: Technology Politics and Power in Everyday Life*, edited by Torin Monahan, 125–147. New York: Routledge, 2006.

Coll, Sami. "The Social Dynamics of Secrecy: Rethinking Information and Privacy through Georg Simmel." *International Review of Information Ethics* 17 (July 2012).

Conrad, Frederick G., and Michael F. Schober, eds. *Envisioning the Survey of the Future.* Hoboken, NJ: John Wiley and Sons, 2008.

Corbett, Ronald, and Gary T. Marx. "Critique: No Soul in the New Machine: Technofallacies in the Electronic Monitoring Movement." *Justice Quarterly* 8, no. 3 (1991): 399–414.

Coser, Lewis. *Functions of Social Conflict.* Glencoe, IL: Free Press, 1956.

Crowe, Timothy D. *Crime Prevention through Environmental Design Applications of Architectural Design and Space and Management.* Boston: Butterworth-Heninemann, 2000.

Culligan, Joseph. *When in Doubt, Check Him Out: A Woman's Survival Guide.* Miami, FL: Hallmark, 1993.

Cunningham, David. *There's Something Happening Here: The New Left, the Klan, and FBI Counterintelligence.* Berkeley: University of California Press, 2004.

Curry, Michael R., David J. Phillips, and Priscilla M. Regan. "Emergency Response Systems and the Creeping Legibility of People and Places." *Information Society* 20, no. 5 (2004): 357–369.

Dahl, Johanne Yttri, and Ann Rudinow Sætnan. "'It All Happened So Slowly': On Controlling Function Creep in Forensic DNA Databases." *International Journal of Law, Crime and Justice* 37, no. 3 (2009): 83–103.

Dalton, Melville. *Men Who Manage.* New York: John Wiley and Sons, 1959.

Dandeker, Christopher. *Surveillance, Power, and Modernity: Bureaucracy and Discipline from 1700 to the Present Day.* Cambridge: Polity Press, 1990.

Davenport, Christian, Hank Johnston, and Carol M. Mueller, eds. *Repression and Mobilization.* Minneapolis: University of Minnesota Press, 2005.

Davis, Andrew. "Do Children Have Privacy Rights in the Classroom?" *Studies in Philosophy and Education* 20, no. 3 (2001): 245–254.

Davis, Mike. *City of Quartz: Excavating the Future of Los Angeles.* London: Verso, 1990.

Davis, Murray. *What's So Funny? The Comic Conception of Culture and Society.* Chicago: University of Chicago Press, 1993.

Decew, Judith W. *In Pursuit of Privacy: Law, Ethics, and the Rise of Technology.* Ithaca, NY: Cornell University Press, 1997.

Deflem, Mathieu. *Policing World Society.* York: Oxford University Press, 2002.

364 REFERENCES

DeLanda, Manuel. *A New Philosophy of Society: Assemblage Theory and Social Complexity*. London: Bloomsbury Academic, 2006.

Deleuze, Gilles. "Postscript on the Societies of Control." *October* 59 (1992): 3–7.

Denzin, Norman K. *The Cinematic Society: The Voyeur's Gaze*. Thousand Oaks, CA: Sage Publishers, 1995.

Derber, Charles. *The Pursuit of Attention: Power and Ego in Everyday Life*. New York: Oxford University Press, 2000.

De Sola Pool, Ithiel. *Technologies of Freedom*. Cambridge: Harvard University Press, 1983.

Dillon, Michael. "Virtual Security: A Life Science of (Dis)order." *Millennium: Journal of International Studies* 32, no. 3 (2003): 531–558.

DiTecco, D., G. Cwitco, A. Arsenault, and M. Andre. "Operator Stress and Monitoring Practices." *Applied Ergonomics* 23, no. 1 (1992): 29–34.

Dollard, John. *Caste and Class in a Southern Town*. 3rd ed. Garden City, NY: Doubleday and Co., 1957.

Douglas, John E. *Crime Classification Manual: A Standard System for Investigating and Classifying Violent Crimes*. Lanham, MD: Lexington Books, 1992.

Douglas, William O. *The Douglas Letters: Selections from the Private Papers of Justice William O. Douglas*. Edited by Melvin I. Urofsky and Philip E. Urofsky. Chevy Chase, MD: Adler and Adler, 1987.

Doyle, Aaron. *Arresting Images: Crime and Policing in Front of the Television Camera*. Toronto: University of Toronto Press, 2003.

Dubrofsky, Rachel, and Shoshana Magnet. *Feminist Surveillance Studies*. Durham: Duke University Press. 2015.

Duhigg, C. "How Companies Learn Your Secrets." *New York Times Magazine*, February16, 2012.

Dumcius, Gintautas. "Casinos to Offer Gamblers Voluntary Bet Limits." *Commonwealth Magazine*, December 4, 2014.

Dupont, Benoit. "Hacking the Panopticon: Distributed Online Surveillance and Resistance." *Sociology of Crime Law and Deviance* 10 (2008): 259–280.

Earl, Jennifer. "Political Repression: Iron Fists, Velvet Gloves, and Diffuse Control." *Annual Review of Sociology* 37 (2011): 261–284.

Edgley, Charles, and Dennis Brissett. *A Nation of Meddlers*. Boulder, CO: Westview Press, 1999.

Eglash, Ron. "Appropriating Technology: An Introduction." In *Appropriating Technology: Vernacular Science and Social Power*, edited by Ron Eglash, Jennifer L. Croissant, Giovanna Di Chiro, and Rayvon Fouche, vii–xxi. Minneapolis: University of Minnesota Press, 2004.

Ekman, Paul. *Telling Lies: Clues to Deceit in the Marketplace, Marriage, and Politics*. New York: Norton, 1985.

Ellul, Jacques. *The Technological Society*. New York: Vintage Books, 1964.

Elmer, Greg. "Panopticon—Discipline—Control." In *Routledge Handbook of Surveillance Studies*, edited by Kirstie Ball, Kevin Haggerty, and David Lyon. London: Routledge, 2012.

Elster, Jon, ed. *Retribution and Reparation in the Transition to Democracy*. Cambridge: Cambridge University Press, 2006.

Emerson, Robert M., Kerry O. Ferris, and Carol B. Gardner. "On Being Stalked." *Social Problems* 45, no. 3 (1998): 289–314.

Etzioni, Amitai. *The Limits of Privacy*. New York: Basic Books, 1999.

———. *Privacy in a Cyber Age: Policy and Practice*. New York: Palgrave Macmillan, 2015.

Ewick, Patricia, and Susan S. Sibley. *The Common Place of Law-Stories from Everyday Life*. Chicago: University of Chicago Press, 1998.

Fairchild, Amy L., Roland Bayer, James K. Colgrove, and Daniel Wolfe. *Searching Eyes*. Berkeley: University of California Press, 2007.

Farrell, John. *Paranoia and Modernism: From Cervantes to Rousseau*. Ithaca, NY: Cornell University Press, 2006.

Feeley, Malcolm M., and Jonathan Simon. "The New Penology: Notes on the Emerging Strategy of Corrections and Its Implications." *Criminology* 30, no. 4 (1992): 449–474.

Fernandez, Luis A. *Policing Dissent*. New Brunswick, NJ: Rutgers University Press, 2008.

Ferree, Myra Marx. "Soft Repression: Ridicule, Stigma, and Silencing in Gender-Based Movements." In *Authority in Contention: Research in Social Movements, Conflicts, and Change*, vol. 25, edited by Daniel J. Myers and Daniel M. Cress, 85–101. West Yorkshire, UK: Emerald Group Publishing Limited, 2004.

Ferrell, Jeff. *Crimes of Style: Urban Graffiti and the Politics of Criminality*. Boston: Northeastern University Press, 1996.

Figes, Orlando. *The Whisperers: Private Life in Stalin's Russia*. New York: Picador, 2006.

Fijnaut, Cyrille, and Gary Marx. *Undercover Police Surveillance in Comparative Perspective*. Norwell, MA: Kluwer, 1995.

Fischer, Claude S. *America Calling: A Social History of the Telephone to 1940*. Berkeley: University of California Press, 1992.

Fitzgerald, F. Scott. "The Crack-Up." *Esquire*, February 1936.

Fogelson, Robert M. *Big-City Police*. Cambridge, MA: Harvard University Press, 1977.

Folsing, Albrecht. *Albert Einstein: A Biography*. New York: Penguin Books, 1998.

Fonio, Chiara, and Stefano Agnoletto. "Controversial Legacies in Post-Fasist Italy." In *Histories of State Surveillance in Europe and Beyond*, edited by K. Boersma, R.Van Brakel, C. Fonio, and P. Wagenaar. New York: Routledge, 2014.

Forster, Edward M. *Howards End*. New York: Vintage Books, 1961.

Foucault, Michel. *Discipline and Punish: The Birth of the Prison*. New York: Pantheon Books, 1977.

———. *The History of Sexuality*. Vol. 1, *The Will to Knowledge*. London: Penguin, 1998.

Fussey, P., and J. Coaffe. "Olympic Rings of Steel: Constructing Security for 2012 and Beyond." In *Security Games: Surveillance and Control at Mega-events*, edited by C. J. Bennett and K. D. Haggerty. Oxon: Routledge, 2011.

Fraser, Antonia. *Mary Queen of Scots*. New York: Random House, 1993.

Frost, Robert. *North of Boston*. New York: Henry Holt and Co., 1915.

Fuchs, Christian. *Internet and Society: Social Theory in the Information Age*. New York: Routledge, 2008.

Fuchs, Christian, and Daniel Trottier. "Towards a Theoretical Model of Social Media Surveillance in Contemporary Society." *Communications* 40, no. 1 (2015): 113–135.

Fuller, Lon L. "The Case of the Speluncean Explorers." *Harvard Law Review* 62, no. 4 (1949): 616–645.

Funder, Anna. *Stasiland: Stories from behind the Berlin Wall*. London: Granta Books, 2004.

Gabriel, Yiannis. "Beyond Happy Families: A Critical Reevaluation of the Control-Resistance-Identity Triangle." *Human Relations* 52, no. 2 (1999): 179–203.

———. "The Glass Cage: Flexible Work, Fragmented Consumption, Fragile Selves." In *Self, Social Structure and Beliefs*, edited by J. C. Alexander, G. T. Marx, and C. L. Williams. Berkeley: University of California Press, 2004.

Gandy, Oscar H. *The Panoptic Sort: A Political Economy of Personal Information*. Boulder, CO: Westview Press, 1993.

———. "Public Opinion Surveys and the Formation of Privacy Policy." *Journal of Social Issues* 59, no. 1 (2003): 283–299.

Garfinkel, Harold. *Studies in Ethnomethodology.* Englewood Cliffs, NJ: Prentice Hall, 1967.

Garfinkel, Simson. *Database Nation.* Sebastopol, CA: O'Reilly, 2000.

Garrow, David J. *Bearing the Cross: Martin Luther King, Jr., and the Southern Christian Leadership Conference.* New York: William Morrow and Co., 1986.

Gibson, James W. *The Perfect War.* New York: Knopf, 1982.

Giddens, Anthony. *The Consequences of Modernity.* Cambridge: Polity Press, 1990.

Gillham, Patrick F., and John A. Noakes. "'More Than a March in a Circle': Transgressive Protests and the Limits of Negotiated Management." *Mobilization* 12, no. 4 (2007): 341–357.

Gilliom, John. *Overseers of the Poor: Surveillance, Resistance, and the Limits of Privacy.* Chicago: University of Chicago Press, 2001.

Gimbutas, Marija. *The Goddesses and Gods of Old Europe.* Berkeley: University of California Press, 1982.

Glassner, Barry. *The Culture of Fear: Why Americans Are Afraid of the Wrong Things.* New York: Basic Books, 1999.

Goffman, Erving. "Embarrassment and Social Organization." *American Journal of Sociology* 62, no. 3 (1956a): 264–271.

———. *The Presentation of Self in Everyday Life.* New York: Doubleday, 1956b.

———. *Asylums: Essays in the Social Situation of Mental Patients and Other Inmates.* Garden City, NY: Anchor Books, 1961a.

———. *Encounters.* Indianapolis: Bobbs-Merrill Co., 1961b.

———. *Stigma: Notes on the Management of Spoiled Identity.* Englewood Cliffs, NJ: Prentice Hall, 1963.

———. *Behavior in Public Places: Notes on the Social Organization of Gatherings.* New York: Free Press, 1966.

———. *Strategic Interaction.* Philadelphia: University of Pennsylvania Press, 1969.

———. *Relations in Public.* New York: Basic Books, 1971.

———. *Frame Analysis: An Essay on the Organization of Experience.* Cambridge, MA: Harvard University Press, 1974.

———. *Gender Advertisements.* Cambridge, MA: Harvard University Press, 1979.

———. "Program Committee Encourages Papers on Range of Methodologies." *Footnotes.* American Sociological Association, 1981.

———. "The Interaction Order: American Sociological Association, 1982 Presidential Address." *American Sociological Review* 48, no. 1 (1983): 1–17.

Goldstein, Jeffrey, David Buckingham, and Gilles Brougère. "Introduction: Toys, Games, and Media." In *Toys, Games, and Media,* edited by Jeffrey Goldstein, David Buckingham, and Gilles Brougere, 1–10. London: Lawrence Erlbaum Associates, 2004.

Grabosky, Peter N. "Unintended Consequences of Crime Prevention." In *Crime Prevention Studies,* vol. 5, edited by Ross Homel, 25–56. Monsey, NY: Criminal Justice Press, 1996.

Graham, Steve. *Cities Under Siege: The New Military Urbanism.* London: Verso, 2010.

Graham, Steve, and Simon Marvin. *Telecommunications and the City: Electronic Space, Urban Places.* London: Routledge, 1996.

Gramsci, Antonio. *The Antonio Gramsci Reader.* Edited by David Forgacs. London: Lawrence and Wishart, 2000.

Grand, Jeffrey S. "The Blooding of America: Privacy and the DNA Dragnet." *Cardozo Law Review* 23 (2001): 2277–2368.

Gray, Eliza. "How High Is Your XQ?" *Time*, June 22, 2015.

Greenberg, Ivan. *The Dangers of Dissent: The FBI and Civil Liberties since 1965.* Lanham, MD: Lexington Books, 2010.

———. *Surveillance in America: Critical Analysis of the FBI, 1920 to the Present.* New York: Lexington Books, 2012.

Greene, Graham. *A Sort of Life.* New York: Simon and Schuster, 1971.

Greenfield, Adam. *Everyware: The Dawning Age of Ubiquitous Computing.* Berkeley: New Riders, 2006.

Grenville, Andrew. "Shunning Surveillance or Welcoming the Watcher? Exploring How People Traverse the Path of Resistence." In *Privacy, Surveillance, and the Globalization of Personal Information: International Comparisons*, edited by Elia Zureik, Lynda H. Stalker, and Emily Smith, 70–86. Montreal: McGill-Queen's University Press, 2010.

Grimes, Sara M., and Leslie R. Shade. "Neopian Economics of Play: Children's Cyberpets and Online Communities as Immersive Advertising in Neopets.com." *International Journal of Media and Culture Politics* 1, no. 2 (2005): 181–198.

Groebner, Valentin, Mark Kyburz, and John Peck. *Who Are You? Identification, Deception, and Surveillance in Early Modern Europe.* New York: Zone Books, 2007.

Gurak, Laura J. *Persuasion and Privacy in Cyberspace: The Online Protests over Lotus Marketplace and the Clipper Chip.* New Haven, CT: Yale University Press, 1997.

Gurstein, Rochelle. *Repeal of Reticence.* New York: Hill and Wang, 1996.

Gusfield, Joseph R. *The Culture of Public Problems: Drinking-Driving and the Symbolic Order.* Chicago: University of Chicago Press, 1984.

Guzik, Keith. *Making Things Stick: Surveillance Technologies and Mexico's War on Crime.* Berkeley: University of California Press, 2016.

Haggerty, Kevin D., and Richard V. Ericson. "The Surveillant Assemblage." *British Journal of Sociology* 51, no. 4 (2000): 605–622.

———, eds. *The New Politics of Surveillance and Visibility.* Toronto: University of Toronto Press, 2006.

Hancock, Jeff. "Honesty and Lying in Different Communication Media." In *Envisioning the Survey Interview of the Future*, edited by Frederick G. Conrad and Michael F. Schober, 179–194. Hoboken, NJ: John Wiley and Sons, 2008.

Handler, Joel F. "Postmodernism, Protest, and the New Social Movements." *Law and Society Review* 26, no. 4 (1992): 697–731.

Harcourt, Bernard. *Against Prediction.* Chicago: University of Chicago Press, 2007.

Hardt, Michael, and Antonio Negri. *Information Empire.* Cambridge: Harvard University Press, 2000.

Harper, David. "The Complicity of Psychology in the Security State." In *Just War Psychology: Terrorism and Iraq*, edited by R. Roberts. Ross-on-Rye, UK: PCCS Books, 2007.

———. "The Politics of Paranoia: Paranoid Positioning and Conspiratorial Narratives in the Surveillance Society." *Surveillance and Society* 5, no. 1 (2008): 1–32.

Harris, Shane. *The Watchers: The Rise of America's Surveillance State.* New York: Penguin, 2010.

Hawthorne, Nathaniel. "The Birthmark." In *The Celestial Railroad and Other Stories*, edited by R. P. Blackmur, 203–220. New York: New American Library, 1980.

Hayden, F. S. *Military Ballooning during the Early Civil War.* Baltimore: Johns Hopkins University Press, 2000.

Hertzel, Dorothy A. "Don't Talk to Strangers: An Analysis of Government and Industry Efforts to Protect a Child's Privacy Online." *Federal Communications Law Journal* 52, no. 2 (2000): 429–451.

Heymann, Philip B. *Terrorism, Freedom, and Security: Winning without War*. Cambridge, MA: MIT Press, 2003.

Hildebrandt, Mireille. "Properties, Property and Appropriateness of Information." In *Freedom and Property of Information: The Philosophy of Law Meets the Philosophy of Technology*, edited by M. Hildebrandt and B. van den Berg. Routledge, 2015.

Hildebrandt, M., and B. van den Berg. *Freedom and Property of Information: The Philosophy of Law Meets the Philosophy of Technology*. Routledge, 2015.

Hilgartner, Stephen, Richard C. Bell, and Rory O'Connor. *Nukespeak: Nuclear Language, Visions, and Mindset*. San Francisco: Sierra Club Books, 1982.

Hill, Kashmir. "How Target Figured Out a Young Girl Was Pregnant before Her Father Did." *Forbes*, February 16, 2012.

Hoffman, Abbie, and Jonathan Silvers. *Steal This Urine Test: Fighting Drug Hysteria in America*. New York: Penguin Books, 1987.

Hofstader, Richard. *The Paranoid Style in American Politics: And Other Essays*. New York: Knopf Publishers, 1965.

Hoogenboom, R. *The Governance of Policing and Security: Ironies, Myths and Paradoxes*. Palgrave MacMillan, 2010.

Horne, Christine, Brice Darras, Elyse Bean, Anurag Srivastava, and Scott Frickel. "Privacy, Technology, and Norms: The Case of Smart Meters." *Social Science Research* 51 (2015): 64–76.

Horowitz, Alexandra. *Inside of a Dog*. New York: Scribner, 2009.

Horowitz, Irving Louis. *Project Camelot*. New Brunswick: Transaction, 1967.

Hosein, Gus. "On Just Surveillance." *Surveillance and Society* 12, no. 1 (2014): 154–157.

Howard, R. *Brave New Workplace*. New York: Viking, 1985.

Howes, David, ed. *The Varieties of Sensory Experience: A Sourcebook in the Anthropology of the Senses*. Toronto: University of Toronto Press, 1991.

Huey, Laura. "Subverting Surveillance Systems: Access to Information Mechanisms as Tools of Counter Surveillance." In *Surveillance: Power, Problems, and Politics*, 219–243. Vancouver, BC: UBC Press, 2009.

———. "Problem with Ethics: Difficulties in Constructing Normative Frameworks." *Surveillance and Society* 12, no. 1 (2014): 140–141.

Hughes, Everett C. "Good People and Dirty Work." *Social Problems* 10, no. 1 (1962): 3–11.

Huxley, Aldous. *Letters of Aldous Huxley*. Edited by Grover S. Huxley. New York: Harper and Row, 1969.

———. *"Brave New World" and "Brave New World Revisited."* New York: Harper Perennial, 2004.

Ifa, Demian R., Nicholas E. Manicke, Allison L. Dill, and R. Graham Cooks. "Latent Fingerprint Chemical Imaging by Mass Spectrometry." *Science* 321, no. 5890 (2008): 805.

Institute for Applied Autonomy. "Defensive Surveillance: Lessons from the Republican National Convention." In *Surveillance and Security: Technological Politics and Power in Everyday Life*, edited by Torin Monahan, 167–176. New York: Routledge, 2006.

Introna, Lucas D., and Amy Gibbons. "Networks and Resistance: Investigating Online Advocacy Networks as a Modality for Resisting State Surveillance." *Surveillance and Society* 6, no. 3 (2009): 233–258.

James, William. *The Principles of Psychology*. New York: Dover Books, 1950.

Jay, Martin. *Downcast Eyes: The Denigration of Vision in Twentieth-Century French Thought*. Berkeley: University of California Press, 1993.

Jeffery, Clarence R. *Crime Prevention through Environmental Design*. Beverly Hills, CA: Sage Publications, 1971.

Joh, Elizabeth E. "Reclaiming 'Abandoned' DNA: The Fourth Amendment and Genetic Privacy." *Northwestern University Law Review* 100, no. 2 (2006): 857–884.

Johnson, John M. "The Stalking Process." In *Postmodern Existential Sociology*, edited by Joseph A. Kotarba and John M. Johnson, 183–200. Walnut Creek, CA: Altamira Press, 2002.

Johnson, S. (1734). In *Oxford Dictionary of Quotations*. 3rd ed. Oxford: Oxford University Press, 1989.

Jorgensen, Vibeke. "The Apple of the Eye: Parents' Use of Webcams in a Danish Day Nursery." *Surveillance and Society* 2, no. 2/3 (2002): 446–463.

Joskow, Paul. "Creating a Smarter U.S. Electricity Grid." *Journal of Economic Perspectives* 26, no. 1 (2012).

Kafka, Franz. "In the Penal Colony" (1919). In *The Metamorphosis, In the Penal Colony, and Other Stories*, by F. Kafka, W. Muir, and E. Muir. New York: Schocken Books, 1995.

Kahn, David. *The Reader of Gentlemen's Mail: Herbert O. Yardley and the Birth of American Codebreaking*. New Haven, CT: Yale University Press, 2004.

Kammere, Dietmar. "Video Surveillance in Hollywood Movies." *Surveillance and Society* 2, no. 2/3 (2004).

———. "Surveillance in Literature, Film and Television." In *Routledge Handbook of Surveillance Studies*, edited by Kirstie Ball, Kevin Haggerty, and David Lyon. London: Routledge, 2012.

Katz, Cindi. "The State Goes Home: Local Hypervigilance of Children and the Global Retreat from Social Reproduction." In *Surveillance and Security: Technological Politics and Power in Everyday Life*, edited by Torin Monahan, 27–36. New York: Routledge, 2006.

Katz, Jack. "On the Rhetoric and Politics of Ethnographic Methodology." *Annals of the American Academy of Political and Social Science* 595, no. 1 (2004): 280–308.

Katzenstein, Peter, ed. *Culture of National Security: Norms and Identity in World Politics*. New York: Columbia University Press, 1996.

Kazin, Michael. *The Populist Persuasion: An American History*. Ithaca, NY: Cornell University Press, 1998.

Keen, M. *Stalking the Sociological Imagination: J. Edgar Hoover's FBI Surveillance of American Sociology*. Westport, CT: Greenwood Press, 1999.

Kelvin, Peter. "A Social-Psychological Examination of Privacy." *British Journal of Clinical Psychology* 12, no. 3 (1973): 248–261.

Kerr, Ian, Jennifer Barrigar, Jacquelyn Burkell, and Katie Black. "Soft Surveillance, Hard Consent." In *Privacy, Identity, and Anonymity: Lessons from the Identity Trail*, edited by Ian Kerr, Valerie Steeves, and Carole Lucock. Oxford: Oxford University Press, 2009.

Kerr, Margaret, and Hakan Stattin. "What Parents Know, How They Know It, and Several Forms of Adolescent Adjustment: Further Support for a Reinterpretation of Monitoring." *Developmental Psychology* 36, no. 3 (2000): 366–380.

Kiss, Simon J. "Cell Phones and Surveillance: Mobile Technology, States, and Social Movements." In *Surveillance: Power, Problems, and Politics*, edited by Sean P. Hier and Joshua Greenberg, 203–218. Vancouver, BC: UBC Press, 2009.

Klockars, Carl B. "The Dirty Harry Problem." *Annals of the American Academy of Political and Social Science* 452, no. 1 (1980): 33–47.

Koestler, Arthur. *Darkness at Noon*. Vintage, 2010.

Koskela, Hille. "You Shouldn't Wear That Body: The Problematics of Gender and Surveillance."

In *Routledge Handbook of Surveillance Studies*, edited by Kirstie Ball, Kevin Haggerty, and David Lyon. London: Routledge, 2012.

Landau, Susan. *Surveillance or Security: The Risks Posed by New Wiretap Technologies*. Cambridge, MA: MIT Press, 2011.

Lane, Jeffery. "The Digital Street: An Ethnographic Study of Networked Street Life in Harlem." *American Behavioral Scientist*, 60, no. 1 (2016): 43–58.

Larkin, Emma. *Finding George Orwell in Burma*. New York: Penguin Press, 2004.

Larson, Mike, and Justin Piche. "Public Vigilance Campaigns and Participatory Surveillance after 11 September 2001." In *Surveillance: Power, Problems, and Politics*, 187–202. Vancouver, BC: UBC Press, 2009.

Latane, Bibb, and John M. Darley. "Group Inhibition of Bystander Intervention in Emergencies." *Journal of Personality and Social Psychology* 10, no. 3 (1968): 215–221.

Latessa, Edward, Francis T.Cullen, and Paul Gendreau. "Beyond Correctional Quackery." *Federal Probation*, September 2002.

Laudon, Kenneth C. "Data Quality and Due Process in Large Record Systems: Criminal Record Systems." *Communications of the ACM* 29, no. 1 (1986a): 4–11.

———. *The Dossier Society: Value Choices in the Design of National Information Systems*. New York: Columbia University Press, 1986b.

———. "Markets and Privacy." *Communications of the ACM* 39, no. 9 (1996): 92–104.

Lee, Alfred McClung, and Elizabeth Briant Lee. *The Art of Propaganda: A Study of Father Coughlin's Speeches*. New York: Harcourt Brace and Co., 1939.

Lehr, Dick, and Gerard O'Neill. *Black Mass: The Irish Mob, the FBI, and a Devil's Deal*. Oxford: PublicAffairs, 2000.

Leman-Langlois, Stephane. "Policing through the Lens." *Surveillance and Society* (2002).

———. *Technocrime: Technology, Crime, and Social Control*. Devon, UK: Willan Publishing, 2008.

———. *Technocrime: Policing and Surveillance*. New York: Routledge, 2012.

Lemert, Edwin. *Social Pathology*. New York: McGraw-Hill, 1951.

Leo, Richard A. "From Coercion to Deception: The Changing Nature of Police Interrogation in America." *Crime, Law and Social Change* 18, no. 1 (1992).

———. *Police Interrogation and American Justice*. Cambridge, MA: Harvard University Press, 2009.

Leo, Richard A., and Kimberly D. Richman. "Mandate the Electronic Recording of Police Interrogations." *Criminology and Public Policy* 6, no. 4 (2007).

Le Roy Ladurie, Emmanuel. *Montaillou: Promised Land of Error*. New York: George Braziller, 1979.

Lessig, Lawrence. *Code: And Other Laws of Cyberspace*. New York: Perseus Books, 1999.

Li, Katy. "The Private Insurance Industry's Tactics against Suspected Homosexuals: Redlining Based on Occupation, Residence and Marital Status." *American Journal of Law and Medicine* 22, no. 4 (1996): 477–502.

Lianos, Michalis. *Le nouveau controle social: Toile institutionnelle, normativité et lien social*. Paris: Harmattan, 2001.

———. "Social Control after Foucault." *Surveillance and Society* 1, no. 3 (2003): 412–430.

Lilly, R. J., and M. Nellis. "The Limits of Techno-Utopianism." In *Electronically Monitored Punishment: International and Critical Perspectives*, edited by M. Nellis, K. Beyens, and D. Kaminski. 2013.

Lindner, Marc, and Ingrid Nygaard. *Void Where Prohibited: Rest Breaks and the Right to Urinate on Company Time*. Ithaca, NY: Cornell University Press, 1998.

Livingstone, Sonia. *Children and the Internet*. Cambridge: Polity Press, 2009.

Locke, John L. *Eavesdropping: An Intimate History*. London: Oxford University Press, 2011.

Los, Maria. "The Technologies of Total Domination." *Surveillance and Society* 2, no. 1 (2004).

Lowenthal, Leo, and Norbert Guterman. *Prophets of Deceit: A Study of the Techniques of the American Agitator*. New York: Harper, 1949.

Lucas, G. *Anthropologists in Arms: The Ethics of Military Anthropology*. New York: Rowman and Littlefield, 2010.

Lyng, Stephen. "Edgework: A Social Psychological Analysis of Voluntary Risk Taking." *American Journal of Sociology* 95, no. 4 (1990): 851–886.

Lyon, David. *The Electronic Eye: The Rise of the Surveillance Society*. Cambridge: Polity Press, 1994.

———. *Surveillance Society: Monitoring Everyday Life*. Buckingham: Open University Press, 2001.

———, ed. *Surveillance as Social Sorting: Privacy, Risk, and Digital Discrimination*. London: Routledge, 2003.

———. *Surveillance Studies: An Overview*. Cambridge: Polity Press, 2007.

———. "Surveillance and the Eye of God." *Studies in Christian Ethics* 27, no 1 (2014): 21–32.

MacCoun, Robert J., and Peter Reuter. *Drug War Heresies: Learning from Other Vices, Times, and Places*. Cambridge: Cambridge University Press, 2001.

Machado, Helena, and Catarina Frois. "Aspiring to Modernization: Historical Evolution and Current Trends of State Surveillance in Portugal." In *Histories of State Surveillance in Europe and Beyond*, edited by K. Boersma, R. Van Brakel, C. Fonio, and P. Wagenaar. New York: Routledge, 2014.

Macnish, Kevin. "Just Surveillance? Towards a Normative Theory of Surveillance." *Surveillance and Society* 12, no. 1 (2014).

Mander, Jerry. *In the Absence of the Sacred: The Failure of Technology and the Survival of the Indian Nations*. San Francisco: Sierra Club Books, 1992.

Mann, Steve, Jason Nolan, and Barry Wellman. "Sousveillance: Inventing and Using Wearable Computing Devices for Data Collection in Surveillance Environments." *Surveillance and Society* 1, no. 3 (2003): 331–355.

Mannheim, Karl. *Ideology and Utopia: And Introduction to the Sociology of Knowledge*. New York: Harcourt, 1955.

Manning, Peter K. "Information Technology in the Police Context: The 'Sailor' Phone." *Information Systems Research* 7, no. 1 (1996): 52–62.

———. "A View of Surveillance." In *Technocrime: Technology, Crime, and Social Control*, edited by Stephane Leman-Langlois, 209–242. Devon, UK: Willan Publishing, 2008.

Marcuse, Herbert. *One Dimensional Man*. New York: Routledge, 2002.

Margulis, Stephen T., Jennifer A. Pope, and Aaron Lowen. "The Harris-Westin's Index of General Concern about Privacy: An Exploratory Conceptual Replication." In *Privacy, Surveillance and the Globalization of Personal Information: International Comparisons*, edited by Elia Zureik, Lynda H. Stalker, and Emily Smith, 91–109. Montreal: McGill-Queen's University Press, 2010.

Marks, Amber. *Headspace: Sniffer Dogs, Spy Bees and One Woman's Adventures in the Surveillance Society*. London: Ebury Publishing, 2009.

Martin, Aaron K., Rosamunde E. van Brakel, and Daniel J. Bernhard. "Understanding Resistance to Digital Surveillance: Towards a Multi-disciplinary, Multi-actor Framework." *Surveillance and Society* 6, no. 3 (2009): 213–232.

Martin, Brian. *Information Liberation.* London: Freedom Press, 1998.

Marvin, Carolyn. *When Old Technologies Were New.* New York: Oxford University Press, 1990.

Marx, Gary T. *Muckraking Sociology: Research as Social Criticism.* Piscataway, NJ: Transaction Publishers, 1972.

———. "Thoughts on a Neglected Category of Social Movement Participant: The Agent Provocateur and the Informant." *American Journal of Sociology* 80, no. 2 (1974): 402–442.

———. "External Efforts to Damage or Facilitate Social Movements: Some Patterns, Explanations, Outcomes and Complications." In *The Dynamics of Social Movements: Resource Mobilization, Social Control, and Tactics,* edited by Mayer N. Zald and John D. McCarthy. Cambridge, MA: Winthrop Publishers, 1979.

———. "Ironies of Social Control: Authorities as Contributors to Deviance through Escalation, Nonenforcement, and Covert Facilitation." *Social Problems* 28, no. 3 (1981): 221–246.

———. "Notes on the Discovery, Collection, and Assessment of Hidden and Dirty Data." In *Studies in the Sociology of Social Problems,* edited by Joseph Schneider and John I. Kitsuse, 78–113. Norwood, NJ: Ablex Publishing, 1984.

———. "The Surveillance Society: The Threat of 1984-Style Techniques." *Futurist* 6 (1985): 21–26.

———. "When a Child Informs on Parents." *New York Times,* August 29, 1986. http://web.mit .edu/gtmarx/www/when.html.

———. *Undercover: Police Surveillance in America.* Berkeley: University of California Press, 1988a.

———. "You'd Better Watch Out! This Is the Year of Spying Kits for Kids." *Los Angeles Times,* December 25, 1988b. http://web.mit.edu/gtmarx/www/kids.html.

———. "The Case of the Omniscient Organization." *Harvard Business Review* 68, no. 2 (1990): 12–20.

———. "Fraudulent Identification and Biography." In *New Directions in the Study of Justice, Law, and Social Control,* by D. Altheide et al. New York: Plenum, 1991.

———. "Some Reflections on Undercover: Recent Developments and Enduring Issues." *Crime, Law and Social Change* 18, no. 1 (1992).

———. "New Telecommunications Technologies Require New Manners." *Telecommunications Policy* 18, no. 7 (1994): 538–551.

———. "The Engineering of Social Control: The Search for the Silver Bullet." In *Crime and Inequality,* edited by John Hagan and Ruth D. Peterson, 225–246. Stanford, CA: Stanford University Press, 1995a.

———. "Social Control across Borders." In *Crime and Law Enforcement in the Global Village,* edited by William F. McDonald. Cincinnati: Anderson, 1995b.

———. "Privacy and Technology." *Telektronik,* January 1996.

———. "The Declining Significance of Traditional Borders (and the Appearance of New Borders) in an Age of High Technology." In *Intelligent Environments: Spatial Aspects of the Information Revolution,* edited by Peter Droege, 484–494. Amsterdam: Elsevier, 1997.

———. "Censorship and Secrecy, Social and Legal Perspectives." In *International Encyclopedia of the Social and Behavioral Sciences,* 2001a.

———. "Murky Conceptual Waters: The Public and the Private." *Ethics and Informational Technology* 3, no. 3 (2001b): 157–169.

———. "What's New about the 'New Surveillance'? Classifying for Change and Continuity." *Surveillance and Society* 1, no. 1 (2002): 9–29.

———. "Seeing Hazily (but Not Darkly) through the Lens: Some Recent Empirical Studies of Surveillance Technologies." *Law and Social Inquiry* 30, no. 2 (2005a): 339–399.

———. "Some Conceptual Issues in the Study of Borders and Surveillance." In *Who and What Goes There? Global Policing and Surveillance*, edited by Elia Zureik and Mark B. Salter, 11–35. Devon, UK: Willan Publishing, 2005b.

———. "Travels with Marty: Seymour Martin Lipset as a Mentor." *American Sociologist* 37, no. 4 (2006): 76–83.

———. "Foreword." In *Theory of Collective Behavior*, by Neil J. Smelser, xxiii–xxvi. New Orleans: Quid Pro, 2011a.

———. "Turtles, Firewalls, Scarlet Letters and Vacuum Cleaners: Rules about Personal Information." In *Privacy in America: Interdisciplinary Perspectives*, edited by William Aspray and Philip Doty, 271–294. Lanham, MD: Scarecrow Press, 2011a.

———. "'Your Papers Please': Personal and Professional Encounters with Surveillance." In *Routledge Handbook of Surveillance Studies*, edited by Kirstie Ball, Kevin Haggerty, and David Lyon, xx–xxxi. New York: Routledge, 2012.

———. "The Public as Partner? Technology Can Make Us Auxiliaries as Well as Vigilantes." *Security and Privacy*, September–October 2013.

———. "Toward an Imperial System of Surveilllance Ethics." *Surveillance and Society* 12, no. 1 (2014): 171–174.

———. "Coming to Terms: The Kaleidoscope of Privacy and Surveillance." In *Social Dimensions of Privacy: Interdisciplinary Perspectives*, edited by Beate Roessler and Dorota Mokrosinska. Cambridge: Cambridge University Press, 2015a.

———. "Genies, Bottled and Unbottled: Some Thoughts on the Properties of Information." In *Freedom and Property of Information: The Philosophy of Law Meets the Philosophy of Technology*, edited by M. Hildebrandt and B. van den Berg. Routledge, 2015b.

———. "Technology and Social Control: The Search for the Illusive Silver Bullet Continues." In *Encyclopedia of the Social and Behavioral Sciences*, 2nd ed. 2015c.

Marx, Gary T., and Glenn W. Muschert. "Personal Information, Borders, and the New Surveillance Studies." *Annual Review of Law and Social Science* 3 (2007): 375–395.

———. "Simmel on Secrecy: A Legacy and Inheritance for the Sociology of Information." In *Soziologie als Gens Möglichkeit 100 Jahre Georg Simmel's Untersuchgen*, edited by Christian Papiloud and Cecile Rol. Weisenbaden, Germany: VS Verlag für Sozialwissenschaften, 2008.

Marx, Gary T., and Nancy Reichman. "Routinizing the Discovery of Secrets: Computers as Informants." *American Behavioral Scientist* 27, no. 4 (1984): 423–452.

Marx, Gary T., and Valerie Steeves. "From the Beginning: Children as Subjects and Agents of Surveillance." *Surveillance and Society* 7, no. 3/4 (2010): 192–230.

Mathiesen, Thomas. "The Viewer Society: Michel Foucault's 'Panopticon' Revisited." *Theoretical Criminology* 1, no. 2 (1997): 215–234.

Mayer-Schonberger. *Delete: The Virtue of Forgetting in the Digital Age*. Princeton, NJ: Princeton University Press, 2011.

Mazzetti, Mark. "The Secret History of SEAL Team 6." *New York Times*, June 7, 2015.

McCahill, Mike. *The Surveillance Web*. Devon, UK: Willan Publishing, 2002.

McCann, Michael, and Tracey March. "Law and Everyday Forms of Resistance: A Socio-political Assessment." In *Studies in Law, Politics, and Society*, vol. 15, edited by Austin Sarat and Susan Silbey, 201–236. Beverly Hills: Sage, 1995.

McDonald, William. *Crime and Law Enforcement in the Global Village*. Cincinnati: Anderson, 1996.

McLuhan, Marshall. *The Gutenberg Galaxy: The Making of Typographic Man*. Toronto: University of Toronto Press, 1962.

McNally, Megan M., and Graeme R. Newman. *Perspectives on Identity Theft*. Monsey, NY: Criminal Justice Press, 2008.

Mead, Rebecca. "Letter from Nevada: 'American Pimp.'" *New Yorker*, April 23, 2001, 74–75.

Mendez, Antonio, Jonna Mendez, and Bruce Henderson. *Spy Dust: Two Masters of Disguise Reveal the Tools and Operations That Could Help Win the Cold War*. New York: Atria Books, 2003.

Merton, Robert K. *Social Theory and Social Structure*. Glencoe, IL: Free Press, 1956.

Michael, M. G., S. J. Fusco, and K. Michael. "A research note on ethics in the emerging age of überveillance." *Computer Communications* 31, no. 6 (2008): 1192–1199.

Mills, C. Wright. *The Sociological Imagination*. Oxford: Oxford University Press, 1959.

Milosz, Czeslaw. *The Captive Mind*. New York: Vintage, 1990.

Moers, Gigi. *How and Why Lovers Cheat and What You Can Do about It*. New York: Shapolsky, 1992.

Monahan, Torin. "Counter-surveillance as Political Intervention?" *Social Semiotics* 16, no. 4 (2006): 515–534.

———. *Surveillance in the Time of Insecurity*. New Brunswick, NJ: Rutgers University Press, 2010.

———. "The Right to Hide? Anti-surveillance Camouflage and the Aestheticization of Resistance." *Communication and Critical/Cultural Studies* 12, no. 2 (2015): 159–178.

Montgomery, Kathryn C. "Digital Kids: The New On-Line Children's Consumer Culture." In *Handbook of Children and the Media*, edited by Dorothy G. Singer and Jerome L. Singer, 635–650. Thousand Oaks, CA: Sage Publications, 2000.

Moore, Dawn, and Kevin D. Haggerty. "Bring It on Home: Home Drug Testing and the Relocation of the War on Drugs." *Social and Legal Studies* 10, no. 3 (2001): 377–395.

Morozov, Evgeny. *The Net Delusion: The Dark Side of Internet Freedom*. New York: PublicAffairs, 2011.

———. "The Real Privacy Problem." *Technology Review*, October 22, 2013.

Mumford, Lewis. *Technics and Civilization*. London: George Routledge and Sons, 1934.

Murray, Harry. "Deniable Degradation: The Finger-Imaging of Welfare Recipients." *Sociological Forum* 15, no. 1 (2000): 39–63.

Muschert, Glenn W., and Anthony A. Peguero. "The Columbine Effect and School Anti-violence Policy." *Research in Social Problems and Public Policy* 17 (2010): 117–148.

Myrdal, Gunnar. *An American Dilemma: The Negro Problem and Modern Democracy*. New York: Harper and Bros., 1944.

Natapoff, Alexandra. *Snitching: Criminal Informants and the Erosion of American Justice*. New York: New York University Press, 2009.

National Commission on Terrorist Attacks upon the United States. *The 9/11 Commission Report: Final Report of the National Commission on Terrorist Attacks upon the United States*. New York: W. W. Norton and Co., 2004.

Navasky, Victor S. "The Selling of the Brethren." *Yale Law Journal* 89, no. 5 (1980): 1028–1035.

Nelson, Margaret K. *Parenting out of Control: Anxious Families in Uncertain Times*. New York: NYU Press, 2010.

Neumann, Peter. *Computer Related Risks*. Reading, MA: Addison-Wesley, 1995.

Newburn, Tim, and Stephanie Hayman. *Policing, Surveillance, and Social Control*. Devon, UK: Willan Publishing, 2001.

Newman, Oscar. *Defensible Space: Crime Prevention through Urban Design*. New York: Macmillan Books, 1972.

Neyland, Daniel. *Privacy, Surveillance and Public Trust*. New York: Palgrave Macmillan, 2006.

———. "Mundane Terror and the Threat of Everyday Objects." *Technologies of Insecurity*, edited by K. F. Aas, H. O. Gundhus, and H. M. Lowell. New York: Routledge. 2008.

Nippert-Eng, Christena E. *Home and Work: Negotiating Boundaries through Everyday Life*. Chicago: University of Chicago Press, 1996.

———. *Islands of Privacy*. Chicago: University of Chicago Press, 2010.

Nisbet, Robert A. *History of the Idea of Progress*. New Brunswick, NJ: Transaction Publishers, 1980.

Nissenbaum, Helen F. "Protecting Privacy in an Information Age." *Law and Philosophy* 17 (1998): 559–596.

———. *Privacy in Context: Technology, Policy, and the Integrity of Social Life*. Palo Alto, CA: Stanford University Press, 2010.

Noble, Greg. "The Discomfort of Strangers: Racism, Incivility and Ontological Security in a Relaxed and Comfortable Nation." *Journal of Intercultural Studies* 26, no. 1 (2005): 107–120.

Nogala, Detlef. "The Future Role of Technology in Policing." In *Comparisons in Policing: An International Perspective*, edited by Jean-Paul Brodeur, 191–210. Aldershot, UK: Avebury, 1995.

Norris, Clive. "The Success of Failure: Accounting for the Global Growth of CCTV." In *Routledge Handbook of Surveillance Studies*, edited by Kirstie Ball, Kevin Haggerty, and David Lyon. London: Routledge, 2012.

Norris, Clive, and Gary Armstrong. *The Maximum Surveillance Society: The Rise of CCTV*. New York: Oxford University Press, 1999.

Norris, Clive, Paul de Hert, Xavier Hoiry, and Antonella Galetta. *The Unaccountable State of Surveillance: Exercising Access Rights in Europe*. New York: Springer, 2016.

Notes. "Anthropotelemetry Dr. Schwitzgebel's Machine." *Harvard Law Review* 403 (1966).

O'Harrow, Robert. *No Place to Hide*. New York: Free Press, 2005.

O'Leary, Brian. *Spygate: The Untold Story*. Dallas: KLR Publishing, 2012.

Oliver, Pamela E., and Daniel J. Myers. "The Coevolution of Social Movements." *Mobilization* 8, no. 1 (2003): 1–24.

Orwell, George. *The Collected Essays, Journalism and Letters of George Orwell*. New York: Harcourt Press, 1968.

———. *1984: A Novel*. Oxford: Clarendon Press, 1983.

———. *Politics and the English Language*. Peterborough: Broadview Press, 2006.

Packard, Vance O. *The Hidden Persuaders*. New York: Pocket Books, 1957.

———. *The Naked Society*. New York: Penguin Books, 1964.

Page, Clarence. "Q&A: Clarence Page on Jesse Jackson." *Columbia Journalism Review* 39, no. 6 (2001): 9–10.

Pager, Devah. "The Mark of a Criminal Record." *American Journal of Sociology* 108, no. 5 (2003): 937–975.

Palidda, Salvatore. "L'anamorphose de l'État-Nation: Le cas italien." *Cahiers internationaux de sociologie* (1992): 269–298.

Palm, Elin. "Conditions Under Which Surveillance May Be Ethically Justifiable" *Surveillance and Society* 12, no. 1 (2014): 164–170.

Pamuk, Orhan. "My First Passport: What It Means to Belong to a Country." *New Yorker*, April 16, 2007, 56.

Parenti, Christian. *The Soft Cage: Surveillance in America from Slavery*. New York: Basic Books, 2003.

Parsons, Talcott. *The Social System*. London: Routledge & Kegan Paul, 1970.

Pasquale, Frank. *The Black Box Society: The Secret Algorithms that Control Information and Money*. Cambridge, MA: Harvard University Press, 2015.

Patillo, Mary E., Daniel F. Weiman, and Bruce Western, eds. *Imprisoning America: The Social Effects of Mass Incarceration*. New York: Russell Sage Foundation, 2004.

Pecora, Vincent P. "The Culture of Surveillance." *Qualitative Sociology* 25, no. 3 (2002): 345–358.

"Peeping Tom." In *New Encyclopedia*. 1990.

Perrow, Charles. *Normal Accidents: Living with High Risk Technologies*. New York: Basic Books, 1984.

Person, Natalie K., Sidney D'Mello, and Andrew Olney. "Toward Socially Intelligent Interviewing Systems." In *Envisioning the Survey Interview of the Future*, edited by Frederick G. Conrad and Michael F. Schober, 195–214. Hoboken, NJ: John Wiley and Sons, 2008.

Petersen, Julie K. *Understanding Surveillance Technologies: Spy Devices, Their Origins and Applications*. Boca Raton, FL: CRC Press, 2001.

Pew Research Center. "Public Perceptions of Privacy and Security in the Post-Era." 2014. http://www.pewinternet.org/2014/11/12/public-privacy-perceptions/.

Pfaff, Steven. "The Limits of Coercive Surveillance: Social and Penal Control in the German Democratic Republic." *Punishment and Society* 3, no. 3 (2000): 381–407.

Philips, David J. "Texas 9-1-1: Emergency Telecommunications, Deregulation, and the Genesis of Surveillance Infrastructure." *Telecommunications Policy* 29, no. 11 (2005): 843–856.

Pickering, Andrew. *The Mangle of Practice: Time, Agency, and Science*. Chicago: University of Chicago Press, 1995.

———. "Decentering Sociology: Synthetic Dyes and Social Theory." *Perspectives on Science* 13 (2005): 3.

Pinch, Trevor J., and Wiebe E. Bijker. "The Social Construction of Facts and Artifacts, or How the Sociology of Science and the Sociology of Technology Might Benefit Each Other." In *The Social Construction of Technology Systems: New Directions in the Sociology and History of Technology*, edited by Wiebe E. Bijker, Thomas P. Hughes, and Trevor J. Pinch, 17–51. London: MIT Press, 1987.

Pistone, Joseph D. *The Way of the Wiseguy: True Stories from the FBI's Most Famous Undercover Agent*. Philadelphia: Running Press Book Publishers, 2004.

Pitt, William. "Speech on the Excise Bill" (1763). In *The Life of William Pitt*, vol. 2, *Earl of Chatham*, edited by Basil Williams, 154. Oxford: Routledge, 1966.

Polgreen, Lydia. "Scanning 2.4 Billion Eyes, India Tries to Connect Poor to Growth." *New York Times*, September 1, 2011.

Post, Emily. *Emily Post's Etiquette Book*. New York: Harper Collins, 1992.

Poster, Mark. *The Mode of Information: Postculturalism and Social Context*. Chicago: University of Chicago Press, 1990.

Postman, Neil. *Technopoly*. New York: Vintage Books. 1992.

Prager, Joshua. *The Echoing Green: The Untold Story of Bobby Thomson, Ralph Branca and the Shot Heard round the World*. New York: Vintage Books, 2008.

Price, David. *Threatening Anthropology: McCarthyism and the FBI's Surveillance of Activist Anthropologists*. Durham, NC: Duke University Press, 2004.

———. *Anthropological Intelligence: The Deployment and Neglect of American Anthropology in the Second World*. Durham, NC: Duke University Press, 2008.

Priest, Dana, and William M. Arkin. *Top Secret America: The Rise of the New American Security State*. New York: Little, Brown and Co., 2011.

Prosser, Dean. "The Torts of Privacy." *California Law Review* 383, no. 48 (1960): 392–398.

Quan-Haase, Anabel. 2015. *Technology and Society*. Don Mills, Ontario: Oxford University Press.

Raine, Adrian. *The Anatomy of Violence*. New York: Pantheon, 2012.

Rawls, John. *A Theory of Justice*. Cambridge, MA: Belknap Press, 1971.

Regan, Priscilla. *Legislating Privacy: Technology, Social Values, and Public Policy*. Chapel Hill: University of North Carolina Press, 1995.

Reiss, Albert J., Jr. "Consequences of Compliance and Deterrence Models of Law Enforcement for the Exercise of Police Discretion." *Law and Contemporary Problems* 47, no. 4 (Autumn 1984): 83–122.

Renzema, M., and E. Mayo-Wilson. "Can Electronic Monitoring Reduce Crime for Moderate to High Risk Offenders?" *Journal of Experimental Criminology* 1 (2005): 215–237.

Reppetto, Thomas A. "Crime Prevention and the Displacement Phenomenon." *Crime and Delinquency* 22, no. 2 (1976): 166–177.

Ressler, Robert K., and Tom Schachtman. *Whoever Fights Monsters*. New York: St. Martin's Press, 1992.

Rhodes, Loma A. *Total Confinement Madness and Reason in the Maximum Security Prison*. Berkeley: University of California Press, 2004.

Roessler, Beate, and Dorota Mokrosinska, eds. *Social Dimensions of Privacy: Interdisciplinary Perspectives*. Cambridge: Cambridge University Press, 2015.

Rooney, Tonya. "Trusting Children: How Do Surveillance Technologies Alter a Child's Experience of Trust, Risk and Responsibility?" *Surveillance and Society* 7, no. 3/4 (2010).

Rosen, Jeffrey. *The Naked Crowd: Reclaiming Security and Freedom*. New York: Random House, 2004.

Rosner, Lisa. *The Technological Fix: How People Use Technology to Create and Solve Problems*. London: Routledge, 2004.

Rotenberg, Marc, Julia Horowitz, and Jeramie Scott. *Privacy in the Modern Age*. New York: New Press, 2015.

Rule, James B. *Private Lives and Public Surveillance: Social Control in the Computer Age*. New York: Schocken Books, 1974.

———. *Insight and Social Betterment: A Preface to Applied Social Science*. Oxford: Oxford University Press, 1978.

———. *Privacy in Peril*. New York: Oxford University Press, 2007.

Rule, James, and Lawrence Hunter. "Towards Property Rights in Personal Data." In *Visions of Privacy: Policy Choices for the Digital Age*, edited by Colin J. Bennett and Rebecca A. Grant, 168–181. Toronto: Toronto Press, 1999.

Rule, James B., Douglas McAdam, Linda Stearns, and David Uglow. "Documentary Identification and Mass Surveillance in the United States." *Social Problems* 31, no. 2 (1983): 222–234.

Rule, James B., Linda Stearns, Douglas McAdam, and David Uglow. *The Politics of Privacy*. New York: New American Library, 1980.

Samatas, Minas. *Surveillance in Greece*. New York: Athens Printing, 2004.

———. *The "Super-Panopticon" Scandal of the Athens 2004 Olympics and Its Legacy*. New York: Pella Publishing, 2014.

Sanchez, Andres. "Facebook Feeding Frenzy: Resistance-through-Distance and Resistance-through-Persistence in the Societied Network." *Surveillance and Society* 6, no. 3 (2009): 275–293.

Sandel, Michael. *What Money Can't Buy: The Moral Limits of Markets*. New York: Farrar Straus and Giroux, 2012.

Sartre, Jean-Paul. *Being and Nothingness*. New York: Washington Square Press, 1993.

Satz, Debra. *Why Some Things Should Not Be for Sale: The Moral Limits of Markets.* New York: Oxford University Press, 2010.

Schneider, Christopher. *Policing and Social Media: Social Control in an Era of New Media.* Lanham, MD: Lexington Books, Rowman and Littlefield, 2016.

Schneier, Bruce. *Beyond Fear: Thinking Sensibly about Security in an Uncertain World.* Göttingen: Copernicus Books, 2003.

————. *Data and Goliath: The Hidden Battles to Collect Your Data and Control Your World.* New York: W. W. Norton, 2015.

Schoenman, F., ed. *Philosophical Dimensions of Privacy.* Cambridge: Cambridge University Press, 1984.

Schuilenburg, Marc. *The Securitization of Society.* New York: New York University Press, 2015.

Scott, James C. *Weapons of the Weak: Everyday Forms of Peasant Resistance.* New Haven, CT: Yale University Press, 1985.

————. *Seeing like a State: How Certain Schemes to Improve the Human Condition Have Failed.* New Haven, CT: Yale University Press, 1998.

Scott, L. V., and Peter D. Jackson. *Understanding Intelligence in the Twenty-First Century.* New York: Routledge, 2004.

Seiber, Sam D. *Fatal Remedies: The Ironies of Social Intervention.* New York: Plenum, 1981.

Seliger, Martin. *Ideology and Politics.* London: Allen and Unwin, 1976.

Selznick, Phillip. *The Communitarian Persuasion.* Washington, DC: Woodrow Wilson Center, 2002.

Sewell, Graham. "Organization, Employees and Surveillance." In *Routledge Handbook of Surveillance Studies,* edited by Kirstie Ball, Kevin Haggerty, and David Lyon. London: Routledge, 2012.

Sewell, Graham, and J. R. Barker. "Coercion versus Care: Using Irony to Make Sense of Organizational Surveillance." *Academy of Management Review* 31 (2006).

————. "Organization, Employees and Surveillance." In *Routledge Handbook of Surveillance Studies,* edited by Kirstie Ball, Kevin Haggerty, and David Lyon. London: Routledge, 2012.

Sewell, William H. "A Theory of Structure: Duality, Agency, and Transformation." *American Journal of Sociology* (1992): 1–29.

Shade, Leslie R., and Diane Y. Dechief. "Canada's SchoolNet: Wiring Up Schools?" In *Global Perspectives on E-Learning: Rhetoric and Reality,* edited by Alison A. Carr-Chellman, 131–144. Thousand Oaks, CA: Sage Publications, 2005.

Shaiken, Harley. *Work Transformed: Automation and Labor in the Computer Age.* New York: Rinehart and Winston, 1985.

Shalin, Dmitri N. "Goffman's Biography and the Interaction Order: A Study in Biocritical Hermeneutics." 2008. http://cdclv.unlv.edu//ega/bios.html (accessed September 1, 2009).

Shearing, Clifford D., and Phillip C. Stenning. *Private Policing.* Newbury Park, CA: Sage Publications, 1987.

————. "From the Panopticon to Disney World: The Development of Discipline." In *Situational Crime Prevention: Successful Case Studies,* edited by Ronald V. Clarke, 249–255. New York: Harrow and Heston, 1992.

Shearing, Clifford D. "Nodal Security." *Police Quarterly* 8, no. 1 (2015).

Sheptycki, James. *In Search of Transnational Policing.* Aldershot, UK: Dartmouth Publishing, 2003.

Shils, Edward. *The Torment of Secrecy*. New York: Free Press, 1956.

Shteyngart, Gary. *Super Sad True Love Story: A Novel*. New York: Random House, 2010.

Shulman, David. *From Hire to Liar: The Role of Deception in the Workplace*. Ithaca, NY: Cornell University Press, 2007.

Silver, Allan. "The Demand for Order in Civil Society: A Review of Some Themes in the History of Urban Crime, Police, and Riots." In *The Police: Six Sociological Essays*, edited by David D. Bordua, 152–169. New York: John Wiley and Sons, 1967.

Simmel, Georg. "The Secret and the Secret Society, Part Four." In *The Sociology of Georg Simmel*, edited by Kurt H. Wolff, 307–378. New York: Free Press, [1908] 1950.

Skloot, R. *The Immortal Life of Henrietta Lacks*. New York: Random House, 2010.

Slovic, Paul. "Perception of Risk." *Science* 236, no. 4799 (1987): 280–285.

Slovic, Paul, Baruch Fischhoff, and Sarah Lichtenstein. "Rating the Risks." *Environment* 21, no. 3 (1979): 14–39.

Smelser, Neil J. *Social Change in the Industrial Revolution: An Application of Theory to the Lancashire Cotton Industry, 1770–1840*. London: Routledge and Kegan Paul, 1959.

Smith, Gavin. *Opening the Black Box: The Work of Watching*. New York: Routledge, 2015.

Smith, H. Jeff, Tamara Dinev, and Heng Xu. "Information Privacy Research: An Interdisciplinary Review." *MIS Quarterly* 35, no. 4 (2011): 989–1015.

Smith, Michael J., Pascale Carayon, Katherine J. Sanders, Soo-Yee Lim, and David LeGrande. "Employee Stress and Health Complaints in Jobs With and Without Electronic Performance Monitoring." *Applied Ergonomics* 23, no. 1 (1992): 17–27.

Smith, Robert E. *War Stories*. Providence, RI: Privacy Journal, 1997.

———. *Compilation of State and Federal Privacy Laws*. Providence, RI: Privacy Journal, 2013.

Solove, Daniel J. *Understanding Privacy*. Cambridge, MA: Harvard University Press, 2008.

Sontag, Susan. *On Photography*. New York: Picador, 1977.

Sorensen, Georg. *Democracy and Democratization: Processes and Prospects in a Changing World (Dilemmas in World Politics)*. Oxford: Westview Press, 1993.

Sorokin, Pitrim A. *Fads and Foibles in Modern Sociology and Related Sciences*. Chicago: H. Regnery, 1956.

Spector, Malcolm, and John I. Kitsuse. *Constructing Social Problems*. New Brunswick, NJ: Transaction Publishers, 2001.

Squires, Kelly. *Spying on Your Spouse: A Guide for Anyone Who Suspects a Partner Is Cheating*. Secaucus, NJ: Citadel Press, 1996.

Stalder, Felix. "Autonomy beyond Privacy? A Rejoinder to Bennett." *Surveillance and Society* 8, no. 4 (2011): 508–512.

Stalder, Felix. "Response to Bennett: Also in Defense of Privacy." *Surveillance and Society* 8, no. 4 (2011).

Staples, William G. *Everyday Surveillance: Vigilance and Visibility in Postmodern Life*. Lanham, MD: Rowan and Littlefield, 2000.

Staples, William G., and Joane Nagel. "Gary's Gone . . ." *Sociological Quarterly* 43, no. 3 (2002): 447–452.

Steeves, Valerie. "It's Not Child's Play: The Online Invasion of Children's Privacy." *University of Ottawa Law and Technology Journal* 3, no. 1 (2006): 169–188.

———. "El niño observado: Vigilancia en tres sitios de juegos de niños en Internet." *Actas de la Conferencia Internacional sobre los Derechos del Niño*. Buenos Aires: Universidad de Buenos Aires, 2007.

————. "Data Protection versus Privacy: Lessons from Facebook's Beacon." In *Contours of Privacy*, edited by David Matheson, 183–196. Newcastle upon Tyne, UK: Cambridge Scholars Press, 2009.

————. "Surveillance of Young People on the Internet." In *Routledge Handbook of Surveillance Studies*, edited by Kirstie Ball, Kevin Haggerty, and David Lyon, 352–360. London: Routledge, 2012.

Stern, Rachel. "Fiercely critical of NSA, Germany now answering for its own spy practices." *Christian Science Monitor*, May 22, 2015.

Stern, Susannah R. "Expressions of Identity Online: Prominent Features and Gender Differences in Adolescents' World Wide Web Home Pages." *Journal of Broadcasting and Electronic Media* 48, no. 2 (2004): 218–243.

Stone-Romero, E. F., D. L. Stone, and D. Hyatt. "Personnel Selection Procedures and Invasion of Privacy." *Journal of Social Issues* 59, no. 2 (2003): 343–368.

Stoddart, Eric. *Theological Perspectives on a Surveillance Society*. Adlershot, UK: Ashgate, 2012.

————. "Challenging 'Just Surveillance Theory': A Response to Kevin Macnish's 'Just Surveillance Theory.'" *Surveillance and Society* 12, no. 1 (2014): 158–163.

Strang, David, and Sarah A. Soule. "Diffusion in Organizations and Social Movements: From Hybrid Corn to Poison Pills." *Annual Review of Sociology* 24 (1998): 265–290.

Sutherland, Edwin H. *White Collar Crime*. New York: Dryden Press, 1949.

Svenonius, Ola, Fredrika Bjorklund, and Pawel Waszkiewicz. "Surveillance, Lustration and the Open Society: Poland and Eastern Europe." In *Histories of State Surveillance in Europe and Beyond*, edited by K. Boersma, R.Van Brakel, C. Fonio, and P. Wagenaar. New York: Routledge, 2014.

Sykes, Gresham M. *The Society of Captives: A Study of Maximum Security Prisons*. Princeton, NJ: Princeton University Press, 1971.

Sykes, Gresham M., and David Matza. "Techniques of Neutralization: A Theory of Delinquency." *American Sociological Review* 22, no. 6 (1957): 664–670.

Tackwood, Louis. *The Glass House Tapes*. New York: Avon Books, 1973.

Tagg, John. "A Means of Surveillance: The Photograph as Evidence in Law." In *The Burden of Representation: Essays on Photographies and Histories*, edited by John Tagg, 60–102. London: Macmillan, 1988.

Tang, Shengming, and Xiaoping Dong. "Parents' and Children's Perceptions of Privacy Rights in China: A Cohort Comparison." *Journal of Family Issues* 27, no. 3 (2006): 285–300.

Tenner, Edward. *Why Things Bite Back: Technology and the Revenge of Unintended Consequences*. New York: Vintage, 1997.

Tennyson, Alfred. *Tennyson: A Selected Edition*. Edited by Christopher Ricks. Berkeley: University of California Press, 1989.

Thomas, Malcolm I. *Luddites: Machine-Breaking in Regency England*. Aldershot: Ashgate, 1993.

Thompson, Edward P. *The Making of the English Working Class*. New York: Knopf Publishing, 1966.

Thompson, John B. *Ideology and Modern Culture: Critical Social Theory in the Era of Mass Communication*. Cambridge: Polity Press, 1990.

Tilly, Charles. *Popular Contention in Great Britain, 1758–1834*. Cambridge, MA: Harvard University Press, 1995.

Tjaden, Patricia G., and Nancy Thoennes. *Stalking in America: Findings from the National Violence against Women Survey*. Washington, DC: US Department of Justice, National Institute of Justice, Office of Justice Programs, 1998.

Toch, Hans. *Cop Watch: Spectators, Social Media, and Police Reform.* Washington, DC: American Psychological Association, 2012.

Torpey, John. "Through Thick and Thin: Surveillance after 9/11." *Contemporary Sociology* 36, no. 2 (2007): 116–119.

Toynbee, Arnold. *War and Civilization, Selections from A Study of History.* Edited by Albert Vann Fowler. New York: Oxford University Press, 1950.

Tower, John, Edmund Muskie, and Brent Scowcroft. *The Tower Commission Report.* New York: New York Times, 1987.

"Trouble over Privacy in Japan." *Economist*, August 8, 2002.

Trottier, Daniel. *Social Media as Surveillance.* Aldershot, UK: Ashgate, 2012.

Tunnell, Kenneth D. *Pissing on Demand.* New York: New York University Press, 2004.

Turow, Joseph. *The Daily You: How the New Advertising Industry Is Defining Your Identity and Your World.* New Haven, CT: Yale University Press, 2012.

Twain, Mark. *The Innocents Abroad.* New York: Penguin Books, 1984.

Underhill, Paco. *Why We Buy.* New York: Simon and Schuster, 1999.

Updike, John. *Just Looking: Essays on Art.* Boston: MFA Publications, 1989.

Vaidhyanathan, Siva. *The Googlilization of Everything (and Why We should Worry).* Berkeley: University of California Press, 2011.

Vamosi, Robert. *When Gadgets Betray Us.* New York: Basic Books, 2011.

Varon, Jeremy. *Bringing the War Home: The Weather Underground, the Red Army Faction, and Revolutionary Violence in the Sixties and Seventies.* Berkeley: University of California Press, 2004.

Vaughan, Diane. *Uncoupling: Turning Points in Intimate Relationships.* New York: Oxford University Press, 1986.

———. *The Challenger Launch Decision: Risky Technology, Culture, and Deviance at NASA.* Chicago: University of Chicago Press, 1996.

Wachtel, Julius. "Production and Craftsmanship in Police Narcotics Enforcement." *Journal of Police Science and Administration* 13, no. 4 (1985): 263–274.

Waever, Ole. "Securitization and Decuritization." In *On Security*, edited by R. D. Lipschutz. New York: Columbia University Press, 1995.

Wagnsson, Charlotte, Maria Hellman, and Arita Holmberg. "The Centrality of Non-traditional Groups for Security in the Globalized Era: The Case of Children." *International Political Sociology* 4, no. 1 (2010): 1–14.

Waldo, James, Herbert Lin, and Lynette Millett. *Engaging Privacy and Information Technology in a Digital Age: Issues and Insights.* Washington, DC: National Academies Press, 2007.

Walker, Sam. "DNA Dragnets: Use and Experience." Presented at the Conference on DNA Fingerprinting and Civil Liberties, American Society of Law, Medicine and Ethics, Boston, MA, May 12, 2006.

Walsh, James P. "From Border Control to Border Care: The Political and Ethical Potential of Surveillance." *Surveillance and Society* 8, no. 2 (2010): 113–30.

Walton, Greg. *China's Golden Shield: Corporations and the Development of Surveillance.* Montreal: International Centre for Human Rights and Democratic Development, 2001.

Walzer, Michael. *Spheres of Justice: A Defense of Pluralism and Equality.* New York: Basic Books, 1983.

Warren, Carol, and Barbara Laslett. "Privacy and Secrecy: A Conceptual Comparison." *Journal of Social Issues* 33, no. 3 (1977): 43–51.

Warren, Samuel D., and Louis D. Brandeis. "The Right to Privacy." *Harvard Law Review* 4, no. 5 (1890): 193–220.

Webb, E. J.; D. T. Campbell, R. D. Schwartz, and L. Sechrest. *Unobtrusive Measures*. Revised ed. Thousand Oaks, CA: Sage Publications, 2000.

Webb, Eugene J. *Unobtrusive Measures: Nonreactive Research in the Social Sciences*. Chicago: Rand McNally, 1966.

Weber, Max. *From Max Weber*. Edited by Hans Gerth and C. Wright Mills. New York: Oxford University Press, 1958.

———. *Economy and Society: An Outline of Interpretive Sociology*. Vol. 1. Berkeley: University of California Press, 1978.

Wegner, Daniel M., Julie D. Lane, and Sara Dimitri. "The Allure of Secret Relationships." *Journal of Personality and Social Psychology* 66, no. 2 (1994): 287–300.

Weinberg, Alvin M. "Can Technology Replace Social Engineering?" *American Behavioral Scientist* 10, no. 9 (1967): 7–10.

Weizenbaum, Joseph. *Computing Power and Human Reason*. San Francisco: W. H. Freeman, 1976.

Wells, Helen, and David Wills. "Individualism and Identity: Resistance to Speed Cameras in the UK." *Surveillance and Society* 6, no. 3 (2009): 259–274.

Welsh, Brandon C., and David P. Farrington. *Making Public Places Safer: Surveillance and Crime Prevention*. New York: Oxford University Press, 2009.

Westin, Alan F. *Privacy and Freedom*. New York: Athenum, 1967.

———. "Social and Political Dimensions of Privacy." *Journal of Social Issues* 59, no. 2 (2003): 431–453.

Whitley, Edgar, Aaron Martin, and Gus Hosein. "From Surveillance-by-Design to Privacy-by-Design: Evolving Identity Policy in the United Kingdom." In *Histories of State Surveillance in Europe and Beyond*, edited by K. Boersma, R.Van Brakel, C. Fonio, and P. Wagenaar. New York: Routledge, 2014.

Wiener, Norbert. *The Human Use of Human Beings: Cybernetics and Society*. New York: Avon Books, 1967.

Wildavsky, Aaron. *Searching for Safety*. New Brunswick, NJ: Transaction, 1988.

Williams, Christine L. *Inside Toyland*. Berkeley: University of California Press, 2006.

Williams, Jay, and Raymond Abrashkin. *Danny Dunn, Invisible Boy*. New York: McGraw-Hill, 1974.

Williams, John. *Stoner*. New York: New York Review Books Classics, 2006.

Williams, R., and P. Johnson. *Genetic Policing: The Use of DNA in Criminal Investigations*. London: Willan Publishing, 2008.

Willis, James, and Susan Silbey. "Self, Surveillance, and Society." *Sociological Quarterly* 43, no. 3 (2002): 439–445.

Wilson, Dean Jonathon, and Tanya Serisier. "Video Activism and the Ambiguities of Counter-surveillance." *Surveillance and Society* 8, no. 2 (2010): 166–180.

Winner, Langdon. *Autonomous Technology: Technics out of Control as a Theme in Political Thought*. Cambridge, MA: MIT Press, 1977.

———. *The Whale and the Reactor: A Search for Limits in an Age of High Technology*. Chicago: University of Chicago Press, 1988.

Wood, Ann. "Omniscient Organizations and Bodily Observations: Electronic Surveillance in the Workplace." Unpublished paper, University of California, Berkeley, 1996.

Wood, David M. "Globalization and Surveillance." In *Routledge Handbook of Surveillance Studies*, edited by Kirstie Ball, Kevin Haggerty, and David Lyon. London: Routledge, 2012.

Wood, David M., David Lyon, and Kiyoshi Abe. "Surveillance in Urban Japan: A Critical Introduction." *Urban Studies* 44, no. 3 (2007): 551–568.

Wood, Jennifer, and Benoit Dupont, eds. *Democracy, Society and the Governance of Security.* Cambridge: Cambridge University Press, 2006.

Wozencraft, Kim. *Rush.* New York: Ballantine Books, 1990.

Wright, David, and Pail de Hert, eds. *Introduction to Privacy Impact Assessment.* New York: Springer, 2012.

Wright, David, and Reinhard Kreissl. *Surveillance in Europe.* London: Routledge, 2014.

Wright, David, Serge Gutwirth, Michael Friedewald, Elena Vildjiounaite, and Yves Punie. *Safeguards in a World of Ambient Intelligence.* New York: Springer, 2010.

Yar, Majid. "Panoptic Power and the Pathologisation of Vision Critical Reflections on the Foucauldian Thesis." *Surveillance and Society* 1, no. 3 (2003).

Young, A. L., and A. Q. Quan-Haase. "Privacy Protection Strategies on Facebook." *Information, Communication & Soceity* 16, no. 4.

Zelizer, Viviana. *The Purchase of Intimacy.* Princeton, NJ: Princeton University Press, 2005.

Zuboff, Shoshana. *In the Age of the Smart Machine.* New York: Basic Books, 1988.

Zureik, Elia, and Mark Salter, eds. *Global Surveillance and Policing.* Portland, OR: Willan, 2005.

Zureik, Elia, Lynda H. Stalker, and Emily Smith. *Privacy, Surveillance and the Globalization of Personal Information: International Comparisons.* Montreal: McGill-Queen's University Press, 2010.

Conference Proceedings

Surveillance: An Exhibition of Video, Photography, and Installations. Los Angeles Contemporary Exhibitions, Los Angeles, 1987.

Government Reports and Documents (National and International)

American Management Association. *1996 AMA Workplace Survey: Workplace Drug Testing and Drug Abuse Policy.* New York: AMA Publications, 1996.

European Commission. *Factsheet on the "Right to be Forgotten" Ruling* (C-131/12). Brussels: European Commission, 2014.

International Labour Office. *Conditions of Work Digest: Workers' Privacy Part II: Monitoring and Surveillance in the Workplace.* Edited by Michele B. Jankanish. Geneva: International Labour Organization, 1993a.

———. *Conditions of Work Digest: Workers' Privacy Part III: Testing in the Workplace.* Edited by Michele B. Jankanish. Geneva: International Labour Organization, 1993b.

National Academy of Sciences. *Engaging Privacy and Information Technology.* Washington, DC: National Academies Press, 2006.

———. *Engaging Privacy and Information Technology in a Digital Age: Issues and Insights.* Washington, DC: National Academies Press, 2007.

National Research Council. *Private Lives and Public Policies.* Washington, DC: National Academy Press, 1993.

———. *The Polygraph and Lie Detection.* Washington, DC: National Academies Press, 2001.

———. *Engaging Privacy and Information Technology in a Digital Age.* Washington, DC: National Academics Press, 2007.

———. *Protecting Individual Privacy in the Struggle against Terrorism: A Framework for Program Assessment.* Washington, DC: National Academies Press, 2008.

Subcommittee on Africa, Global Human Rights and International Operations, Committee on International Relations, House of Representatives. *The Internet in China: A Tool for Freedom or Suppression?* Washington, DC: US Government Printing Office, 2006.

US Congress Office of Technology Assessment. *Federal Government Information Technology: Electronic Surveillance and Civil Liberties.* Washington, DC: US Government Printing Office, 1985.

US House of Representatives, Subcommittee on Commerce, Trade and Consumer Protection. *The Drug Free Sports Act.* Washington, DC: US Government Printing Office, 2005.

Legal Cases and Court Documents

Children's Online Protection Privacy Act, 15 U.S.C. §§ 6501 (1998)

Electronic Communications Privacy Act of 1986, 18 U.S.C. § 2510–2522 (1986).

Entick v. Carrington, 19 Howell's State Trials, 1029 (1765).

Griswold v. Connecticut, 381 U.S. 479 (1965). Retrieved from LexisNexis Academic database.

Katz v. United States, 389 U.S. 347 (1961). Retrieved from LexisNexis Academic database.

Kyllo v. United States, 533 U.S. 27 (2001). Retrieved from LexisNexis Academic database.

Moore v. Regents of the University of California, 793 P.2d 479 (1990). Retrieved from LexisNexis Academic database.

NAACP v. Patterson, 357 U.S. 449 (1958). Retrieved from LexisNexis Academic database.

Roe v. Wade, 410 U.S. 113 (1973). Retrieved from LexisNexis Academic database.

Smith v. Maryland, 442 U.S. 735 (1979). Retrieved from LexisNexis Academic database.

News and Media Articles

BBC News. "Reid Heckled during Muslim Speech." *BBCNews.com*, September 20, 2006. http://news.bbc.co.uk/2/hi/5362052.stm (accessed September 1, 2009).

———. "Chinese Artist Ai Weiwei Ordered to Stop Webcam Project." *BBCNews.com*, April 4, 2012. http://www.bbc.co.uk/news/world-asia-17615810 (accessed July 2, 2012).

Belluck, Pam. "DNA Test Leads, at Last, to Arrest." *New York Times*, April 16, 2005.

Belson, Ken. "Your Call (and Rants on Hold) Will Be Monitored." *New York Times*, January 11, 2005, A1.

Bernard, Tara Siegel. "Giving Out Private Data for Discount in Insurance." *New York Times*, April 8, 2015.

Booker, Christopher. "Thames Fishermen Get Gangsters' Sentences." *Telegraph*, August 3, 2008. http://www.telegraph.co.uk/comment/columnists/christopherbooker/3561174/Thames-fishermen-get-gangsters-sentences.html (accessed September 1, 2009).

Branigin, William. "Cartels Shipping 'Black Cocaine; Bricks of Drug Look Like Metal Moldings." *The Washington Post*, April 28, 1999.

Clark, Kim. "Professors Use Technology to Fight Student Cheating." *US News and World Report*, October 3, 2008. www.usnews.com/articles/education/2008/10/03/professors-use-technology-to-fight-student-cheating.html (accessed September 1, 2009).

Daily Mail. "Scientists Discover That Eyes Really Are 'the Window to the Soul.'" *Daily Mail*, February 19, 2007.

Davis, Richard H. "NYPD Use Strobe Lights to Stop Occupy Wall Street Filming." *Economic*

Voice, October 17, 2011. http://www.economicvoice.com/nypd-use-strobe-lighting-to-stop
-occup-wall-street-filming/50024706#ixzz1isiZw2Vu (accessed January 13, 2012).

Decourcy, Michael. "F.B.I. Arrests Reputed Leader of Philadelphia Mob and 23 Others." *New York Times*, March 18, 1994.

de Lama, George. "Drug Tests to Start at the Top." *Chicago Tribune*, August 8, 1986.

Dershowitz, Alan M., Harvey A. Silverglate, and Jeanne Baker. "The JDL Informer and the Bizarre Bombing Case." *Civil Liberties Review*, April/May 1976.

Dreifus, Claudia. "A Conversation with—David Wong; A Bloodless Revolution: Spit Will Tell What Ails You." *New York Times*, April 19, 2005.

Dwyer, Jim. "Videos Challenge Accounts of Convention Unrest." *New York Times*, April 12, 2005, A1.

Essoyan, Susan. "Two Marines Challenge Pentagon Order to Give DNA Samples." *Los Angeles Times*, December. 27, 1995.

Farrell, Michael B. "Who's Taping Whom? Video Cameras Clash with Civil Rights at Protests." *Christian Science Monitor*, September 15, 2004. http://www.csmonitor.com/2004/0915/p16s01-usju.html (accessed September 1, 2009).

Feder, Barnaby J., and Tom Zeller. "Identity Badge Worn under Skin Approved for Use in Health Care." *New York Times*, October 14, 2004. http://www.nytimes.com/2004/10/14/technology/14implant.html?pagewanted=print&position (accessed June 15, 2012).

Goetz, Bob. "Gasquet Is Cleared to Play Again." *New York Times*, July 15, 2009.

Gwartney, Debra. "Seared by a Peeping Tom's Gaze." *New York Times*, July 21, 2012.

Hall, Carla, and Tami Abdollah. "Private Eye to the Stars Is Guilty." *Los Angeles Times*, May 16, 2008.

Jarvis, Steve. "CMOR Finds Survey Refusal Rate Is Still Rising." *Marketing News*, February 4, 2002.

Klein, Naomi. "China's All-Seeing Eye: A Nation under Surveillance." *Rolling Stone*, May 29, 2008. http://www.cfr.org/china/rolling-stone-chinas-all-seeing-eye/p17048 (accessed September 1, 2009).

Liptak, Adam. "Full Constitutional Protection for Some, but No Privacy for the Poor." *New York Times*, July 16, 2007.

Marx, Gary T. "Raising Your Hand Just Won't Do." *Los Angeles Times*, April 1, 1987. http://articles.latimes.com/1987-04-01/local/me-665_1_restroom-trip-policy (accessed September 1, 2009).

———. *Trade 'Ya a Sinbad for a Marauder: Drug Fighting, '90s Style (a Stillborn Op-Ed Article).* 2009. http://web.mit.edu/gtmarx/www/sinbad.html (accessed September 1, 2009).

Maschke, George W., and Gino J. Scalabrini. "The Lie behind the Lie Detector." *Antipolygraph.org*, 2005. http://www.antipolygraph.org/lie-behind-the-lie-detector.pdf (accessed September 1, 2009).

McCullagh, Declan. "Court to FBI: No Spying on In-Car Computers." *CNET News*, November 19, 2003. http://news.cnet.com/2100-1029_3-5109435.html (accessed September 18, 2011).

Montopoli, Brian. "ACORN Sting Lands Housing Group in Conservative Crosshairs." *CBS News*, September 16, 2009. http://www.cbsnews.com/8301-503544_162-5315657-503544.html (accessed October 13, 2009).

Moss, Michael, and Ford Fessenden. "America Under Surveillance: Privacy and Security; New Tools for Domestic Spying." *New York Times*, December 10, 2002.

Press Association. "Greek Sprinters Kenteris and Thanou Cleared of Faking Motorcycle Crash."

Guardian, September 6, 2011. http://www.guardian.co.uk/sport/2011/sep/06/greek-sprinters
-cleared-motorcycle-crash (accessed January 17, 2012).

Ramadan, Saud A. "Trading Cards Give War on Drugs a Friendly, Furry Face." *Washington Post*,
August 7, 1997, M02.

Rimer, Sara. "In Rap Obscenity Trial, Cultures Failed to Clash." *New York Times*, October 22,
1990.

Rosen, Steven. "Old Mug Shots Fuel Art and a Debate on Privacy." *New York Times*, August 28,
2011.

Safire, William. "You Are a Suspect." *New York Times*, November 14, 2002.

Seper, Jerry. "'Black Cocaine' Able to Avoid Detection: Drug Smugglers' New Tactics Described."
Washington Times, April 28, 1999.

Sokolove, Michael. " To the Victor, the Drug Test." *New York Times*, August 3, 2008.

Steinhauer, Jennifer. "Scouts Train to Fight Terrorists, and More." *New York Times*, May 14,
2009, A1.

Vilain, E. "The Line Between Male and Female Athletes: How to Decide?" *New York Times*,
June 18, 2012.

Wilcockson, John. "The New Passport: A Conversation with Anne Gripper." *VeloNews*, October
24, 2007. http://velonews.competitor.com/2007/10/news/the-new-passport-a-conversation
-with-anne-gripper_13563 (accessed September 1, 2009).

Web Sites

cartome.org. *Harry Recon: Ace Photo Pigeon*. 2009. http://cartome.org/recon-pigeon.htm (accessed September 1, 2009).

Climate Cops. *Climate Cops*. 2009. http://www.climatecops.com/ (accessed September 1, 2009).

Club Penguin. *The F.I.S.H. (Factual Informative Spy Handbook): Your Duty*. 2009. http://play
.clubpenguin.com/index.htm (accessed September 1, 2009).

Electronic Privacy Information Center. *EPIC*. N.d. http://epic.org/ (accessed October 21, 2011).

Federal Bureau of Investigation. *Kids Page: Kindergarten to 5th Grade*. 2009a. http://www.fbi
.gov/kids/k5th/kidsk5th.htm (accessed September 1, 2009).

———. *Special Agency Undercover*. 2009b. http://www.fbi.gov/kids/games/undercover.htm (accessed September 1, 2009).

———. *The SA Challenge*. 2009c. http://www.fbi.gov/kids/6th12th/sachallenge/sachallenge.htm
(accessed September 1, 2009).

———. *What We Do*. 2009d. http://www.fbi.gov/kids/k5th/whatwed01.htm (accessed September 1, 2009).

Hoofnagle, C. J., J. King, S. Li, and J. Turow. "How Different Are Young Adults from Older Adults
When It Comes to Information Privacy Attitudes and Policies?" Available at SSRN 1589864,
2010. http://papers.ssrn.com.

IRISS. *Handbook on Increasing Resilience in Surveillance Societies*. http://irissproject.eu/?page_id
=610&utm_source=IRISS_June2014&utm_campaign=8a7a98fc5a-IRISS_PR_Surveillance
_in_Europe_10_10_2014&utm_medium=email&utm_term=0_a05fc7983f-8a7a98fc5a
-174015249 (accessed October 1, 2014).

National Reconnaissance Office. *NRO Jr.* 2009. http://www.nrojr.gov/ (accessed March 1, 2009).

National Security Agency. *America's CryptoKids: Future Codemakers and Codebreakers*. 2009a.
http://www.nsa.gov/kids/ (accessed 2009 йил 1–September).

———. *CSS Sam's Operation: Dit-Dah.* 2009b. http://www.nsa.gov/kids/games/gameMorse.htm (accessed September 1, 2009).

OperationCheckpoint.com. *Operation Checkpoint.* 2009. http://www.OperationCheckppoint .com (accessed March 1, 2009).

Privacy Rights Clearinghouse. *Privacy Rights Clearinghouse.* 2011. http://www.privacyrights.org/ (accessed October 21, 2011).

Toys to Grow On. *Top Secret Spy Gear.* 2009. http://www.toystogrowon.com/sku998 (accessed September 1, 2009).

WeTip Inc. *WeTip Inc. for a Safer America.* 2009. http://www.wetip.com/ (accessed September 1, 2009).

Wikipedia, s.v. "Streisand Effect." June 25, 2012. http://en.wikipedia.org/wiki/Streisand_effect (accessed June 26, 2012).

———, s.v. "Toilets in Japan." June 3, 2011. http://en.wikipedia.org/wiki/Toilets_in_Japan (accessed September 15, 2011).

Wizard Industries. *Scan-It Operation Checkpoint Toy X Ray Machine.* 2009. http://samplerewards .com/index.cfm?fuseaction=product.display&Product_ID=2075 (accessed September 1, 2009).

Index

Page references followed by *f* denote figures. Page references followed by *t* denote tables.

Lightning Source UK Ltd.
Milton Keynes UK
UKOW06f2357030817
306650UK00006B/24/P